THE ASTROLOGICAL AUTOBIOGRAPHY OF
A MEDIEVAL PHILOSOPHER
HENRY BATE'S NATIVITAS (1280-81)

ANCIENT AND MEDIEVAL PHILOSOPHY

DE WULF-MANSION CENTRE
Series I

XVII

Series Editors

Russell L. Friedman
Jan Opsomer
Carlos Steel
Gerd Van Riel

Advisory Board

The "De Wulf-Mansion Centre" is a research centre for Ancient, Medieval, and Renaissance
philosophy at the Institute of Philosophy of the KU Leuven,
Kardinaal Mercierplein, 2, B-3000 Leuven (Belgium).
It hosts the international project "Aristoteles latinus" and
publishes the "Opera omnia" of Henry of Ghent and the "Opera Philosophica et Theologica" of
Francis of Marchia.

THE ASTROLOGICAL AUTOBIOGRAPHY
OF A MEDIEVAL PHILOSOPHER

Henry Bate's Nativitas (1280-81)

Edited and introduced by
Carlos Steel, Steven Vanden Broecke,
David Juste and Shlomo Sela

LEUVEN UNIVERSITY PRESS

Published with the support of Universitaire Stichting van België

© 2018 by the De Wulf-Mansioncentrum – De Wulf-Mansion Centre
Leuven University Press / Presses Universitaires de Louvain/ Universitaire Pers Leuven
Minderbroedersstraat 4, B-3000 Leuven / Louvain (Belgium)

ISBN 978 94 6270 155 7

eISBN 978 94 6166 269 9
D/2018/1869/45
NUR: 732

Cover: Geert de Koning

PREFACE

In *Die Kultur der Renaissance in Italien* (1860), Jacob Burckhardt famously claimed that "much of what, till the close of the Middle Ages, passed for biography, is actually nothing but contemporary narrative, written without any sense of what is individual in the subject of the memoir" (trans. Middlemore). Only in Renaissance Italy, Burckhardt continued, did "a keen eye for individuality" first emerge, with the astrological autobiographer Girolamo Cardano (1501-1576) as one of its foremost examples.

This book discloses the riches of an astrological autobiography that preceded Cardano's famous efforts by almost 300 years, and which is in fact the earliest preserved self-analysis to use astrology as an interpretive device. This *Nativitas* was written by Henry Bate of Mechelen (Malines) (1246-after 1310). Bate trained as a philosopher in Paris before embarking on a successful career as a courtier and Church dignitary. In 1280, at the age of 35, Bate was anxiously trying to prepare the next step in his ecclesiastical career. It was precisely at this time that Bate decided to engage in self-analysis, and his philosophical and mathematical skills allowed him to use one of the most powerful tools available: astrology.

Although the historical importance of Bate's *Nativitas* was already recognised in the nineteenth century by scholars like Emile Littré (1801-1881), no edition of this text existed until now. Upon resuming the editing of another one of Bate's works, the *Speculum divinorum*, Carlos Steel encountered the late father Emiel Van de Vyver, librarian of the Benedictine abbey of Dendermonde and an eminent medieval scholar. While Van de Vyver had given up on the edition of the *Speculum*, he maintained a strong interest in Bate's *Nativitas*, having made a transcription of the text from MS Paris, BnF, lat. 10270 and collated it with the other Paris manuscript (lat. 7324). However, Van de Vyver also realised the amount of additional work that would be necessary to prepare a scholarly edition and abandoned this project in view of the frightfully large number of sources used by Bate, most of which were (and still are) unpublished. For a long time, Van de Vyver's handwritten copy remained in a library safe. In the meantime, David Juste got interested in Bate's *Nativitas* while working on his comprehensive catalogue of Latin astrological manuscripts. What frightened dom Van de Vyver in Bate was exactly what thrilled David: the wealth of newly discovered astrological sources. David urged Carlos to start working on the edition of the *Nativitas*, but Carlos said that he could only undertake this task if seconded by experts on medieval astrology. Steven Vanden Broecke agreed to collaborate on the project together with David. In dealing with the labyrinth of Bate's quotations from the work of Abraham Ibn Ezra, Shlomo Sela subsequently joined as the fourth member of our team.

The resulting book consists of two parts. On the one hand, it offers the first edition of Bate's *Nativitas*. This edition of the *Nativitas* was primarily prepared by Carlos Steel (text) and Steven Vanden Broecke (textual sources), with the assistance of David Juste and Shlomo Sela. On the other hand, it soon became clear that the full story of the *Nativitas*, its genesis and its context, was so complex that it required an introductory monograph, whose final coordination and editing were taken in hand by Steven Vanden Broecke. Over the course of seven chapters, this introduction covers four essential dimensions of Bate's *Nativitas*.

Chapter 1, by Carlos Steel and David Juste, lays out the basis of the text edition. It provides a complete inventory of the extant manuscripts of the *Nativitas*, and reconstructs the intricate but fascinating textual tradition. One of the most important results of this exploration is the discovery that not only Bate's astrological self-analysis and predictions have been preserved, but also his subsequent records for empirical verification of these predictions.

Chapter 2, by Carlos Steel and Steven Vanden Broecke, rewrites Bate's biography on the basis of a wealth of new documents and information. It also documents Bate's stunningly long, detailed and penetrating attempt at decoding his life and idiosyncrasies in the *Nativitas*. His philosophical and mathematical skills, musical prowess, love of dance and poetry, sense of solitude, dreams, social conflicts, illnesses, fears of death, love of women: the text of the *Nativitas* reveals all of these and more through Bate's reading of his own horoscope. Finally, chapter 2 reconstructs the immediate biographical context that prompted Bate to undertake this exercise.

Chapter 3, authored by David Juste, likewise rewrites Bate's bibliography. It offers a new, complete catalogue of Bate's known astrological and astronomical works, both original works and translations.

Chapter 4, by Steven Vanden Broecke, presents the intellectual and cultural context of Bate's *Nativitas*. This chapter focuses on Bate's *Nativitas* as an exercise in autobiography. On the one hand, it seeks to delineate Bate's own possible motivations for authoring the *Nativitas*, as well as the precedents and subsequent reception of this remarkable practice. On the other hand, it offers a critical reflection on the applicability of a notion like 'autobiography' to the *Nativitas*, using Bate's text as an illustration of key differences between medieval and modern notions of autobiographical writing.

Chapter 5, by David Juste, goes even deeper by exploring Bate's personal and intellectual connections to the astrological tradition on the one hand, and to the Parisian astrological scene of the second half of the thirteenth century on the other. This chapter demonstrates the extraordinary breadth of Bate's knowledge of astrology and astrological literature. By 1280, most astrological texts that were to become the vulgate until the sixteenth century were already available in Latin, and it is no exaggeration to say that Bate knew virtually all of them. Not only did he know and use them, but he thoroughly mastered their content, scope and significance as well. Indeed, few European scholars before 1300 demonstrate such knowledge and command of astrology. Through a thorough analysis of the relevant manuscript sources, this chapter also reveals the close ties between Bate and the Parisian scholarly scene, on which it casts an entirely new light.

Chapter 6, by Shlomo Sela, focuses on another dimension of Bate's historical importance: his role in the transmission of Hebrew learning to the Latin West. On the one hand, this chapter explains that it was Bate who brought the astrological treatises of Abraham Ibn Ezra (c. 1089-c. 1161), one of the foremost Hebrew scholars of the Middle Ages, to the attention of the Latin West. On the other hand, this chapter documents and disentangles Bate's complex relation to the astrological corpus of Ibn Ezra in the *Nativitas*.

Chapter 7, by Steven Vanden Broecke, leaves the intellectual and cultural context of the *Nativitas*, and focuses on some of the main astrological techniques and concepts that Bate deployed in constructing his self-analysis. In doing so, the chapter casts a privileged light on some of the methods used by one of the most accomplished working astrologers of the 13th century.

The cooperation among four editors through hundreds of mails was as productive as it was complicated. In dealing with the many faces of Henry Bate, we were also fortunate in being able to draw on the expertise of other scholars. Charles Burnett freely shared his extraordinary knowledge of astrological texts with us, allowing us to identify source references by Bate that would otherwise have remained unidentified. Through David Juste, we could also draw on the riches of the database of the *Ptolemaeus Arabus et Latinus* (*PAL*) project of the Bayerische Akademie der Wissenschaften. Guy Guldentops, expert editor of Bate's *Speculum divinorum*, was always ready to assist us with his unparalleled knowledge of Bate's intellectual and linguistic idiosyncracies. Our heartfelt thanks also go out to Pasquale Arfé (Università degli Studi di Bari Aldo Moro), Jean-Patrice Boudet (Université d'Orléans), David Burn (KU Leuven), Godfried Croenen (University of Liverpool), Benjamin Dykes (The Cazimi Press), Russell Friedman (KU Leuven), Kenan van de Mieroop (Ghent University) and Philipp Nothaft (All Souls College, Oxford) for their invaluable advice and assistance on specific astrological, astronomical, biographical, linguistic and musicological problems.

We also thank the two anonymous readers of "Universitaire Stichting/Fondation Universitaire" for their valuable comments and suggestions, which kept us from making even more mistakes and helped us to improve the edition. We thank Universitaire Stichting/Fondation Universitaire for its financial assistance in making this book possible. In the past, Leuven University Press published four volumes of Bate's *Speculum divinorum*. We are very proud to have our edition of the *Nativitas* accepted as part of their series on Ancient and Medieval Philosophy, which is its natural place indeed.

Our one remaining frustration is that we were as yet unable to complement our edition with a full annotated translation of this remarkable text, written in a complicated Latin and larded with the daunting technical vocabulary of ancient astronomy and astrology. We hope that this can be the goal of another project.

Completum Lovanii in vigilia Assumptionis beatae Mariae Virginis anno Domini 2018, die Martis, ascendente Libra in qua Luna coniuncta Veneri.

Carlos Steel
Steven Vanden Broecke
David Juste
Shlomo Sela

TABLE OF CONTENTS

Abbreviations

App. I	Henricus Bate, *Nativitas*, Appendix I
App. II	Henricus Bate, *Nativitas*, Appendix II
Nat.	Henricus Bate, *Nativitas*

INTRODUCTION

Chapter 1
Manuscripts and Text Tradition of the Nativitas

1.1. Manuscripts (David Juste)

Munich, Bayerische Staatsbibliothek, Clm 3857 (*M*)

s. XIII^ex for fols. 47-48 (the core of the MS dates from the second half of the thirteenth century). Or.: probably the University of Paris. Prov.: cathedral of Augsburg.

Parchment, 48 fols., a single neat hand copied the core of the MS (fols. 1-46). Fols. 47-48 contain added notes in two or three hands, the first of which (fol. 47r) might be that of the main scribe, albeit in a more cursive script.

Astrology: Albumasar, *Flores* (1ra-5ra); Gergis, *De significatione septem planetarum in domibus* (5ra-6ra); Jafar, *De pluviis et ventis* (6rb-7ra); astrometeorology, at least partly from the *Liber novem iudicum* "Aomar: Ex conventu itaque vel oppositione vel ex Solis..." (7ra-8rb); Albumasar, *Introductorium maius*, tr. John of Seville, VI.1 (9ra-11rb); Ptolemy, *Quadripartitum*, tr. Plato of Tivoli (11va-43va); Pseudo-Ptolemy, *Liber proiectionis radiorum stellarum* (43va-43vb); Pseudo-Ptolemy, *De iudiciis partium* (43vb-46vb). According to a table of contents added by another hand in the top margin of fol. 1r, the MS also contained Alcabitius's *Introductorius* after fol. 46. The added notes fols. 47-48 include **Henry Bate, *Nativitas*, excerpts (47r)**; a list of the 28 lunar mansions (47v); *Liber Alchandrei*, 19-20 (47v); the horoscope of a nativity of 16 March 1265 (47v); two horoscopes of a nativity of 23 December 1267 (48r); an unfinished *rota* meant to show the 12 signs and the 28 lunar mansions (48v).

The excerpts from the *Nativitas* consist of three horoscopes with tables and notes, including Bate's nativity, the horoscope of the syzygy preceding birth and the revolution for the 35th year, i.e. *Nat.* 375-471, 483-489, 511-512,507, 513, 508-509 and 2793-2810, with the following section added between *Nat.* 489 and 511: "Saturnus retrogradus, Iupiter retrogradus, Mars directus, Venus directa, Mercurius directus, Luna tarda cursu".

Lit. Karl Halm and Georg von Laubmann, *Catalogus Codicum Latinorum Bibliothecae Regiae Monacensis*, vol. 1.2: *Clm 2501-5250* (München: Sumptibus Bibliothecae Regiae, 1871), p. 147; David Juste, *Catalogus Codicum Astrologorum Latinorum*, vol. 1: *Les manuscrits astrologiques latins conservés à la Bayerische Staatsbibliothek de Munich* (Paris: CNRS éditions, 2011), pp. 99-100.

Oxford, Bodleian Library, Digby 210 (O)

s. XVI. Or.: Italian hand.

Paper, 93 fols., a single hand.

Astrology: Lorenzo Bonincontri, *De revolutionibus nativitatum* (1r-33v); astrological notes (33v-35r); "De morte natorum. Pronosticatio mortis nascentium laudem maximam astronomo prestat..." (35v-39v); Lorenzo Bonincontri, star table verified 1480 (39v-41r); Albumasar, *De revolutionibus nativitatum* (42r-87v); **Henry Bate, *Nativitas*, excerpts 5-373 and 562-571** (87v-91r), followed without a break by astrological notes "Sed quoniam aspectus et huiusmodi figure..." (91r-91v); added horoscopes for 1556 and 1497 with notes (91^{bis}r-91^{ter}r). Blank: 41v.

The excerpts from the *Nativitas* are identical to those in *Vat.*

Lit. William D. Macray, *Catalogi codicum manuscriptorum Bibliothecae Bodleianae*, vol. 9: *Codices a viro clarissimo Kenelm Digby* (Oxford: Clarendon Press, 1883), cols. 225-226.

Paris, Bibliothèque nationale de France, lat. 7324 (P)

s. XIV² (for fols. 1-90; after 1362, cf. fols. 50v-51v; fols. 91-102 were added in the fifteenth century). Or.: France or northern Italy (for fols. 1-90, see Boudet). Prov.: Louis de Langle, who copied fols. 91-102; anonymous astrologer working in Lyons in the 1470s; Simon de Phares; King Francis I.

Paper, 104 fols., composite MS made of two parts: fols. 1-90 (two hands: fols. 1-49 and 50-89) and fols. 91-102 (a single hand).

Astrology and astronomy: Albumasar, *De revolutionibus nativitatum*, attr. Messahallah (1ra-24va); **Henry Bate, *Nativitas* (24va-47ra)**; William of Saint-Cloud, *Nativitas* (47ra-49va); star table verified 1362 in Barcelona (50va-51va); another star table (51vb); Messahallah, *De revolutionibus annorum mundi* (52r-58v); John of Saxony, commentary on Alcabitius's *Introductorius*, Book IV (59r-68v); Messahallah, *De nativitatibus*, anonymous tr. (73r-76ra); "Dixit Tholomeus quod si domini triplicitatis Solis... Explicit liber Ali de qualitate nati" (76rb-86r); "Alius tractatus. Capitulum in nativitate hoc est ad sciendum nativitatem..." (86v-88r); "Luna iuncta cum Saturno aut ipsam 4 aspectu vel oppositione..." (88r-89r); Guido Bonatti, *Liber introductorius ad iudicia stellarum*, IX.3 (91r-102v); table of contents of the volume, added at the end of the fifteenth century (103r-104v). Blank: 50r, 69r-72v, 89v-90v.

Lit. *Catalogus codicum manuscriptorum Bibliothecae Regiae*, vol. 4: *Cod. Latini 7226-8822* (Paris: E Typographia Regia, 1744), p. 341; Jean-Patrice Boudet, *Lire dans le ciel. La bibliothèque de Simon de Phares, astrologue du XVe siècle* (Bruxelles: Centre d'Etude des Manuscrits, 1994), pp. 62-68; David Juste, *Catalogus Codicum Astrologorum Latinorum*, vol. 2: *Les manuscrits astrologiques latins conservés à la Bibliothèque nationale de France à Paris* (Paris: CNRS éditions, 2015), pp. 103-104.

Paris, Bibliothèque nationale de France, lat. 10270 (*Par*)

s. XV². Or.: Naples, copied under the supervision of Arnald of Brussels. Prov.: Bernard Collot (d. 1755), canon of Notre-Dame of Paris.

Paper, 102 fols. numbered 83-184 by Arnald of Brussels, a single hand. All texts and excerpts in this MS, including the horoscopes fols. 83r, 84v and 86v, are found to be identical and in the same order in *V.*

Astrology: two horoscopes (83r); *Liber Salcharie Albassarith*, end only "... in ascendenti debet esse humilis boni cordis..." (83v-84r); onomancy "Quia omnes verissime prescire soli Deo subtiliter constituta existit neminem contradicere..." (84r); horoscope (84v); "Si volueris habere unam mulierem et volueris scire utrum possis habere eam vel non, aspice dominum ascendentis et dominum septimi..." (84v-86v); horoscope (86v); Albumasar, *De revolutionibus nativitatum* (87r-139r); **Henry Bate, *Nativitas* (139v-177v)**; William of Saint-Cloud, *Nativitas* (178r-183v). Blank: 184.

Lit. Léopold Delisle, *Inventaire des manuscrits conservés à la Bibliothèque Impériale sous les numéros 8823-11503 du fonds latin* (Paris: A. Durand, 1863), p. 68; Emmanuel Poulle, *La bibliothèque scientifique d'un imprimeur humaniste au XVe siècle. Catalogue des manuscrits d'Arnaud de Bruxelles à la Bibliothèque nationale de Paris* (Genève: Droz, 1963), pp. 87-88; Charles Samaran and Robert Marichal, *Catalogue des manuscrits en écriture latine portant des indications de date, de lieu ou de copiste*, vol. 3: *Bibliothèque Nationale, fonds latin (Nᵒˢ 8001 à 18613)* (Paris: Centre national de la recherche scientifique, 1974), p. 634; David Juste, *Catalogus Codicum Astrologorum Latinorum*, vol. 2: *Les manuscrits astrologiques latins conservés à la Bibliothèque nationale de France à Paris* (Paris: CNRS éditions, 2015), p. 193.

Segovia, Archivo y Biblioteca de la Catedral, B 349 (84) (*S*)

s. XV² (after 1455 for fols. 33r-35v, cf. fol. 33r: "ab anno Christi 1455 usque ad annum in quo es..."). Or.: unknown. Prov.: "Es del archivo de la cathedral de Segovia", 17ᵗʰ c.-hand (fol. 1r).

Paper, 106 fols. formerly paginated 490-699, several hands.

Astrology and astronomy: **Henry Bate, *Nativitas* (1r-28v)**; Antonius de Murellis de Camerino, prognostication for 1432 (29r-32v); "Cum planeta cuius est negotium est in medio celi..." (33r-35v); table: properties of the 12 signs (36v); Firminus de Bellavalle, *De mutatione aeris* (37r-75v); Pseudo-Ptolemy, *De cometis* (75v-76r); Messahallah, *Liber interpretationum* (76v-78v); "Domus prima, prima est illa que ascendit in oriente, demonstrat vitam..." (79r-84v); Eustachius de Eldris, *De directionibus* (85r-89r); notes (89v); solar table dated 1331 in Paris (90r); "Ad retrogradationem sciendam opportet querere..." (91r-96v); astronomical tables (97r-106v). Blank: 36r, 90v.

Lit. Guy Beaujouan, "Manuscrits scientifiques médiévaux de la cathédrale de Ségovie", in *Actes du XIe Congrès international d'histoire des sciences (Varsovie,*

Toruń, Kielce, Cracovie, 24-31 août 1965) (Wrocław: Ossolineum, 1968), vol. 3, pp. 15-18 (p. 17) [reprinted in Guy Beaujouan, *Science médiévale d'Espagne et d'alentour* (Aldershot: Variorum, 1992), art. IV].

Seville, Biblioteca Capitular y Colombina, 5-1-38 (*L*)

s. XV. Or.: unknown. Prov.: Padua until 1531, cf. fol. 60v: "Este libro costó 16 beços en Padua a 15 de abril de 1531 y el ducado de oro vale 280 beços."

Paper, 60 fols., a single hand. The first six folia have been damaged, apparently by water, so that the upper part (about 30-50%) of the folia concerned is illegible.

Astrology: **Henry Bate, *Nativitas* (1r-50r)**; William of Saint-Cloud, *Nativitas* (50r-56r); added astrological notes (60v). Blank: 56v-60v (except provenance note fol. 60v).

Lit. José Francisco Sáez Guillén and Pilar Jiménez de Cisneros Vencelá, *Catálogo de manuscritos de la Biblioteca Colombina de Sevilla* (Sevilla: Cabildo de la Santa, Metropolitana y Patriarcal Iglesia Catedral de Sevilla, 2002), vol. 1, p. 72.

Vatican, Biblioteca Apostolica Vaticana, Vat. lat. 12732 (*Vat*)

s. XV^2 (fols. 105-239) and XVI^{in} (for the rest of the MS). Or.: Italy, perhaps Naples (fols. 105-239). The core of the MS consists of fol. 105-239, copied in a single neat hand. Most of the rest of the MS has been copied by two alternating hands, one of which signed "... finit 1502, per me Iohannem de Basilea Magna cum diligentia scriptus" (fol. 83r), while the other left notes and glosses throughout the entire volume.

Paper, 279 fols. (new foliation in lower right corner), three main hands.

Astrology: fols. 105-239 contain Albohali, *De nativitatibus*, tr. Plato of Tivoli (beginning) and Johannes Toletanus (end) (105r-130v); Firmicus Maternus, *Mathesis*, excerpts from Books IV and III (130v-153r); astrological notes (153r-153v); Haly Abenragel, *De iudiciis astrorum*, excerpts (154r-167r); astrological notes (167r-167v); Albumasar, *De revolutionibus nativitatum* (168r-231v); **Henry Bate, *Nativitas*, excerpts 5-373 and 562-571 (232r-236v)**, followed without a break by astrological notes "Quoniam aspectus et huiusmodi figure eorumque virtus et efficacia ad stellarum radiorum naturam spectat..." (236v-237r); Hermes, *Liber de stellis beibeniis* (237v-239v). The rest of the MS is made of texts, excerpts and notes dealing mainly with nativities and including, among others, Lorenzo Bonincontri, star table verified 1480 (8r-12v) and Lorenzo Bonincontri, *Liber nativitatum* (22r-83r).

The excerpts from the *Nativitas* are as follows: *Nat.* 5-373 "Quoniam ut testatur Philosophus Politicorum tertio, fere quidem plurimi... (236v) in ergo his omnibus protestor me aut parum aut nihil de meo positurum" and *Nat.* 562-571 "Dicit enim Avenezre in suo libro equationum (sic) quod omnes aspectus Solis ad Lunam boni sunt... et benignitatis suae gaudio illustrat."

Lit. *Codices manu scripti Vaticani Latini 12345-12847 ex Archivo in Bybliothecam Vaticanam translati anno 1920 aliique qui in dies accesserunt* [handwritten catalogue available *in situ*], fol. 915r; Paul Oskar Kristeller, *Iter Italicum*, vol. 2 (London/ Leiden: Brill, 1977), p. 348.

Venice, Biblioteca Nazionale Marciana, lat. VI.108 (2555) (*V*)

s. XV² (perhaps c. 1463, date mentioned in the upper margin of fol. 41r). Or.: unknown (northern Italy?). Prov.: Venice, Cardinal Domenico Grimani (1461-1523).

Paper, 145 fols., several hands. The MS was bound in disorder: fols. 1-40 originally took place — or were meant to take place — after fol. 112v (cf. catchwords on that folio "Sole nativitatis tempore", which correspond to the incipit of Albumasar's *De revolutionibus nativitatum*). Once the correct order is restored, the sequence of texts and excerpts in this MS (fols. 110v-112 + 1-40 + 113-145) matches that of *Par*, fols. 83-183 exactly.

Astrology: Albumasar, *De revolutionibus nativitatum* (1r-40r); Albubater, *De nativitatibus* (41r-110r); "Nota quod omnes beiberne [sic] que reperiuntur in libro Hermetis de beibeniis currente anno Ihesu Christi 1185..." (110r); two horoscopes, the positions of the second of which correspond to 29 October 1201 (110v); *Liber Salcharie Albassarith*, end only "... in ascendenti debet esse humilis boni cordis..." (111r); onomancy "Quia omnes verissime prescire soli Deo subtiliter constituta existit neminem contradicere..." (111r); horoscope, whose positions are roughly correct for 1 or 2 November 1234 (111v); "Si volueris habere unam mulierem et volueris scire utrum possis habere eam vel non..." (111v-112v); horoscope (112v); **Henry Bate, *Nativitas* (113r-141v)**; William of Saint-Cloud, *Nativitas* (141v-145v). Blank: 40v.

Lit. Giuseppe Valentinelli, *Bibliotheca manuscripta ad S. Marci Venetiarum. Codices MSS. Latini*, vol. 4 (Venezia: Ex Typographia Commercii, 1871), pp. 288-289 (XI.110).

Vienna, Österreichische Nationalbibliothek, 10583 (*W*)

s. XVI.

Paper, 100 fols., a single hand.

Astrology: Albumasar, *De revolutionibus nativitatum* (1r-90r); **Henry Bate, *Nativitas*, excerpts 5-373 and 562-571 (90r-98v)**, followed without a break by astrological notes "Quoniam aspectus et huiusmodi figure..." (98v-99v). Blank: 100.

The excerpts from the *Nativitas* are identical to those in *Vat*.

Lit. *Tabulae codicum manu scriptorum praeter Graecos et Orientales in Bibliotheca Palatina Vindobonensi asservatorum*, vol. 6: *Cod. 9001-11500* (Wien: Gerold, 1873), p. 208.

?Unknown location, *olim* Greenville (Miss.), Public Library, 1 (*G*)

s. XV^ex ("1480. Deo gracias", at the end of Albumasar's text). Or.: unknown. Prov.: Constantin August Naumann (d. 1852), professor of mathematics at Freiberg, who had acquired many manuscripts in Germany; Guglielmo Libri, who bought the MS in 1854 and sold it in London in 1859; Greenville (Miss.), Public Library, 1 (De Ricci). The MS is no longer in Greenville and appears to be lost.

Paper, 61 or 62 fols.

Astrology: Albohali, *De nativitatibus*, tr. Plato of Tivoli (12 fols.); Albumasar, *De revolutionibus nativitatum*, (35 fols.); "Tractatus astrologicus (?) incerti auctoris" (15 fols.). The last item (labelled "Ms. astrologicum incerti auctoris" in Naumann's catalogue, "Astrologia incerti Auctoris" in Libri and "Tractatus astrologicus (?) incerti auctoris" in De Ricci) might correspond to **Henry Bate's *Nativitas***, also found after Albumasar's *De revolutionibus nativitatum* in *Par* and *V*, as well as, for the excerpts 5-373 and 562-571, in *O*, *Vat* and *W*. Only Naumann's catalogue gives the number of folia for each text.

Lit. *Catalogue de la bibliothèque de feu Mr. Auguste Const. Naumann, professeur de mathématiques à l'école des mines à Freiberg, dont la vente se fera mardi le 6 juin 1854 et jours suivants dans la salle de Mr. T. O. Weigel à Leipzig* (Paris, 1854), p. 2, no. 9; Guglielmo Libri, *Catalogue of the Extraordinary Collection of Splendid Manuscripts, Chiefly upon Vellum, in Various Languages of Europe and the East, Formed by M. Guglielmo Libri, The Eminent Collector, who is obliged to leave London in consequence of ill health, and for that reason to dispose of his Literary Treasures* (London: J. Davy and Sons, 1859), p. 8, no. 25; Seymour de Ricci, *Census of Medieval and Renaissance Manuscripts in the United States and Canada*, vol. 2 (New York: H. W. Wilson, 1937), p. 1142.

Lost manuscript

A copy of the *Nativitas* once belonged to the library of Charles V of France, as seen in the inventory of the "librairie du Louvre" made by Gilles Malet in 1373: "Nativitas cujusdam Dyonisii, episcopi Silvanentis, **Exemplum nativitatis Henrici de Mechlinia**, Nativitas cujusdam imperatoris Constantinopolis, Albertus [i.e., Albumasar?] De revolutionibus nativitatum, et quasdam determinationes sive questiones, escript en pappier, de tres menue lettre, couvert de parchemin, sans aiz" (ed. Boudet 2015, p. 396, no. 677; see also Delisle 1868-1881, vol. 3, p. 148, no. 731). The same MS reappears in the subsequent inventories of the librairie du Louvre in 1411, 1413 and 1424 (see Delisle, *ibid.*). This MS has not been found.

1.2. Text tradition (Carlos Steel)

Bate's *Nativitas* is transmitted in five manuscripts, one of which dates from the 14th century (*P*), while the four others are from the late 15th century (*L Par S V*). Moreover, three manuscripts copied around 1500 (*O Vat W*) contain the introduction until the first nativity figure. Finally, the first three horoscopes were copied in *M*. An examination of the relations between the copies will demonstrate that we have to assume that at least two now lost manuscripts were used as models.

The Segovia manuscript (*S*) exhibits a textual tradition that is different from the four other manuscripts. Moreover, this manuscript contains an alternative version of the events occurring in Bate's 35th year (with a wealth of autobiographical material), which is very different from the standard text in the four other manuscripts (see below 1.2.2). As we shall see, these four manuscripts have many errors in common, in particular omissions, which is proof that they all derive from a lost common model (α). As we shall further show, *Par* is a direct copy of *V*, while *L* and *P* depend upon a lost model (β), which was itself copied from α. Finally, immediately after Bate's *Nativitas*, these four manuscripts offer another autobiographical nativity of someone born in Paris in 1255 (the son of a certain Petrus Fabri). As David Juste demonstrates in section 5.3.4 below, the author of the latter text is William of Saint-Cloud (*fl.* 1285-1292). However, the manuscripts give no indication that a new text by a different author starts here. On the contrary, what follows in the next paragraph ("inveni per scripta") might initially appear to be the continuation of Bate's own *Nativitas*. Interestingly, the copyists of manuscripts *P* and *L* put the concluding title "Explicit natiuitas magistri Henrici Machliniensis cum quibusdam reuolutionibus" after the *Nativitas* of William of Saint-Cloud, because they were unaware that another nativity had been added to Bate's text. This explicit must have been on the same (incorrect) place in their common model β. The most plausible explanation for the presence of this nativity after Bate's nativity is that William had obtained a copy of Bate's *Nativitas* from Bate himself. Having read Bate's text with great interest, he started working on his own nativity, following Bate's magnificent example. He probably wrote down his nativity on the manuscript he owned, which contained Bate's *Nativitas*. As William's *Nativitas* can be dated 1285, he must have obtained his copy of Bate's *Nativitas* directly from its author. We should therefore assume that the scholars were in close contact with each other.

1.2.1. *The two traditions of the* Navitas

As stated previously, Bate's *Nativitas* is transmitted in two textual traditions, one represented by the Segovia manuscript, the other by four manuscripts originating from a copy that once may have belonged to Willam of Saint-Cloud. Both traditions are differentiated by a great number of disjunctive errors.

1.2.1.1. Errors in *PV* (and their copies *Par L*) against *S*

Samples of omissions: 61 nominato *om. PV* | 144 mediam *om. PV* | 161 imparis *om. PV* | 257 reuolutionis *om. PV* | 640 ut...infra *om. PV* | 859 Non...864 coniunctionem *om. PV* | 923 magis...infortunatus *om. PV* | 997-8 ex...eius *om. PV* | 1015 ex...eius *om. PV* | 1166 hoc proposito *om. PV* | 1192 homo *om. PV* | 1223 uel maleuolos *om. PV* | 1246-7 Baltheus...pectus *om. PV* | 1327 quomodo ... prudentiam *om. PV* | 1338-9 unum ... operibus *om. PV* | 1474 hominum *om. PV* | 1553 et negligit *om. PV* | 1672 receptus *om. PV* | 1711-2 Mars ... infirmitatum *om. PV* | 3307-9 Iouem ... ad *om. PV* | 3362 nisi — ille *om. PV*

Other errors: 653 penes] ponere *PV* | 766 regales] regulares *PV* | 781 habitudinis] habitationis *PV* | 782 habentes] homines *PV* | 870 bene...dispositus] bone fuerit dispositionis *PV* | 1461 improuiso] impulso *PV* | 1863 oportunum] optimum *PV* | 2521 magisterii] ingenii *PV* | 2532 qui idem] quidem *PV* | 2548 coincidunt] quo incidit *PV* | 2568 sufficienter] supra *PV* | 2601 Sagittarius] Saturnus *PV* | 2626 ob imimicitias] ab inimicis *PV* | 2863 ludis] laudis *PS*

1.2.1.2. Errors in *S* against *PV* (and their copies)

11 neque...habentibus *om. S* | 68 partum...aptum *om. S* | 77-8 reuoluendo...compotistarum *om. S* | 108-10 illo...gradu *om. S* | 277 habebat...natiuitatis *om. S* | 899 etiam] quoque *S* | 900 scilicet Saturni *inv. S* | 905 interrogationum] retrogradationum *S* | 909 minus] nimis *S* | 914 Vnde...Hispalen*sis om. S* | 917 tardus est *inv. S* | 918 simpliciter] in omnibus *praem. S* | 920 alkocoden] *post* natiuitatibus *S* | 1024 fuisset...infortunatus *om. S* | 1315-1317 cantionum...et *om. S* | 1387 quod] dicitur *add. S* | 1389 iam *om. S* | 1391 que domus *om. S* | 1393 mysteria] in scientia *S* | 1397 Saturnus est *inv. S* | 1405 Saturni *om. S* | 1429 c̊uius...luminaris *om. S* | 1444-1446 et alii...non *om. S* | 1770 Venus...1772 Hispalensis *om. S* | 1802-1803   Dorotheus...nubere *om. S* | 2355 coniunctionis *om. S* | 2359 libro *om. S* | quod Saturnus *om. S* | 2658 domini *om. S* | etiam dicit *inv. S* | 2663 dubius] indubius *S* | 2665-6 mortis...possumus *om. S* | 2715 proptera...cognouerunt *om. S* | 3221 Circa...retrogradationis *om. S* | 3368 renouabit] remouebit *S* | 3371 operatio] oppositio *S* | 3374 operabitur aliquid] comparabitur idem *S* | 3381-2 Leonis...propriam *om. S* | 3382 Leoni] locum *S* | 3385 inimicorum] amicorum *S*

1.2.1.3. *Par* a copy from *V*

Par is a superb manuscript, beautifully written with the utmost care by a professional copyist working under the supervision of Arnald of Brussels, who was established as a printer in Naples between 1472 and 1477. While residing in Naples, Arnald collected copies of astronomical treatises out of personal interest in the topic; these are now partially preserved in Paris at the BnF.[1] When Emiel Van de Vyver (1921-2000) started work on an edition of Bate's *Nativitas*, he took *Par* as his "Leithandschrift". Van de Vyver's handwritten copy of *Par* was the starting point of our own collations. However, the discovery of the Venetian manuscript (*V*) undermined the authority of *Par*, which is in fact an excellent copy of *V*. Both

---

[1]   See Poulle 1963; Edmunds 1991, pp. 29-30.

manuscripts contain the same collection of astrological texts and excerpts in the same order. This common content could be explained in three ways: *Par* is a copy of *V*, *V* a copy of *Par*, or both *Par* and *V* have a common model. Evidence confirms the first hypothesis: *Par* follows *V* in its particular errors (although some minor errors are corrected in writing), and it adds some further errors, which are not found in *V*.

Examples of errors in both *V* and *Par* (not including errors that come from the model α common to *PV* + *Par*):

215-6 huiusmodi ... propositum *om. V Par* | 1119 spiritu...omnia *om. V Par* | 1836-7 quia...confirmat *om. V Par* | 2028-9 in proposito autem dominus secundi qui auxiliatores nati significat *om. V Par* | 2143 et separationum *om. V Par* | 2316 suos...quomodocumque *om. V Par*

Errors in *Par* not present in *V*:

562 electionum] equationum *Par* | 569 omnibus *om. Par* | 570 sororem] uxorem *Par* | 590 ubique *om. Par* | 711 ad presens *om. Par* | 720 dominus uite est *om. Par* | 769 nato *om. Par* | 781 magnitudinis] bone conseruationis *add. Par* | 875 respectu] natiuitatis *add. Par* | 1325 efficere et musicam morem qualem quondam *om. Par* | 1512 stabilitatem] iustitie et *add. Par* | 1671 felicitatem *om. Par* | 1866 conscripserit] in scriptis *praem. Par* | 1903 aduersitatem] diuersitatem *Par* | 2194 amicabilis *om. Par* | 2195 magne] intelligentiae et *add. Par* | 2289-90 potius uidetur *inv. Par* | 2298 uidelicet] unde licet *Par* | 2317 non uideo *om. Par* | 2321 in gradu] gradus *Par* | 2334-5 angulus tamen *inv. Par* | 2342 Iouis et Saturni *inv. Par* | 2367 refrenata] reformata *Par* | 2433-4 uim suam] unus itaque *Par* | 2442 reges significat *inv. Par* | 2449 dominus *om. Par* | 2519 ut uult Auicenna *om. Par* | 2572 amicos habere *inv. Par* | 2642 dicit Hispalensis *inv. Par* | 2643 eandem *om. Par* | 2702 ut uult Avicenna *om. Par* | 2932-3 et celestibus *om. Par* | 2975 ut est hic *om. Par* | 3040 conturbari magis *inv. Par* | 3295 bonitate] ueritate et] *praem. Par*

From all these examples, it becomes evident that *Par* is a copy of *V*, and not the other way around. There is a counterargument however. *V* only has the first two natal charts (i.e., for Bate's time of birth and for the syzygy preceding his birth), not the figures of the revolution of Bate's birth chart for his 35th and 36th year; in the two latter cases, the scribe of *V* left a blank space, but he never entered the figures. *Par* has all four figures however. This raises the question of where the scribe found the latter two? Moreover, *Par* has a full title, while *V* only has a title in the margin, probably written by another hand. However, the full title in *Par* is probably an addition of Arnald of Brussels, as we will show below, section 1.2.3. If this is the case, Arnald may also have intervened in the text and asked the copyist to add the two missing charts in the open spaces. The figures for Bate's 35th and 36th year in *Par* have all their features in common with *L P* and *M* (in the latter case only for the figure of 35th year). Therefore, Arnald must have found the missing figures in another manuscript of the α tradition. It could have been β, the lost model of *L* and

P, which was circulating in Italy at that time (see below). Or he may have had access to α from which *V* itself had been copied.

On fol. 152v Arnald (?) noted in the margin a quote from the *Picatrix* which corresponds to a passage of Albumasar quoted by Bate in *Nat.* 1240-1243: "Nota secundum Piccatricem: ascendit enim secunda facie Geminorum vir cuius vultus est similis aquile et eius caput panno linteo aptatum, lorica plumbea indutus et munitus et in eius caput galeam ferream, supra quam est corona Sirica, et in eius manu balistam et sagittas habens".[2]

1.2.1.4. *P* and *L* copies of a common model

P and *L* share a large number of various errors, including many omissions. *P* is a meticulous copy, whereas *L* is a mediocre and hastily made copy. Because of their many common errors, and the multiplication of errors in *L* not present in *P*, one could easily surmise that *L* is just a bad copy of *P*. However, this hypothesis could not be confirmed. *P* has a number of particular errors that are absent from *L*. Although these errors are not very numerous (compared to the mass of errors in *L*), they definitely exclude a dependence of *L* on *P*.

Examples of particular errors in *P* not present in *L*:

658 esse *om. P* |1570 natus *om. P*|1641 ad subduplum *om. P* |1788 in septimal *om. P* |1812 aliqua *om.* P |2158 generaliter *om. P* | 2672 insuper et aspicientes *om. P* | 3334 domum occupabit *om. P*

The strongest argument against *L*'s dependency on *P* is the fact that *P* omitted a very long section of the text. On fol. 36vb (modern numbering), after "aduersantes" (*Nat.* 1974), the whole section "moderator .... premonstratum est" (*Nat.* 1974-2020) is lacking in *P*. The copyist simply continues after "aduersantes" with "nam testimonia adversariorum" without noticing that he skipped a page. Was the page lacking in his model, or did he inadvertently turn two pages at once? The second hypothesis seems most probable. Surprisingly, the omitted text was added by a later hand on two strips of paper (one folium cut in half vertically). This text begins with "moderator" and ends on the second strip with "premonstratum est. Nam testimonia aduersariorum *et cetera ut sequitur*". The addition of the supplementary strips of pages led to a new numbering of the folia. The *Nativitas* begins on fol. 24v in a modern numbering which replaces the older medieval numbering (which had one number less: 23v). Folio 33 in the medieval numbering thus becomes 34, 34 becomes 35, 35 becomes 36 (where the omission occurs); but 36 becomes 39, 37 becomes 40, etc. The medieval numbering simply continues, but the modern numbering required adding the two supplementary strips of paper. One of these is numbered 38, the other has no numbering, but the librarian may -erroneously- have considered it to be 37. This proves that the long omission, which probably corresponds to one page,

---

[2]   Pingree 1986, p. 76:23-26.

was not noticed when the first numbering of the folia was made. The addition of the extra half leaves came later.

L also omits a long section of the text. After "dirigendo a parte fortune" (*Nat.* 2833), there immediately follows "Luna hyleg" (*Nat.* 2971). The entire section "peruenitur hoc anno ... loco in quo fui" is lacking in *L*, with no indication whatsoever. It is most likely that a folio disappeared from its model. There are numerous errors on all folia; what follows is a full collation of fol. 14v:

968 profectionis] perfectionis *L* | 970 que fuit *om. LP* | 976 arismetica] arismetrica *LV* | 977 ex compositione] expositione *L* | 978 delectationis] -nem *P* dilectionem *L* | 980 aularum] uillarum *P* | 981 infortunia] -nium *LP* | 982 et] in *L* | 983 huius] eius *LP* | 985 iudicum] et *add. L* | 986 eorum] illorum *LP* | seu] siue *L* | etiam et *om. LP* | conuiuia] communia *L* | 987 ergo] igitur *LP* | domus uite *om. L* | 989 | coniunctionum] -nis *LP* | 990 iuxta *om. LPV* | 992 quidem *om. L* | uel] et *L* 994| orizonte] oriente *P* | 995 omnium cardinum] *spat. vacuum in L* lib. deficit *mg. notauit* | 996 semper *om. P* | 997 ex...eius *om. LPV* | 1000 quoque *om. LPV.*

We may conclude that *L* and *P* derive from a common lost exemplar β. This cannot be *V* since *V* has its own errors that are neither present in *P* nor *L*. *P* is an accurate copy of this lost model, the work of a professional copyist, while *L* is a dreadful copy, full of mistakes. We fully collated manuscript *L*, but decided not to include its multiple variant readings in the apparatus. These never offer a valuable reading that is preferable to what is found in the other manuscripts. Moreover, the first six folia are seriously damaged: only half the text, or less, is decipherable. We only quote *L* in the horoscope figures and when *S* is not present (notably in the section where *S* has an alternative version of Bate's revolution for his 35th year).

The Spanish owner of *L* mentions that he bought the manuscript in Padua in 1521. It is plausible that *L* was copied in northern Italy from its model β. If this is the case, we must suppose that β had been moved from Paris, where it was used to copy *P*, to northern Italy, where it served as model for *L*.

1.2.1.5. Another witness of β: Munich, BSB, Clm 3857

This manuscript collection of astrological texts was copied during Bate's lifetime, at the end of the 13th century, probably in Paris. Some notes were added on the last leaves of this parchment codex (fol. 47-48). On fol. 47r one finds three astrological charts with the corresponding tables and notes from Bate's *Nativitas*: Bate's own nativity chart, the figure of the syzygies preceding his birth, and the chart of the solar revolution for Bate's 35th year. This is undoubtedly the earliest textual witness of the *Nativitas*. An unknown scholar with an interest in astrology must have encountered a manuscript of the *Nativitas* and copied the first three figures with the corresponding notes from it. It is clear that the manuscript he used belonged to the tradition of *LPV Par*. Moreover, there are some indications that he used manuscript

β, from which both *P* and *L* derive. Thus *M* shares with *L* and *P* the following addition in the tables accompanying the second chart: "Ascensiones gradus ascendentis
280 gr. 44 min. correspondentes 12 gr. 20 min. Sagittarii. Equatio dierum 12 min.
hore" (441-443) . See also 376 equatis] equalibus *LP+M* | 402 27.8] 27 *LP+M* | 435 56]
secunda *add. LP + M* | 436 6.52] 6 min. 52 sec. *LP + M*. If the scribe used sub-arche-
type β (a copy of a copy of Bate's original text), one should assume that the figures
were copied in *M* at the earliest at the end of the 13th century in Paris.

1.2.1.6. Three copies of the introduction of the *Nativitas*

At the end of the 15th century, an Italian scholar, probably in Naples, read the introduction of the *Nativitas* with interest and had a copy made of it. This partial copy
is found in three manuscripts, which were copied late 15th/early 16th centuries in
Italy (*O Vat W*).

Bibliotheca Apostolica Vaticana, Vat. lat. 12732 (Vat)

The Vatican codex is a convolute containing diverse texts related to astrology, which
were copied by different scribes at different times. In its original state (fols. 105-239),
it contained a series of astrological texts copied by a hand of the late 15th century.
To this ancient core, two later hands, copying alternately, added two works of the
astronomer Lorenzo Bonincontri (1410-c. 1491).[3] The partial copy of the *Nativitas*
is found in the original core, on fols. 232r-236v, directly following upon Albumasar,
De revolutionibus nativitatum (168r-231v) and copied by the same scribe. Bate's
text begins without any title: "Quoniam ut testatur Philosophus Politicorum tertio
fere quidem plurimi", and ends on fol. 236v: "protestor me aut parum aut nihil de
meo positurum" (373). It is clear that the scribe (or his patron) was only interested
in the introduction of the *Nativitas,* in which Bate explains how he establishes
the exact date of his birth and conception using different indications (cf. a later
scholar's note on fol. 233r: "loquitur de mora in utero matris"). The copy ends just
before the insertion of the first horoscope chart. However, after a space of three
lines, a different hand added another passage from the *Nativitas* taken from lines
562-571: "Dicit enim Auenezre in suo libro equationum (*sic*) quod omnes... gaudio
illustrat". Moreover, this other hand continued with the following comment which
is not found in Bate's *Nativitas*:

> "Sed quoniam aspectus et huiusmodi figure eorumque uirtus et efficacia ad
> stellarum radiorum naturam spectat et ad illorum proprietatem referri uidetur –
> dum enim in predictis figurarum locis planete discurrunt, radiorum potentia et
> uirtus, sed etiam ipsius stellaris corporis uis atque benignitas diuino quodam nutu
> per rectam lineam ad alterius stelle dirigitur corpus – , de radiis eorundem pauca
> subicio. Notandum itaque stellarum lumen bipartitum esse, ante scilicet et retro

---

3   On Bonincontri, see Grayson 1970, Heilen 1999.

per medium. Solis enim radii 30 graduum, 15 ante et totidem retro, Lune siquidem 24, 12 ante et totidem retro, Saturni nanque et Iouis 18, refulgent nouem ante et nouem retro equaliter. Martis sexdecim uindicauit potentia, 8 ante et totidem retro. Cum itaque stella ad stellam applicans gradum illius proprio lumine contingerit, applicata dicitur. Si enim nundum attingit, ad applicationem uidetur accedere. Et in conuentu similiter. Nec unquam separari dicetur stella ab alia eiusue applicatione donec ad medium sue lucis eandem suosue radios transierit. Deinceps si quidem separata iudicari potest."

Finally, yet another hand (presumably the scholar who also made some comments in the margins) added more comments: "In conuentu uerum est non in aspectibus: scito quod in eclipsi Sol non potest fieri quin significetur aliquod magnum accidens..." until "Si eclipsis facit in gradu Solis uel Lune radicis uel prope per unum gradum abc:"

Oxford, Bodleian Library, Digby 210

Besides the two works of Lorenzo Bonincontri, which are found in *Vat*, this manuscript also contains Albumasar, *De revolutionibus nativitatum* (fol. 42r-87r), followed, as in *Vat*, by the introduction of Bate's *Nativitas*, 5-373 (87v-91r). The same scribe continues on fol. 91r with the other extract of the *Nativitas* (562-571), which in *Vat* had been added by another hand, and with the comment "Sed quoniam aspectus et huiusmodi figure.... Deinceps si quidem separata iudicari potest". However, he does not continue with the comment added by the third scholarly hand in *Vat*, which reads:"In conuentu uerum est non in aspectibus, etc.". The rare combination of the introduction of the *Nativitas* with a second extract of this work and supplementary astrological comments, which are found in *Vat* written by different hands, is proof that the scribe of the Oxford manuscript used *Vat* as model for its copy. At the moment the scribe of *O* made his copy, the third hand in *Vat* had not yet added the extra comment "In conuentu uerum est non in aspectibus, etc." However, the copyist of *O* added some extra material himself. After "Deinceps si quidem separata iudicari potest" he added a title: "Infallibiles et notande Gaurici regule vere et probate de commento ex verbis Centiloquii 60. Hore figurate primi concubitus — habuerit in radice et in aliquo reuolutionis anno reiterauerit, morbum in partibus obscenis denotat, et eo maxime cum habuerit in: ". This reference to a work of the celebrated astronomer Luca Gaurico (1475-1558) is proof that the copy in *O* was made after c. 1530.

Vienna, Österreichische Nationalbibliothek, 10583 (W)

This manuscript contains Albumasar's *De revolutionibus nativitatum* (1-90r) followed without title by the introduction of Bate's *Nativitas* and the other additional comments as in *O* (90r-99v). There is no doubt that *W* was copied from *O*. It is, alas, a dreadful copy and contains numerous errors.

As *Vat* is the origin of this partial textual tradition, we only collated this copy of the *Nativitas*. The collations demonstrate that this partial copy of the *Nativitas* undoubtedly derives from the manuscript that was once in the possession of Arnald of Brussels when he was residing in Naples (= *Par*). Not only does it have the particular errors of *Par* (setting it apart from its own model *V*), it also has some of the corrections that were introduced in the first pages of the text in *Par* by another hand (= *Par*^c)

11 altera] odienti *add. mg. Par*^c *Vat* | 12 magnitudinem] amoris *s.l. Par*^c *Vat*^c 16 potentes] de se *add. Par*^c *Vat* | 96 nam] tantum *Par Vat* | 105 alterius *om. Par Vat* | 111 uel] aut *Par Vat* | 114 uel] aut *Par Vat* | 133 emergeret] contingeret *Par Vat* | 134 illius] ipsius *Par Vat* | 142 qua de causa] qua de re *Par Vat* |144 mediam *om. PV s.l. Par*^c *in textu Vat*| 145 horam integram *inv. Par Vat* | 146 1 gr. 38 min.] in 30 *Par Vat* | 147 eufortuniorum et infortuniorum] eufortuniorum *Par* infortuniorum *Vat* | 148 poteram] possunt *Par Vat* | 157 inter Hermetem et Ptolomeum] Ptolomei et Hermetis *Par Vat* | 227-228 comprobetur. Hec est enim uia uocata] nota. Probetur enim estimatiua *ex. corr. Par, sic in textu Vat* | 250 etiam] autem *Par Vat* | 251 testatur] dicit *Par Vat* | 252 causare] creare *Par Vat* | 255 in *om. V s.l. add. Par*^c *in textu Vat*| eiusdem] illius *Par Vat* | 259 causabat] procreabit *Par Vat* | 277 habebat *exp. Par om. Vat* | 562 libro Electionum] libro Equationum *Par Vat*.

As is the case in *Par* and in all other manuscripts deriving from α, Bate's *Nativitas* follows in *Vat* immediately after Albumasar's *De revolutionibus nativitatum*. However, in *Vat* and its copies, Bate's *Nativitas* begins without a title, and seems to be a continuation of Albumasar's text. This may indicate that the *Nativitas* in *Par* had not yet received its full title ("liber servi Dei etc."), when it was copied by the scribe of *Vat*. (on this title, see below section 1.2.3). From these indications we may conclude that the partial copy in the Vatican manuscript was made in Naples, probably before Arnald inserted the title, i.e. before 1477 (end of stay of Arnald in Naples).

Since *Vat* entirely depends on *Par*, which is itself a copy of *V*, this partial tradition of the *Nativitas* contributes nothing to the constitution of the text in the edition. However, it reveals some interest for Bate's work in Italy at the end of the 15th century.

1.2.2.   *Two different versions of the revolution of the 35th year*

In the last part of his work, after having established and analysed his nativity, Bate turns to the discussion of the revolutions for the current and following years. He first discusses the indications of the revolution for his 35th year, followed by those for his 36th year. An alternative version of the events following from the revolution for the 35th year is found in the Segovia manuscript (edited in *App. I* after the text of the *Nativitas* and translated below). The relation of this document to the other version, present in the four other manuscripts, poses many problems of interpretation.

The divergence in the tradition is only found in the last section (corresponding to *Nat.* 3089-3169). In the preceding section starting with the chart for the 35th year (*Nat.* 2796-3088), both traditions offer the same version. Bate first examines at length the exact configurations for the revolution of the 35th year and the influence of the different astrological signifiers for his fortune or misfortune. His 35th year is mainly ruled by Venus, notwithstanding hindrances caused by Saturn and Mars. Referring to astrological authorities, and above all, to Albumasar, Bate infers that he will enjoy happiness and prosperity in this year ("significat prosperitatem in illo anno", *Nat.* 2857), mainly through women. Nevertheless, Bate also finds counter-indications: he will suffer from women through envy, quarrels, slander ("infamia et suspicio praua" 2894-2895), and will even suffer accusations of fornication ("rixas cum feminis et accusationes de fornicatione", *Nat.* 2884-2885). Other elements in the solar revolution are found to suggest that Bate will be plagued by all kinds of diseases ("egrotabit egritudine pessima", *Nat.* 2920), particularly in his eyes and in his head. On the authority of a large number of astrological authors, Bate tries to show that, while these misfortunes may cause anxiety and sorrow, they will fail to hinder a positive outcome for the coming year. For instance, one text by Albumasar predicts a difficult year, with victories for Bate's enemies and a serious injury ("significant malitiam anni et difficultatem et inimicorum uictoriam et uulnus a ferro ... ac damnum", *Nat.* 2949-2951). However, Bate manages to sidestep this indication by arguing that Albumasar's text might be corrupt ("truncatus"): "God's servant" will eventually escape these evils and impediments after some 80 days. Accordingly, he concludes (following Albumasar) that "some good will happen around the end of the [35th] year".

After this conclusion, we have two different versions of the events of the 35th year. In the manuscripts of the α tradition we find an astrological prediction of the events to come. In the *S* version, on the contrary, the events of the 35th year are described and assessed as having already happened in the past. Moreover, the Segovia account contains a wealth of autobiographical information that is missing in the other tradition. After the divergent version, both *S* and the α manuscripts give the chart of the 36th year followed by an explanation of what will happen in that year, when "the good that was indicated at the end of the previous year will receive its fulfilment" ("bonum in fine precedentis insinuatum consummationem recipiet", *Nat.* 3188). From there on, there are no more divergences between the two traditions, except for the usual accidents due to copying errors.

We shall first present the text of the α tradition and then the *S* version. Finally, we will try to explain why there are two different versions of the events of the 35th year.

1.2.2.1 The α version

The standard version begins with a somewhat solemn announcement of good tidings:

> "The year had then reached the angle of the tenth house of the root nativity, where two superior planets were both within the [astrological] terms of the conjunction, together with a fixed star and the 'lot of friends' in the house of Venus, who is now lord of the year and participating in the division. Given that [Venus] had such dignity in the root nativity, as was explained above, it appears that the prosperity and honour which, according to all philosophers, was indicated by these signifiers, may come about through female persons of high or royal rank, and this around the end of the year" (*Nat.* 3089-3097).

However, Bate continues, there will also be hindrances and misfortunes in the second quarter of the year due to the presence of the Moon and Saturn between the twin angles of mid-heaven and the West. Bate also expects to be affected by Mars around the beginning of the fourth quarter of that year. Furthermore, he needs to be on guard for the effects of an imminent Saturn-Mars conjunction (*Nat.* 3097-3106)

With Albumasar and Ibn Ezra, Bate finally determines that his misfortunes will be not fatal, but that he will have to be vigilant about a Saturnine disease, i.e. a tertian or quartian fever ("quartana aut tertiana", *Nat.* 3118). He must also beware of constipation, injuries in the eyes, and maladies of the entire head "unless the directions are not concordant" with the configurations (*Nat.* 3125-3126). Around Christmas 1280, a conjunction of the Moon with both Saturn and Mars also portends evil, and Mercury's simultaneous association with these planets reinforces the dangers (*Nat.* 3133-3140). Bate also finds cause for worry in Venus being combust at that time, even though Mercury's receding from Saturn and Mars and application to Jupiter should bring relief for the greater part of these evils (*Nat.* 3140-3144). Another cause for hope by the end of the year is given by Venus's return to the place it previously occupied in the revolution at the beginning of the year, and because the Sun will then have entered the degree of the lot of fortune (*Nat.* 3144-3149). Bate adds many more astrological indications of a prosperous end to the year.

> "Briefly, the height of the [native's] prosperity depends on Venus, and it is with her that we sealed off (*sigillauimus*) this year" (*Nat.* 3167-3169).

1.2.2.2. The S version

In view of the exceptional biographical (see below, sections 2.2 and 2.3) value of the S version of Bate's revolution for his 35th year, we here offer a full translation of this text, as found in *App. I* of our edition.

"Having first considered and examined these matters, let us now add the more notable events of this [current] year in an orderly manner. At the beginning of this year, after about three days [i.e., 27 March 1280], he whose revolution is cast here hastened himself to a monastery of nuns in Brabant along with the lord of his land. Having found there the relative and counsellor of the queen of France, his lord pleaded with her, imploring her, as if she was obliged, not to renege on her promise about the promotion of this servant of God [i.e., Bate], which she too had steadfastly approved.

However, to pass over this period quickly, during the whole first quarter of that year this person indulged in pleasures and delight, leading a jolly good life through various forms of corporeal pleasure, except that around Easter he suffered from an abscess in his throat. Afterwards, however, his reputation was spreading and it was rumoured among known and unknown people that this man, the subject of the revolution [of the 35th year], full with nourishing philosophy,[4] having rejected the dignity of heaven, was battling Jupiter's offspring, the venerable Pallas and contrived to crush the innate dignity of philosophy under the feet of Pluto by taking her captive into the freedom of matrimony, or rather into a servitude below matrimony.[5] And it was said that he had fallen into such insanity that he not only detested the worthy matrimony of Mercury and Philosophy, about which Martianus -called Capella- sang so admirably, but that he even plotted the perverse divorce of a sanctified and lawful matrimony, and that he had managed to let Mercury himself sink into the underworld by having an adulterous relationship with infernal Proserpina — God forbid!

Around the beginning of the second quarter of the year [i.e. around 23 June 1280] an accusation and reproach was raised [against him] with regard to some woman, which was made credible with innumerable assurances. As a result, some people in the entourage of the queen of England and her peers tried to make his reputation even worse. Moreover, rancour and jealousy were increasing among the malevolent people, and those who were hostile, both men of letters and merchants, did overrule the authority of friends.[6] The servant of God now had to be cautious and on guard against such people. The upsurge of this misfortune lasted about three months. It was at this time that he composed that vernacular poem on his all too numerous incredible hardships, addressing God in the forecourt of his heart: "Lord, how those that harass me have multiplied; many are rising against me". Furthermore, in these days he suffered from migraine, which is an excessive pain in the head. There was

---

4 "Satur almc philòsophic" (*App. I* 14). By using the term "satur" Bate may have wished to assimilate himself to Saturn. See Augustine, *De consensu evangelistarum*, I.23.35: "philosophi recentiores platonici … Saturnum aliter interpretari conati sunt dicentes appellatum cronon uelut a satietate intellectus eo, quod graece satietas coros, intellectus autem siue mens nûs dicitur". (We owe this reference to G. Guldentops).

5 Noticeable is the allegorical use of the "matrimony of Mercury and Philology" in *App. I* 15-24. Bate is not simply accused of bringing the virgin Pallas into matrimony ("libertas"), but even of forcing here into a sexual relation that does not have the status of a legal matrimony, but is a slave relation. A few lines further down it is said that he managed to make Mercury fornicate with Proserpina, which may refer to accusations of magic.

6 In *App. I* 30-31 we read instead of "animarum austeritate" (S) "amicorum auctoritate". See Cicero, *Laelius De amicitia* § 44: "plurimum in amicitia amicorum bene suadentium ualeat auctoritas".

also an evil imbalance of the entire body, about which the doctors were in doubt for not knowing its cause. [This happened] mainly around the beginning of the third quarter of the year [i.e., around 23 September 1280]. This person then suffered from an inflammation around the left eye, indeed almost of his entire jaw, due to an abscess in the left part of his nose.

In that third quarter of the year, when Venus reached the sign of profection, he took the road to Paris, leaving on the exact hour on which he was born – that is, when the sign of profection entered the seventh house, which contained the Moon with Cancer in the *Imum Coeli*. However, before he reached Paris, he suffered a great many troubles and nuisances, despite being as cautious as possible. After his departure from his region, during the three days when Venus was conjoined with Mars in Scorpio [10 November 1280], a new malicious rumour arose, now on the occasion of the misfortune of some lady who was once righteous, but who had been misled and deceived in a fraudulent manner. However, seeing that the disgrace was so blatantly false, the innocence of the accused [i.e., Bate] was immediately obvious. Moreover, because Saturn occupied his ascendant at birth, this person suffered from unusual constipation in his belly, and from a faintness of the head, along with continuous ringing and hissing in his ears and vertiginous disorder. Furthermore, at the time of the conjunction of Mercury with Mars and Saturn [c. 25 December 1280], he suffered difficulty in speaking because of an impediment of the tongue and some pain in the left side [of his tongue]. This happened especially when the Moon was conjoined with these [planets] for three days, right before Christmas. At that time, he also suffered from a widening of the uvula. Just prior to this, an affection of the eyes started which was countered through regimen and diet. Summarizing things, [it appears that] he suffered a weakening of the principle that is the head of Aries, for an unusual constipation of the belly is one of the affections most repugnant to the head.

Finally, near the beginning of the last quarter of the year, there was no disease, febrile or worse. This is empirical proof that revolutions of the years since birth do not add much force to the nativity if they are not especially strengthened by the concordance of directions and similar [celestial configurations]. Furthermore, the impediments of Saturn and Mars determining one another enacted their signification, each in proportion, at that time. For it happened twice in that quarter of the year that there was an abscess on the left nostril, albeit not a very serious one, while the hissing and vertigo in his head continued until the next year. His right ear was most affected because of Saturn, and his left nostril because of Mars, and this agrees with the sayings of the scholars. However, his eyes were not affected at that time. For the matter that should have caused this, was sufficiently contained in the ears and the nose instead. When Saturn was approaching its station [March 1281], the constipation of his belly began to cease. Indeed, these events and others [offer] sufficient evidence of the truthfulness of the claim, made by Ibn Ezra and others, that the latitude of conjoined [celestial] signifiers considerably weakens the force of the [astrological] testimonies.

But let us complete the year. Around the middle of February [1281], a man from Huy came forth with great insistence on behalf of some nephew to the king to make contact with him [=Henricus Bate]. Although there had already been talk about the same matter around the feast of St. Nicholas [i.e., 6 December 1280], it was thought that it would not come about, although (as it later transpired) this nobleman had a firm plan, long conceived from the innermost benevolence of friendship. For it is incumbent upon friends to finally give a suitable response to an urgent request by delaying it. Moreover, on 2 March [1281], which was Torch Sunday, around the twelfth hour of the day, this man had a conversation with the queen's counsellor, as had happened at the beginning of the year, and another conversation took place concerning this promotion on the following Thursday, around the third or fourth hour. This lady was initially backtracking on certain points. However, having convened a meeting, she promised anew that she would loyally aim to realize what she promised. And then, after three days, the 35th year was completed [23 March 1281]".

"In a margin of the book from which this nativity was taken, almost towards the end of the book, it was written: 'after Saturn made an ingress into the ascendant degree of the birth chart, up until its egress [i.e. November 1280 until January 1282], he suffered pain in the arm when moving it and a chronic paralysis accompanied by some pain.' See where this should be added [to the text], since such was not marked".

As will be fully explained below (see section 2.2), Bate tells us how, in the beginning of that year, he travelled with the lord of his land to a monastery in Brabant to see a nun, who was a relative and "counsellor" of the queen of France. Bate's lord asked her to intercede on the matter of an important benefice for Bate, something which she had already promised to do before. Although the intervention was initially unsuccessful, Bate was not overly worried and continued to have a good time. The second quarter of the year, however, brought a succession of problems: defamation, accusations by women of improper behaviour, perhaps even of magical practices. This difficult period lasted for about three months (see *App. I*, 32-34) – the afore-mentioned 80 days. Bate used this period to write a poem in vernacular about his misfortunes. This episode is followed by an extraordinarily detailed enumeration of Bate's diseases in that period: afflictions of his eyes, abcesses on the cheek and nose, problems in the head, constipation, a disordered equilibrium, and tinnitus. His poor health improved a little at the beginning of the fourth quarter. Finally, at the very end of the year, on the Sunday before Lent, after another intervention at the Brabant monastery, the queen's relative finally agreed to intervene on Bate's behalf.

1.2.2.3. Why are there two versions of the revolutions for the 35th year?

Both the *S* version and the α version deal with the revolutions for the 35th year, but they consider them from different perspectives. In the *S* version, Bate gives an extraordinary detailed and personal account of the events of his 35th year as if these had already happened. In fact, he is writing from the perspective of the end of his 35th year, i.e. March 1281, when he was probably completing his *Nativitas*. In other words, the *S* version offers empirical verifications of predictions rather than astrological predictions as such.

In the α version, however, Bate offers future events that might occur in his 35th year – things to be feared or hoped, and against which precautions should be taken. He writes from the perspective of someone entering his 35th year (i.e., on 23 March 1280), with the appropriate revolution chart laid out before him. As is usual in such astrological judgements, the future tense is used to describe the future configurations between 23 March 1280 and 23 March 1281, and gerundial forms or conjunctives are used to exhort the native to react to these celestial dispositions in a particular way: "one should take care", "one should guard against", "one should fear", "one should hope". Consider the following excerpts:

> "*manifestabitur* uirtus Iouis in tertia quarta anni. Impedimentum quoque Martis (...) *afficiet* seruum Dei uersus ultime quarte principium. Circa illud itaque tempus *caueat* sibi. (...) idcirco *caueat* homo Dei ab egritudine Saturnina, (...). *Cauendum* est etiam a constipatione uentris. (...) non *oberit* tamen, si *precaueatur* secundum Hermetis consilium (...). *Erit* autem circa Natale Domini in hoc anno Luna coniuncta ambobus. Verum quia Mercurius eisdem infortuniis consimiliter *associabitur* ad idem tempus, tanto magis *est timendum*,. (...). Item *timendum* est ad idem tempus (...). Verumtamen Mercurius a Saturno et Marte defluens Ioui *applicabit* cum mutua receptione, ratione cuius *consolandum est* de periculi parte maiori. Preterea *sperandum est* de meliori uersus finem anni, ut dictum est (...). Vnde motus significationis huius *esse debet* (...). Item Solis propinquitas (...) *exauget* promissum. Postremo autem (...) Veneris *stabitque* dispositio (...). *Disponet* igitur Venus principaliter (...)".

Despite the difference in perspective (one version writing about what may happen, the other about what has already happened), the two versions do have common content. First, both insist on the essential role of Venus in the positive outcome at the end of the year. The α version formulates this in a cryptic manner: "uidetur huiusmodi proficuum seu honor... procedere a mulieribus personis alti gradus seu regalibus et hoc uersus finem anni" (*Nat.* 3094-3096). This prediction was indeed realised at the end of the year, as we learn from the *S* version, where we are informed about the role of a nun who was "consiliaria regine Francie" and who accepted to intervene on behalf of Bate. Secondly, both versions discuss at length, the hindrances effected by the combined influence of Saturn and Mars, which would seem to hinder this positive outcome. Thirdly, both versions contain ample references to diseases (constipation, disorder of the eyes, of the whole head), again, as things to be feared in the α version, and as actual events in the *S* version. However, the *S* version is much more elaborate and detailed in its description of the diseases affecting Bate. Fourthly, we may note the reference of the α version to the Moon's conjunction with Saturn and Mars (with Mercury being associated to both) around Christmas 1280 (*Nat.* 3133-3135: "Erit autem circa Natale Domini in hoc anno Luna coniuncta ambobus..."). The prediction of a possible danger around Christmas is verified in the *S* version (*App. I* 62-63: "cum Luna ipsis coniuncta fuit quasi per triduum ante natale Domini"). However, whereas the α version relates a Saturnine disease to this Christmas conjunction (i.e., a tertian or quartan fever), the *S* version knows better: what really happened was some hindrance in the mouth which made it difficult to speak, and a widening of the uvula.

Interestingly, Bate characterizes the experiences of his 35th year as empirical confirmation of some of his earlier predictive claims, including "that the revolutions of the year to not add many force to the nativity if they are not strengthened by the concordance of the directions". Compare, for instance, *Nat.* 3125-3126 (α version, "nisi quia directiones et ea que prius dicta sunt non concordant" with *App. I* 69-72 ("*experimento* inuestigari potest quod annorum reuolutiones) natalium non magnam superaddunt radici fortitudinem nisi per directionum et consimilium consonantiam specialiter fuerint roborate").

In short, the *S* version is an empirical confirmation of the astrological prediction of the α version. Having finished his predictions for his 35th year (as we have them in the α version), Bate presumably kept a careful record of the actual events in that year. At the end of that 35th year, Bate appears to have done two things. First, he went back to his initial predictions and wrote the alternative version preserved in *S*. Secondly, there is evidence that Bate carefully compared prediction and actual events, and that he rephrased (perhaps even rewrote) some of his earlier predictions accordingly. Consider, for instance, *Nat.* 317-328, which Bate must have inserted in an earlier version of the *Nativitas* having experienced a dreadful disease at the beginning of his 35th year:

> "Moreover, some hindrances [to his promotion] are signified in the 35th year of this native, which has now just started (...) for at the beginning of that year he suffered from a rather harmful abscess on the upper jaw and throat, accompanied by a feverish heat".

That Bate suffered from a dangerous abscess in his throat is also mentioned in the *S* version of the 35th year, where we read that around Easter (i.e., "ineunte 35° anno"), the native suffered from an abscess in his throat ("passus est in faucibus apostema *App. I* 12). When Bate predicted the 35th year in the α version, he as yet did not know about this abscess, since he did not mention it.

We may conclude, then, that the *S* version was written at the end of Bate's 35th year (i.e., around March 1281), when Bate was happy to see that the positive outcome about his promotion, which he previously predicted through astrology, was finally realized. However, it remains unclear whether he intended the *S* version to replace the α version. The fact that the *S* version is not just a personal diary describing various diseases and other misfortunes, but that it is written in an amplified style, suggests that Bate intended to insert it in his *Nativitas* all along. He may have copied the *S* version in the margin of the α version without deleting the latter.

This leaves us with the question why the copy made for William of Saint-Cloud, which stands at the origin of the entire α tradition, does not have the version we find in *S*. One might think that the removal of this alternative version was intentional. Once Bate had obtained his long-awaited promotion, he may have been reluctant to make the details of the events of 1280-81 public. These could have been considered embarrassing for Bate, his worldly lord, and the counsellor of the French queen. But there is a simpler explanation. If the *S* version was indeed written in the margin of the corresponding α version, it is possible that the scribe who made the copy for William did not add what he found in the margin, while the copyist of the Segovia text thought that the marginal text had to replace the main text, even if this was not absolutely clear in the autograph. Anyway, it is fantastic that we have a copy of the two versions. It allows us to see how an astrologer like Bate attempted to empirically verify his predictions.

1.2.2.4. Is *S* a direct copy of Bate's autograph?

The presence of Bate's earlier predictions for his 35th year leads us to conclude that the Segovia manuscript goes back to Bate's original copy of the *Nativitas* in its primitive version. Might *S* have been a direct copy of Bate's autograph? A note written by the scribe of *S* after the text of the *Nativitas* (fol.28v) allows us to answer in the affirmative. The scribe claims to have found the following note in the margin of the book from which he copied the *Nativitas*:

> "After Saturn reached the ascendant degree of the root nativity and until it went out of Sagittarius [i.e. November 1280 until January 1282], he suffered pain in the arm when moving it and a chronic paralysis accompanied by some pain" (*App. I* 105-108).

This observation undoubtedly came from Bate himself, who usually traced his illnesses and bodily discomforts back to astral causes. Bate may have intended to integrate this additional experience in his version of the events of his 35th year. Interestingly, the remark was added later (1282), after the *Nativitas* had been written. Our scribe mentions that it was written *in margine* "near the end of the book". However, as this particular note lacked a clear reference sign, the copyist presumably did not know what to do, and simply added Bate's note to the end of the text.

After this marginal note, the scribe also copied a calculation for the duration of pregnancy, in which he differentiated between males and females, and between "minor, middle, and greater durations ("mora minor, media and maior", resp. 8 months and 18 days; 9 months and 3 days; 9 months and 18 days). This calculation corresponds to Bate's discussion of different methods for calculating the time between conception and birth (the so-called "trutina siue animodar") at the beginning of the *Nativitas*: "Corresponding to this are the different delays (*morae*) of the foetus in the maternal womb according to the different situation of the Moon at these two times" (*Nat.* 94-96). To be sure, one cannot exclude the possibility that a later scholar added the aforementioned calculations, having read Bate's discussion of the "trutina hermetis" method. However, it seems more probable that they come from Bate himself, since they immediately follow the marginal note mentioning pain in his arms, which was certainly written by him.

Our hypothesis that *S* is a direct copy of Bate's autograph might seem implausible in view of the fact that this copy was made after 1455 (this date is mentioned in a text on fol. 33r). Besides Bate's *Nativitas*, the Segovia manuscript contains a collection of astrological texts written by different scribes. There is a pagination on the inferior margin from p. 490 to 699, which seems to imply that a large part of the original codex was lost. However, the manuscript has an older quire numbering (9 quires of 12 folia each, labeled from *a* to *i*), showing that in fact nothing was lost from the original codex. The original quire numbering proves that this heteroclite collection of astrological treatises, short notes and astronomical tables were copied by different scribes around the same time, even if the texts themselves originated at different points in history. Thus, we have a prognostication for 1432, composed for the horizon of the city of Camerino, by Antonius de Murellis, "doctor artium et medicinae"[7] ; a solar table dated in Paris in 1331. The manuscript also contains a rare treatise *De directionibus* by Eustachius de Eldris (*fl.* 1390), a Liège astronomer working in the late 14th century.[8] De Eldris dedicated it to Gerlacus de Ghemert (*fl.* 1365-1415), who was court physician to Duchess Joan of Brabant (1355-1406) between 1365 and 1393.[9] Perhaps Eustachius acquired Bate's *Nativitas* along with other related materials (such as the Parisian solar table dated 1331), which later came into the hands of Antonio Murelli. While this is all very speculative, it remains a fascinating fact that Bate's autographed version of the *Nativitas* was copied somewhere in Italy in the late 15th century.

1.2.3.   *Title*

There is no title in *S V P* (while *L* is deficient at the beginning). However, an inscription in the margin of *S*, written in a hand other than the scribe's own, reads: "liber Henrici Baten cantoris Leodiensis de nativitate propria". In *P*, again in another hand, one finds in the margin "natiuitas magistri Henrici Macliensis cum quibusdam reuolutionibus". This marginal title corresponds to what we find in *P* and *L* at the end of the *Nativitas* (which also includes the *Nativitas* of William of Saint-Cloud): "Explicit natiuitas magistri Henrici Machliniensis cum quibusdam reuolutionibus"

---

[7]   On Antonius de Murellis, see Lanza 2001.

[8]   On Eustachius de Eldris, see Boudet 1997-9, p. 546, note 29c. There is one other copy known of this work, preserved in Paris, BNF, lat. 7279.

[9]   On Gherlacus de Ghemert, see Wetzer 2017.

The later hand in *P* probably derived his marginal title from this explicit. Moreover, the Segovia manuscript adds "Explicit natiuitas. Incipiunt reuolutiones presentis natiuitatis" just before the section on the solar revolutions for Bate's 35th and 36th years [i.e., after "sublimis" (*Nat.* 2781)].

Only in *Par* do we find the long title "liber serui Dei de Mechlinia de ducatu Brabantie super inquisitione et uerificatione natiuitatis incerte ex indiciis ac subsequentibus nato post natiuitatem". Scholars usually refer to Bate's work by this title, but the title seems to have been added by another hand in *Par*. The original copy of the text may have had no title at all, as was the case in its model *V*. One may suppose that the scholar who ordered the copy of the *Nativitas* to be made (Arnald of Brussels) composed the title. Inspiration for this title might have been drawn from Bate's nativity chart, which reads: "Natiuitas serui Dei ... in corde Brabantie opido Machelini". Indeed, the proposed title nicely summarizes what Bate attempts to do in the first part of his treatise (sections 2 and 3 of our edition). Here, Bate begins by determining the exact date and hour of his birth, for which he uses many "indicia": the testimony of his mother and aunt; the tomb of a deceased local lord in Mechelen's Franciscan church, etc. Finally, Bate draws upon his own personal history to verify the correctness of his proposed date of birth (see below, sections 4.1, 7.2, 7.3). Nevertheless, Bate's *Nativitas* contains much more than what this title suggests, and it seems improbable that he would have given his work this ambitious yet incomplete title. Maybe the marginal title in S comes closest to what Bate would have used as a title to name his treatise. As we shall see (below, section 2.2) Henry presented himself as "cantor Leodiensis", a status he only obtained in 1282 after the *Nativitas* had been composed. Maybe he used this title once he had obtained the long-anticipated benefice.

1.2.4. *Conclusion: a short text history*

There are undoubtedly two traditions of the *Nativitas*. One is represented by the Segovia manuscript, the other tradition by all other manuscripts. The Segovia manuscript goes back to Bate's autograph in its primitive version. It may have passed through the hands of Eustachius de Eldris at the end of the 14th century in Liège, and circulated in the 15th century in Italy. The four other manuscripts go back to a copy of the text [α] that Guillaume de Saint-Cloud obtained from Bate between 1280 and early 1285 (before he composed his own *Nativitas* in 1285). This manuscript may also have contained Albumasar's *De revolutionibus* (as it is present in *P Par* and *V*). From the exemplar α, another copy (β) was made from which *P* in Paris and later *L* (in Italy ?) were copied. It was also used around 1300, probably in Paris, by a scholar who added three astrological charts in *M*. In the 15th century, *P* belonged to the French astrologer Louis de Langle (d. 1463 or 1464), who added a section from Guido Bonatti's *Liber introductorius ad iudica stellarum*. After him, the manuscript passed to the famous astrologer Simon de Phares (1444-after 1499) before entering the Royal Library. *L* was bought in Padua in 1531 and may have been copied in northern Italy. Its model, the lost manuscript β, was then already circulating in Italy, as was manuscript α, from which the *Marcianus* was copied. Giovanni Pico della Mirandola (1463-1494) had a copy of Bate's *Nativitas* and *Speculum* (see below, section 4.3). The partial copy in *Vat* (and the manuscripts deriving from it) is also of Italian origin. It may have originated in the circle of Lorenzo Bonincontri (1410-c. 1491).

1.2.5. *Stemma codicum*

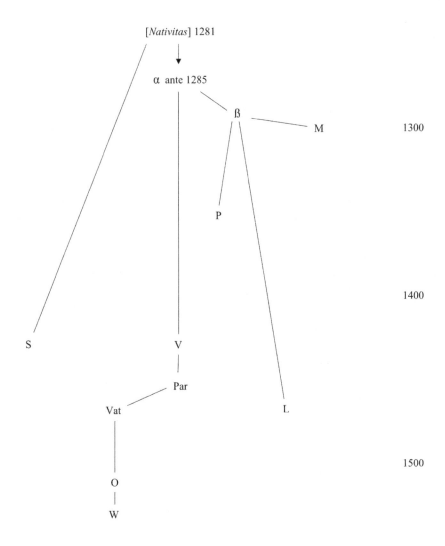

1.3. Editorial principles (Carlos Steel)

The text is transmitted by S and by the α tradition, which is represented by four manuscripts (L P Par V). As Par is a direct copy of V, we do not use it for the edition of the text, except for the horoscopes and in rare cases where V is uncertain. We had the benefit of a full transcription of the text in Par made by Van de Vyver, which served initially as the reference text for the collations of the other manuscripts. As was said before, we do not indicate the multiple errors of L in the apparatus, as it is a careless copy of the same model (β) used by P. The editor is thus confronted with a simple choice: S versus α represented by V (direct copy) and P (indirect copy). S, which is closer to Bate's original version, as is evident from the fact that it is the sole manuscript to preserve the version of the events of the year 1280-1281, makes it possible to correct the numerous errors of the α tradition, particularly its omissions. However, S is a mediocre copy in and of itself, with all sorts of errors, omissions, inversions, errors in reading abbreviations, etc. These can be corrected via the α manuscripts. Hence the editor must often choose between the readings of S and those of PV. In many cases the choice is obvious, as when omissions are made or when there are scribal errors. When Bate gives long and literal quotations of Aristotle, Albumasar, or Firmicus Maternus, it is easy to determine the right reading. Cases in which there is no external authority and where both readings are possible *ad sensum* are more difficult. Here we have taken, as our guiding principle, Bate's idioms and phrases as they appear elsewhere in the text. In the case of indifferent readings (e.g., inversions, ergo/igitur, seu/siue), we follow the α tradition, because S is a single manuscript and its scribe made many individual errors, even modifications of the text, whereas the lost α model is represented by two manuscripts copied by careful scribes, who did not intervene in the text. Only in exceptional cases did we take a reading of P against SV, or of V against PS. Rare are the cases where we had to intervene in the text and make conjectures. This shows that the twofold tradition allows us to come rather close to Bate's original text. This is remarkable, given Bate's idiosyncratic Latin and penchant for long and tortuous sentences, which offer ample opportunity for scribal errors. In Appendix I, where we have to rely upon the sole testimony of S, more conjectures were needed.

Given that all copies stem from the late 14th (P) or late 15th century (S V), we did not try to establish a consistent medieval orthography, but chose to normalize the spelling according to standard Latin dictionary lemma's. Moreover, S is often deviant. Thus, we write *imago* (P mostly ymago), *somnia* (sopnia SV sompnia P), *damnum* (dampnum PV), *uerumtamen* (uerumptamen PV). We kept word endings on -tio, -tia, as in S, though PV write *reuolucio, mencio, translacio*, etc. However, we do not introduce diphthongs (ae or oe) and do not distinguish between u/v, using -u- for both the vowel u and the consonant v, while keeping V only for capitals.

Proper names also pose a problem, as there are many variations in the manuscripts. *P*, which is the earliest copy of the text, best represents the medieval usage. Here again we have standardized the spelling, taking what seems to be the dominant form in the manuscripts. Thus, we always write Auenezre (though there are forms with -sre), Abraham (though there are some Habraham), Messehallah (though mostly Messehalah in *V*, and Mesahallach in *S*), Ptolomeus (though there are occasional forms with Pthol-) and Capitula Almansoris (sometimes Almassoris in *V*, Alma(s)sor in *S*), Zael (though *P* has mostly Zahel). We also uniformise technical astrological terms coming from the Arabic such as *almutas, alkocoden, firdaria, hyleg*. As in many medieval manuscripts, it is often difficult to distinguish *hec/hic/hoc*: we only note variations in the manuscripts when the non-abbreviated form is used. Bate likes to use the expression *huiusmodi*, which appears 45 times in the *Nativitas*. Here again, it is often difficult to distinguish abbreviations of *huius* from those of *huiusmodi*. We follow the usage of *V*, which is the most consistent. Variations in the manuscripts are only indicated when the full form is used.

The presentation of the four astrological charts raises a special problem. The figures in the manuscripts offer a considerable amount of astronomical data on matters like the house cusps, planetary positions, and a large variety of astrological lots – so much, in fact, that we found it materially impossible to represent all of these data in our versions of these charts, as included in our introduction (chapter 7) and text. Instead, our edition offers slightly simplified models of the charts (the originals of which can be found below, pp. 119-121). These include the necessary information concerning house cusps and planetary positions. Our edition offers the additional information provided by Bate on the content of the different houses in a list below each chart, numbered I-XII, following the twelve houses. The modern reader can form a good idea of the manuscript versions of the charts through the images, also included in this volume, of the original charts in BnF, lat. 10270 (*Par.*), which once belonged to Arnald of Brussels.

The critical apparatus is negative: we only indicate deviations from the accepted text. The only exceptions are editorial interventions. Orthographica are not mentioned. The titles and subtitles in the edition of the *Nativitas* are our own, as is the punctuation of the text.

Identifying the sources which Bate references proved to be an arduous task for at least two reasons: first, there is the sheer volume and breadth of Bate's references, which encompass the astrological literature of his time (on the latter, see below, section 5). The second obstacle is the absence of reliable modern editions for many of the astrological sources that Bate references (not to mention the almost complete absence of easily searchable digital versions). Despite many new editions that made important texts available in the past decades, we have often been forced to rely on non-critical editions from the 15th and 16th centuries. These were often based on incomplete texts, or on texts that differed substantially from the versions used by

Bate (notable examples include the *Liber novem iudicum*, Johannes Hispalensis's *Epitome*, Aomar's *De nativitatibus*, or Alcabitius's *Introductorius*). Despite these obstacles, we managed to identify almost all source references, though some references remain problematic when Bate is rephrasing his source in his own way.[10] For some texts we used a MS source to supplement what was lacking in the edition (thus Vat. lat. 6766 for the *Liber novem iudicum*, and Vat. Reg. lat. 1452 and Erfurt Ampl. O.84 for the *Isagoge* of Hispalensis).

The numerous quotations from the works of Ibn Ezra offer another problem. To our surprise, Bate never quotes from the translations he published later. Wherever it was possible, we checked the quoted text in MS Leipzig Univ. 1466, which is the oldest collection of Bate's translations. What we read in the manuscript was similar the text quoted in the *Nativitas*, but different in vocabulary and style. The most probable explanation is that Bate used the French translation that the Jewish scholar Hagins had made in his house in Mechelen in 1273 (see below, sections 2.2 and 6.1), and that he made an *ad hoc* Latin translation whenever he needed to quote a passage. Consider the following example, Ibn Ezra's *Reshit Ḥokhmah*, where we have the Hebrew original as well as the Old French and Bate's translations. We first give the Hebrew text with English translation in the edition of Sela (2017), then the Old French in the edition of Levy Cantera (1939), then the translation as found in the Leipzig MS, and finally the quotation in the *Nativitas*.[11]

> Ibn Ezra, *Reshit Ḥokhmah*, § 2.9:26, pp. 112-113: והנולד בו מבני אדם תהיה קומתו ישרה, והוא
> צהוב, ופחדיו ארוכים, ושוקיו עבות, והוא אדם שמח, וגבור, ונדיב, מצחו מחודד, וככה זקנו, ושערו דק,
> ובטנו גדולה, והוא קל לדלג, ואוהב הסוסים, וחכם במדות, ובעל מרמות ואינו עומד על דרך אחת, וקולו
> דק, ולא ירבו בניו.

> "A person born in it [Sagittarius], will be of medium height; he will be yellow, with long thighs and thick shanks; he will be happy, mighty, generous, with a pointed forehead, and so too his beard; he will have thin hair and large abdomen; he will skip switfly; he will be a lover of horses, learned in geometry, a liar, fickle, his voice will be thin, and he will not have many children.

> Et celi qui est né en li d'enfans d'ome il sera s'estande droit et il cler, et sen vit et si coullion sont lons et ses jambes espesses, et il home goieus et fort et volentif, et son front aguisié et ausinc sa barbe, et son poil menu et son ventre grant, et il ert legier a saillir et amans les chevaus, et sages en mesures, et sires d'engingnement, et ne se tient mie sur une voie, et sa vois basse et non croistront ses enfans. (*Commencement*, p. 64)

> At uero qui natus fuerit ex hominibus in hoc signo erit statura rectus et ipse splendidus, [ueretrum eius et testiculi longi,] tybie eius grosse, et ipse homo

---

[10]   Unidentified is a reference to Hermannus (*Nat.* 211-215) and a reference to the *Liber novem iudicum* (*Nat.* 910-912). In one passage Bate refers erroneously to Avicenna (=Albohali) (*Nat.* 176).

[11]   I thank Shlomo Sela for the references to the Hebrew text.

gaudiosus et fortis seu robustus et placidus, [frons eius acuta et similiter barba eius et capelli minuti, uenter eius magnus, et ipse agilis erit ad saliendum, equos amabit,] et sapiens erit in mensuris atque cauillosus, secundum unam uiam non se tenebit, et uox eius humilis seu grauis, et filii eius pauci. (MS Leipzig 1466, fol. 8vb:32-41)

Qui natus fuerit sub Sagittario erit eius statura recta et ipse clarus et tibie eius grosse et ipse hilaris et fortis et liberalis et sapiens in mensuris et ingeniosus et non tenens se super uiam | unam et uox eius humilis siue submissa et filii eius parum uiuent" (*Nat.* 821-825).

The Leipzig MS gives an accurate translation of the full text by Ibn Ezra, whereas the quotation in the *Nativitas* is much shorter than the original text. In fact, Bate often intentionally skips passages in the sources he quotes, because he considers them to be irrelevant ("equos amabit") or not appropriate ("ueretrum eius et testiculi longi") (On this self-censuring, see below, sections 2.3 and 4.1). But apart from that, both translations share similar vocabulary and phrases that point to the same translator. Consider "sapiens in mensuris", corresponding to the Hebrew חכם במדות, and "not tenens se super uiam unam", corresponding to the Hebrew ואינו עומד על דרך אחת, and "uox humilis", corresponding to the Hebrew וקולו דק. But there are also many differences: "clarus/splendidus" "hilarus/gaudiosus", "liberalis/placidus", "ingeniosus/cauillosus", "humilis/submissa", Moreover, it seems that Bate in the translated quotations is closer to the Old French translation than in the Leipzig translation. Consider the last phrase "filii eius parum uiuent" in the *Nativitas* ("non croistront ses enfans") whereas the Leipzig translation ("filli eius pauci") corresponds better to the Hebrew ולא ירבו בניו; or "clarus ("cler") versus "splendidus", "ingeniosus" (sires d'engingments") versus "cauillosus", which corresponds better to the Hebrew בעל מרמות. It is evident that the later 'published' translation is an improvement vis à vis the quotations in the *Nativitas*.

As said, it seems as if Bate made *ad hoc* translations from the French, whenever he quoted Ibn Ezra. However, it is also possible that he already had a draft Latin translation for some texts, which he edited later to produce a proper 'publication' with dates and colophons. An interesting case is *Nat.* 944-946. When discussing the affinity of the retrograde motion of the planets to the more divine beings, Bate refers to his commentary on Ibn Ezra's *Te'amim* I: "quemadmodum a nobis latius est expositum super *Libro rationum* Auenezre". This reference in fact corresponds to Bate's long digression in his translation of the treatise found in MS Leipzig Univ. 1466, fols. 69v-70r (and in Limoges BM 9 fols.37v-39r). We added a full transcription of this digression in *App. II*. The literal parallels with the *Nativitas* show that, at least for this treatise, Bate must have already made a Latin translation with digressions, which he later edited.

Given the fact that no Latin translation fully corresponds to the quotations from Ibn Ezra, we decided to refer to the editions of the Hebrew texts by Shlomo Sela, with the exception of those treatises that have only been transmitted in Latin, as the *Liber nativitatum* and *De nativitatibus*. However, whenever one of Bate's own translations exists, our source apparatus gives the Latin text according to MS Leipzig 1466; in the case of Ibn Ezra's *Reshit Ḥokhma*, we also include Bate's French translation, according to the edition of that translation by Levy and Cantera (Ibn Ezra, *Commencement*).

Given the fact that access to the sources Bate used is problematic, it is also difficult to distinguish exactly between quotations and paraphrases or modifications of the source text. As we know from the edition of the *Speculum divinorum* Bate is usually rigorous in his quotations. This is also the case in the *Nativitas*, at least where he quotes from Aristotle, Firmicus Maternus or Albumasar, but for other texts, such as Albohali or Iohannes Hispalensis, Bate takes much more liberties and often rewrites his sources, as he uses them to formulate what he considers to be his own character (see below, section 2.3). When quotations are literal (or parts of them) we use italics, even if words and verbs are somehow modified (v.g. different endings because a quoted sentence has been restructured).

Chapter 2
A portrait of Henry Bate
(Carlos Steel and Steven Vanden Broecke)

2.1. Introduction

Building on the example of Emile Littré (1801-1881), Aleksander Birkenmajer (1890-1967) identified the *Nativitas* as the single most important source for Bate's biography before 1280-81.[12] One can readily understand why: in this unique text, one finds Bate obsessively searching for reliable evidence of the precise time of his birth, of other important events in his life, in order to confirm the predictions based on his nativity chart. Bate's self-analysis sought to triangulate the evidence of historical events, the "supercelestial disposition" signified in his natal chart, and "the teachings of the philosophers".[13] Convinced that his nativity chart never failed to reveal the life story into which he was born, Bate provided his readers with an unusual amount of biographical and personal detail. The following biography thoroughly exploits the information found in the *Nativitas,* while supplementing it with data from both archival sources and his other works.[14]

2.2. Bate's biography

2.2.1. Family background

Bate was born in the city of Mechelen on Saturday the 24th of March 1246, shortly after midnight, after a pregnancy that was hardly noticeable to his mother's acquaintances.[15] Both of his parents died before 1280,[16] although Bate considered them to have had a rather long life.[17] Friendship between Bate and his parents was signified in the former's nativity.[18] There were at least four children in the Bate household, of which Henry Bate was the second youngest.[19] There was one older brother, whose nativity Henry Bate cast as well.[20] His older sister was born on the 11th of November, 1244.[21] We know nothing about Henry's younger sibling.

Bate was clearly from a well-to-do patrician family. In 1259, a "Henricus dictus Bate" —probably his father or uncle— is mentioned as one of the landlords of Grim-

---

12   Birkenmajer 1970, p. 109.
13   *Nat.* 345-346.
14   See also Wallerand 1931, pp. 7-13.
15   *Nat.* 72-73; *Nat.* 237.
16   *Nat.* 33-34; *Nat.* 1529-1530.
17   *Nat.* 690-691.
18   *Nat.* 1533, 1537.
19   *Nat.* 1516.
20   *Nat.* 1529-1530.
21   *Nat.* 53-55.

bergen abbey.²² Nicolas Bate, who was either Bate's brother or nephew, is regularly mentioned as dean of the St. Rumbold's chapter in Mechelen between 1290 and 1297.²³ The wife of his maternal uncle used the death of Walter IV Berthout, member of a long line of noble overlords of Mechelen, on 10 April 1244, as her private chronological reference point for the birth of Bate's older sister.²⁴ As we shall see, there is also evidence that Walter V Berthout intervened on Bate's behalf to obtain an ecclesiastical prebend.

2.2.2. *Studies in Paris*

This family background allowed Bate to move to Paris for his studies. In the colophons of his works, Bate typically refers to himself as *magister* (see below, chapter 3), which indicates that he obtained at least a master's degree from the Paris arts faculty. According to the university statutes, Bate could not have started his studies there before the age of fourteen (i.e. before 1260), nor could he have obtained a master's degree before the age of twenty (i.e., 1266). As for the end of Bate's Parisian studies, we are certain that Bate completed them before 1273, when we find him back in Mechelen, ready for an ecclesiastical career.

One further piece of evidence might allow us to push our *terminus ante quem* further back, to 1271 or so. As we will see below, Bate called Guy of Avesnes (c. 1253-1317), bishop of Utrecht between 1301 and 1317, his former disciple (*discipulus*) in philosophy. Guy of Avesnes fully embraced an ecclesiastical career between 1271 (around which time he became a canon of St. Lambert in Liège) and 1281 (when he became sacristan of St. Lambert and archdeacon of Hainaut). If we assume that Bate tutored Guy in philosophy prior to this career (i.e., around the age of 18), and if we assume that this happened after Bate's return from Paris, then we could plausibly date Bate's return to c. 1271.

Yet another possibility is that Guy himself studied at Paris (which he could have done, under the aforementioned statutes, by c. 1267), and that his 'discipleship' in fact refers to some form of being tutored by Bate while studying at the arts faculty. One problem with this scenario is that we have no that evidence Guy of Avesnes studied in Paris. Another problem is the language of a master-pupil relationship which Bate adopted towards Guy: this seems to imply a deeper intellectual *rapport* than could be expected from mere university tutoring. All things considered, it

---

²² Archief Abdij Grimbergen, MS Cl. 1,9 (dd. 7 February 1259): "Henrico dicto Bate, tanquam domino fundi". See Guldentops 2001, vol. 1, p. 4

²³ See Jamees 1991, p. 176 (doc. 225, dd. 6 July 1290); p. 180 (doc. 228, dd. 7 June 1291); p. 206 (doc. 260, dd. 6 December 1295); p. 227 (doc. 285, dd. 18 October 1297). See Guldentops 2001, vol. 1, pp. 4-5.

²⁴ On the Berthouts, see Croenen 2003. On the correct year of Walter IV Berthout's death, see ibidem, p. 312 note 3. Croenen situates Walter IV's death in 1243, criticizing Emmanuel Poulle's suggestion that Bate's testimony about the epitaph data for Walter IV's death refers to 1244 (n.s.). After weighing the arguments of Croenen against the evidence of Bate's interpretation of the chronology surrounding Walter IV's death, we decided to retain Poulle's interpretation.

seems safe to suggest that Bate obtained his Parisian master's degree between 1266 and c. 1271.

The *Nativitas* repeatedly suggests that Bate was well acquainted with medical science.[25] External confirmation is offered by *De diebus creticis*, in which Bate examined the astronomical conditions, in particular of the moon, for the development of certain diseases (see below, section 3.1). Bate's interest in medicine is equally apparent in parts VIII-X of his encyclopedic *Speculum divinorum*, where Bate refers to an impressive range of medical authorities. One might suppose, then, that he also attended classes in medicine as a student in Paris. The claim that he went on to study theology is unsubstantiated and perhaps even implausible, as he never shows any sustained interest in theological topics.[26]

Little is known about Bate's intellectual circle in Paris, but it seems very likely that he was connected to a thriving local community of celestial practitioners, which comprised, amongst others, Peter of Limoges, who was dean of the faculty of medicine between 1267 and 1270 (see below, section 5.3.2), and William of Saint-Cloud (1285-1292).[27] In the aforementioned *Speculum divinorum* (XVIII.15), Bate gives a detailed description of the passage of a comet between June and October 1264.[28] However, further research on contemporary observations of this comet will be necessary before we can securely establish whether Bate's description was based on personal observation, and whether it allows us to place him in Paris in 1264.

Pierre d'Ailly (1350/51-1420), Simon de Phares and Giovanni Pico della Mirandola all refer to Bate as a pupil of Albertus Magnus (1200-1280). This is implausible, given that Albert left Paris for Germany in 1254; the connection was probably made on the basis of Albert's reputation as an astrological authority. Still, the *Speculum divinorum* reveals that Bate was influenced by Albert's views on the intellect, and that he can be considered as the first representative of a tradition of thought later labeled as 'Albertism'.[29] Bate certainly came to know Thomas Aquinas (1225-1274), who taught in Paris between 1268 and 1272. The *Speculum divinorum* is replete with long quotations of Thomas's works, mostly his commentaries on Aristotle. Bate calls him the "novus expositor" and often confronts Thomas with the ancient commentator, Averroes. Very often, however, Bate criticizes Thomas's Aristotelian views, particularly on the intellective soul and its capacity to know intelligible objects, and defends a more Platonic view instead. Occasional remarks suggest a measure of envy towards the famous master.[30] The discussion on the intellective soul in *Specu-*

---

[25]   *Nat.* 2518-2519; *Nat.* 2535. For other references to Bate and medicine in the *Speculum*, see Van der Lugt 2004. For the strong sociological and disciplinary connection between medicine and the sciences of the stars until the 16th century, see Westman 1980.

[26]   Birkenmajer 1970, p. 4; Wallerand 1931, p. 9.

[27]   Wallerand 1931, p. 9.

[28]   On this comet, see Kronk 1999-2017, vol. 1, pp. 218-222.

[29]   Guldentops 2001a.

[30]   On Bate and Thomas, see Wallerand 1934 and Guldentops 2005.

lum divinorum (III.17 and V.14) also shows Bate to have been well acquainted with the views of his compatriot Siger of Brabant (1240-1282), whom Aquinas attacked in his *De unitate intellectus* (1270).[31] Although Bate's studies were probably completed by c. 1271, he returned to Paris after his studies, since the *Nativitas* places him there in the autumn of 1280.[32]

2.2.3. *Return to the Low Countries: courtly connections, astrology, and an ecclesiastical career*

In another passage of the *Nativitas*, Bate qualifies himself as a philosophy teacher and princely secretary[33], a function which we know he fulfilled for the aforementioned Guy of Avesnes, brother of John II of Avesnes, who was the count of Hainaut (1247-1304).[34] In fact, Bate dedicates his *Speculum* to Guy, addressing the bishop as follows:

> "To Lord Guy, brother of the count of Hainaut and Holland, bishop of the church of Utrecht by God's grace, who is now our reverend father, but previously was the son or pupil of philosophical doctrine and our beloved disciple; Henry of Mechelen, who is called Bate in the vernacular (meaning progress in Latin), cantor of the church of Liege, wishes him a blessed life burning of love for true and perfect Sophia, that is, uncreated and created wisdom. May he measure his active life with unfailing prudence, so that speculative wisdom may always rise above it and the best part never be taken away".[35]

Even taking into account rhetorical emphasis, there can be no doubt that Bate and his disciple continued to have a close relationship throughout their lives.

The *Nativitas* tells us that Bate obtained his first ecclesiastical prebend in his 28th year (i.e. in 1273).[36] The colophons of four translations of works of Ibn Ezra (see below, section 3.2) show that he was residing in his native Mechelen at that time. This suggests that the benefice was tied to the local church of St. Rumbold. Bate's first ecclesiastical advancement coincided with his initial ventures in astrological authorship. In 1273, four astrological treatises by Abraham Ibn Ezra were translated into French in his house in Mechelen, in a joint venture with "Hagins le Juif" (i.e., Chajjim, responsible for translating from Hebrew into French) and a certain Obert de Montdidier (who wrote down Hagins's oral translation).[37] There may have been more translations, as is clear from other references in the *Nativitas*. Bate may have become acquainted with Hagins in Paris. In 1278, Bate made a translation of *De*

---

[31]   See Nardi 1945, pp. 175-177.
[32]   *Nat.* 44.
[33]   Tutorship: *Nat.* 2507-2508. Secretary: *Nat.* 1129-1130; *Nat.* 2522.
[34]   On this topic, see Van de Vyver 1960, pp. xiv-xv.
[35]   Van de Vyver 1960, p. 3:1-11.
[36]   *Nat.* 280-281.
[37]   Wallerand 1931, p. 14.

iudiciis revolutionum annorum mundi, a treatise attributed to al-Kindi, "ad preces Iohannis de Milana" (see below, section 3.2.1). Thanks to a legal document made in Mechelen on February 1259, we can identify the commissioner of this translation as John of Milanen, alderman of Mechelen and possibly Bate's uncle.[38]

In 1274, Bate participated in the council of Lyons (7 March-17 July), where he established a solid friendship with the famous translator William of Moerbeke OP, whose translation of Ptolemy's *Tetrabiblos* was used by Bate throughout the *Nativitas*.[39] It was to Moerbeke that Bate addressed his treatise on the astrolabe, in a letter from Mechelen dated 11 October 1274.[40] It was also in Mechelen that Bate composed his treatise on the equatorium and his own astronomical tables, the *Tabulae Machlinienses*.[41]

One may wonder why Henry, who was not a bishop, was invited to attend the council of Lyons. A possible explanation may lie in his connections with the court of the count of Hainaut. Among the decisions taken by the council was the deposition of the prince-bishop of Liège, Henry III of Guelders (d. 1285). One of the candidates for Henry III's succession was John of Enghien (d. 1281), a bishop of Tournai with good connections at the court of Pope Gregory X (1271-1276). John of Enghien most probably attended the council in Lyons to promote his (successful) bid for the Liège position; if this was so, he may have been assisted by the young Henry Bate, since Bate played a similar role when promoting the candidacy of Guy of Avesnes in Orvieto in 1292 (see below, section 2.4). After all, the Enghien and Avesnes families were closely related: the mother of John of Enghien was a cousin of count John of Avesnes, brother of Bate's pupil Guy of Avesnes.

As we learn again from the *Nativitas*, Bate received a second, "fatter" ecclesiastical benefice,[42] apparently involving "various disturbances and difficulties",[43] near the end of May 1276[44], when Bate was in his 31st year.[45] Gaston Wallerand and others have suggested that it was this second benefice that brought him to the cathedral chapter of St. Lambert in Liège.[46] The fact that John of Enghien was bishop of Liège probably played a role in this appointment. The earliest explicit evidence connecting Bate to Liège comes from the colophon of his translation of Abraham Ibn Ezra's *'Olam I [De mundo vel seculo]* of 1281, which states that he began the translation

[38] See Goetschalckx 1907, p. 318, nr. 444: "Vniversis presentes litteras visuris Everardus de Ralenbeca, Iohannes de Milana, Walterus de Stadiken, Scabini Machlienses". Also see below, note 68.
[39] Wallerand 1931, p. 11.
[40] On the nature of Bate's friendship with Moerbeke, see Guldentops 2001, vol. 1, pp. 6-7 n 32.
[41] Poulle 2008; Poulle 1964; d'Alverny and Poulle 1956.
[42] *Nat.* 286.
[43] *Nat.* 314-315, 318; also see *Nat.* 1017-1023.
[44] *Nat.* 290.
[45] *Nat.* 309-310.
[46] Wallerand 1931, p. 11; Renardy 1981, p. 291; Guldentops 2001, vol. 1, p. 7.

in Liège, presumably sometime around 1279/80, but finished it in Mechelen.[47] Bate apparently kept his residence in Mechelen.

Bate candidly admitted the importance of worldly connections to his career. The *Nativitas* tells us that he obtained his first two benefices (i.e., in 1273 and 1276) through the aid of the same[48] "illustrious martial prince"[49], and mentions that he obtained many goods from women as well.[50] Although the identity of these patrons remains unclear, there is evidence suggesting that Bate's "illustrious prince" was in fact the powerful Walter V Berthout (d. after 1286)[51], who also intervened to help Bate obtain the third and most important benefice (in 1281).

Berthout was married to a niece of Henry II, duke of Brabant (1207-1248), and thus closely related to the court.[52] In the absence of the duke, Berthout even took on the role of regent of Brabant for a while. On the other hand, Berthout also acted as 'advocatus ecclesiae', expected to defend the privileges of the church of Liège in Mechelen. In actual fact, Berthout was more interested in establishing his own seigneurial position in Mechelen, and got into armed conflicted with prince-bishop Henry III of Guelders.[53] Relations improved during John of Enghien's tenure at Liège (1274-1281).[54] It is around this time that Berthout may have intervened on behalf of Bate.

As for Bate's reference to the role of female patrons, a fascinating glimpse of these connections is offered by the alternative, retrospective version of Bate's astrological analysis for his 35th year in *S*.[55] In this version, Bate recounts negotiations concerning a new (his third?) benefice, which happened in the year beginning on 24 March 1280:

> "In the beginning of this year, after three days or so, he whose revolution is cast here, hastened himself to a monastery of nuns in Brabant along with the lord of his lands. Having found there a relative and counsellor of the queen of France, the lord pleaded with her, imploring her as if she was obliged, not to renege on her promise about the promotion of this servant of God [i.e., Bate], which she herself had steadfastly approved".[56]

Near the end of his *versio altera*, Bate reports the outcome of these negotiations:

> "Around the middle of February [1281], a man from Huy came forth with great insistence on behalf of some nephew to the king to make contact with him. Although

---

[47] Wallerand 1931, p. 16 note 16; Sela 2010, p. 5.
[48] *Nat.* 286-287.
[49] *Nat.* 289.
[50] *Nat.* 1773-1774.
[51] On Walter V Berthout, see Croenen 2003, pp. 325-331.
[52] Croenen 2003, p. 53.
[53] Croenen 2003, pp. 99, 102.
[54] Croenen 2003, p. 100.
[55] See above, section 1.2.2.2, and below, *App. I*.
[56] *App. I* 2-9.

there had already been talk about the same matter around the feast of St. Nicholas [i.e., 6 December 1280], I had little hope about its outcome, although (as it later transpired) this nobleman had a firm plan, long conceived from the innermost benevolence of friendship. For it is incumbent upon friends to finally give a suitable response to an urgent request by delaying it. Moreover, on 2 March [1281], which was Torch Sunday, around the twelfth hour of the day, this man had a conversation with the queen's counsellor, as had happened at the beginning of the year, and another conversation concerning this promotion was had on the following Thursday, around the third or fourth hour. Although this lady was initially backtracking on certain points, having convened a meeting, she promised anew that she would loyally aim to realize her promise. And then after three days the 35th year was completed".[57]

Which monastery might this be? And who was the *consiliaria* whom Bate's friends targeted there throughout the year? One tentative answer can be developed through the reference to the queen of France. In 1281, this was Mary of Brabant (1254-1322), daughter to Henry III, duke of Brabant (c. 1231-1261) and second wife of the French king Philip III (1245-1285). Assuming that the Brabant monastery which Bate visited in 1281 had a special relation with Mary, we might consider the Dominican monastery of Val Duchesse (Hertoginnedal) in Auderghem, near Brussels, as a likely option. Val Duchesse was founded in 1262 by Mary's mother, Aleidis of Brabant (1233-1273), and Mary of Brabant is mentioned several times, between 1275 and 1293, in charters related to Val Duchesse.[58]

Who was Mary's "familiar counsellor" ("familiaris consiliaria")? Only four 13th-century members of the Val Duchesse community have been identified with certainty, among whom only the prioresses might seem to qualify for this type of relation to the queen of France.[59] In 1281, this prioress was Aleidis of Burgundy, niece of the founder Aleidis of Brabant. An alternative possibility, however, is indicated by the text of a donation made to Val Duchesse in 1293. In this charter, the donor Beatrice of Jodoigne is explicitly identified as maid of honour to Mary of Brabant ("damoysselle a ... madamme Mary, reyne de Franche").[60] One could surmise that Beatrice of Jodoigne was related to the aforementioned John of Enghien, then prince-bishop of Liège, and that it was she who intervened on Bate's behalf.

This third benefice, so difficult to obtain in 1281, must have been the position of "cantor" at the cathedral chapter in Liège. The cantor was the second in dignity after the dean of the chapter, and a fat prebend was usually attached to such a position. The first solid proof of Bate holding this position dates from 1289, when he is mentioned as cantor and canon of St. Lambert cathedral, acting on the authority

---

[57]   *App. I* 86-100.
[58]   Information kindly supplied by Godfried Croenen.
[59]   See Bogaerts 1979, pp. 144 and 234.
[60]   A copy of this charter is preserved in Algemeen Rijksarchief Brussel, Kerkelijke archieven Brabant, nr. 11465, fol. 91r. See Uyttebrouck and Graffart 1979, p. 52, nr. 51. We thank Godfried Croenen for bringing this document to our attention.

of the cathedral chapter in a legal dispute with prince-bishop John of Flanders (1282-1292).[61] This shows that Bate already enjoyed great authority in Liège at that time. We also find this title in the colophons of his translations of Ibn Ezra, made in Orvieto (see below, section 3.2). In the aforementioned dedication letter of the *Speculum* too, Bate presents himself as "Leodiensis ecclesie cantor".

2.2.4. *After the* Nativitas

Since the *Nativitas* was composed in 1280-81, information for the later period of Bate's life is relatively scarce. Early in 1292, Bate accompanied Guy of Avesnes to Orvieto to assist him in defending his interests at the papal court. The occasion was a dispute about the succession to the episcopal see of Liège, which Guy was now hoping to obtain following the death of prince-bishop John II of Dampierre (1282-1292).[62] Pope Nicholas IV (1288-1292) died on 4 April, not long after their arrival; discussion about the election of a new pope was drawn out and only Bate stayed on, probably to keep an eye on his patron's interests. Bate benefited from this prolonged stay to complete his translations of astrological works by Abraham Ibn Ezra.[63] The last of these translations was dated 29 October 1292.

It was also in Orvieto that Bate came to know Adam, bishop of Aversa, to whom he dedicated his translation of *De luminaribus* in 1292.[64] Adam, a native of Picardie and former "rector ecclesie de Brayo" (Braye-sur-Somme), is mentioned in the *Registri* of Charles I of Anjou (1226/7-1285) as "consiliarius et medicus regis". With the support of this royal patron, Adam became bishop of Aversa at the end of 1276, holding this position until his death in 1293. Adam probably stayed in Orvieto for some time, as did many members of the curia, during the prolonged conclave after the death of Nicholas IV. It is there that he may have become acquainted with Henry Bate, with whom he could converse in Picardian on matters of common interest.

---

[61]   Wallerand 1931, p. 11. Renardy 1981, p. 291 situates Bate's first Liège prebend in May 1276, his preceptorship of Guy of Avesnes in 1281, and his Liège cantorship on 6 April 1289.

[62]   Wallerand 1931, pp. 12-13; Van de Vyver 1960, pp. xiv-xvi.

[63]   Wallerand 1931, pp. 16-7.

[64]   See the colophon of the translation of *De luminaribus*, below, section 3.2, with the dedication to "reverendo patre domino N presulo Aversano". "N" as found in the MS of Limoges is certainly an error for "A" (as is found in the colophon of the Glasgow MS). In fact, between 1276 and 1293, Adam of Bray was bishop of Aversa (see Birkenmajer 1970, p. 108). Filangieri di Candida 1950-2000 gives several references to Adam de Aversa. Most of these relate to disputes about property and the payment of tithes. See vol. 18 (1277-78), n. 405: "pater A. Adversanus episcopus, dilectus consiliarius et familiaris noster"; vol. 19 (1277-78), n. 15: "consiliarius et medicus regis"; vol. 21 (1278-79), n. 46: "Adam rector ecclesie de Brayo"; vol. 25 (1280-82), n. 52: "Adam episcopus Aversanus familiarius et consiliarius regis"; vol. 27 (1283-85), n. 13: "Adam episcopus Aversanus consiliarius et familiarius". Adam remained as bishop active as "medicus". In vol. 23 (1279-1280), n. 126 and 152, Adam is mentioned as member of a committee to examine a candidate bachelor in medicine. Vol. 19 (1277-78), n. 390 is also interesting. It is an order of the king to his treasurer asking him to make a copy of a book to be sent -without delay- to the bishop "transcribendum per eum ad opus suum accommodare per quinternum sine difficultate procuretis". We owe a debt of gratitude to Dr. Pasquale Arfé (Naples), who provided copies of all relevant pages in the *Registri*.

Given Adam's interest in medical matters, it is possible that Bate also composed his *De diebus creticis* for him (see below, section 3.1).

After returning to the Low Countries, Bate probably went back to residing in Mechelen rather than Liège, where Hugh of Chalon (1260-1312) became prince-bishop in 1296. At the end of his life, Bate devoted himself to the writing of a philosophical encyclopedia called the *Speculum divinorum*, dedicated to Guy of Avesnes, who had, in the meantime, become bishop of Utrecht in 1301.[65] From the dedicatory letter, it appears that Bate remained in close relations with his former noble pupil: Bate claims to have composed the *Speculum* upon Guy's request.

The work was completed between 1301 and c. 1305.[66] However, Bate must have started working on this monumental project much earlier, collecting materials as early as his Paris student years. It is also clear that Bate had an extraordinarily rich collection of scientific and philosophical works. Some references in the *Speculum* indicate that Bate resided in Mechelen while was working on the last volumes. In part XIX, he recounts stories about strange events happening in Leuven and Relegem, a small village close to Brussels. In an addition to the *Speculum*, Bate tells a story about ghostly appearances occurring in Berlaar, a village close to Mechelen, in 1305-6.[67]

His presence in Mechelen is again attested in a legal document from 1308.[68] Another biographical reference from that year is found in an addition to part XXII, chapter 18, which Bate wrote some years after the *Speculum* was completed. In this addition, Bate refers to a solar eclipse he observed on 31 January 1310 [i.e., 1309].[69] According to Bate, this eclipse confirms the astronomical tables he had composed and corrected "tertio et ultimo" (*add.* 44).

> "Still, our own tables, which have been corrected by taking ancient and modern observations into account, insofar as this was possible for us while assuming the principles of astronomy, are found to agree with the appearances much more than do the other tables. This has been clearly ascertained and observed, through sense perception, from a solar eclipse on the last day of January 1309. In the middle of the [visibility of] that eclipse, a kind of circle of solar radiance appeared, shining equally all around the Moon through the intermediate transparency of a quite pervious cloud. Finally, our aforementioned tables should not at all be despised. For by means

---

[65] It has been generally accepted that the title of Bate's magnum opus is *Speculum divinorum et quorundam naturalium*. However, Guldentops (2002, pp. 395-396) convincingly argued that *Speculum divinorum* is the original title of the work.

[66] Poulle 2008; Van de Vyver 1960, pp. xiv-xv.

[67] Guldentops 1997.

[68] Guldentops 1997; Guldentops 2001, vol. 1, p. 8 (with reference to Erens 1950, pp. 174-175; nr. 401 dd. 13 August 1308). This document (along with Erens 1950, nr. 402) shows that Bate inherited a property on the Nieuwe Bruul in Mechelen from the aforementioned John of Milanen, who was perhaps his uncle.

[69] Bate himself dates the eclipse to 1309, following the calendar convention of starting the new year on Easter: see *Nat.* 40-42.

of these [tables], which are harmonized with the observations done previously by Ptolemy and later by us and which agree with truthful experience, it is possible to find the places of the planets and their conjunctions, as well as the revolutions of the year and its seasons; I mean at least those conjunctions about which it is primarily worthwhile or necessary to have some certitude without the vain effort of searching out the proportional longer or nearer longitudes, in which, as we have said, [the hypothesis of] eccentricity is brought in".[70]

This is Bate's astronomical testament, written when he was in his sixties. He clearly took great pride in his astronomical tables, considering them superior to other tables. Yet we also sense some disappointment concerning their reception ("demum neque spernandae sunt omnino"). The text also demonstrates his ongoing interest in the sciences of the stars; as late as 1298, Bate was receiving astronomical eclipse reports from Paris (see below, section 5.3.3). His ongoing interest in the effects of the visible heavens on human life is also evident from many sections in the part XIX of the *Speculum*, which covers extraordinary natural phenomena.[71]

Bate may have spent his last years at the abbey of Tongerlo.[72] He is mentioned in three necrologia: those of the abbey of Tongerlo, of the abbey of St. Bernard in Hemiksem, and of the cathedral chapter of Liège. Unfortunately, only the day of Bate's death is mentioned (resp. as October 20, 21, and 25) — not the year.[73] More research is required to determine the subsequent fate of Bate's extraordinary library.

2.3. Bate's self-portrait

Born in spring, Bate found his appearance agreeable due to the dominance of humid and hot qualities in his complexion. Healthy, white in color[74], Bate claimed to enjoy good eyes, height, and bodily bearing.[75] The Moon's disposition and an ascendant in Sagittarius[76] signified a rotund face, upright posture, almost converging brows and swift motions, despite certain Saturnine influences.[77] The only clear blot on Bate's virile constitution[78] were some nutritional difficulties brought on by the Moon's oppositional aspect to the ascendant degree of Bate's nativity.[79]

---

[70]   See Steel and Guldentops 1996, p. 347-348 (*Additio*, 51-66), translation by Guy Guldentops, modified.

[71]   See the discussion *in Speculum*, pars XIX, c. 10: "de generatione portentorum seu monstrorum ad finem aliquam a cura diuina per uirtutem celestem causatorum secundum astrologorum iudicia et exempla", which contains long quotations from Haly Abenragel.

[72]   According to Sanderus 1659, pp. 21-22, Bate was friends with abbot Godfrey of Herentals and stayed in the abbaye at 1309.

[73]   Guldentops 2001, p. 8.

[74]   *Nat.* 817.

[75]   *Nat.* 780-782.

[76]   *Nat.* 821-824.

[77]   *Nat.* 816-820.

[78]   *Nat.* 810.

[79]   *Nat.* 785-786.

Despite this positive outlook, Bate's *Nativitas* often reads as the narrative of someone in worryingly ill health. In order to verify his birth time through the astrological technique of primary directions, Bate was able to draw on his experience of several grave illnesses. At 21 and 24, he suffered from serious bouts of *disinteria*.[80] At the age of 30, Bate was struck by a dangerous disease of the eyes[81], followed by "a rather harmful abscess on the upper jaw and throat, accompanied by a feverish heat" as he reached the age of 35.[82]

The aforementioned *versio altera* (see *App. I* and above, section 1.2.2.2) offers a more detailed account of Bate's health in his 35th year. Around Easter 1280, Bate's swelling of the throat returned. The summer brought him severe headaches of which physicians could not determine the cause, while an abscess on the left nostril spread to his entire jaw, causing an inflammation of the left eye. In the autumn of 1280, Bate was constipated while suffering from a constant ringing in his head, aggravated by bouts of vertigo. A conjunction of Mercury with Mars and Saturn made it difficult for him to speak and, some three days before Christmas, gave him pain in the left side of his tongue. Around the same time, Bate experienced a loosening of the tonsils and another eye disease. These were successfully treated with regimen and diet. Finally, the winter of 1280/1 brought fever, two light abscesses of the left nostril, while the ringing in Bate's ears persisted. On the positive side, his eyes were momentarily fine, while his constipation relaxed by the following spring.

According to Bate, most mercurial properties and conditions had been impressed on him. In Albumasar's *Introductorium maius*, he found that this led him towards "probable inductions, necessary syllogisms, the study of philosophy, poetry, as well as medicine, several mathematical arts such as arithmetic, geometry and astronomy, as well as music, poetry, and dance".[83] In each of these sciences, he felt particularly drawn towards practical use and application,[84] novel inventions and the comprehension of secret things.[85] After Easter 1280, Bate was surrounded by rumors of his engagement with the dark arts.[86] Bate also admitted to having frequent dreams of flying.[87]

It has been pointed out that music played a substantial role in Bate's life, both as cantor at Liège cathedral and in his philosophical *Speculum*.[88] Bate's *Nativitas* strongly confirms this:

---

[80] *Nat.* 242-243; *Nat.* 263-264.
[81] *Nat.* 269-270.
[82] *Nat.* 324-325.
[83] *Nat.* 1150-1155; *Nat.* 2241.
[84] *Nat.* 1179-1180.
[85] *Nat.* 1154-1155; *Nat.* 1194-1195.
[86] *App. I* 12-24.
[87] *Nat.* 2273.
[88] On Bate and music, see: Goldine 1964, Page 1986, pp. 59-61, Jeffreys 2009, 90-91, Silan 2008. We are grateful for the advice of Prof. David Burn (KU Leuven, Dept. of Musicology) in translating these passages.

"From childhood, this servant of God gladly listened to people playing on flutes and pipes and to every kind of musical instrument, finding so much pleasure in them that he acquired a share in almost every one of these arts. He knew how to modulate air through pipes, flutes and diverse kinds of reeds, and also how to elicit melodic tunes with organs and strings by striking keys.

This man knew how to carry the melodious fiddle, handling the touch of its snares and the drawing of the bow in due proportion, how to skilfully touch the citola with fingers and plectrum. Using a double feather, he knew how to bring out in harmony pleasant melodies from the sweet-sounding psaltery, and how to replicate the delightful sound of the Lycian trumpet by playing the tympan with beats replicated in turn. Moreover, he mastered every kind of singing and diverse kinds of popular songs in various languages, and was himself fond of singing. He was a merry inventor of poems and songs, a playful and delightful leader of dances, a master of outdoor dances who enjoyed preparing plays, feasts and jokes, initiating playful dance in company".[89]

By his own admission, Bate lost interest in flute playing when he decided to study philosophy and became more obedient to the intellect.[90] He refers to what Aristotle recounts about Athena in his *Politics* (VIII 7): "she threw away the flute, because its practice did not contribute to knowledge". Nevertheless, he found consolation in the same Aristotle praising a moderate practice of music in a well-educated young man. Interestingly, we find Bate composing a vernacular song on his misfortunes in the summer of 1280.[91]

Another frequent source of pleasures and tensions was Bate's professed weakness for women, including young girls.[92] Bate's analysis of the fifth house confirmed these inclinations, which ran counter to the philosopher's traditional *persona*.[93] Most embarrassing for Bate was the fact that his nativity chart clearly predicted that he should become legally married; an impossibility in view of his clerical status. Bate found a satisfactory solution:

"Even if we grant that the configuration of the signifying stars predict that this person should become legally married, it does not necessarily follow that he should go under the female yoke. For as Ptolemy says in his *Centiloquium*: when one knows the nature of the stars, one can avert many of their influences".[94]

Nevertheless, venereal matters were marked out as a frequent source of adversity and tribulation.[95] Bate's subsequent discussion of the events of his 35th year appear

[89] *Nat.* 1308-1320. For other references to Bate's singing, see *Nat.* 1701-1702; *Nat.* 2497.
[90] *Nat.* 1292-1295; *Nat.* 1327-1328.
[91] *App. I* 33-35.
[92] *Nat.* 1791-1792.
[93] *Nat.* 1011-1012.
[94] *Nat.* 1866-1872.
[95] *Nat.* 1678-1680.

to confirm this. In the summer of 1280, female relations led Bate to become the object of much gossip. This problem recurred around 10 November 1280, when Venus was conjoined with Mars in Scorpio. At this point, Bate once again claimed his innocence and victimization by "a woman who had been misled and deceived in a fraudulent manner".[96] Bate preferred to be discreet about his affairs, on his own account for fear of becoming prolix and because of his natural desire for secrecy.[97] His self-analysis betrays a clear tendency towards censorship concerning astrological significations with overly explicit sexual implications.[98]

Despite Bate's talents as an extraverted *bon vivant*, he also confessed to a measure of loneliness in his social environment, where he claimed to have many friends but few confidants.[99] Indeed, the *Nativitas* contains several references to "detractors and jealous people", possibly occasioned by Bate's steady rise in ecclesiastical and courtly *milieux*.[100] Beyond these worldly contingencies, however, Bate suggested a "sadness" inside of himself,[101] which he counteracted by privileging that "noble love of the sciences, *trivium*, moral philosophy, and the others, as well as the three theoretical philosophical disciplines of mathematics, natural philosophy, and theology".[102]

As was customary in the analysis of astrological nativities, Bate commented at length on his manner and time of death. Concerning the latter topic, he remained surprisingly vague, determining a life expectancy of some 80 years.[103] Although Bate's analysis eventually suggested a gentle death between family and friends,[104] he still considered it necessary to take specific precautions against the possibility of dying abroad or from a fall, especially while horse riding.[105]

---

[96]   *App. I* 51-52.

[97]   *Nat.* 1299-1303; on Bate's tendency to secrecy, see also *Nat.* 1863-1866 and *Speculum*, XIX, 24 (the latter has the same reference to *Albumasar in Sadan*).

[98]   Notable examples include: Bate's omission of the passus "ueretrum eius et testiculi longi" when quoting Ibn Ezra in *Nat.* 821-825; omission of the passus "in coitu et in vestimentorum ornatu et in unguentorum unctione" when quoting Albumasar in *Nat.* 2862-2865; omission of the passus "et multiplicabitur coitus eius" and "diuersis vestibus delectabitur" when quoting Albumasar in *Nat.* 2868-2873.

[99]   *Nat.* 1356-1357.

[100]   *Nat.* 1934-1950; *Nat.* 2180-2189.

[101]   *Nat.* 1372-1373.

[102]   *Nat.* 1365-1368.

[103]   *Nat.* 712-725.

[104]   *Nat.* 2702-2703.

[105]   *Nat.* 2708-2709; *Nat.* 2732.

CHAPTER 3
BATE'S ASTROLOGICAL AND ASTRONOMICAL WORKS
(David Juste)

3.1. Original works

3.1.1. Magistralis compositio astrolabii (1274)[106]

Completed on 11 October 1274 at the request of William of Moerbeke, this text describes the construction and uses of an original astrolabe especially designed for astrological purposes (projection of rays and directions, ascensions of zodiacal signs for the latitude of Mechelen, planetary longitudes and latitudes). Authorities include Ptolemy, Geber, Albategni, Abraham Iudeus, Albumasar, as well as unnamed "magistri probationum" and "magistri considerationum". All five manuscripts were copied on the 1485 edition.

Text sample (ed. Venice 1485) "[TITLE] Magistralis compositio astrolabii Hanrici Bate ad petitionem fratris Wilhelmi de Morbeka ordinis predicatorum domini pape penitentiarii et capellani etc. [PREFACE] Prologus. Universorum entium radix et origo Deus qui nobiliora entia… [INC.] Accepi ergo cum Dei adiutorio pulchri eris et mundi laminam unam — [EXPL.] Valeat semper vestra dilectio que Deo annuente mei nequaquam obliviscatur. [COLOPHON] Expletum est hoc opusculum ab Hanrico Bate in villa Machlinensi, Luna coniuncta Iovi in domo septima, ascendente Leone, anno domini 1274, quinto idus Octobris, ad petitionem fratris Wilhelmi de Morbeca ordinis predicatorum, domini pape penitentiarii et capellani".

ED.: Venice, Erhard Ratdolt, 1485, sigs. [C5]r-[D4]r.

MSS: Munich, BSB, Clm 125, s. XV, fols. 181ra-184vb

New York, New York Public Lib., Spencer Collection 51, s. XVI, fols. 131r-137v

Oxford, BL, Digby 48, s. XV, fols. 143v-152r

Paris, BnF, lat. 10269, s. XV, fols. 151ra-157bv

Vienna, ÖNB, 5143, s. XV, fols. 20r-28v

3.1.2. [Equatorium planetarum] (date unknown)[107]

This short text describes the uses of an equatorium, an instrument which allows one to find the position of the planets mechanically and without calculations. This is the second earliest account of an equatorium in Latin literature, after Campanus

---

[106] Birkenmajer 1970, pp. 108-109; Wallerand 1931, pp. 19-20 (B.2); Poulle 1954, pp. 93-94; Poulle 2008. The text is edited in Gunther 1932, II, pp. 368-376 (from ed. Venice 1485).

[107] Birkenmajer 1970, p. 110; Wallerand 1931, p. 20 (B.3); Poulle 1980, pp. 210-214 and 802; Poulle 2008.

of Novara's *Theorica planetarum* (1261-64).[108] The text bears no title and Bate simply calls his device "instrumentum (nostrum)", as Campanus did before him. The date of the text is unknown, but it was composed after the Tables of Mechelen, which are referred to twice.[109] Authorities include Azarchel, Ptolemy, Geber, Albategni, Abraham Iudeus, Azophius [al-Ṣūfī], the "magistri probationum"[110] and Albumasar, and Bate demonstrates that he is acquainted with most astronomical tables available in his time, including the Toledan Tables, the Tables of Novara (by Campanus), the Tables of Hereford, Ptolemy's tables, Albategni's tables, Abraham's Tables of Pisa and Winchester, the Tables of Toulouse "and many others".[111] The text immediately follows the *Magistralis compositio astrolabii* in the 1485 edition and in all five manuscripts.

Text sample (ed. Venice 1485) "[INC.] Volentes quidem vera loca planetarum coequare per instrumentum nostrum ad hoc specialiter ingeniatum — [EXPL.] semper tamen est unus modus operandi in instrumento nostro".

ED.: Venice, Erhard Ratdolt, 1485, sigs. [D4]r-[D6]r.

MSS: Munich, BSB, Clm 125, s. XV, fols. 184vb-186ra

New York, New York Public Lib., Spencer Collection 51, s. XVI, fols. 137v-139v

Oxford, BL, Digby 48, s. XV, fols. 152v-155v

Paris, BnF, lat. 10269, s. XV, fols. 158ra-160rb

Vienna, ÖNB, 5143, s. XV, fols. 28v-31r

---

[108]   On which see Benjamin and Toomer 1971; Poulle 1980, pp. 41-63.

[109]   "Et quamcumque hoc nostrum instrumentum super octavam speram fundatum sit, nihilominus valet ad motus planetarum hac secunda via coequandos que est secundum nonam speram. Si igitur placuerit hac secunda via locum Solis invenire ex tabulis ad hoc constitutis, ut sunt tabule Machlinenses vel Pisane..." (ed. Venice, 1485, sig. [D4]v) and "et argumentum ex tabulis Machlinensibus aut Pisanis vel consimilibus, que secundum nonam speram currunt" (sig. [D5]r).

[110]   The "magistri probationum" (i.e. astronomers who based their tables and calculations on observation) and al-Ṣūfī are repeatedly quoted in the so-called *Liber de rationibus tabularum* associated with Abraham Ibn Ezra (ed. Millás Vallicrosa 1947), a text which Bate refers to in his *Speculum divinorum* as "Abraham Iudeus in libro de opere tabularum" (XXII.17, eds. Steel and Guldentops 1996, p. 337).

[111]   "Est enim instrumentum hoc super motus planetarum ad octavam speram relatos ingeniatum et radicatum, secundum quod Açarkel et alii consideratores quamplures tabulas suas fundaverunt, ut patet in tabulis Toletanis, Novariensibus, Herfordensibus et aliis pluribus. Ptholemeus vero et Geber, Albategni, Abrahamque Iudeus et Açophius, ceteri quoque magistri probationum et maxime orientales astronomi motus planetarum secundum nonam speram considerantes radices suas super hoc fundaverunt, et hoc patet in tabulis Ptholomei, Albategni et Abrahe in tabulis Pisanis, Wintoniensibus et aliis, propter quod et iudicia sua ad instar huius protulerunt, ut apparet precipue in principe iudiciorum Albumaçar" (ed. Venice, 1485, sig. [D4]r-[D4]v). "Ex tabulis igitur Tolosanis aut consimilibus, centro Saturni extracto ab auge equantis..." (sig. [D5]r).

3.1.3. Tables of Mechelen — Tabule Machlinienses *(first version before 1280)*[112]

The Tables of Mechelen were inspired by and are partly based on Abraham Ibn Ezra's Tables of Pisa, which means that they are set upon the ninth sphere (tropical zodiac) instead of the eighth sphere (sidereal zodiac).[113] This contrasts with most astronomical tables in use during the thirteenth century, in particular the Toledan Tables and their derivatives, like the Tables of Toulouse, but foreshadows the still-to-come Alfonsine Tables. Bate drew a first version of the Tables of Mechelen before 1280, which he used to cast his own nativity (*Nat.* 347-352 and 417), and kept correcting them throughout his life on the basis of his own observations, as he tells us in the *Speculum divinorum*.[114] The three known manuscripts present essentially the same material with, however, varying parameters, probably reflecting Bate's own corrections. This material is restricted to planetary tables (mean motions) and contains no canons. The Tables of Mechelen were used by William of Saint-Cloud[115] and, in the second half of the fourteenth century, by Heinrich Selder.[116]

MSS: Bernkastel-Kues, Cusanusstiftsbibl., 210, s. XIV, fols. 84v-87r

Paris, BnF, lat. 7421, s. XIII-XIV, fols. 211r-220r

Paris, BnF, n.a.l. 3091, s. XIII, fols. 79v-80v

3.1.4. Nativitas *(1280-81)*

3.1.5. De diebus creticis periodorumque causis *(after 1281, perhaps 1292)*[117]

This substantial work in 18 chapters deals with astrological medicine, and more specifically with the critical days, periods and periodicities of illnesses. Bate's authorship

---

[112]   Birkenmajer 1970, p. 109; Wallerand 1931, p. 19 (B.1); d'Alverny and Poulle 1958; Poulle 1964, pp. 799-801 and *passim*; Poulle 2008; Nothaft (forthcoming).

[113]   As Bate actually implies in his *Equatorium planetarum* (see n. 109 above). In MS Paris, BnF, lat. 7421, the last table (fol. 220r) bears the title "Argumentum Mercurii secundum Abraham Evenzare [sic] in annis Christi ad meridiem Machlinie". The Tables of Mechelen were believed to derive from the Toledan Tables, see Poulle 1980, pp. 20-21 (no indication of origin in Poulle 1964), and Nothaft 2016, p. 274. A full study of Bate's tables is about to be published, see Nothaft (forthcoming).

[114]   "Sane secundum omnes tabulas astrologicas quae ad nos hucusque pervenerunt, ac etiam nostras Machlinenses tertio iam et ultimo correctas, eas inquam quae super astrologicas radices et principia fundatae sunt... Nostrae [tabulae] tamen quae per antiquarum quidem et modernarum observationum deprehensionem correctae sunt" (*Speculum divinorum*, XXII.18, *Additio*, eds. Steel and Guldentops 1996, p. 347).

[115]   See section 5.3.4 below.

[116]   Nothaft 2016, pp. 273-274.

[117]   Thorndike 1944, p. 300; Dell'Anna 1999, vol. 1, pp. 213-214; Poulle 2008. The text is briefly mentioned, though not discussed, in Birkenmajer 1970, p. 110, and Wallerand 1931, p. 21 n. 46. Critical edition in Dell'Anna 1999, vol. 2, pp. 97-127 (from all MSS, except Luzern P 7 fol., Stuttgart HB XI 9 and Vat. Pal. lat. 1407).

has been questioned,[118] but a mere glance at the astrological sources quoted in the text would suffice to remove any doubt: Abraham Ibn Ezra's *Liber causarum seu rationum, Liber electionum, Liber luminarium* and *Liber nativitatum*; Albumasar's *De revolutionibus nativitatum* and *Introductorium maius*; Aomar; Haly Abenrudian's commentary on Ptolemy's *Quadripartitum*; Hermes's *Centiloquium*; the *Liber novem iudicum*; Ptolemy's *Quadripartitum* in William of Moerbeke's translation; Pseudo-Ptolemy's *Centiloquium*; and Sadan's *Excerpta de secretis Albumasar*. The use of Haly Abenrudian[119] shows that this text was written after the *Nativitas* and it was perhaps composed in 1292, in connection with Bate's translation of Abraham Avenezra's *De luminaribus* (no. 3.2.3 below), which deals with the same topic. Alongside the astrological sources, Bate uses texts pertaining to natural philosophy (various works by Aristotle, Averroes's *Commentum super libro de celo et mundo Aristotelis*, Beda's *De temporum ratione* and Isidore of Seville's *Etymologiae*) and displays a remarkable knowledge of medical texts, citing various works by Hippocrates and Galen, Avicenna's *Canon*, Alkindi's *Liber graduum*, Isaac's *Liber febrium* and the *Liber pantegni*.

Text sample (ed. Dell'Anna 1999) "[TITLE] Incipit libellus magistri Henrici de Maglinia dicti Bate de diebus creticis periodorumque causis. [INC.] De diebus creticis periodorumque causis aliqua summatim colligere temptantes, in primis cum Avicenna supponamus quod — [EXPL.] quorum causa satis est tacta superius. Tot ergo dicta sunt de diebus creticis peryodorumque causis. Explicit" (followed by a table).

MSS: Limoges, BM, 9 (28), s. XIV, fols. 51v-65v

Luzern, Zentral- und Hochschulbibl., P 7 fol., s. XIV, fols. 235rb-242ra

Modena, Bibl. Estense Universitaria, lat. 175 (Alfa O.6.8), s. XIII-XIV, fols. 139ra-148rb

Stuttgart, Württembergische Landesbibl., HB XI 9, s. XIV, fols. 135vb-141ra

Vatican, BAV, Pal. lat. 1116, s. XV, fols. 118ra-125ra

---

[118]   Wallerand 1931 did not include it among Bate's works and only briefly alludes to it (p. 21 n. 46). Thorndike 1944, p. 300, writes: "Against Bate's authorship may be cited Limoges 9 (28)... attributed to Hugh of Lucca" (same in Dell'Anna 1999, vol. 2, p. 97 n. 1a: "Ugo da Lucca"). In fact, no such name occurs in Limoges, BM, 9, whose explicit reads "Explicit tractatus de diebus creticis a mag[istro] H. Luce compilatus", where "H. Luce" must be a misreading for "H. Bate". The text is unambiguously attributed to Bate in MSS Luzern, ZHB, P 7 fol. ("Tractatus magistri Heinrici de Malinis... Explicit tractatus de diebus creticis a magistro H[enrico] compilato, dicto de Malinis"); Modena, BEU, lat. 175 ("Incipit libellus magistri Henrici de Maglima dicti Bate...", apud Dell'Anna 1999, vol. 2, p. 97 n. 1a); and Vatican, BAV, Pal. lat. 1211 ("Incipit tractatus magistri Hainrici de Malinis... Explicit tractatus de diebus creticis a magistro Hainrico compilatus dicto de Malinis. Requiescat in pace"), and is anonymous in the other MSS. MS Stuttgart, WLB, HB XI 9, has not been checked.

[119]   "unde Haly in commento super Quadripartitum Ptholomei, quarto capitulo primi libri, inquit: Et Galienus probavit quod omnes naturales virtutes tali calore, qualis est complexio ista Solis omnia sua opera operantur. Idem 13° eiusdem: Virtus Lune sequitur virtutem Solis et sic contingit quod ut sicut motus naturalis virtutis sequitur motum Solis sic motus particularis, qui fit omni mense cursum Lune sequitur" (c. 12, ed. Dell'Anna 1999, vol. 2, p. 119; these are accurate quotations from Haly's commentary to *Quadripartitum*, I.4 and I.13, see MS Paris, BnF, lat. 16653, fols. 17v and 29v).

Vatican, BAV, Pal. lat. 1211, s. XIV, fols. 89ra-99rb

Vatican, BAV, Pal. lat. 1407, s. XIV-XV, fols. 63r-71v

Vienna, ÖNB, 5337, s. XIV-XV, fols. 185r-193v

3.1.6. Commentary on Albumasar's De magnis coniunctionibus (lost)[120]

This text is known only through quotations by Pierre d'Ailly in his *Elucidarium astronomice concordie cum theologica et historica veritate* (1414) and *De concordantia discordantium astronomorum* (1415).[121] The nature of the quotations confirms Bate's authorship beyond doubt and the mention of the Tables of Mechelen "verified for the last time" ("Inveni per tabulas Machlinienses ultimo verificatas") suggests a late date.

[3.1.7.] †Tractatus in quo ostenduntur defectus tabularum Alfonsi[122]

This text is attributed to Bate by Nicholas Cusanus and by Simon de Phares, as well as in two of its five known manuscripts: Wolfenbüttel, HAB, 81.26 Aug. 2° (2816), s. XV, fols. 9r-12r ("magistro Henrico Bate de Machlinia" in both the title and the explicit), and Paris, BnF, lat. 7281, s. XV, fols. 172v-174v (the scribe wrote next to the explicit: "credo per Gaufredum de Meldis", to which another hand added: "Vel verius per Henricum Batem Machlinensem, ut circa finem tractatus a domino de Cusa sibi ascriptus scriptum invenitur"). This text, dated 1347, is definitely not by Bate.

---

[120] Birkenmajer 1970, p. 110; Poulle 2008.

[121] *Elucidarium astronomice concordie cum theologica et historica veritate*, c. 1 (ed. Leuven, Johannes de Westfalia, c. 1477-1483 [Hain *836], sig. ee1r-ee1v): "Unde nota quod de hac coniunctione Henricus de Machlinia, magnus Alberti Magni discipulus, supra librum magnarum coniunctionum Albumasar, differentia prima, ita scribit: "Inveni per tabulas Machlinien[ses] ultimo verificatas annum coniunctionis significantis Diluvium 3382 annis ante annum incarnationis dominice [...]"; c. 19 (sig. ff2r): "Et concordat in hoc Albumasar primo De coniunctionibus magnis differentia prima. Nota quod ibi dicit Henricus de Machlinia quod Albumasar magnam facit vim de signis orbium et dominiis eorum, necnon de consequentibus ad hoc. Et quia huiusmodi rei fundamentum consistit in verificatione numeri annorum coniunctionis significantis super Diluvium, ideo diligenter considerat per tabulas ad meridiem Mechlinie compositas, quas ipsemet correxerat, utrum evenerit illa coniunctio per 3958 annos ante annum coniunctionis significantis super sectam Arabum et reperit in illo anno Saturnum a Iove distare quasi per 4 signa [...]"; c. 33 (sig. gg1v): "Hic sequitur triplicitas aerea. Nota quod anno ab incarnatione domini 1225, in eius mense ultimo, fuit coniunctio Iovis cum Saturno per mutationem triplicitatis in 20 gradu Aquarii, ut dicit Henricus de Machlinia"; *De concordantia discordantium astronomorum* (ed. *ibid.*, sigs. hh5v-hh8r): "Quantum ad secundum principale sciendum est quod quondam Henricus de Machlinia, magnus Alberti Magni discipulus, predictam discordiam nititur concordare — Et hec recollecta sint ex dictis prememorati Henrici propter concordiam philosophorum super dissolutione perplexitatis predicte" (this long section quotes a large number of sources: Abraham Avenezre, "Abraham Collector" ("Item per alium Abraham qui dictus est Collector in principio sui libri de nativitatibus", sig. hh5v), Ptolemy, Albumasar, the *Liber novem iudicum*, Firmicus Maternus, Messahallah, Zael, Aristotle, Avicenna, Hippocrates, Galen and Johannes Hispalensis); (sig. hh8v) "Quantum ad tercium principale sciendum quod ad confirmationem premissarum dicit idem Henricus quod cum intento studio magnaque diligentia et vehementi consideravit pluries et mente revolvit quod dicit Albumazar de triplicitatibus super fortificatione [...]".

[122] Birkenmajer 1970, p. 111; Wallerand 1931, pp. 21-22 (B.6); Poulle 2008; Nothaft 2015, esp. p. 87.

3.2. Translations

3.2.1. *Alkindi,* Liber de iudiciis revolutionum annorum mundi *(1278)*

This previously unnoticed text, was translated "de Hebreo in Latinum" in Mechelen on 3 September 1278 at the request of John of Milanen, alderman in Mechelen (see 2.2 above). The Arabic original has not been identified,[123] although traces of it are found in various sources, in particular in Abraham Ibn Ezra's *Sefer ha-ʿolam I*, cf. "Yaʿqub al-Kindī said in his Book of the Revolution…" (§ 44.1) and "Yaʿqub al-Kindī said…" (§ 60.1).[124] What is puzzling is that the relevant passages are not found in our Latin text, whereas other passages from *Sefer ha-ʿolam*, which are not attributed to al-Kindī, correspond closely to sections of the Latin text.[125] The work is said to have been translated from Arabic into Hebrew and it seems clear that the translator intervened with comments and additions of his own, which makes the identification of al-Kindī's material somewhat difficult. For example, the zodiacal chorography attributed to the Babylonians includes Pisa and Lucca,[126] and speaking about the great conjunctions, the text mentions the shift of triplicity from fire to earth (fol. 58r), something that happened in 1007 A.D. (modern computation). These elements point to Abraham Ibn Ezra, or someone close to him, as the translator from Arabic into Hebrew.

In the Vatican manuscript, this text is preceded by another work (fols. 55r-58r) attributed to al-Kindī in a note added in the margin by another hand ("Liber Iacob Alkindi de revolutionibus annorum mundi"). This work has nothing to do with al-Kindī and deals instead with the calculation (in retrospect) of the horoscope of the great conjunction of 1067 for the longitude of Winchester on the basis of astronomical tables said to have been composed by the author ("in hoc loco qui est Wintonia… secundum tabulas quas ego composui", fol. 57v). This is interesting because several sources, including Bate himself (see 3.1.2 above), attribute a set of tables for Winchester to Abraham Ibn Ezra. The authorities quoted in this text are reminiscent of the *Liber de rationibus tabularum* associated with Abraham Ibn Ezra,[127] and sentences such as "secundum Christianos" (fol. 57v) and "anni 1067 secundum annos Christianos" (fol. 58r) suggest that the author was not a Christian.

---

[123] A *Maqāla taḥāwīl al-sinīn* ("Discourse on the Revolutions of the Years") is attributed to al-Kindī in MS Escorial, Real Bibl. del Monestario de San Lorenzo, 918, fols. 10-11, but this is a different work, judging from the Spanish translation in Muñoz 1979. See also Travaglia 1999, p. 122, no. 29, who does not list any other Arabic work by al-Kindī dealing with the revolutions of the world-years.

[124] Tr. Sela 2010, pp. 83 and 91, and comments pp. 133-134.

[125] E.g. "Et semper compara Solem regibus et principibus — Luna vero cum Virgine super partes Aspii" (fol. 58v) = *Sefer ha-ʿolam I*, §§ 36-37, tr. Sela 2010, p. 77.

[126] "Pisarum Aquarium, Luce Cancer" (fol. 59r), compare with *Sefer ha-ʿolam I*, § 38.9 and *II*, § 15.24-25, tr. Sela 2010, pp. 77 and 167, and comments pp. 207-208.

[127] These sources include Ptolemy, Alkindi, "Liber tabularum", "Avenezre", "sapientes Persarum", "sapientes Indorum", "compotus Indorum", "Liber figurarum", "sapientes Sarracenorum", "magistri probationum", Albategni, "Almamoni", "Alzophi" and "Almazkar".

These two texts seem to be unique in the Latin manuscripts, but they survive in a fragmentary English version in MS London, Royal College of Physicians, 384, s. XV-XVI, pp. 83-85, which also ascribes the translation to Bate: "I have wryten these thingis of the boke of domes of revolucions of the yeris of the world, the whiche Jacob the sone of Ysaak Alkyndi compiled, of the booke that was translate out of Ebrewe into Latyne be Henry Bate" (p. 83). This English version has been analysed by John North,[128] who dismissed the attribution to Abraham Ibn Ezra on the ground that the calculations are closer to the Toledan Tables than to Ibn Ezra's tables and tentatively attributed the text to ʿAbd al-Masīḥ of Winchester, who is the only other known astronomer associated with Winchester. This question should be re-examined in light of the Latin texts.

Text sample (Vatican, BAV, Pal. lat. 1407) "[INC.] Dixit translator: Interpretabor quidem nunc tractatum unum ex Arabico in Hebraycum ydeoma de iudiciis annorum mundi quem collegit Iacob filius Ysaac Alkindi. Et hoc est inicium sui tractatus: Quia concordati sunt omnes astrorum iudices quod universalium iudicia seu communium dependent a coniuctione duorum superiorum a principio inquam coniunctionis eorum in signis triplicitatum. De signis enim igneis mutantur ad signa terrea. Et tu debes aspicere ad figuram dispositionis orbis signorum — [EXPL.] et poteris scire constellationem eius in hora edificationis civitatis secundum viam rationis. [COLOPHON] Explicit liber de iudiciis revolutionum annorum mundi quem compilavit Iacob filius Ysaac Alkindi. Expletus est libellus iste ascendente Cancro, in quo Luna coniuncta Iovi, die tertia Septembris anno domini 1278° in Mechlinia, translatus ex Hebrayco in Latinum per Henricum Bate ad preces Iohannis de Milana."

MS: Vatican, BAV, Pal. lat. 1407, s. XIV-XV, fols. 58r-62r.

3.2.2. *Abraham Avenezra,* De mundo vel seculo I *[Sefer ha-ʿolam I] (1281)*[129]

A work on the influence of the great conjunctions on mundane affairs (weather conditions, natural disasters, wars etc.), whose translation was begun in Liège and completed in Mechelen on 20 October 1281. Bate added a lengthy preface to it.

Text sample (Oxford, BL, Digby 212) "[TRANSLATOR'S PREFACE] Tractatus Avenesre de planetarum coniunctionibus et annorum revolutionibus mundanorum translationem aggressuri... [INC.] Si tu inveneris librum Albumasar — [EXPL.] ad aspectus autem semper intendas. [COLOPHON] Explicit liber de mundo vel seculo, completus die Lune post festum beati Luce, hora diei quasi decima, anno Domini 1281, inceptus in Leodio, perfectus Machlinia, translatus a magistro Henrico Bate de Hebreo in Latinum".

---

[128] North 2003.
[129] Wallerand 1931, pp. 14-16 (A.2); Thorndike 1944, pp. 294-295; Smithuis 2006, pp. 248 and 293; Sela 2017a, pp. 167-168; Steel (forthcoming). Critical edition and translation of the Hebrew text in Sela 2010.

ED.: Venice, Petrus Liechtenstein, 1507, sigs. LXXVIra-LXXXVra.

MSS: Basel, UB, F.II.10, s. XV, fols. 82ra-90rb

Berlin, SBPK, lat. fol. 54 (964), s. XV, fols. 170r-176vb

Cambridge, Emmanuel Coll., 70, s. XV, fols. 137v-143v

Cambridge, Pembroke Coll., 204, s. XV, fols. 78ra-83vb (incomplete)

Cracow, BJ, 610, s. XV, fol. 350r (last chapters only)

Cracow, BJ, 1843, s. XV, fols. 195v-196v (last chapters only)

Douai, BM, 715 (957), s. XIV, fols. 59r-69v

Erfurt, UFB, Amplon. Q. 352, s. XIV, fols. 1ra-6rb

Florence, BML, Ashburnham 1133, s. XV, fols. 1r-8v

Florence, BNC, Conv. Soppr. J.III.28 (San Marco 180), s. XIV, fol. 75ra-75va (excerpt)

Ghent, UB, 2 (417/152), s. XV, fols. 45v-54r

Klagenfurt, Archiv der Diözese Gurk — Bischöfliche Mensalbibl., XXX b 7, s. XV, fols. 202v-209r

Leipzig, UB, 1466, s. XIV, fols. 24ra-30va

Limoges, BM, 9 (28), s. XIV, fols. 135v-143v

London, BL, Sloane 312, s. XV, fols. 70v-96v

Milan, BA, D.331 inf., s. XV, fols. 31ra-37vb

Munich, BSB, Clm 25004, s. XV, fols. 145r-146v (last chapters only)

Naples, Bibl. Statale Oratoriana dei Girolamini, 15.11, s. XIV-XV, fols. 167vb-172vb

Oxford, BL, Canon. Misc. 190, s. XV, fols. 64r-72r

Oxford, BL, Digby 114, s. XIV, fols. 165r-175r

Oxford, BL, Digby 212, s. XIV, fols. 48v-52v

Paris, BnF, lat. 7336, s. XV, fols. 98v-109r

†Paris, BnF, lat. 7413, s. XIII

Paris, BnF, lat. 7438, s. XV, fols. 151r-168v

Paris, BnF, lat. 10269, s. XV, fols. 88ra-99rb

Paris, BnF, n.a.l. 3091, s. XIII, fols. 107vb-113rb

Paris, Bibl. de la Sorbonne, 1037, s. XV, fols. 83r-89v (excerpt)

Prague, NKCR, VI.F.7 (1144), s. XV, fols. 128v-129r (last chapters only)

Vienna, ÖNB, 4146, s. XV, fols. 257r-264r

Vienna, ÖNB, 5275, s. XV-XVI, fols. 187ra-192vb (excerpts, ends incomplete)

Vienna, ÖNB, 5309, s. XV, fols. 256rb-264rb

Vienna, ÖNB, 5335, s. XIV, fols. 49r-54v

Wolfenbüttel, HAB, 42.3 Aug. 2° (2505), s. XV, fols. 215va-216vb (beginning and end missing)

Zürich, Zentralbibl., B.244 (769), s. XV, fols. 80vb-88ra

3.2.3. *Abraham Avenezra*, De luminaribus *[Sefer ha-me'orot] (1292)*[130]

A work on astrological medicine, whose translation was completed in Orvieto on 4 June 1292 and dedicated to Adam of Amiens, bishop of Aversa.

Text sample (Limoges, BM, 9) "[TITLE] Incipit liber Abrahe Avenesdre de luminaribus. [INC.] Dominum Deum meum simpliciter oro quamdiu in me est anima mea ut in cor meum — [EXPL.] hec duo addunt aliquid et minuunt. Sic ergo facere debes de anno in annum. [COLOPHON] Explicit liber de luminaribus. Pulcherrimas laudes habeat ille qui omnes creat creaturas. Perfectus 4 die iunii anno domini 1292, die Mercurii, Sole occidente in Urbe Veteri, translatus in Latinum a magistro Henrico de Malinis, dicto Bate, pro reverendo patre domino N. [A. in MS Glasgow, UL, Hunterian Museum 461] presule Aversano".

    EDS: Padua, [Matthaeus Cerdonis,] 7 Feb. 1482/1483; Lyon, Johannes Trechsel, 1496, sigs. f$_{vi}$v-f$_{viii}$r; Lyon, Johannes Cleyn, 1508, sigs. h$_i$rb-h$_{iii}$rb; Lyon, 1614.

    MSS: Glasgow, UL, Hunterian Museum 461, s. XV, fols. 108r-114r (beginning gone)
        Leipzig, UB, 1466, s. XIV, fols. 30va-34rb
        Limoges, BM, 9 (28), s. XIV, fols. 66r-71v
        Naples, BN, VIII C 45, s. XV, fols. 71r-80v
        Paris, BnF, lat. 16195, s. XIV, fols. 5ra-6vb
        Paris, BnF, n.a.l. 1524, s. XVI, fols. 10r-15r
        Prague, NKCR, III.C.2 (433), s. XV, fols. 118vb-123ra
        Prague, NKCR, VI.F.7 (1144), s. XV, fols. 144r-147r
        Vicenza, Bibl. Civica Bertoliana, 208 (132), s. XV, fols. 95r-103v
        Warsaw, Bibl. Ordynacji Zamojskiej, 59, s. XV, item 4

3.2.4. *Abraham Avenezra*, Introductorius ad astronomiam *[Reshit ḥokhmah] (1292)*[131]

A general introduction to astrology, of which Bate completed the translation in Orvieto on 22 August 1292.

Text sample (Leipzig, UB, 1466) "[INC.] Initium sapientie timor domini. Huius aut verbi seu dicti sensus hic est quod dum homo nec post oculos suos — [EXPL.] ut commemorat Ptholomeus in libro fructus, id est Centiloquii. [COLOPHON] Complete sunt 10 partes libri huius quem compilavit magister Abraham Avenezre, quod interpretatur magister adiutorii et magister Hynricus de Malinis, dictus Bate, cantor Leodiensis, transtulit. Et translationem complevit in Urbe Vetere anno domini M CC XCII° in octava assumptionis beate Marie virginis gloriose. Laudationes illi domino qui extendit aera sive celos et qui scientiam ampliviavit Avenezre".

---

[130] Wallerand 1931, p. 17 (A.4); Thorndike 1944, p. 300 ("Liber luminarium"); Smithuis 2006, pp. 248 and 291-292; Sela 2017a, p. 168. Critical edition and translation of the Hebrew text in Sela 2011.

[131] Wallerand 1931, p. 17 (A.3); Thorndike 1944, p. 296; Smithuis 2006, pp. 248 and 277-278; Sela 2017a, p. 168. Critical edition and translation of the Hebrew text in Sela 2017.

MSS: Berlin, SBPK, lat. fol. 192 (963), s. XV, fols. 152ra-163ra (c. 4-9)
    Gloucester, Cathedral Lib., 21, s. XV, fols. 37r-68r (without c. 1)
    Leipzig, UB, 1466, s. XIV, fols. 2ra-23va
    Vatican, BAV, Pal. lat. 1377, s. XV, fols. 21ra-37va
    Wolfenbüttel, HAB, 81.26 Aug. 2° (2816), s. XV, fols. 84r-111v

3.2.5. *Abraham Avenezra,* Liber rationum *I* [Sefer ha-ṭeʿamim *I] (1292)*[132]

A work on the reasons behind astrological doctrines, whose translation was completed in Orvieto on 15 September 1292. This translation includes a long digression by Bate, which is edited below, as *App. II* to the *Nativitas*.

Text sample (Leipzig, UB, 1466) "[TITLE] Incipit Liber causarum seu rationum super hiis que dicuntur in introductorio Abrache Dau (?). [INC.] Incipit sapientie timor domini capitulum primum. Excelsus dominus et metuendus adaperiat et illuminat oculos nostros in Libro rationum et dirigat gressus nostros (?) invidet veritatis. Circulus 360 partes habet eo quod non invenerunt numerum — [EXPL.] regulare quedam et artificiosum ac breve tradidimus documentum. [COLOPHON] Explicit Liber rationum et completus est, eius translatio perfecta est a magistro Hynrico de Malinis, dicto Bate, in Urbe Veteri anno domini 1292° in octavis nativitatis beate Marie virginis".

MSS: Leipzig, UB, 1466, s. XIV, fols. 60vb-73va
    Limoges, BM, 9 (28), s. XIV, fols. 24r-44r (beginning gone)

3.2.6. *Abraham Avenezra,* Liber rationum *II* [Sefer ha-ṭeʿamim *II]* *(1292)*[133]

Another work on the reasons behind astrological doctrines, different from no. 3.2.5 above. Bate completed the translation in Orvieto on 23 September 1292.

Text sample (Leipzig, UB, 1466) "[TITLE] In nomine Dei manentis in excelsis incipiam librum rationum seu causarum fundamentum quidem volo ponere Libro initii sapientie. [INC.] Scito nempe quod omnis creatura subsistere nititur ex Dei consilio — [EXPL.] angulorum cum Sole de die et cum Luna de nocte. [COLOPHON] Translatio partis huius perfecta est 23 die mensis Septembris anni domini 1292".

MSS: Leipzig, UB, 1466, s. XIV, fols. 49vb-60vb
    Limoges, BM, 9 (28), s. XIV, fols. 1r-23v (end gone)

---

[132] Wallerand 1931, p. 17 (A.6); Thorndike 1944, p. 297; Smithuis 2006, pp. 248 and 279; Sela 2017a, p. 169. Critical edition and translation of the Hebrew text in Sela 2007.
[133] Wallerand 1931, p. 17 (A.6); Thorndike 1944, p. 297; Smithuis 2006, pp. 248 and 281-282; Sela 2017a, p. 169. Critical edition and translation of the Hebrew text in Sela 2007.

3.2.7.   *Abraham Avenezra,* **Liber introductionis ad iudicia astrologie** [Mishpeṭei ha-mazzalot] *(1292)*[134]

Another general introduction to astrology (see no. 3.2.4), whose translation was completed in Orvieto on 29 October 1292.

Text sample (Leipzig, UB, 1466) "[TITLE — in the margin] Ysagoge magistri Abrahe ducis seu principis vocati Hebrayce Nati Hezkia. [INC.] Spera maior honorabilis in qua totus est exercitus Dei gloriosi et sublimis celum celorum notata est — [EXPL.] tu considerare debes arcum oppositum. Et consimiliter est de principio tertie domus. [GLOSSATOR'S ADDITION, FOL. 48rb] Hec Abraham princeps. Glosator autem super verbis huius capituli de aspectibus circa principium ubi dicitur. Vide si fuerit planeta inter domum decimam et gradum ascendentem — gradus planete fuerit collocatus. Explicit. [COLOPHON] Explicit liber introductionis ad iudicia astrologie. Deo gratias et laudes, cuius nomen (?) magistrum (?) et qu... (?) opera sunt ...ata (?). Perfecta quidem et translatio libri huius in Urbe Veteri a magistro Hynrico de Maclinis dicto anno domini 1292 in crastino apostolorum Sym[onis] et Iude etc."

MSS: Leipzig, UB, 1466, s. XIV, fols. 37rb-49va

Prague, NKCR, III.C.2 (433), s. XV, fols. 123ra-125rb (incomplete)

Vatican, BAV, Pal. lat. 1377, s. XV, fols. 37vb-43vb (second part)

[3.2.8]   †De fortitudine planetarum[135]

This is not an independent translation, but only a section of the *Liber introductionis ad iudicia astrologie* (no. 3.2.7 above).

---

[134]   Wallerand 1931, p. 17 (A.5); Thorndike 1944, p. 296; Smithuis 2006, pp. 248 and 279-280; Sela 2017a, pp. 168-169. Critical edition and translation of the Hebrew text in Sela 2017.

[135]   Thorndike 1923, p. 928 n. 5; Wallerand 1931, p. 18 (A.7).

Chapter 4
Bate's *Nativitas*: the earliest known astrological autobiography

(Steven Vanden Broecke)

4.1. Purpose

Why did Bate write the *Nativitas*? There are at least three possible answers to this question. The first answer approaches the *Nativitas* as a didactic tool for students of astrology. One piece of evidence for this interpretation is the title given to Bate's treatise in Paris, BnF, lat. 10270. This title reads "Book (...) on the inquiry into, and verification of, an uncertain nativity through clues and events [happening to] the native after his birth". This suggests a didactic treatise teaching prospective astrologers how to perform *a posteriori* verification of nativities, in cases where the time of birth is determined with insufficient precision — as was indeed the case with Bate's own nativity. Another clue for the first answer lies in the immediate reception and circulation of Bate's *Nativitas*, which consistently points to the circle of Parisian astronomer-astrologers to which Bate belonged (see below, section 5.3). However, the evidence for the first answer also has one major flaw, in that the aforementioned title appears to be a later addition to Bate's own text (see above, section 1.2.3).

A second possible answer emphasizes the immediate psychological benefits of the *Nativitas* to its author. This answer sets out from the closing analyses of the solar revolutions of Bate's natal chart for his 35th and 36th years on the one hand, and the Segovia appendix on the other.[136] More specifically, this evidence points towards a very specific biographical context as providing the immediate impetus for Bate's exercise. Composition of the *Nativitas* began around the beginning of Bate's 35th year, in the first months of 1280. The text stops in March 1281, although a subsequent marginal note references health problems that only ceased in January 1282.[137] The aforementioned appendix also shows that this was a period of intense high-level negotiation about Bate's ecclesiastical career.

This context explains Bate's frequent reflections, throughout the *Nativitas*, on the necessities and challenges of worldly advancement. We already saw how the opening sections of the *Nativitas* highlighted the role of princely patronage in ob-

---

[136] *Nat.* 2782-3400 and *App. I.*

[137] The opening section of the *Nativitas* refers to the revolution of Bate's 35th year (23 March 1280) as "now current and begun" (*nunc instante et ingresso*), see *Nat.* 318-319, 324. The *versio altera* (see "Appendix I") discusses actual events in this year and ends the narrative around Thursday 6 March 1281 (135:97). However, in a marginal note, Bate mentions an injury of the arm, general weakness and recurring pains while Saturn was between Sagittarius 12°20' (Bate's ascendant degree) and the end of Sagittarius, i.e., from November 1280 until January 1282. See *App. I* 105-108.

taining ecclesiastical benefices (see above, section 2.2). These princely relations recur in Bate's analysis of the fourth, seventh, and tenth houses of his nativity.[138] Interestingly, Bate presents these relations as the solution to a tension between the promise of material advancement on the one hand, and of difficulties and tribulations on the other.[139] It is therefore not unlikely that parts of Bate's *Nativitas* functioned as a means of coming to terms with the actual events and tensions pervading his life as a high-profile ecclesiastic with strong personal ties of support with Guy of Avesnes (see above, section 2.2).[140]

This interweaving of astrological art and personal life is confirmed by evidence that Bate rewrote earlier parts of the *Nativitas* in light of the meaning they acquired during the events of his 35th year. One possible example of such rewriting occurs in Bate's analysis of the seventh house, where he remarks that the opposition between the lord of the ascendant and Mercury (the lord of Bate's seventh house) signifies conflict and adversity, especially from men of letters and merchants.[141] Despite their obvious association with Mercury, Bate's focus on the danger of merchants remains somewhat surprising, in view of his clerical status and overall mode of life. Our surprise is softened, however, when Bate later unveils that in 1280, certain "men of letters and merchants" from the circle of the queen of England were spreading malicious rumours about him.[142]

Our second answer also carries an important disadvantage. As we have seen (see above, section 2.3), Bate was not above censoring astrological significations when these were too damning for his astrological self-image. Why do this if this was an intensely private exercise of working through personal fears and hopes?

A third answer also emphasizes the importance of 1280-1 as a crucial moment in Bate's career, but highlights the potential worldly uses of the *Nativitas*. Indeed, the princely context of the *Nativitas* raises the question whether the intended purpose of our text was a kind of medieval counterpart to the modern *curriculum vitae*. A specific audience of prospective employers interested in Bate's philosophical and negotiating skills may be intended, for instance, where Bate emphasizes his facility and moderation in conversations and speeches,[143] or where his soul is characterized as "perfect" with "reason commanding appetite", showing that Bate "will always act with discretion and equity".[144] One may also consider how Bate naturalized his functioning as a churchman, princely counsellor, and semi-prophet

---

[138] See *Nat.* 1628-1629 (4th house); *Nat.* 1965-1969 (7th house); *Nat.* 2402, 2422-2423 (10th house).

[139] *Nat.* 1620-1629.

[140] See *Nat.* 2071-2072: "Non contristent ergo nimis hunc seruum Dei tribulationes et pressure".

[141] *Nat.* 1901-1902.

[142] *App. I* 29-31.

[143] *Nat.* 1073-1074, 1090, although a sextile aspect between Mars and Mercury threatened to have this collapse into indiscretion (*Nat.* 1158).

[144] *Nat.* 1171-1173. At the same time, Bate acknowledged a tendency towards secrecy and concealment in the realms of knowledge, rumors, and books (*Nat.* 1059-1060; *Nat.* 2213-2214; *Nat.* 2248), but also towards verbal indiscretion (*Nat.* 1158).

through Sagittarius, his ascendant sign,[145] through Saturn's retrograde motion,[146] or through Libra's position in midheaven (see below, section 7.5).[147] One important disadvantage of this explanation lies in the sheer prolixity and twistedness of Bate's self-analysis. If the *Nativitas* was designed to instill trust in Bate among his courtly protectors and supporters, then it remains to be explained why he wrote the text in the way he did.

Some combination of these answers might point us in the right direction. In the last instant, however, it seems difficult to avoid the impression that our second interpretation best matches the actual text of the *Nativitas*, which offers a self-analysis that is both intensely personal, meandering and exploratory. Writing the *Nativitas* allowed Bate to come to terms with the events and tensions he experienced at what was clearly an important point in his career.

4.2. 'Autobiography' and astrological meaning-making in the *Nativitas*

This exploratory nature in turn calls for caution when calling Bate's *Nativitas* 'autobiographical'. What did it mean for someone like Bate to "come to terms" with events and tensions? What did it mean for Bate to compose an 'astrological autobiography'? Once again, our answer to these questions can only be provisional and incomplete. Nevertheless, it seems possible to point out at least three ways in which the *Nativitas* departs from our modern notions of 'autobiography', and in which it highlights some of the ways in which medieval life writing was different.

4.2.1. Astrological judgment and self-guidance

Like all astrological analyses, Bate's *Nativitas* was a judgment rather than a narration of life events. On the one hand, this means that we are firmly in the realm of practical reason and preparation for action. On the other hand, it also means that Bate turned to astrology as a kind of tribunal of the self, citing astrological authorities as one cites witnesses before a court. Bate is explicit about this in the introduction of the *Nativitas*, where he immediately characterizes the central goal of his text as "judging things that are his own (*propria*)" — more specifically "accidents and events".

---

[145] *Nat.* 830-832.

[146] Despite Saturn's retrograde motion at his time of birth, Bate managed to find an interpretation that portended fortunate things for his soul (*Nat.* 946-948). On this basis, he went on to associate his nativity with the promise of prophecy, display of miracles, and the wondrous pursuit of sublime things (*Nat.* 949; *Nat.* 957; *Nat.* 959; *Nat.* 963-968). Further mention of sublime things at *Nat.* 998; *Nat.* 2212. Further mention of astrology and divination at *Nat.* 2252-2253; *Nat.* 2474.

[147] The position of Jupiter and Saturn in Libra at the time of Bate's birth announced his talents in mathematics, music and the arts of conviviality (*Nat.* 984-987).

The problem for which astrological analysis offered a solution was a coincidence of "my self" (*meipsum*) with its judge. Motivated by natural self-love[148], Bate claimed, such coincidence led the self towards a "poor and unjust" (*pravus et iniustus*) judgment. Astrological self-analysis organized judgment through an alternative relationship: that between *meipsum* and "the philosophers" (i.e., the astrologers). As an alternative to the "I" that is its own judge, Bate thus recommended a "faithful" following of the philosophers.[149] The self could only assume the "office of the judge" (*officium iudicis*) on this basis, effectively turning the mathematician who cast the necessary natal charts into "an extraneous other".[150] Bate thus portrayed astrological judgment as a profoundly disinterested and philosophical art, which allowed the self to assume the voice of the philosophers in judging itself.[151] Accordingly, Bate found that "the aforementioned philosophical teachings *compel us* [my italics]",[152] or called on endless arrays of authorities to confirm something which he already knew to be the case for himself.[153]

Over and above the task of detecting and inventorying personal qualities and future events, the *Nativitas* was ultimately geared for action. More specifically, it sought to assess the most prudent attitude that Bate should take in relation to the various possibilities signified in his birth chart.[154] One example of this is Bate's apprehensiveness about the potential negative impact of Saturn on his soul – a theme to which he constantly returns in his lengthy discussion of the qualities of the native's soul and the significations of the second house in his birth chart (see below, section 7.5).[155] The same applies to Bate's interest in Mars: here too, we find Bate carefully weighing and working through all the possibilities signified by the red planet, craftily resolving these into the promise of a philosophical, temperate character instead.[156]

The theme of astrological self-guidance also shines through in Bate's rambling investigation of the seventh house's indications concerning marriage. Feverishly working his way through a wealth of contradictory significations,[157] we find Bate slowly determining a position[158] from which he can distance the prospect of mar-

---

[148] For Bate's emphasis on *amor et odium* standing in the way of *recta iudicia*, see e.g. *Nat.* 372-374; *Nat.* 1283-1284.

[149] See *Nat.* 531-533.

[150] *Nat.* 25.

[151] The resulting attitude is exemplified in, among other passages, *Nat.* 646-649: "Nam hic natus in principalioribus actionibus suis Mercurialis est. Accidentia quoque eius et euentus ab hoc non discordant, secundum quod superius aliqualiter tactum est et inferius palam fiet ex dicendis".

[152] *Nat.* 339.

[153] Examples of this abound throughout the *Nativitas*. See e.g. *Nat.* 1061; *Nat.* 1149-1150; *Nat.* 1300; *Nat.* 1351-1353; *Nat.* 1355; *Nat.* 1426-1427; *Nat.* 1678; *Nat.* 2273.

[154] See *Nat.* 2319-2320.

[155] See e.g. *Nat.* 1023 sqq.

[156] See e.g. *Nat.* 1091-1092; *Nat.* 1156 sqq.; *Nat.* 1201-1210.

[157] See *Nat.* 1759-1825.

[158] See *Nat.* 1851-1853.

riage, under the aegis of philosophical advice on the mastering of the passions.[159] A third example is Bate's frequent concern with the question of whether negative significations signify fearful things or actual bodily impediment.[160] Finally, it is also clear that Bate often used astrological authorities to deliver a more hopeful message about himself, whether about his relation to the passions or about his ability to withstand enmity and strife.[161]

Bate's notion of self-guidance may also have carried a religious dimension. There is, of course, Bate's constant referral to himself as a "servant of God": *servus Dei* or *servus Dei gloriosi (et sublimis)*. Medieval hagiography often used the expression *servus Dei* to denote saints. However, it would be surprising to have Bate styling himself as a saint in light of his personal confessions throughout the *Nativitas*. It is far more likely that he took the expression from either the *Nativitas* of Richard of Fournival (see below, section 5.3.2) or from the title of Alcabitius's *Introductorius* in the translation of John of Seville: "Libellus ysagogicus Abdilazi, id est servi gloriosi Dei, qui dicitur Alchabitius".[162]

More relevant for the possible presence of a religious horizon in Bate's astrological self-understanding, are a number of passages in which he identifies divine grace as one component of the negotiation of celestial conditions. Near the end of the *Nativitas*, Bate writes that "this servant of God will evade such evils, divine grace assisting", and similar passages can be found elsewhere in the *Nativitas*.[163] Moreover, Bate at least once seems to suggest a role for providence in the very work of astrological self-analysis, when he claimed that a divine command (*nutum Dei*) led him to interview his mother before she died, thus securing essential resources for determining his precise time of birth.[164] If nothing else, this serves as a salutary reminder that despite the capacity of medieval astrologers to develop a thoroughly naturalizing analysis of their situation, they also embedded such analyses in an ulterior horizon defined by religion.[165]

4.2.2. *Particularity and notions of selfhood*

A second dimension of the *Nativitas*'s notion of autobiographical life writing may initially appear to be paradoxical. Despite the stunning amount of personal detail that Bate uncovers by way of astrological self-analysis, one could argue that he lacks a robust notion of human particularity.

---

[159] *Nat.* 1883-1896.

[160] See e.g. *Nat.* 2885-2886, 2888; *Nat.* 2894-2895; *Nat.* 2943-2944; *Nat.* 2996, 2998, 3003; *Nat.* 3017.

[161] See *Nat.* 1707-1709; *Nat.* 2065-2100.

[162] See Burnett, Yamamoto and Yano 2004, p. 192.

[163] See e.g. *Nat.* 124; *Nat.* 342; *Nat.* 3028-3029; *Nat.* 3372; *Nat.* 3388

[164] *Nat.* 32.

[165] On Christian aspects of Bate's philosophical ideal, see the thoughtful comments of Guldentops 2001b, pp. 675-681.

Bate did use the first person singular when denoting the object of his analysis, as when he uses the phrase "my own self" (*memetipsum*).[166] On the whole, however, he appears to prefer third-person expressions like "servant of the glorious God" (*seruus Dei gloriosi*), "the native [whom we have before us]" (*natus [quem pre manibus habemus]*)[167], "he whose revolution this is" (*hic/is cuius est reuolutio*), this one here (*hic aliquis*) or "he who is under discussion here" (*eum de quo est sermo*).[168] On the one hand, one can surmise that such language simply adopts the conventions of astrological judgment. On the other hand, such conventions may themselves rest on widely shared notions of selfhood.

It may be helpful to point out that pre-modern astrological discourse tended to reduce human particularity to human variety. The set of qualities that inhere in an individual human being *qua* irreducibly particular, were typically treated by astrologers as an epiphenomenon of a variable but universal human relation to an equally universal visible heaven.

One excellent example of this reduction is the famous astrological chorography of the second book of Ptolemy's *Tetrabiblos*, where Ptolemy posits a basic and optimum relation of humans to the Sun, and then goes on to treat human *diversity* across the inhabited world as *variety inside* this universal model. Ptolemy thus traces the phenomenon of human particularity back to the variable *temperatio* of a universal celestial power. One could argue that, *mutatis mutandis*, this pattern also obtains in natal astrology, where human particularity is ultimately approached as the effect of one's being born at one time rather than another. There too, human particularity is reduced to (chronological) variety.

Astrologers thus premised their analysis of particulars on the notion that human particularity ultimately inheres in a single, universal model of humanity. Interestingly, this squares with Caroline Walker Bynum's penetrating remarks concerning the specificity of medieval notions of human selfhood. The Middle Ages, Bynum reminded us, "did not have our twentieth-century notions of "the individual" or "the personality"". Looking inside of oneself was a quest for universal humanity.[169] Similarly, medieval autobiographical life writing approached human particularity as a springboard for exploring one's relation to universal humanity. Conversely, Bate's autobiographical exercise illustrates how universalizing astrological anthropologies provided a quintessential starting point for exploring human particularity.

---

[166] For other explicit first-person references, see e.g. *Nat.* 89; *Nat.* 352, 359; *Nat.* 661; *Nat.* 1273; *Nat.* 3075.

[167] *Nat.* 745-746.

[168] E.g. *Nat.* 702 *passim*.

[169] Walker Bynum 1982, p. 87.

4.2.3. *The inhabitable birth chart*

Finally, we should say a few words about the relation between self and text in the *Nativitas*. Intuitively, one could be inclined to think of Bate's self-analysis as the portrait of a 'self' that exists outside and before the text. One might also surmise that this pre-textual reality provides the historian (at least in principle, if not in practice) with a benchmark against which to measure the objectivity or subjectivity of Bate's analysis. It is true that many features of the *Nativitas* support such an interpretation. There can be no doubt that confrontation with the authoritative significations encoded in his natal chart, often moved Bate towards a process of public self-fashioning. We can see this happening when astrological indications of sexual proclivity or dandy-esque behaviour led Bate to censor relevant passages by Albumasar or Ibn Ezra (see above, sections 2.3 and 4.1).

However, this is not the entire story. Other features of the *Nativitas* seem to go in the opposite direction, and suggest that Bate's self-analysis did not simply naturalize or authorize a self-portrait that was already in place. Quite to the contrary, self-analysis also assisted Bate in acknowledging and articulating less visible or attractive character traits, such as obsequiousness or the fact of having many friends, but few trustees.[170]

How can we describe this more ambiguous, two-way relation between self and text in Bate's *Nativitas*? More than 600 years after Bate, Sigmund Freud (1856-1939) confronted a very similar set of challenges when analysing his own dreams as the basic empirical material for *The Interpretation of Dreams* (1899). One of the key messages that Freud was trying to convey in this book, of course, concerned the fact that just as dreams were productions rather than representations, so the practice of dream-interpretation served life rather than knowledge of the self. Freud famously expressed this two-way relationship between life and interpretation, between self and text, in his metaphor of "the navel of the dream". With this metaphor, Freud emphasized that interpretation was primarily a task of making dreams 'inhabitable' by their subjects. The entire point of dream analysis lay in personal meaning-making, not public self-fashioning. This may be a salutary consideration for anyone trying to come to grips with Bate's *Nativitas*.

4.3. Precedents and reception

Henry Bate's *Nativitas* is the earliest known example of an astrological autobiography. Although Richard of Fournival (1201-1260) authored his own *Nativitas* before 22 October 1239, it offers little more than a determination of Fournival's nativity, its main signifiers and lots, and a basic overview of relevant primary directions and profections. A complete auto-analysis of the kind that we find in Bate's *Nativitas*

---

[170] See e.g. *Nat.* 1058-1061; *Nat.* 1350-1353; *Nat.* 1356-1357.

is wholly lacking in the case of Fournival.[171] Indeed, a subsequent commentary by Peter of Limoges shows Fournival's text being used as the pedagogical basis for expounding and practicing various astrological operations and techniques.[172]

Another 13th-century astrological autobiography was authored, as David Juste shows in section 5.3, by William of Saint-Cloud in 1285. As we have seen, William's *Nativitas* follows Bate's *Nativitas* in all of the manuscripts containing the latter text, with the exception of *S*. William of Saint-Cloud's text has neither incipit, nor title, nor explicit authorship.[173] Apparently, he added his self-analysis to a copy of Bate's *Nativitas* that he owned himself. This, combined with the further fact that William's *Nativitas* uses Bate's *Tabulae Machlinienses* alongside the Toledan tables, makes it very likely that the later *Nativitas* was inspired by the example of Bate.

Most of the evidence for the subsequent reception of Bate's *Nativitas* comes from the five known manuscripts of this text. The two Parisian manuscripts situate Bate's *Nativitas* in the world of 15th-century astrological practitioners. BnF lat. 7324 (*P*) was owned by the astrologers Louis de Langle and Simon de Phares (see above, section 1.1). BnF lat. 10270 (*Par*) was made under the supervision of Arnald of Brussels, the scribe and printer working in Naples, who had a particular interest in geography, astrology, astronomy, medicine and alchemy (see above, section 1.2.1.3). The Seville and Venice manuscripts both show how Bate's *Nativitas* was available in the Veneto region in the late 15th and early 16th centuries.

Finally, a series of interesting references to Bate's *Nativitas* appear in book IX of Giovanni Pico della Mirandola's famous *Disputationes adversus astrologiam divinatricem* (1496). Pico appears to be referencing Bate's *Nat.* 2642-2649 in *Disputationes* IX.7, and *Nat.* 775-778 in *Disputationes* IX.12.[174] Another reference occurs in chapter IX.3, where Pico invokes the authority of *Nat.* 83-85 in order to attack the Ptolemaic *animodar* for rectifying nativities (see below, section 7.2):

"We also mention Henry Bate, a discipline of Albert the Great, who — examining his own nativity while hiding his name under the epithet 'servant of God' — said that Ptolemy's *animodar* has been rejected by wise men. Others, like Aomar, have corrected, not rejected, this dogma while also disagreeing with Ptolemy".[175]

---

[171]   Lucken and Boudet (forthcoming). Note that the only judgment made by Richard of Fournival concerns his length of life.

[172]   Lucken and Boudet (forthcoming).

[173]   Poulle 1964, p. 794.

[174]   Pico 1946-1952, vol. 2, p. 316: "Quod Hispanus, Abraam, praeceptor Avenazrae, et Henricus Batensis observant, non minus ex loco pronunciantes in quo planeta sit, facta per aequales gradus distributione, quam ubi communi more divisionibus annotates"; vol. 2, p. 350: "Henricus Batensis observat eam configurationem planetarum ratione locorum ut trigonus sit horoscopo qui locum quintum tenuerit, nulla interim habita signi ratione, atque ita de reliquis".

[175]   Pico 1946-1952, vol. 2, p. 296: "Henricus Batensis, Alberti Magni discipulus, suam examinans genituram, quamquam nomine dissimulato servum dei se nominans, mittamus, inquit, Animodar Ptolemaei a sapientibus reprobatum; alii dogma non expungunt sed castigant, ut Omar, nonnihil a Ptolemaeo dissentiens".

Pico's (incorrect) reference to Bate as a pupil of Albert the Great may have been borrowed from Pierre d'Ailly's astrological work (see section 3.3), which Pico certainly read. The reference to Bate's *Nativitas*, however, appears to be Pico's own. If so, it is possible that Pico learned of the *Nativitas*'s existence while studying in Paris (July 1485-March 1486), or that he managed to acquire one of the Italian copies that were already circulating in the 15th century (see above, section 1.2.4).[176]

4.4. Structure and synopsis of the *Nativitas*

5-29	Introduction	
30-346	Determining Bate's ascendant at birth	
347-529	Casting Bate's nativity and the chart of the New Moon preceding his birth	
530-2781	Judgment of Bate's nativity	
	530-663	Determination of hyleg and alcochoden
	664-750	Bate's life expectancy
	751-1390	First house

751-756	Introduction
757-811	Complexion of the body
812-841	Form of the body
842-1390	Quality of the soul

1391-1505	Second house
1506-1523	Third house
1524-1648	Fourth house
1649-1702	Fifth house

---

176 See Dorez and Thuasne 1897.

CHAPTER 5
BATE'S *NATIVITAS* IN CONTEXT
(David Juste)

5.1. The *Nativitas* in the history of astrology

Within the vast and varied field of astrological literature, Bate's *Nativitas* stands as an exceptional document in several respects. First of all, it is a practical text in which Bate endeavours to interpret a birth horoscope ("nativity"), namely his own, in a systematic and thorough manner. Strictly speaking, such an examination belongs to the genre of "judgements on nativities" (*iudicia nativitatum*).[177] While handbooks on the subject (*De nativitatibus*, *Liber nativitatum*, etc.) began to circulate in Europe in the twelfth century, mainly through translations from Arabic, surprisingly few judgements on nativities have come down to us for the period prior to 1450, only four of them dating from the period prior to Bate. The earliest instance is that of a native of 23 August 1135 attributed to Abraham or based on Abraham's judgements, most probably Abraham Ibn Ezra.[178] Another judgement, very brief and of an elementary nature, is that of an unnamed boy ("puer") born on 29 October 1135, by one "Abraham Iudeus" in Béziers.[179] Two judgements concern the nativities of another unnamed boy ("puer") born on 30 December 1160[180] and of one Hubertus born in Florence on 14 October 1259.[181]

Bate's *Nativitas* is also remarkable because it is one of the very few instances of examination of one's own nativity, i.e. an "astrological autobiography", as it is sometimes called. Other examples of this genre include Richard of Fournival's *Nativitas* (before 1239),[182] William of Saint-Cloud's *Nativitas* (1285)[183] and Nicolaus Gugler's *Prognosticon* (1539).[184] Richard of Fournival provides an antecedent to Bate, but

---

[177]   For an edition and technical commentary of a typical judgement on a nativity, see Juste 2015a.

[178]   On this text, used by Bate (*Nat.* 707-710), see Appendix no. 1.

[179]   This text is edited from the only known manuscript (Paris, BnF, lat. 16208, s. XII, fol. 1v) in Lipton 1978, pp. 221-222. New edition with an English translation in Burnett 2017, pp. 198-203. Abraham Ibn Ezra was in Béziers in 1148, but the judgement is so crude that it is hard to believe that he might be the author.

[180]   MSS Roma, Bibl. Vallicelliana, F 86, s. XIII, fols. 28v-39r and 42v-47v; and Dijon, BM, 1045 (116), s. XV, fols. 107v-119r.

[181]   MS Paris, BnF, n.a.l. 398, s. XV, fols. 76vb-80ra.

[182]   See Boudet and Lucken 2018. Full study and edition in Lucken and Boudet (forthcoming).

[183]   See below 5.3.4.

[184]   MSS Paris, BnF, lat. 7417, s. XVI, fols. 112r-143v, and Tübingen, UB, Mc 64, s. XVI, fols. 121r-129r. Of course, the examples given here do not exhaust the list of authors who examined their own horoscope. The most famous case is perhaps Girolamo Cardano in his *De propria vita* (1576), on which see Ernst 1994, pp. 180-184; Grafton 1999, pp. 178-198; Giglioni 2001; Ernst 2010; Faracovi 2012, pp. 101-115.

it is important to note that his *Nativitas* is restricted to the technical elements necessary for the establishment of the horoscope (the rectification of the ascendant by way of the animodar) and its interpretation (hyleg, alcochoden, profections and directions). The text does not include any interpretation *per se*, beyond a few facts listed in relation to the profections and directions. For example, Richard writes: "the direction of Venus reached the sextile aspect to Mars in the year when mother died". Likewise, William of Saint-Cloud and Nicolaus Gugler mainly limit themselves to technical elements and do not offer proper interpretation. Bate, by contrast, provides a dense and elaborate narrative of all aspects of his life. This makes the *Nativitas* a unique work in the history of Latin literature, and possibly even in the history of literature in general, for no such text has been brought to light in any other language.

5.2. Bate's astrological sources

But the *Nativitas* stands out in particular for the extraordinary breadth of Bate's knowledge of astrology and astrological literature. By 1280, most astrological texts that were to become the vulgate until the sixteenth century were already available in Latin, and it is no exaggeration to say that Bate knew virtually all of them. Not only did he know and use them, but he thoroughly mastered their content, scope and significance. He was able to find his way through the most obscure and intricate texts and extract from them the tiniest element that could illuminate his own *Nativitas*, and he did not hesitate to compare two or several translations of the same text when facing perplexing readings.[185] Few European scholars before 1300 demonstrate such knowledge and command of astrology.

Bate used at least 40 astrological texts represented by some 20 authors (see Appendix, 5.4 below). These are, in alphabetical order, Abraham Ibn Ezra, Abraham bar Ḥiyya, Albohali, Albumasar, Alcabitius, Aomar, Firmicus Maternus, Gergis, Guillelmus Anglicus, Haly Embrani, Hermann of Carinthia, Hermes, Johannes Hispalensis (Pseudo-), Messahallah, Ptolemy (and Pseudo-Ptolemy), Sadan and Zael.[186] The texts concerned cover all branches of astrology, not only treatises on

---

[185]   *Nat.* 1065-1078, 1128-1134 and 2713-2725. See also *Nat.* 730-743, 1610-1615, 2313-2327, 2957-2958 and 3075-3083.

[186]   Further authorities include Alkindi, Aristotle and Dorotheus, quoted from the *Liber novem iudicum* [Appendix, no. 31]; "Haly" and "Abuiafar" as the commentator(s) of Pseudo-Ptolemy's *Centiloquium* [36]; "Enoch" (*Nat.* 86 and 1757) found in several of Abraham Ibn Ezra's works; "Alendruzagar" (*Nat.* 1379 and 1642), i.e. the Persian astrologer Andarzaghar, quoted from Abraham Ibn Ezra's *Sefer ha-moladot* [8]; and "Benneka Indus" (*Nat.* 2511-2512), whose name occurs once in *Sefer ha-moladot II* [9] as "Bonneca Alhendi" (MS Erfurt, UFB, Amplon. O. 89, fol. 67r) and twice in Alkindi's *Liber de iudiciis revolutionum annorum mundi* (3.2.1 above) as "Bennek(h)a Indus" (MS Vatican, BAV, Pal. lat. 1407, fols. 59v and 61r). Bate also refers to purely astronomical texts (these are not listed in the Appendix): Ptolemy's *Almagest* (*Nat.* 1931), translated by Gerard of Cremona before 1187; Alpetragius [al-Biṭrūjī] (*Nat.* 358), whose *De motibus celorum* was translated by Michael Scot in 1217; and Albategni [al-Battānī] (*Nat.* 2828), whose canons for astronomical tables were translated by Plato of Tivoli in the 1130s.

nativities [Appendix, nos. 1-2, 8-9, 15, 17, 21, 24, 37], but also general introductions [3-4, 12-13, 18-20], full treatises [23, 29, 35, 40], collections of aphorisms [22, 28, 36, 38], as well as works dealing specifically with elections [6-7, 26], interrogations [11, 27, 31, 34], mundane astrology [10, 14, 16, 32-37, 39], astrological medicine [5, 25] and astral magic [30].

With the exception of Firmicus Maternus's *Mathesis* [23], written in Antiquity, most of these texts originated in the twelfth or early thirteenth century, either as translations from Arabic [15-16, 18-22, 24, 26, 32-36, 39-40] or as Latin compilations based on Arabic sources [25, 27, 29, 31]. Yet Bate was aware of more recent works. First and foremost comes his favourite author, Abraham Ibn Ezra (and Abraham bar Ḥiyya), whose various texts [1-14] first became known through Bate's translations undertaken in 1273.[187] Bate also used all three astrological texts translated or compiled in Sicily by Stephen of Messina around 1262, namely Albumasar's *De revolutionibus nativitatum* [17], Hermes's *Centiloquium* [28] and Sadan's *Excerpta de secretis Albumasar* [38]. For Ptolemy's *Quadripartitum* [35], while he was aware of Plato of Tivoli's translation from the Arabic (1138), he preferred the translation made from the Greek by William of Moerbeke between 1266 and 1269.[188] It is probably through William of Moerbeke that he had access to a translation from the Greek of Pseudo-Ptolemy's *Centiloquium* [36] which has not been identified in extant manuscripts. Bate also appears to be one of the earliest users of two older texts, i.e. Pseudo-Johannes Hispalensis's *Epitome totius astrologie* [29] and Pseudo-Ptolemy's *De iudiciis partium* [37]. But the most unexpected source to feature in the *Nativitas* is the *Liber Aldaraia sive Soyga* [30], a lengthy and enigmatic astro-magical text, which was so far known to us only through two sixteenth-century English manuscripts and quotations by John Dee (1527-1609). It is more difficult to pinpoint texts that escaped Bate's attention. In the field of nativities, one can mention Messahallah's *De nativitatibus*, translated by Hugo Sanctelliensis before 1151, and Albubater's *De nativitatibus*, translated by Salio of Padua in Toledo in 1218, omissions for which Bate cannot be blamed, for these texts were virtually unknown in his time.[189] Bate also ignored the recent translations made by Aegidius de Tebaldis at the court of Alfonso X in Toledo, i.e. Haly Abenragel's *De iudiciis astrorum* (after 1253) and Haly Abenrudian's commentary on Ptolemy's *Tetrabiblos* (after 1257), but he became aware of these works after writing the *Nativitas*.[190]

---

[187] See chapter 6 below.

[188] Vuillemin-Diem and Steel 2015, esp. pp. 39-44 for Bate's uses of William's translation.

[189] Messahallah's text is extant in two manuscripts only. Albubater's *De nativitatibus* was to enjoy great popularity in the fifteenth- and sixteenth centuries, with some 20 extant manuscripts and four printed editions between 1492 and 1540, but no manuscript prior to the end of the fourteenth century is known to exist. This text was known, however, to William of Saint-Cloud (see n. 235 below).

[190] Bate quotes Haly Abenrudian in his *De diebus creticis periodorumque causis* (see 3.1.5 above) and both Haly Abenrudian and Haly Abenragel in his *Speculum divinorum*, XIX.10 (MS Saint-Omer, BM, 587, fol. 320v).

5.3. Bate and the University of Paris

5.3.1. Introduction

Where did Bate acquire his astrological knowledge? We know that Bate was friend to William of Moerbeke, whom he had met in 1274, and we can surmise that it is through personal contact that he procured William's translation of Ptolemy's *Tetra-biblos* (and, probably, the *Centiloquium* translated from the Greek). We also know that Bate had access to a corpus of Abraham Ibn Ezra's Hebrew writings, whose translation into French by Hagins le Juif he supervised in Mechelen in 1273. Yet these two channels account for only a small portion of the large astrological library he must have assembled in order to write the *Nativitas*. Where did he find the books? We do not have a definite answer to that question, but it is likely that the University of Paris played an instrumental role. Bate graduated in Paris sometime between 1266 and 1273 and it is soon after this Parisian period that his first astrological and astronomical activities are documented, i.e. the translation of Abraham Ibn Ezra's treatises in 1273 and the writing of his *Magistralis compositio astrolabii* in 1274.

5.3.2. Peter of Limoges

In the second half of the thirteenth century, Paris was one of the most vibrant centres for astronomical and astrological studies in Europe. Between 1266 and 1273, we find there at least one man who possessed a knowledge of astronomy and astrology comparable to Bate's: Peter of Limoges. Little is known about Peter of Limoges's life.[191] He is first attested in Paris in 1260-61, when he copied a large collection of sermons, including some given by Robert de Sorbon. He was dean of the faculty of medicine from 1267 to 1270 and appears to have spent most of his life in Paris until his death in 1306. A brilliant polymath, he was versed in theology as well as in all secular subjects, including mathematics, optics, medicine and, above all, astronomy/astrology (his Sorbonne obituary portrays him as a "magnus astronomus"). While he is best known for his *De oculo morali* composed between 1274 and 1289, he also authored a couple of astrological pieces, including a commentary on Richard of Fournival's *Nativitas*, a judgement on the comet of 1299,[192] and, probably, a judgement on the comet of 1301.[193] He may also have been involved in casting the nativity horoscope of the future Louis X, born on 8 October 1289.[194] His interest

---

[191]   On Peter of Limoges, see Delisle 1868-1881, vol. 2, pp. 167-169; Birkenmajer 1949; Thorndike 1950, pp. 196-198; Mabille 1970; Mabille 1976; Bériou 1986, esp. pp. 68-70; Bataillon 1988.

[192]   Thorndike 1950, pp. 196-201 (with edition).

[193]   Thorndike 1950, pp. 202-207 (with edition).

[194]   This horoscope, together with four other horoscopes related to that nativity and to the great conjunction of 1285, is found on a bifolium appended to Peter's own copy of his collection of sermons of 1260-61 (Paris, BnF, lat. 15971, fols. 233r-234r). These horoscopes have been analysed by Poulle 1999, who noted that they were cast on the basis of the Tables of Toulouse, except for the horoscope of the great conjunction of 1285 or, more precisely, of the syzygy preceding that conjunction (fol. 234r).

in scientific subjects can be traced back to the early 1260s at least. Around 1263, he worked in close collaboration with Roger Bacon on optical matters[195] and it is perhaps in the same year that he heavily glossed the complete text of Ptolemy's *Almagest* in what is now MS Paris, BnF, lat. 16200.[196]

Yet Peter's profound expertise in both astronomy and astrology is best exhibited in the large collection of manuscripts copied by him or under his supervision, most of which are glossed in his hand. According to the Sorbonne obituary, he bequeathed over 120 manuscripts to the College of Sorbonne in 1306, of which more than 70 have been identified, mainly at the Bibliothèque nationale de France.[197] Many of his glosses consist of cross-references given in the most precise fashion, not only to texts and chapters, but also to folio numbers and pages (recto/verso) of his own manuscripts.[198] Sometime after 1262, he commissioned a massive volume of essential astrological works, which he himself refers to in his glosses as the *"Liber magnus iudiciorum"*. This volume, which amounted to at least 339 folia, has regrettably disappeared for the most part and what is left (92 folia) today forms MS Paris, BnF, lat. 7320. The texts still in the manuscript include Albumasar's *De revolutionibus nativitatum* (*) (fols. 1r-24v, now at the end of the manuscript); the *Capitula Almansoris* (*) (fols. 37r-40v); Guillelmus Anglicus's *De urina non visa* (*) (fols. 40v-43v); the *Astronomia Ypocratis* (fols. 44r-47v); Abraham Avenezra's *De terminatione morborum* (fols. 44r-46r, as glosses to the previous text); Messahallah's *Liber receptionis* (*) (fols. 48r-58v); and Ptolemy's *Quadripartitum* in Plato of Tivoli's translation (*) (fols. 61r-104v). Thanks to Peter's glosses referring to this volume, we know that the *Liber magnus iudiciorum* also contained at least the following texts: Peter's commentary on Richard of Fournival's *Nativitas*; Albohali's *De nativitatibus* (*); Albumasar's *Introductorium maius* (*), *De magnis coniunctionibus* (*) and *De revolutione annorum nativitatum*; Pseudo-Johannes Hispalensis's *Epitome totius astrologie* (*); and Pseudo-Ptolemy's *Centiloquium* (*). The making of the *Liber*

This horoscope puzzled Poulle because it was cast for 27 December 1285, while according to Tables of Toulouse, the great conjunction took place in the first half of December (Poulle 1999, p. 265 n. 21). The answer to this question is in fact provided by William of Saint-Cloud, who carefully observed the great conjunction on 28 and 29 December 1285 (as he explains in detail in his *Almanach planetarum* of 1292, canons, § 11, ed. Pedersen 2014, pp. 12-13). It follows that this horoscope was based on William's observations and, therefore, that William was perhaps also involved in casting the horoscopes found in Peter's manuscript. For further connections between Peter of Limoges and William of Saint-Cloud, see n. 218 and 222 below.

[195] Hackett 1998.

[196] This manuscript has not been identified so far as belonging to Peter, but many of the glosses, as well as the foliation are his. This sumptuous manuscript was copied in Paris in 1213, as a note on fol. IIv informs us, but someone changed the date into 1263 (see Samaran and Marichal 1974, p. 738), which nicely falls within Peter's period of activity. At any rate, Peter somehow inherited or appropriated the manuscript for himself, as his own foliation shows.

[197] His astrological manuscripts are Paris, BnF, lat. 7320, 7434, 15971, 15972, 16206, 16210, 16653 and 16658 (on these, see Juste 2015), as well as Paris, BnF, fr. 24276; Vatican, BAV, Reg. lat. 1191; and Vatican, BAV, Reg. lat. 1261.

[198] Birkenmajer 1949; Mabille 1976.

magnus iudiciorum cannot be dated precisely, but its nature as a compendium, its function as a textbook designed with large margins for glosses, as well as the fact that Peter refers to it in most of his other astrological manuscripts, all suggest that it was completed at an early stage of his scholarly career. Another manuscript likely to be from Peter's early period is MS Paris, BnF, lat. 7434, which includes, among various scientific texts, Gerard of Feltre's *Summa de astris* (fols. 1r-12v, incomplete at beginning and end due to missing folia) and Roger of Hereford's *Liber de tribus generalibus iudiciis astronomie* (fols. 76r-79r). When Peter became aware of the Alfonsine translations, he commissioned splendid copies of both Haly Abenragel's *De iudiciis astrorum* (*) and Haly Abenrudian's commentary on Ptolemy's *Tetrabiblos* (*) (now MSS Paris, BnF, lat. 16206 and 16653 respectively). Peter also refers to further texts which have not been found in his manuscripts: Haly Embrani's *De electionibus horarum* (*), Pseudo-Ptolemy's *Iudicia*, Zael's *Liber iudiciorum* (*) and one "liber Leopoldi" — probably Leopold of Austria's *De astrorum scientia*, written c. 1271 —, among others that cannot be clearly identified. It should be kept in mind that the list given here is certainly not complete, as many of Peter's manuscripts are lost or still to be found.[199]

Texts marked with an asterisk above were also known to Bate. Now, it is fair to say that access to these texts was nothing exceptional, as many of them were already bestsellers by the middle of the thirteenth century. There are, however, more striking similarities between Peter of Limoges and Bate.

First, Peter and Bate are the earliest attested users of the translations made by Aegidius de Tebaldis in Toledo (after 1253/1257) and by Stephen of Messina in Sicily (c. 1262).[200] Among these, Albumasar's *De revolutionibus nativitatum* was held in high esteem by both men, for it is the opening text of Peter's *Liber magnus iudiciorum* (Paris, BnF, lat. 7320, fols. 1r-24v) and the single most quoted source in Bate's *Nativitas* (52 references). Strikingly, there was some uncertainty regarding the authorship of this text and this uncertainty is echoed by both. In the *Liber magnus iudiciorum*, the text is anonymous, but Peter recognised that the author was Albumasar on doctrinal grounds, as he tells us in a gloss on fol. 20r: "Nota quod ex hoc quod hic dicitur patet quod actor huius libri est Albumasar, qui etiam composuit Introductorium astrologie, sed planissime patet ex titulo libri huius abreviati

---

[199]   At least one astrological manuscript is missing, for Peter refers to texts in his own "quodam parvo volumine iudiciorum astrorum", which contained a corrected version of the *Astronomia Ypocratis* (i.e., perhaps in the new translation from the Greek by either William of Moerbeke or Peter of Abano), followed by Haly Embrani's *De electionibus horarum* (see Paris, BnF, lat. 7320, fol. 44r, in a gloss edited by Birkenmajer 1949, p. 24). Elsewhere, Peter refers to a *Tractatus de dispositione aeris* found "in libro parvo astronomie ligato" (see gloss in Paris, BnF, lat. 16653, fol. 23r), presumably the same volume. This manuscript has not been found.

[200]   But note that, in his *Opus maius* (1266-1267), Roger Bacon cites "Haly Abenragel" in a list of essential introductions to astrology (ed. Bridges 1897, p. 389). Haly Abenragel was also an important source for Guido Bonatti, in his *Liber introductorius ad iudicia stellarum*, written after 1277.

infra fol. 310".[201] On two occasions in the *Nativitas*, Bate expresses doubts about the authorship. He writes: "In libro etiam revolutionum nativitatum, qui dicitur Albumasar" (*Nat.* 679-680) and "In libro quoque de revolutionibus annorum nativitatum, qui dicitur Albumasar" (*Nat.* 1030-1032).

Second, in the field of astrological medicine, both Peter and Bate refer to the same rare material, namely a commentary on *verbum* 60 of Pseudo-Ptolemy's *Centiloquium* in connection to an octogonal (or hexadecagonal) diagram showing the critical days.[202] This commentary is known in six manuscripts, only two of which have the octogonal diagram: Berlin, SBPK, lat. fol. 192 (963), s. XV, fols. 79vb-81v (diagram fol. 81r), and Vatican, BAV, Pal. lat. 1116, s. XV, fols. 125v-126v (diagram fol. 126v).[203] The latter copy is clearly connected to Bate, where the text in question immediately follows his *De diebus creticis periodorumque causis* (fols. 118ra-125ra).

Third, Peter of Limoges was actively involved in the nativities business. This is best exemplified by his thorough enquiry into Richard of Fournival's *Nativitas*. This enquiry took several forms: Peter recalculated Richard's nativity horoscope, glossed Richard's text and wrote a full-length commentary on it.[204] The commen-

---

[201] Peter refers to Albumasar's *Introductorium maius* and *De revolutione annorum nativitatum*. The latter is indeed another translation of the *De revolutionibus nativitatum* (from the Arabic, probably by John of Seville), which includes only Book I and the first chapters of Book II, hence Peter's label of "libri huius abreviati". For a comparison of the two translations, see Burnett 2009.

[202] Peter: "Et nota quod dictum modum Abrahe de creticis diebus tangit et ponit Ptolomeus in Centiloquio proposicione 60a, ut patet per commentum ibi, ut patet per figuram 8 angulorum, de qua ibi loquitur et de qua ibi notavi, scilicet libro magno iudiciorum 339 folio, pagina prima" (gloss in Paris, BnF, lat. 7320, fol. 44r, ed. Birkenmajer 1949, p. 24). Bate: "Angulorum quidem proprietas idem comvincit quod dictum est ut patet intuenti partes scientie geometrice propter quod dicit Ptholomeus, 60 propositione Centilogii, et suus commentator quod crises laudabiles fiunt in oppositione Lune ad locum principii egritudinis secundum quartum aspectum. Deinde secundum figuram octogonam aut secundum sedecagonam ita quod dies figurationum debilioris virtutis indicativi sunt respectu fortioris" (*De diebus creticis periodorumque causis*, ed. Dell'Anna 1999, vol. 2, p. 114).

[203] On this commentary, see Dell'Anna 1999, vol. 1, pp. 343-346, and edition, vol. 2, pp. 128-131 (from Vatican, BAV, Pal. lat. 1116). The other manuscripts are Bergamo, BCAM, MA 388, s. XV, fols. 59r-60r; Darmstadt, Hessische Landes- und Hochschulbibl., 739, s. XIV, fols. 182rb-183vb; London, BL, Harley 13, s. XIII-XIV, fols. 229ra-230rb; and Vatican, BAV, Reg. lat. 1452, s. XIV, fols. 121r-121v. The text, of unknown origin, is attributed to "Hispalensis" in the earliest copy (Harley 13), to "Linconensis" (*sic*), i.e. Robert Grosseteste, in Vatican, BAV, Pal. lat. 1116, and is anonymous in the other manuscripts. The octagonal diagram is also found, together with a canon describing its use (inc. "Circulus 16 angulorum describit dies creticos..."), in MSS Berlin, SBPK, lat. fol. 646, s. XIII, fols. 19v-21r, and Munich, BSB, Clm 244, s. XIV, fols. 140v and 146r; and the canon alone occurs in Vatican, BAV, Pal. lat. 1116, where it precedes the comm. on *verbum* 60 (this canon is edited in Dell'Anna 1999, vol. 2, pp. 202-205).

[204] See Birkenmajer 1949. The recalculations (autograph notes and two horoscopes) are found in Paris, BnF, lat. 16658, fols. 31v-32r; the glosses in Vatican, BAV, Reg. lat. 1261, s. XIII, fols. 59r-60v (a manuscript that contains a wealth of scientific texts glossed by Peter throughout); and the commentary in Oxford, Hertford Coll., 4, s. XV, fols. 160r-166r (preceded by Richard's text on fols. 159r-160r); Vatican, BAV, Pal. lat. 1380, s. XIV, fols. 184r-187r (with Richard's horoscope alone on fol. 188r); Vatican, BAV, Pal. lat. 1443, s. XIV, fols. 211r-221v (followed by Richard's text on fols. 221v-222v), as well as in Peter's *Liber magnus iudiciorum* (now lost). Richard's *Nativitas* also occurs alone in London, BL, Sloane 3281, s. XIII-XIV, fols. 14r-15v. All of these texts will be edited and discussed in Lucken and Boudet (forthcoming).

tary consists of detailed guidelines for casting nativities (including the calculation of the animodar, hyleg, alcochoden, profections and directions) and provides precise references to the relevant authorities for each topic. A polished work with a distinctive didactic timbre, it was not meant for Peter's own use, but as a teaching text for students or more advanced scholars in astrology. Whether Bate was inspired by Peter's commentary we cannot say, but it is fairly certain that he knew Richard's *Nativitas*. This is revealed by the same unusual formula used by both to denote their nativity in the central panel of their respective horoscope: "Nativitas servi Dei gloriosi".[205] If Bate knew Richard's *Nativitas*, it would seem almost inevitable to conclude that it was through Peter of Limoges, who appears to have been the main agent in the circulation of Richard's work.[206] Unfortunately Peter's commentary cannot be dated with any certainty,[207] but as an aside, I note that already in the late 1250s and in the 1260s, Parisian scholars were concerned with recording the time of birth as precisely as possible, as reflected by a set of notes found in an astronomical/astrological manuscript which provides the birth data (date and time) of five individuals born between 1258 and 1266.[208]

Fourth, Peter of Limoges knew Abraham Ibn Ezra's astrological works. In the margins of his *Liber magnus iudiciorum*, he himself copied a "Liber Abraham de

---

[205] *Nat.* 375. In the *Nativitas*, Bate never gives his name and repeatedly calls himself "servus Dei (gloriosi)", see *Nat.* 31-32, 225, 242, 281, 288, 290, 347-348,418, 1286, 1935, 2066, 2072, 2153, 2780, 3029, 3040 and 3102; *App. I* 7 and 33.

[206] All manuscripts of Richard's *Nativitas* are accompanied by Peter's glosses or commentary, with the only exception of London, BL, Sloane 3281 (see n. 204 above). But even this MS can be somehow linked to Peter, for it contains, immediately after Richard's *Nativitas*, a series of eclipse predictions for the years 1282-1311 in Saint-Quentin (fols. 16ra-16vb), one of which (fol. 16rb19-26) occurs almost word for word as one of Peter's glosses in MS Paris, BnF, lat. 16210, fol. 222v, i.e. in his copy of William of Saint-Cloud's *Almanach planetarum*, under July 1311 (this gloss is edited by Pedersen 2014, p. 64).

[207] Birkenmajer (1949, p. 28) tentatively dated Peter's work on the *Nativitas* to between 1267 and 1295, on account of autograph notes found on fol. 38v of Paris, BnF, lat. 16658. The notes in question give an *exemplum* of the calculation of the date of Easter within a 28-year cycle starting in 1267. However, Peter glossed his manuscripts at various times throughout his life, so that this *exemplum* is of little help in dating his recalculations of Richard's nativity, which are found elsewhere in the manuscript (fols. 31v-32r), let alone in dating his commentary. The presence of Peter's commentary towards the beginning of his *Liber magnus iudiciorum* (fols. 29-31, see Birkenmajer 1949, p. 20 n. 18) suggests an early date.

[208] London, BL, Harley 4350, s. XIII, fol. 2rb. The names of these individuals have been erased and replaced by cryptic, perhaps partly Hebrew, characters, evidently to prevent identification. The hand is not that of Peter of Limoges. The author, who was an astronomer, indicates the time of birth in accurate terms, twice by giving the altitude of a star (§§ 1 and 4), which supposes the use of an astrolabe or a kindred instrument: "[1] *** fuit natus anno domini M° IIc et LVIII°, octavo idus Ianuarii, die dominico in nocte, Aldebarem erat in altitudine 34 graduum ex parte occidentis et erat F littera dominicalis. [2] *** fuit natus anno domini M° IIc LXI°, primo idus Februarii, die Lune primis gallis cantantibus. [3] *** fuit *** anno domini M° IIc 63°, mense Iulii, undecimo kalendas Augusti, die dominico in crepusculo noctis et erat festum Madalene. [4] Anni (?) *** anno domini 1264°, primo idus Februarii, die Veneris, in nocte et erat Pleiades in altitudine 13 graduum ex parte occidentis. [5] *** fuit natus anno domini 1266, tercio nonas Marcii, die Sabati in fine hore secunde et in principio tercie vel circiter". The manuscript, copied in northern France and most probably in Paris, in the 1250s or 1260s, contains several added notes c. 1266 referring to Paris (e.g. fols. 25v, 119v).

terminacione morborum". This text is none other than a previously unidentified translation of Ibn Ezra's *Sefer ha-me'orot* ("Book of Luminaries"), dealing with the critical days.[209] This translation is found in two further copies: Limoges, BM, 9 (28), s. XV, fols. 75v-79v, and Leiden, UB, Voss. Chymici Q.27, s. XVI, fols. 91r-99r. In the latter copy, it is immediately followed by a text opening "In libro Abraham de iudiciis...", which turns out to be another previously unidentified translation of Ibn Ezra, this time of selected chapters from *Sefer ha-moladot* ("Book of Nativities").[210] This *Liber Abraham de iudiciis* occurs in two other manuscripts: Oxford, Hertford Coll., 4, s. XV, fols. 133v-135r, and Vatican, BAV, Pal. lat. 1380, s. XIV, fols. 187r-188r. These two manuscripts also contain Peter's commentary on Richard of Fournival's *Nativitas* and it is striking that in the Vatican manuscript, both texts form a single unit, where Peter's commentary (fols. 184r-187r) is followed by *Liber Abraham de iudiciis* (fols. 187r-188r) and, without a break, by the nativity horoscope of Richard (fol. 188r). This connection with Richard's *Nativitas* makes perfect sense, for the *Liber Abraham de iudiciis* deals with the rectification of the ascendant by way of the *trutina Hermetis* and with the revolutions of nativities, two topics which are absent from Richard's *Nativitas* (and from Peter's commentary), but which most appropriately supplement it. It seems reasonable to assume that Peter himself selected the chapters from Ibn Ezra's *Sefer ha-moladot* and appended them to his commentary on Richard's *Nativitas*.

The question arises how Peter got hold of Ibn Ezra's astrological works. We can provide an answer to that question. As already noted, a corpus of Ibn Ezra's astrological texts was translated from Hebrew into French under Bate's supervision in Mechelen in 1273. The details of this episode are known to us thanks to a colophon found in the earliest manuscript of these translations, MS Paris, BnF, fr. 24276, which reads (fol. 66rb): "Ci define li livres du commencement de sapience que fist Abraham Evenazre ou Aezera, qui est interpretes maistre de aide, que translata Hagins li Iuis de ebrieu en romans, et Obers de Mondidier escrivoit le romans, et fu fait a Malines en la meson sire Henri Bate, et fu fines l'en de grace 1273° lendemein de la seint Thomas l'apostre [22 December]". But what has not been realised up to now is that this manu-

---

[209] Paris, BnF, lat. 7320, fols. 44r-46r: "Incipit liber Abraham de terminacione morborum. Quesierunt medici causam creticorum dierum in infirmitatibus qui sunt dies 7a vel 14a vel 20a vel 21a vel 27a vel 28a — et sic debes facere de anno in annum". The translation omits the first chapter of *Sefer ha-me'orot*.

[210] Leiden, UB, Voss. Chymici Q.27, fols. 99r-101v: "In libro Abraham de iudiciis ita dicit Abraham: Dicit Enoch quod in nativitate hominis semper ita est quod locus Lune in hora nativitatis est gradus ascendens in hora conceptionis... (100v) Idem in libro de revolutionibus nativitatum. Si vis scire principium revolutionis anni — et simili modo semper debes operari ad inveniendam horam revolutionis. Explicit". This manuscript is clearly related to Peter, for it also contains (1) the *De Antichristo* (here entitled "De terminacione durationis mundi", fols. 115r-118v), an eschatological-astrological text known so far in a unique copy, which belonged to Peter: Paris, BnF, lat. 15972, s. XIII, fols. 83ra-84va (see study and edition from that manuscript in Bériou 1986); and (2) "De diebus creticis pro pronosticanda mutatione aeris. Ut dicitur in comento super Ipocratis de diebus creticis periodorum quos complent dies creticis quidam sunt particulares..." (fols. 119r-129r), a text on critical days otherwise found uniquely in Limoges, BM, 9 (28), fols. 79v-84r, where it follows Abraham's *De terminatione morborum*.

script is glossed in a hand familiar to us, which is none other than Peter of Limoges's. Not only did Peter add notes in the margins of fols. 104r, 109r, 113r, 113v and 118r, but he also foliated the whole volume and drew up a table of contents in the margin of fol. 1r. In other words, this manuscript belonged to him and was, in all likelihood, the very copy sent to him by Bate, probably in or shortly after December 1273.[211]

We thus have material evidence of a connection between Peter of Limoges and Bate. This should not prompt us to conclude, however, that Peter became acquainted with astrology under Bate's influence after 1273. The similarities outlined above would rather be the result of prolonged contacts between the two men. After all, they were in Paris at the same time and, presumably, over a period of several years. In those conditions, it is hardly conceivable that they failed to meet sometime before 1273. Considering that Peter was older than Bate and already a well-established scholar (dean of the faculty of medicine 1267-1270) when Bate was still a student, it is reasonable to assume that Peter was, generally speaking, the source of inspiration for his younger fellow, rather than the other way around. At any rate, the beginning of Bate's attested astrological activities (1273-74) more or less coincides with the end of his curriculum in Paris and cannot be independent from it. Even in the case of Ibn Ezra, it is hard to believe that after graduating in Paris, Bate returned to Mechelen, where he discovered a corpus of Hebrew astrological writings and engaged in translating activities with Hagins le Juif. The most likely scenario is that Bate came across Ibn Ezra's works in Paris, possibly through Peter of Limoges,[212] to whom he could have returned the favour by sending him a copy of Ibn Ezra's translations.

5.3.3. *Other scholars and opportunities*

Peter of Limoges was of course not the only supplier of astrological/astronomical books and learning in Paris. A decisive moment in the history of the College of Sorbonne occurred in 1272, when Gerard of Abbeville, master of theology, died and bequeathed his collection of some 300 manuscripts to the college. The major part of this collection came from the library of Richard of Fournival (d. 1260), which included a large number of scientific manuscripts. Richard's manuscripts that have

---

[211] The manuscript later belonged to the Sorbonne (see ex-libris fol. 1r and Delisle 1868-1881, vol. 3, p. 69, no. 74). Shlomo Sela compared the Hebrew, French and Latin versions and confirmed to us that the *Liber Abraham de iudiciis* is indeed a translation of the *Livre des jugemens des nativites* (=*Sefer ha-moladot*) as found in Paris, BnF, lat. 24276, fols. 66rb-100va. It should be noted, however, that this manuscript does not include a French translation of *Sefer ha-me'orot*, so that the *De terminatione morborum* came from a different source, perhaps another manuscript prepared by Bate. These questions will be fully treated in Sela (forthcoming b).

[212] Note that Peter knew at least some Hebrew. See the evidence assembled by Bataillon 1988, p. 268, and Federici Vescovini 1992, p. 403, to which the following passage from Peter's judgement on the comet of 1299 should be added: "illa comete que vocatur dominus ascone, quod in Arabico et in Ebraico idem significat quod dominus mortis in Latino" (ed. Thorndike 1950, p. 199).

been identified so far contain over 30 astrological texts[213] and it is interesting to note that five of them were known to Bate but (apparently) not to Peter of Limoges: the *Liber novem iudicum* in its complete version (Paris, BnF, lat. 7344A, fols. 1ra-51vb), Aomar's *De nativitatibus* (Paris, BnF, lat. 16204, in a section now lost), Gergis's *De significatione septem planetarum in domibus* (Paris, BnF, lat. 16204, pp. 428b-432b; Paris, BnF, lat. 16208, fols. 50va-51vb), and Messahallah's *Epistola de rebus eclipsium* (Paris, BnF, lat. 16204, pp. 387b-391b, and Paris, BnF, lat. 16208, fols. 49va-50va) and *De revolutionibus annorum mundi* (Paris, BnF, lat. 16204, pp. 391b-404a). 1272 was probably too late for Bate to have taken (full) advantage of Richard's library during his student years in Paris, even though the possibility that he would have accessed it before 1272, i.e. directly through Gerard of Abbeville, cannot be ruled out. Moreover, Bate may also have consulted the newly acquired books on the occasion of a later visit to Paris, which happened in the autumn of 1280 (*App. I* 44), when the *Nativitas* was about to be completed.

While in Paris in the 1260s, Bate would have had the opportunity to meet other scholars working on astronomy and astrology, like Roger Bacon and Giles of Lessines.[214] There is also a group of astronomers whose biographies are poorly documented, but who appear to have been active in Paris mainly in the 1280s and 1290s. This group includes Franco of Poland, William of Saint-Cloud, John of Sicily, Peter of Dacia, Peter of Saint-Omer, Bernard of Verdun, Peter of Abano and the anonymous author of a commentary on the canons of the Toledan Tables in 1290.[215] After his graduation, Bate remained in contact with Paris. As just noted, he returned there in the autumn of 1280. Much later, in his *Speculum divinorum*, he tells us that he received from Paris a report of the observation of the solar eclipse of 12 April 1298.[216] Elsewhere in the *Speculum*, he recounts contemporary measurements of the altitude of the Sun made in Paris by two men who used large quadrants.[217] The two men are not named and no date is given, but as luck would have it, this experiment

---

[213]   MSS Paris, BnF, lat. 7344A, 16203, 16204, 16205, 16208, 16652, 16657 and 16659. On these MSS, see Juste 2015.

[214]   Giles of Lessines wrote his *Summa de temporibus* in Paris between 1260 and 1264 and his *De essentia, motu et significatione cometarum* in or shortly after 1264. See Thorndike 1950, pp. 87-103; Nothaft 2014; Nothaft 2014a. For Roger Bacon, see n. 195 above.

[215]   On Franco, see Birkenmajer 1972, pp. 444-448, and Poulle 1964a; on William, see below; on John, Pedersen 1986; on Peter of Dacia and Peter of Saint-Omer, Pedersen 1983-1984; on Bernard of Verdun, Poulle 1964a; on Peter of Abano, Federici Vescovini 1992; on the anonymous of 1290, Pedersen 1984 and Pedersen 2001-2002. For general accounts on astronomical activities in Paris in the second half of the thirteenth century, see Chabás and Goldstein 2003, pp. 244-248, and especially Nothaft 2017, pp. 218-223 and 226-227.

[216]   *Speculum divinorum*, XXII.18, *Additio* (ed. Steel and Guldentops 1996, p. 346).

[217]   "Nostro quoque tempore Parisius artificiosi viri duo simul, duobus maximis quadrantibus artificiose factis et ingeniose verificatis, elevationem Solis maximam in meridie solstitii scilicet aestivalis acceperunt, quam alter quidem illorum invenit esse 64 gradus 42 minuta, alter vero 64 gradus 45 minuta, eratque sic illorum differentia 3 minutorum" (*Speculum divinorum*, XXII.17, ed. Steel and Guldentops 1996, p. 337).

has come down to us via one of Peter of Limoges's glosses, where the missing data are disclosed: this experiment was performed jointly by Franco of Poland and Peter of Limoges in 1283, and the results obtained were later used by William of Saint-Cloud in his *Almanach planetarum* of 1292.[218]

5.3.4. *William of Saint-Cloud*

This shows that Bate kept abreast of the astronomical activities carried out in Paris in the 1280s and 1290s. It is unclear whether he attended the experiment of 1283, nor do we know who his informant concerning the eclipse of 1298 was. It is possible, however, to show that he was in contact with at least one of the scholars mentioned above: William of Saint-Cloud. William of Saint-Cloud ("Guillelmus de Sancto Clodoaldo") was a central figure among the Parisian astronomers of the last two decades of the thirteenth century.[219] He is known to have performed a large number of astronomical observations between 1285 and 1292 and has been identified as the author of three works: (1) the *Directorium*, a bilingual (Latin-French) set of instructions for the use of a magnetic compass, which he dedicated to a queen sometime before 1292 (probably Mary of Brabant, widow of Philip III the Bold);[220] (2) the *Kalendarium regine*, an astronomical calendar with canons, which he dedicated to Mary of Brabant around 1292 and later translated into French for Joan of Navarre (wife of Philip IV the Fair);[221] (3) the *Almanach planetarum*, a set of tables with canons for finding the planetary longitudes for every single day from 1292 to 1311.[222]

---

[218] "Anno domini 1281, 15 die Iunii, littera dominicalis E, dominica eadem die in meridie altitudo Cancri 64 gradus et 43 minuta. Eodem anno, Decembris die 14 dominica altitudo Capricorni in meridie Parisius 17 gradus, 37 minuta. Hec observavit Franco. 1283, in die sancte Lucie, ego cum ipso inveni 17 gradus, 35 minuta. Hec fecimus cum magno quadrante, cuius latera erant de ligno et limbus de latone divisus usque ad 5 minuta". This passage is part of a longer gloss, also reporting similar observations made in Paris in 1290, found on an originally blank folio within Giles of Lessines's *Summa de temporibus* in MS Vatican, BAV, Reg. lat. 1191, fol. 139r. The gloss was edited in full by Delorme 1936 (p. 559), who attributed it to William of Saint-Cloud on the ground that the very same observations for 1290 are reported as William's own observations in his *Almanach planetarum* (see canons, § 5, ed. Pedersen 2014, pp. 9-10). However, the handwriting is unmistakably that of Peter, as Federici Vescovini 1992, p. 402, had already recognised. The attribution to Peter is in fact confirmed, rather unexpectedly, by the presence of virtually the same gloss, in a contemporary hand, in MS Vienna, ÖNB, 2311, fol. 96v, where we read "ipse cum Petro" instead of "ego cum ipso". The Vienna glossator is certainly William of Saint-Cloud, for the observations of 1290 are said to have been made not in Paris (as in the Vatican gloss), but 'apud Sanctum Clodoaltum', i.e. in Saint-Cloud. The whole gloss lies in the background of the opening chapters of William's *Almanach planetarum* (canons, §§ 2-5, ed. Pedersen 2014, pp. 8-10). As to "Franco", he is evidently to be identified with Franco of Poland, who is known mainly as the author of a treatise on the turquetum or turketum (*Tractatus de turketo*, composed in Paris in 1284), an instrument which Peter of Limoges used to observe the position of the comet of 1299. On these astronomical observations, see also Nothaft 2017, pp. 219-220.

[219] For general accounts on William of Saint-Cloud, see Harper 1966 and Poulle 2008a.

[220] Harper 1966, pp. 4-5, 22-23 and 56-58.

[221] Both versions are edited in Harper 1966.

[222] The canons are edited, translated and discussed in Pedersen 2014. See also Harper 1966, pp. 40-56, and Mancha 1992. The tables themselves occur in only two manuscripts from the late thirteenth

But there is more. In sections 1 and 5.1 of this volume, we ascribed to William of Saint-Cloud a *Nativitas* of 1285, and this requires some justification. This *Nativitas* immediately follows Bate's *Nativitas* in four manuscripts and has not been found in any other context.[223] It concerns someone born in Paris on 18 January 1255 and since the author also provides the revolution horoscope for the 30th year of his life, it can be safely dated to 1285. The text is anonymous in all four copies, but the author mentions the name of his father, a certain "Petrus Fabri".[224] This led Emmanuel Poulle to tentatively identify the author with Robertus Faber/Fabri, or Robert le Febvre, physician to Philip IV and Joan of Navarre.[225] But Poulle was not aware that "Faber" is also the name by which William of Saint-Cloud calls himself in the colophon of his *Directorium*: "Versiculos Faber hos ego Guillelmus fabricavi / Quorum Romanum regine sic reservavi".[226] The date of the *Nativitas* matches the period of activity of William, who first appears on the scene with his astronomical observations of 1285, as we have seen. By contrast, Robert le Febvre is not credited with any astronomical or astrological activity, as Poulle himself admitted. If we add that William composed his *Almanach planetarum* explicitly for casting nativities and other astrological purposes,[227] we are left to conclude either that there were two astrologers named Faber and active in Paris in 1285, or that William of Saint-Cloud is the author of *Nativitas* of 1285.

The *Nativitas* of 1285 (let us now call it William of Saint-Cloud's *Nativitas*) is of special interest to us because it presents one of the rare instances of the use of Bate's Tables of Mechelen. In the process of casting his nativity, William performed all calculations twice, first according to the Tables of Toulouse (as was common among Parisian astronomers), then according to the Tables of Mechelen. The final result, displayed in the horoscope, agrees with the Tables of Mechelen, even though, re- grettably, William does not explain the reasons behind this choice. It is interesting to note here that in his *Almanach planetarum*, William demonstrated, on the basis of his observations of the longitude of Saturn, Jupiter and Mars, that the Tables of Toulouse (and the Toledan Tables, from which the Tables of Toulouse derive) were

---

century: Paris, BnF, lat. 16210, fols. 2r-229v (a manuscript commissioned by Peter of Limoges; wrongly reported as "lat. 16201" in Pedersen 2014, p. 58 and *passim*) and Vatican, BAV, Vat. lat. 4572, fols. 1r-102v.

[223] Paris, BnF, lat. 7324, fols. 47ra-49va; Paris, BnF, lat. 10270, fols. 178r-183v; Seville, BCC, 5-1-38, fols. 50r-56r; Venice, BNM, lat. VI.108 (2055), fols. 141v-145v.

[224] "pater meus... sub isto nomine Petrus Fabri" (Paris, BnF, lat. 7324, fol. 47ra).

[225] Poulle 1964, pp. 794-795 and n. 4.

[226] MS Paris, Bibl. de l'Arsenal, 1037, s. XIII, fol. 8va (see also Harper 1966, pp. 4-5, who mistran- scribed the colophon). This splendidly illustrated manuscript is likely to be the presentation copy to the queen. Poulle later became aware of this colophon but nevertheless asserted "Nor are there grounds for calling William of Saint-Cloud by the name of Lefebvre" (Poulle 2008a), without justification. In the colophon, "Faber" can only denote the author's name and not a noun meaning "maker" or "craftsman", for this would render the verse embarrassingly redundant ("faber" + "fabricavi").

[227] See canons, §§ 31-33, ed. Pedersen 2014, pp. 22-23, and, for a practical application, n. 194 above.

severely wrong, so much so that, as he concludes, calculations based on those tables would lead to despicable errors in astrological judgements.[228]

There is another context in which the Tables of Mechelen were used. MS Oxford, New College, 282, s. XV, fols. 197r-198r, contains a set a notes and calculations by an astronomer who verified the data of the nativity of Haly Abenrudian. These notes immediately follow Haly Abenrudian's commentary on Ptolemy's *Quadripartitum* (tr. Aegidius de Tebaldis), where Haly's nativity is indeed found.[229] Our astronomer recomputed Haly's horoscope and provided all calculations on the basis of the Tables of Mechelen, but he also tells us that he compared these results with those of the Tables of Toulouse.[230] On closer examination, it becomes clear that this astronomer and the author of the *Nativitas* of 1285 are one and the same person, not only because of the comparison between the Tables of Mechelen and the Tables of Toulouse, but also because the calculations are carried out in exactly the same way, and in a way which, for that matter, differs from Bate's own calculations.[231] While Oxford, New College, 282 is a fifteenth-century manuscript, these notes are undoubtedly much older, for they also occur, albeit in a shorter version omitting

---

[228] Canons, §§ 11-12, 14, 17 and 20 (ed. Pedersen 2014, pp. 13-16) and conclusion § 22 (ed. p. 17): "Consideret igitur ex predictis quilibet, qui penitus tabulas imitatur, quam turpiter possit errare in iudiciis quibuscumque. Non enim est mirum si eas imitando in iudiciis sint decepti, cum coniunctiones et applicationes et separationes planetarum adinvicem, nec non et directiones, multo diverse sint secundum veritatem ab his que per tabulas habentur, ut potest cuilibet per predicta faciliter apparere".

[229] The commentary ends with an appendix in which Haly provides, by way of a didactic example, an interpretation of three nativities, including his own, see Oxford, NC, 282, fols. 191r-196v: "Volo tibi in hoc dare exemplum trium nativitatum ut melias intendas quidquid locuti sumus, et prima est nativitas mea. Ego natus fui...".

[230] "Volui probare utrum actor iste iudicaret secundum octavam speram vel secundum nonam, et inveni per loca planetarum que posuit in figura sue nativitatis quod ipsa fuit annis Christi perfectis 986, 10 mensibus, 15 die Ianuarii, qua die equavi planetas secundum tabulas et inveni sic. [Table:] Medius motus Solis 9.29.3.55. Verus Solis 10.0.12.27. Medius Lune 7.12.45.6. Argumentum medium Lune 3.11.26.53. Centrum Lune 6.25.22.22... [48 positions are given altogether]. /197v/ Per istas equationes, que facte sunt ad tempus predicte nativitatis per tabulas Mach[linienses], que sunt ad nonam speram, patet actorem per nonam iudicasse, quamvis loca aliquorum planetarum non conveniant locis ipsis nativitatis. Tamen Sol et Luna, per quos maxime postest probari quod dictum est, conveniunt eidem. Quidem vero accidit equando per tabulas compositas secundum octavam speram, quia tunc per additionem 6 graduum, qui tunc erant motus octave spere, pervenient loca planetarum scripta in predicta nativitate ut apparet /198r/ superius. Equavi etiam per tabulas Tholose et secundum utrasque tabulas concordant loca Solis, Lune et Veneris et Saturni cum locis figure, sed in loco Iovis discordant in signo integro, unde credo esse errorem scriptoris. Et hoc apparet per Haium [read: Halum] cum dicat Iovem coniunctum Saturno et in sextili Lune et quod sit in decima. Si enim esset in 29 Capricorni, hec non essent vera. Tamen quod dicit Iovem in suo casu (?) in capitulo fratrum videtur per hoc quod Iupiter fuerit in Capricorno. Loca etiam Martis et Mercurii non concordant cum locis nativitatis" (Oxford, NC, 282, fols. 197r-198r).

[231] The relevant positions (mean motion, argument, centre etc.) are labelled in the same way and given in the same order for each planet in turn (Sun, Moon, Caput, Saturn, Jupiter, Mars, Venus, Mercury). For example, William's *Nativitas* reads "Medius motus Solis... Verus eius... Medius Lune... Argumentum medium [Lune]... Centrum eius..." etc. (Paris, BnF, lat. 7324, fol. 48va; compare with previous note). By contrast, Bate does not follow the order of the planets and lists all apogees, centres, arguments, mean motions etc., see *Nat.* 490-529.

the calculations and the reference to the Tables of Toulouse, in a dozen of other manuscripts of Haly's commentary,[232] the earliest of which is MS Vienna, ÖNB, 2311, copied in the late thirteenth century. Strikingly, this Vienna manuscript was glossed by someone who reported astronomical observations made in Saint-Cloud in 1290, that is, in all likelihood, by William of Saint-Cloud himself.[233]

We thus have two new documents (the *Nativitas* of 1285 and the verification of Haly Abenrudian's nativity) which can be attributed to William of Saint-Cloud. These documents have something to reveal about the nature of the relationship between William and Bate. William held Bate's works in high esteem. Both documents attest that William deemed the Tables of Mechelen to be superior to the Tables of Toulouse.[234] It is also apparent that William shaped his own *Nativitas* on Bate's model. Like Bate, he provides a comprehensive account of the intricate investigations that led him to establish the date and time of his birth, gives all the details of the calculations of his nativity and casts the revolution horoscope for the year of writing. Yet William was by no means a novice astrologer in 1285. Even though his *Nativitas* is brief and includes no proper interpretation, it exhibits a good command of the subject and cites various sources, including a very important source that was unknown to Bate, namely Albubater's *De nativitatibus*.[235] Elsewhere, William distances himself from his model. For instance, he rectifies his nativity by way of the animodar only, and does not even mention the *trutina Hermetis*, which was the method favoured by Bate. It is likely that William obtained a copy of both the *Nativitas* and the Tables of Mechelen directly from Bate. Born in 1255, William was still a child when Bate first studied in Paris, so that we must assume that they

---

[232] "Volui probare utrum iste actor iudicaret secundum nonam speram vel secundum octavam, et inveni per loca planetarum que ponit in figura sue nativitatis quod ipsa fuit annis Christi perfectis 986, 10 mensibus, 15 die Ianuarii, qua die equavi planetas secundum tabulas Mach[linienses] et inveni sic" (Vienna, ÖNB, 2311, fol. 95rb). Same text in MSS Cambridge, UL, Kk 4.7 (2022), s. XIV, fol. 88ra; Chicago, The Newberry Lib., Ayer Collection 744, s. XV, fol. 226va-226vb; Florence, BNC, Magliabech. XX.22, s. XV, fol. 204va-204vb; Klagenfurt, Archiv der Diözese Gurk — Bischöfliche Mensalbibl., XXXI b 10, s. XV, fol. 73v; Leipzig, UB, 1474, s. XV, fol. 138va; Paris, BnF, lat. 7305, s. XV, fol. 353r; Paris, BnF, lat. 7432, s. XV, fol. 134r; Paris, Bibl. de la Sorbonne, 593, s. XV, fol. 187vb; Venice, BNM, lat. VIII.16 (3382), s. XV, fol. 104rb; Vienna, ÖNB, 2271, s. XIV, fol. 422va; Vienna, ÖNB, 3105, s. XV, fol. 36vb; Wroclaw, BU, R 44, s. XV, fol. 133rb.

[233] MS Vienna, ÖNB 2311, fol. 96v. For the glosses in question, see n. 218 above.

[234] In the *Almanach planetarum*, William only names the Tables of Toulouse (six times) and the Toledan Tables (once), and he does so only to criticise them (see references n. 228 above). The Tables of Mechelen do not feature there, but it would be interesting to ask whether William used them at all for drawing his own tables. The *Almanach* opens with the value of the precession, which William asserts to be 10°15' in 1292 ("Hanc enim distantiam pono temporibus istis 10 gradus et 15 minuta", canons § 2, ed. Pedersen 2014, p. 8). Oddly enough, the same value is attributed to Bate in a note added in MS London, BL, Royal 12.C.IX, s. XIV, fol. 29v: "Henricus de Machilinio ponit pro motu octave spere 10 gradus et 15 minuta".

[235] "Albubetri in nativitatibus" (Paris, BnF, lat. 7324, fol. 49ra). On Albubater, see n. 189 above. The other sources quoted by William are Ptolemy (*Quadripartitum*), Albumasar's *De magnis coniunctionibus*, Pseudo-Ptolemy's *Centiloquium*, "Hispalensis" (i.e. Pseudo-Johannes Hispalensis's *Epitome totius astrologie*), Aomar, Alcabitius and Albohali, all of which were known to Bate.

only met later. In any case, it is between 1280 and early 1285 that he received Bate's *Nativitas*. This event would not be without historical significance, for it prevented Bate's *Nativitas* from falling into almost complete oblivion.

5.4. Appendix: Bate's astrological sources

This appendix lists the astrological sources used in the *Nativitas*. Bestsellers (texts extant in over 25 manuscripts) are referenced in Juste 2016, where available editions and additional bibliography can be found. For nos. 2-14, see also Shlomo Sela's contribution in this volume (section 6) and Sela 2017a. For the other texts, the authoritative study is given, together with the manuscripts prior to 1300. Nos. 3-14 are referred to in the Hebrew original, because it is unclear whether Bate quotes them from an Old French version, from a draft of his own Latin translations, or even directly from the Hebrew text (with or without the help of a Hebrew scholar).[236] Bate translated at least six of these works into Latin after writing the *Nativitas*: no. 10 in 1281, and nos. 3-5 and 12-13 in 1292.

[1] Abraham Avenezra [Abraham Ibn Ezra], jugement on a nativity of 23 August 1135. This text, titled "Hec est nativitas quedam ad instruendum te in aliis nativitatibus et est de iudiciis Abraham", is found among Ibn Ezra's astrological works in MSS Erfurt, UFB, Amplon. O. 89, s. XIV, fols. 72v-76r, and Vienna, ÖNB, 5442, s. XV, fols. 220vb-223va (for these MSS, see also nos. 7 and 9).[237] No date is given, but the planetary positions in the accompanying horoscope correspond to 23 August 1135. Bate refers to this work once, as "secundum modum Avenezre in quodam exemplo nativitatis cuiusdam ab ipso iudicate" (*Nat.* 707-710).

[2] Abraham Avenezra [Abraham Ibn Ezra], *Liber de nativitatibus*. This text derives from Ibn Ezra's *Sefer ha-moladot* (see also nos. 8-9) and shares the same terminology as the other Latin texts which were associated with Ibn Ezra's name since the middle of the twelfth century, like the so-called *Liber de rationibus tabularum* (1154) and *De astrolabio*. See Smithuis 2006a and Sela (forthcoming). The *Nativitas* is the earliest attestation of this text. Bates refers to it 17 times and ascribes it (as "Liber nativitatum" when the title is given) to either "Abraham Iudeus" or "Abraham Compilator" (or both, see *Nat.* 673-675 and 713).

[3] Abraham Avenezra [Abraham Ibn Ezra], *Mishpeṭei ha-mazzalot* ("Book of the Judgements of the Zodiacal Signs"). Bate refers to this work once, as "secundum testimonium Abrahe Principis" (*Nat.* 694).

[4] Abraham Avenezra [Abraham Ibn Ezra], *Reshit ḥokhmah* ("The Beginning of Wisdom"). 17 references as "Initium sapientie" or "Liber initii sapientie" ascribed to "Avenezre".

---

[236] On Bate's knowledge of Hebrew, see Sela 2017a, pp. 170-171.

[237] Thorndike 1944, p. 298, and Smithuis 2006, pp. 254 and 298, briefly report this text as "Excerpta quaedam ex libro iudiciorum Abraham deprompta" (a title not found in the manuscripts), but they did not see that it was a judgement on a nativity.

[5] Abraham Avenezra [Abraham Ibn Ezra], *Sefer ha-me'orot* ("Book of Luminaries"). Five references as "Liber luminarium" ascribed to "Avenezre".

[6] Abraham Avenezra [Abraham Ibn Ezra], *Sefer ha-mivḥarim* II ("Book of Elections"). Two references as "Liber electionum" ascribed to "Avenezre".

[7] Abraham Avenezra [Abraham Ibn Ezra], *Sefer ha-mivḥarim* III ("Book of Elections"). This text corresponds to a lost version of *Sefer ha-mivḥarim*, of which a Latin translation survives in two manuscripts under the title "Liber electionum" and attributed to "Abraham Additor": Erfurt, UFB, Amplon. O. 89, fols. 39v-46v, and Vienna, ÖNB, 5442, fols. 192vb-198va. See Smithuis 2006, pp. 252-272 and 295, and Sela 2017a, pp. 179-180. Bate refers to this text three times, as "iuxta consilium Abrahe cognomine Principis" (*Nat.* 86-87), "alterius Abrahe cognomine Principis in suo De electionibus tractatu" (*Nat.* 105-107) and "in Libro electionum Abrahe Principis" (*Nat.* 603-604). However, Bate's quotations do not correspond *verbatim* to the Latin translation found in the Erfurt and Vienna manuscripts, so that he must have accessed this text in another form, probably in the Hebrew or Old French version (see also no. 9 below).

[8] Abraham Avenezra [Abraham Ibn Ezra], *Sefer ha-moladot* I ("Book of Nativities"). 52 references, as "Liber nativitatum" (or "Liber de nativitate" in *Nat.* 89 and "Liber de nativitatibus" in *Nat.* 682) ascribed to Avenezre, or simply as "Avenezre". See also nos. 2 and 9.

[9] Abraham Avenezra [Abraham Ibn Ezra], *Sefer ha-moladot* II ("Book of Nativities"). This text corresponds to a lost version of *Sefer ha-moladot* (see also nos. 2 and 8), which, like no. 7 above, is extant in MSS Erfurt, UFB, Amplon. O. 89 (fols. 53r-68v) and Vienna, ÖNB, 5442 (fols. 203va-217vb), where it is entitled "Liber nativitatum" and attributed to "Abraham Additor". See Smithuis 2006, pp. 252-272 and 295, and Sela 2017a, p. 179. Bate refers to this text 22 times, as the "Liber nativitatum" of "Abraham Princeps". Like in no. 7 again, Bate's references do not correspond *verbatim* to the translation found in the Erfurt and Vienna manuscripts, so that he must have accessed this text in another form, probably in the Hebrew or Old French version.

[10] Abraham Avenezra [Abraham Ibn Ezra], *Sefer ha-'olam* I ("Book of the World"). Three references as "Liber revolutionum annorum mundi" ascribed to Abraham (*Nat.* 234) or "Liber coniunctionum" ascribed to "Avenezre" (*Nat.* 381 and 2049).

[11] Abraham Avenezra [Abraham Ibn Ezra], *Sefer ha-she'elot* II ("Book of Interrogations"). Four references as "Liber interrogationum" (or "in suis Interrogationibus" in *Nat.* 1107) ascribed to "Avenezre".

[12] Abraham Avenezra [Abraham Ibn Ezra], *Sefer ha-ṭe'amim* I ("Book of the Reasons"). 10 references as "Liber rationum" ascribed to "Avenezre".

[13] Abraham Avenezra [Abraham Ibn Ezra], *Sefer ha-ṭe'amim* II ("Book of the Reasons"). 15 references as "Liber rationum" ascribed to "Avenezre". Bate does not

explicitly distinguish between *Sefer ha-ṭeʿamim* I and II, except on four occasions: "in secunda parte Libri rationum" (*Nat.* 160), "In Libro rationum, 2ª particula" (*Nat.* 593), "in Libro rationum, capitulo 6°, prima particula" (*Nat.* 620), "in 1° Rationum" (*Nat.* 767).

[14] Abraham bar Ḥiyya ha-Naśiʾ, *Megillat ha-megalleh* ("Scroll of the Revealer"). Composed between 1120 and 1129. Bates refers to this text once, as "Hispanus Abraham cognomine Princeps in suo tractatu Coniunctionum" (*Nat.* 2357). There exists a Latin translation of the fifth part (dealing with the great conjunctions and referred to by Bate) made at an unknown date by one Theodoricus de Northem or Northen via an Old French intermediary. See Federici Vescovini 1991. This Latin translation is extant in three fifteenth-century manuscripts, including Leipzig, UB, 1467, fols. 214ra-227ra, where the work is titled "Abraham de coniunctionibus magnis tractatus" and followed (fols. 228r-239v) by Abraham Avenezra's *Liber de nativitatibus* (no. 2 above); and Wolfenbüttel, HAB, 42.3 Aug. 2° (2505), fols. 199ra-215va, where it is attributed to Abraham Avenezra and followed by excerpts from Bate's translation of Abraham Avenezra's *De mundo vel seculo*. The third manuscript is Wolfenbüttel, HAB, 444 Helmst. (479), fols. 177ra-183vb. However, Bate's quotation does not correspond to Theodoricus's Latin translation, so that we must suppose that, here too (see nos. 7 and 9), he had access to this text in another form, probably in the Hebrew or Old French version.

[15] Albohali [Abū ʿAlī al-Khayyāṭ], *De nativitatibus*. Translated twice in the twelfth century, by Plato of Tivoli in 1136 and by one "Johannes Toletanus" in 1152/53. See Juste 2016, p. 191 no. 37. Bate used both translations and refers to the author as "Avicenna", except once as "Albuhaly, qui et Avicenna" (*Nat.* 1037). 51 references, including *Nat.* 1128-1134, where Bate compares both translations. Bate also quotes Albohali (under the name "Albenaiach") as one of the authors of the *Liber novem iudicum*.

[16] Albumasar [Abū Maʿshar], *De magnis coniunctionibus*. Translated by John of Seville in the first half of the twelfth century. See Juste 2016, p. 192 no. 40. Five references.

[17] Albumasar [Abū Maʿshar], *De revolutionibus nativitatum*. Translated from Arabic into Greek in the tenth century, then from Greek into Latin by Stephen of Messina in 1262. See Burnett 2014, pp. 162-164. This work is extant in at least 18 manuscripts, two of which date from the thirteenth century: Paris, BnF, lat. 7320, fols. 1r-24v (Peter of Limoges's *Liber magnus iudiciorum*) and Vatican, BAV, Pal. lat. 1406, fols. 45ra-91rb. 52 references.

[18] Albumasar [Abū Maʿshar], *Introductorium maius*. Translated twice in the twelfth century, by John of Seville in 1133 (?) and by Hermann of Carinthia in 1140. See Juste 2016, p. 189 no. 18. Bate used Hermann's translation only. 24 references.

[19] Albumasar [Abū Maʿshar], *Ysagoga minor*. Translated by Adelard of Bath probably before 1133. See Burnett, Yamamoto and Yano 1994. This text survives in

seven manuscripts, two of which predates 1300: Avranches, BM, 235, s. XII, fol. 78r (last page only) and London, BL, Sloane 2030, s. XII, fols. 83r-87r. Bate refers to this work once, as "Zafo [i.e., Jafar] in Ysagogis" (*Nat.* 1003).

[20] Alcabitius [al-Qabīṣī], *Introductorius*. Translated by John of Seville, probably before 1135. See Juste 2016, p. 185 no. 1. Three references.

[21] Aomar ['Umar ibn al-Farrukhān al-Ṭabarī], *De nativitatibus*. Translated by John of Seville in the first half of the twelfth century. See Juste 2016, p. 190 no. 29. Seven references. Bate also quotes Aomar as one of the authors of the *Liber novem iudicum*.

[22] *Capitula Almansoris*. Translated by Plato of Tivoli in 1136. See Juste 2016, p. 190 no. 29. 14 references.

[23] Firmicus Maternus, *Mathesis*. Composed in 337 A.D. See Juste 2016, p. 191 no. 32. 21 references.

[24] Gergis, *De significatione septem planetarum in domibus*. Translated, most probably from Arabic, in the first half of the twelfth century. See Juste 2016, p. 187 no. 13. An alternative translation of this work occurs in the introduction of the *Liber novem iudicum*. Bate refers to both versions, as "Iergis... in libello De significationibus planetarum in domibus" (one reference, *Nat.* 1612-1613) and "Iergis in 9 Iudicum" (two references, *Nat.* 1610 and 1729) respectively.

[25] Guillelmus Anglicus, *De urina non visa*. Composed in 1220. See Juste 2016, p. 187 no. 12. Bate refers to this work twice, as an anonymous "liber De iudicio urine (non vise)" (*Nat.* 333 and 1217).

[26] Haly Embrani ['Alī b. Aḥmad al-'Imrānī], *De electionibus horarum*. Translated by Abraham bar Ḥiyya in 1133. See Juste 2016, p. 191 no. 31. Bate refers to this work four times, as "Haly in Electionibus" (*Nat.* 233 and 1855), "Haly in suo Libro electionum" (*Nat.* 887-888) or simply "Haly" (*Nat.* 2103).

[27] Hermann of Carinthia, *De occultis*. Compiled from Arabic sources c. 1140. See Burnett 1978, pp. 118-121. This works survives in a dozen of manuscripts, two of which date from the thirteenth century: St Petersburg, Rossijskaja Nacionalnaja Biblioteka, F. 8 (XXA^b/III^1), fols. 155ra-169v, and Vatican, BAV, Vat. lat. 4079, fols. 11ra-22va. Bate refers to this work four times, as Hermannus's "Liber cogitationum et rerum absconditarum" (*Nat.* 211), "Liber de rebus absconditis" (*Nat.* 2063), "Liber rerum absconditarum" (*Nat.* 2485) or without title (*Nat.* 3018).

[28] Hermes, *Centiloquium*. Compiled from Arabic sources by Stephen of Messina c. 1262. See Burnett 2014, pp. 155-157, and Juste 2016, p. 191 no. 32. Seven references, as "Hermes in Floribus" or simply "Hermes".

[29] Johannes Hispalensis (Pseudo-), *Epitome totius astrologie*. Composed in 1142, perhaps by or in collaboration with Abraham Ibn Ezra, this work consists of an introduction ("Ysagoge") and four books ("Quadripartitum") devoted to revolutions, nativities, interrogations and elections respectively. See Juste 2016, p. 189 no. 21. 37 references, as "Hispalensis" or "Iohannes Hispalensis", with only occasion-

al mention of a title ('in suis tractatibus nativitatum', *Nat.* 578; "in suis Ysagogis", *Nat.* 660-661, 964-965 and 1186). Bate appears to be one of the first users of this work, which was also known to Peter of limoges and to the author of the *Speculum astronomie*, composed around the middle of the thirteenth century (see Zambelli 1992, pp. 226, 230, 230-231, 234 and 236). A different version of the *Epitome* is extant in MS Vatican, BAV, Reg. lat. 1452, s. XIV, fols 58ra-76va, and, partially (second part on nativities only), in Madrid, BN, 10009, s. XIII, fols. 39ra-46vb and Berlin, SBPK, Hdschr. 95, s. XV, fols. 58r-74v and 40r-46v. Bate used both versions (cf. "alia littera eiusdem Iohannis", *Nat.* 732).

[30] *Liber Aldaraia sive Soyga.* This work, of unknown origin, is extant in two sixteenth-century manuscripts. See Reeds 2006. Bate refers to it twice, as "Liber Soyga" (*Nat.* 1187-1192).

[31] *Liber novem iudicum.* Compiled towards the middle of the twelfth century, at least partly by Hugo Sanctelliensis, on the basis of nine authorities (i.e. the "nine judges") carefully named in the text whenever relevant: Albohali (called "Albenai-ach" by Bate), Albumasar, Alkindi, Aristotle, Aomar, Dorotheus, Gergis, Messahal-lah and Zael. See Juste 2016, p. 189 no. 23. 50 references, generally as "9 iudicum".

[32] Messahallah [Māshā'allāh], *De revolutionibus annorum mundi.* Translated at an unknown date, but no later than the first half of the thirteenth century. See Juste 2016, p. 192 no. 39. Bate refers to this work once (*Nat.* 907).

[33] Messahallah [Māshā'allāh], *Epistola de rebus eclipsium.* Translated by John of Seville in the first half of the twelfth century. See Juste 2016, p. 186 no. 7. One reference as "Liber coniunctionum" (*Nat.* 955-960).

[34] Messahallah [Māshā'allāh], *Liber receptionis.* Translated by John of Seville in the first half of the twelfth century. See Juste 2016, p. 189 no. 20. Bate refers to this work three times, as "Messehallah in Libro interrogationum" (*Nat.* 610) or, simply, as "Messehalah" (*Nat.* 1555 and 1574).

[35] Ptolemy, *Quadripartitum.* At least six Latin translations of this work were available by 1280. See Juste 2016, pp. 186-187 no. 9. 26 references, mainly to William of Moerbeke's translation, but also from Plato of Tivoli's translation made in 1138. Bate compares the two translations in *Nat.* 2713-2725.

[36] Ptolemy (Pseudo-), *Centiloquium.* Translated at least five times from the Arabic in the twelfth century, by Adelard of Bath (c. 1120), Plato of Tivoli (1138), Hugo Sanctelliensis (before 1151) and two anonymous translations denoted "Mundanorum" and "Iam premisi" from their incipits. See Juste 2016, p. 185 no. 2. The "Mundanorum" translation includes two distinct versions for each *verbum*, referred to as "Mundanorum 1" and "Mundanorum 2". Bate refers to this work 13 times (as "Centilogium/Centiloquium", "Liber arboris", "Liber fructus" or "Liber 100 verborum"), including in *Nat.* 1065-1078, where he compares five translations, i.e., respectively, Plato of Tivoli's, "Mundanorum 1", Adelard of Bath's, "Mundanorum 2" and a translation from the Greek, which has not been found. This translation from

the Greek is also referred to in *Nat.* 3079 and turns out to be the main source of Bate's quotations, for these do not correspond to any of the known medieval versions. This is confirmed by his quotation from v. 95, where we find the Greek word "decanus" (*Nat.* 1235) for "decan", instead of "facies", typically given in translations from Arabic. The translator from the Greek is, in all likelihood, William of Moerbeke (see no. 35 above), whose style can be discerned in Bate's quotations (information Carlos Steel). All translations from Arabic, with the exception of Adelard's, include the commentary by Abū Ja'far Aḥmad ibn Yūsuf, who became known in the Latin tradition as "Haly". Bate also refers to this commentary, but he seems to have made up two distinct authors for it, cf. "et sui expositores" (*Nat.* 811) and "eius expositores Haly et Abuiafar Hamet filius Ioseph filii Abrahe" (*Nat.* 1029-1030).

[37] Ptolemy (Pseudo-), *De iudiciis partium*. This text was excerpted from Messahallah's *De nativitatibus* in the translation of Hugo Sanctelliensis (before 1151) and circulated independently under Ptolemy's name. It is extant in nine manuscripts, the earliest of which date from the second half of the thirteenth century: Munich, BSB, Clm 3857, fols. 43vb-46vb (which also contains excerpts from Bate's *Nativitas*) and Madrid, BN, 10063, fols. 22va-23va (copied by Alvaro de Oviedo in Toledo). In both manuscripts, as well as in others, it is appended to Ptolemy's *Quadripartitum*, without mention of an author in the Munich MS and under the title "Liber partium Ptholomei in iudiciis partium 12 domorum" in the Madrid MS. Bate refers to this work three times, as an anonymous "Liber de partium locorumque iudiciis" (*Nat.* 1488) or "Liber partium" (*Nat.* 2262 and 2559-2560).

[38] Sadan [Abū Saʿīd Shādhān ibn Baḥr], *Excerpta de secretis Albumasar*. This text was translated into Greek in the tenth century and from Greek into Latin by Stephen of Messina c. 1262. See Burnett 2014, pp. 158-162. 13 manuscripts are known, none prior to 1300. 26 references.

[39] Zael [Sahl b. Bishr], *Fatidica*. Translated by Hermann of Carinthia in 1138. See Burnett 1978, pp. 115-118. This text is known in seven manuscripts, all dating from the fourteenth and fifteenth centuries. Two references.

[40] Zael [Sahl b. Bishr], *Liber iudiciorum*. A corpus of five texts (*Introductorium, Quinquaginta precepta, De interrogationibus, De electionibus* and *Liber temporum*), translated before 1141, most probably by John of Seville. See Juste 2016, p. 186 no. 6. Ten references, to *Introductorium* (2), *Quinquaginta precepta* (4) and *De interrogationibus* (4), in all cases without mention of a book title, except twice, as "Zael in suis Interrogationibus" (*Nat.* 1252) and "Zael et alii in libris interrogationum" (*Nat.* 1835-1836). Zael is also quoted as one of the authors of the *Liber novem iudicum*.

CHAPTER 6
BATE AND ABRAHAM IBN EZRA[238]
(Shlomo Sela)

6.1. Introduction

Abraham Ibn Ezra (c. 1089-c. 1161) was born in Muslim Spain, but he made the bulk of his literary career in Latin Europe, after he left his homeland and arrived in Rome in 1140, when he was 50 years old. From then on he led the life of the vagabond scholar, roaming through Italy, France, and England, where he wrote profusely in Hebrew, on an extremely wide variety of subjects. Abraham Ibn Ezra's reputation rests on his outstanding biblical commentaries, but his intellectual interests extended to the sciences, especially astrology. Ibn Ezra's most significant contribution in this field is the creation of the first comprehensive corpus of Hebrew astrological textbooks that address the main systems of Arabic astrology. Today we know of nineteen treatises by him.[239]

This relatively large number reflects the multiple versions, or recensions, of each individual work that he produced. This phenomenon is typical of his literary career. The multiple versions of most of his biblical commentaries, scientific treatises, and astrological writings are an artifact of his nomadic existence and reflect the fact that he supported himself by his pen. He would write a new version of an old work for a new patron when he arrived in a new town and continued to stimulate the attention and curiosity of readers all along his itinerary through Latin Europe. Although some of Ibn Ezra's works became known to Christian scholars shortly after his death and were then translated or elaborated for Latin readers,[240] his astrological writings remained outside the mainstream of Latin astrological literature until the last decades of the thirteenth century.[241] But then, Ibn Ezra was "reborn" and brought to the knowledge of the Latin West thanks to the translational and literary work of Henry Bate.

---

[238] This section is an abridged version of Sela 2017a.

[239] For a list of these astrological treatises, sorted according to the main genres of Greek and Arabic astrological literature to which they belong, and accompanied by references to editions in which these treatises are available today, see Sela 2017, pp. 2-5.

[240] Lévy and Burnett 2006; Smithuis 2006; Millás Vallicrosa 1947; Millás Vallicrosa 1940. See also Burnett (forthcoming).

[241] This emerges from the fact that neither Ibn Ezra's name nor references to any of his works are found in the exhaustive catalogue of astrological writings in the *Speculum astronomiae* (Mirror of astronomy), composed around the middle of the thirteenth century, and so too in the *Liber introductorius ad iudicia stellarum*, the most important astrological work of the thirteenth century, composed by Guido Bonatti around 1270.

Three main stages may be discerned in the development of the Henry Bate-Abraham Ibn Ezra connection, as follows. In 1273, Henry Bate commissioned a Jewish scholar named Hagins le Juif to translate a collection of Ibn Ezra's astrological works from Hebrew into Old French. Preserved in two manuscripts, they include the following four items: (1) *Li livres du commencement de sapience*, (2) *Livre des jugemens des nativités*, (3) *Le livre des elections Abraham*, and (4) *Le livre des interrogations*.[242] These are translations of respectively (1) *Reshit Ḥokhmah* (Beginning of wisdom); (2) *Sefer ha-Moladot* (Book of nativities; henceforth *Moladot*); (3) the second version of *Sefer ha-Mivḥarim* (Book of elections; henceforth *Mivḥarim* II); and (4) the second version of *Sefer ha-She'elot* (Book of interrogations; henceforth *She'elot* II).

Later on, Henry Bate carried out the translation into Latin of a collection of Ibn Ezra's astrological writings. First, in 1281, *De mundo vel seculo*, a Latin rendering of the first version of *Sefer ha-'Olam* (Book of the World, henceforth *'Olam* I). Then, in 1292, Bate produced five more Latin translations of astrological treatises by Ibn Ezra in Orvieto, as follows: (1) *Introductorius ad astronomiam*, a translation of *Reshit Ḥokhmah*. (2) *De luminaribus seu de diebus creticis*, a translation of *Sefer ha-Me'orot* (Book of the luminaries; henceforth *Me'orot*). (3) *Liber introductionis ad iudicia astrologie* is *Mishpeṭei ha-Mazzalot* (Judgments of the zodiacal signs). (4) *Liber causarum seu racionum super hiis que dicuntur in Introductorio Abrahe qui incipit Sapiencie timor domini* (Book of causes or reasons on what has been said in the Introduction by Abraham, which begins "the beginning of wisdom is the fear of the Lord") is the Latin of the first version of *Sefer ha-Ṭe'amim* (Book of reasons; henceforth *Ṭe'amim* I). (5) *Liber causarum seu racionum* (Book of causes or reasons), the Latin translation of the second version of *Sefer ha-Ṭe'amim* (Book of reasons; henceforth *Ṭe'amim* II).

But in 1280-81, in between the Old French and the Latin translations, Henry Bate composed an astrological autobiography commonly known as *Nativitas*, in which he evinced an extraordinary acquaintance with Ibn Ezra's astrological work. To anchor the astrological interpretation of his own life, Bate incorporated at least 140 paraphrases, translations, and quotations from twelve astrological treatises written by or attributed to Abraham Ibn Ezra. These references are the first known in the Latin West.

6.2. The Triple Abraham

A perplexing feature of the Henry Bate-Ibn Ezra astrological connection is that when Bate refers to astrological treatises that we now know were written by, or are attributed to, Abraham Ibn Ezra, he assigns them to one of three different authors. All three are "Abraham," but they are distinguished by their cognomens.

---

[242] MSS Paris, BnF, fr. 24276, fols. 1ra-66rb; and Paris, BnF, fr. 1351, fols.1ra-66rb.

One is *Abraham Avenezra*, the latinized form of Abraham Ibn Ezra; the second is *Abraham Princeps*, the Latin translation of the Hebrew name by which Abraham Bar Ḥiyya (c. 1065-c. 1136) was known within Jewish society: *Abraham ha-Naśi'*, i.e., Abraham the Prince; the third is *Abraham Compilator*, an otherwise unknown Latin name. When Henry Bate mentions any of the three Abrahams on his own, the name Abraham is usually accompanied by the name of an astrological treatise of which the relevant Abraham is taken to be the author. In many cases, these references are accompanied by passages that turn out to be translations, quotations, or paraphrases of excerpts from astrological treatises by Ibn Ezra. This allows us to establish which part of Ibn Ezra's corpus was associated with each Abraham. All in all, *Nativitas* incorporates at least 140 separate passages from twelve treatises by Abraham Ibn Ezra or attributed to him. We now examine the references to each of the Abrahams separately.

6.3. Abraham Avenezra

Abraham Avenezra, the latinized form of Abraham Ibn Ezra, accounts for 107 of the 140 separate references in *Nativitas*; this makes him the most important of the three Abrahams as well as the name Henry Bate applied to the historical Abraham Ibn Ezra. A look at these references, the names of the treatises associated with "Abraham Avenezra," and particularly the identification of the astrological treatise behind the passages associated with these references proves that Henry Bate excerpted these passages from eight of Ibn Ezra's astrological treatises.

(1) *Liber nativitatum = Moladot*, with 52 references in Henry Bate's *Nativitas*.[243] (2-3) *Liber rationum = Ṭeʿamim* I and *Ṭeʿamim* II, with 25 references in the *Nativitas*, 10 to *Ṭeʿamim* I[244] and 15 to *Ṭeʿamim* II.[245] (4) *Liber initii sapientiae = Reshit Ḥokhmah*, with 17 references in Henry Bate's *Nativitas*.[246] (5) *Liber luminarium = Meʾorot*, with five references in the *Nativitas*.[247] (6) *Liber revolutionum annorum mundi* or *Liber coniunctionum* or *Tractatus Avenesre de planetarum Coniunctionibus et annorum revolutionibus mundanorum = ʿOlam* I, with three references in the *Nativitas*.[248] (7) *Liber interrogationum = Sheʾelot* II, with four references in the *Nativitas*.[249] (8) *Liber electionum = Mivḥarim* II, with two references in the *Nativitas*.[250]

---

[243] For examples, see *Nat.* 88-91; 91-94; 103-104; 258-260; 328-331; 546-549; 564-567; 574-577; 602-603; 651-655; 681-684; 742-745; 775-778, et passim.

[244] See *Nat.* 621-624; 768-769; 944-946; 1112-1116; 1637-1640; 1722-1723; 2160-2162; 2329-2333; 2385-2387; *App. I* 84-85.

[245] See *Nat.* 159-165; 593-595; 704-706; 853-854; 966; 990-991; 1084-1087; 1089-1091; 1109-1110; 1280-1283; 1683-1686; 1961-1963; 2285-2286; 2380-2387; 2407-2409.

[246] See *Nat.* 249-250; 615-619; 699-701; 707-710; 821-825; 825-827; 827-829; 829-831; 869-876; 984-987; 1023-1026; 1349-1351; 2188-2190; 3001-3111.

[247] See *Nat.* 2987-2981; 3019-3022; 3119-3121; 3131-3132; 3137-3140.

[248] See *Nat.* 233-235; 380-382; 2049-2051.

[249] See *Nat.* 604-605; 903-905; 1104-1107; 1910-1914.

[250] See *Nat.* 562-563, 605-607.

6.4. Abraham Princeps

Abraham Bar Ḥiyya (c. 1065-c. 1136), who vanished from the scene just before Abraham Ibn Ezra began his literary career, was known to medieval Jewish society as *Abraham ha-Naśiʾ*, Abraham the Prince. In his Hebrew oeuvre, Ibn Ezra mentions Abraham Bar Ḥiyya a number of times, always adding the appellative *ha-Naśiʾ* to his name.[251] Given that Henry Bate translated these passages into Latin, his renderings of these loci are germane for determining how the Abraham Princeps-Abraham Avenezre connection was shaped in Henry Bate's mind. In one reference, for example, Henry Bate translates "the aforementioned Prince," used by Ibn Ezra to refer to Abraham Bar Ḥiyya, as "Princeps predictus".[252] It is therefore understandable that Henry Bate might have thought that Abraham Princeps was the historical figure known to us as Abraham Bar Ḥiyya.

Henry Bate assigns four treatises to Abraham Princeps in the *Nativitas*. The first is the fifth chapter of *Megillat ha-megalleh* (Scroll of the revealer), a genuine work by Abraham Bar Ḥiyya which incorporates a Jewish and universal astrological history and an astrological prognostication of the coming of the Messiah, based on the interpretation of horoscopes cast at the vernal equinox of years in which conjunctions of Saturn and Jupiter took place.[253] This work is designated in the *Nativitas* as *Tractatus coniunctionum*, the Book of the Conjunctions,[254] a name that reflects the historical analysis in this work based on examination of the Saturn-Jupiter conjunctions.

Abraham Ibn Ezra is the author of the other three treatises Bate attributed to Abraham Princeps. One is *Mishpeṭei ha-Mazzalot*, translated into Latin by Henry Bate in 1292. In a title at the beginning of the translation we read: "Ysagoge magistri Abrahe Ducis seu Principis notati hebrayce Nati Hezkia"[255] = "Introduction by Master Abraham, the Commander or the Prince, known in Hebrew as Bar Ḥiyya". This is the only instance in Henry Bate's entire work where Abraham Bar Ḥiyya appears as the author of one of the astrological treatises he translated or referred to. There is also one reference to a passage of *Mishpeṭei ha-Mazzalot* in the Nativitas.[256] The other two treatises by Ibn Ezra that Bate assigned to Abraham Princeps are works whose Hebrew original is lost but that are extant in Latin translations. Henry Bate refers to them only in his *Nativitas*.

---

[251] See Goodman 2011, Hebrew part, p. 36, English part, pp. 66-67; long commentary on Daniel 11:31; Sela 2007 (*Ṭeʿamim* I, 10.3:6, 98-99, 10.4:3, 98-99).

[252] See MS Leipzig, UB, 1466, fol. 72ra:19-20; See *Ṭeʿamim* I, § 10.4:3, 98-99.

[253] Abraham Bar Ḥiyya 1924, pp. 111-155.

[254] *Nat.* 2357-2358.

[255] See MS Leipzig, UB, 1466, fol. 27rb: 1-2.

[256] See *Nat.* 694-697; see Sela 2017, § 29:1, 512-513.

There are 21 references to *Liber nativitatum* (Book of the nativities), one of the treatises Bate assigned to Abraham Princeps, in the *Nativitas*.[257] A scrutiny of the translations or paraphrases accompanying these references demonstrates that this *Nativitatum* is identical with Ibn Ezra's second version of *Sefer ha-Moladot*.[258] Bate's *Nativitas* also assigns twice a work on the doctrine of elections to Abraham Princeps, under two slightly different names: *Tractatus de electionibus* and *Liber electionum*.[259] This work corresponds to the third version of Ibn Ezra's *Sefer ha-Mi* *vḥarim*.[260]

6.5. Abraham Compilator

The most intriguing of the three Abrahams is Abraham Compilator, mentioned sixteen times in the *Nativitas*.[261] In one of these Abraham Compilator is referred to as "Iudeus,"[262] and in two other loci the name "Abraham Iudeus" appears alone.[263] The latter designation is also found once in Bate's philosophical encyclopedia, *Speculum divinorum*.[264] A close look at this passage that the *Speculum divinorum* assigns to Abraham Iudeus reveals that it is a verbatim quotation from a Latin astronomical work known today as *Liber de rationibus tabularum* (Book of the reasons of astronomical tables), which Henry Bate calls *Liber de opere tabularum* (Book on the use of [astronomical] tables). This work, which is extant in eight manuscripts, two of them from the end of the twelfth century, is a Latin version of the canons of Ibn Ezra's astronomical tables, whose Hebrew original is now lost.[265]

That Bate held Abraham Compilator and Abraham Iudeus to be the same person is proven by the fact that he assigns one work, *Liber nativitatum* (Book of Nativities), to both of them.[266] All 18 passages from *Liber Nativitatum* that Henry Bate's *Nativitas* assigns to Abraham Compilator or Abraham Iudeus[267] were excerpted from *Liber Abraham Iudei de nativitatibus* (henceforth *De nativitatibus*), a Latin

---

[257]   See *Nat.* 602-603; 655-676; 682-684; 735-736; 812-814; 1054-1057; 1196-1200; 1584-1586; 1595-1596; 1684-1686; 1737-1740; 1759-1760; 1774-1776; 1787-1788; 2249-2251; 2236-2237; 2237-2239; 2650-2652; 2662-2664; 2765-2767.

[258]   The Hebrew original of *Moladot* II is lost but survives today in a Latin translation, available in two manuscript copies and entitled *Liber nativitatum*. See MSS Erfurt, UFB, Amplon. O. 89, fols. 53r-68v; Vienna, ÖNB, 5442, fols. 203va-217vb.

[259]   See *Nat.* 106-117; 603-604.

[260]   This Latin translation, entitled *Liber Eleccionum*, is extant in two manuscript copies: Erfurt, UFB, Amplon, O. 89, fols. 39v-46v; Vienna, ÖNB, 5442, fols. 192vb-198va.

[261]   See *Nat.* 332; 659; 674; 713; 1146; 1273; 1533; 1543; 1682; 2175; 2287; 2449; 2494; 2645; 2688; 3340.

[262]   *Nat.* 712-713

[263]   *Nat.* 178; 712-713.

[264]   Steel and Guldentops 1996, p. 337.

[265]   See Millás Vallicrosa 1947, esp. pp. 11-70; Sela 2003, pp. 22-27.

[266]   See *Nat.* 332-333; 177-178, *et passim*.

[267]   See *Nat.* 177-178; 332-333; 578-80; 655-659; 674-677; 712-715; 1146-1148; 1270-1273; 1538-1540; 1542-1545; 1681-1683; 2174-2175; 2287; 2439-2441; 2491-2494; 2645-2649; 2688-2691; 3340-342.

astrological treatise on nativities traditionally assigned to Ibn Ezra.[268] Here it is noteworthy that 10 of these 18 passages are verbatim quotations from *De nativitatibus*.[269] These ten verbatim quotations are the earliest evidence of the existence of *De nativitatibus*.

De nativitatibus was transmitted in four different versions, of which only one reflects the text known to Henry Bate, which exists in ten manuscripts and print witnesses. This version, which is the one known to modern scholarship through the edition printed by Erhard Ratdolt in Venice in 1485,[270] was probably written by Henry Bate.[271] Whereas all the incipits and explicits of the manuscript and print editions of *De nativitatibus* make Abraham Iudeus its author, at least one manuscript gives the author as both Abraham Iudeus and Abraham Compilator.[272] This explains why Henry Bate called the third Abraham both Abraham Iudeus and Abraham Compilator and why he assigned *De nativitatibus* to both.

Finally, let us ask: why did Henry Bate split Abraham Ibn Ezra into three Abrahams and divide Ibn Ezra's astrological oeuvre among them? I would suggest that Bate invented the three Abrahams principally to accommodate the fact that in his *Nativitas* he was working with three different treatises called *Liber nativitatum*, each written by a Jew whose name was Abraham. Henry Bate did not know that a main feature of Ibn Ezra's modus operandi was the production of two or more versions or recensions of each treatise (see above). Because Henry Bate was drawing on three Hebrew treatises in the same branch of astrological literature, nativities, and because he found it odd that they were all written by the same person, the best solution he could find was to attribute each of the three to a different Abraham.

---

[268] Abraham Ibn Ezra 1485, sig. a2r-c4v.

[269] *Nat.* 178-183; see Ibn Ezra 1485, sig. a2v: 21-25; *Nat.* 578-80, see Ibn Ezra 1485, sig. a7v: 14-15; *Nat.* 1146-1148, see Ibn Ezra 1485, sig. a6r: 8-11; *Nat.* 712-715, see Ibn Ezra 1485, sig. a8r:12-14; *Nat.* 1542-1545, see Ibn Ezra 1485, sig. b4r: 17-20; *Nat.* 1538-1540, see Ibn Ezra 1485, sig. b6v: 33-35; *Nat.* 1681-1683, see Ibn Ezra 1485, sig. b2v: 13-14; *Nat.* 2174-2175, see Ibn Ezra 1485, sig. c1v:22; *Nat.* 2439-2441, see Ibn Ezra 1485, sig. c3r: 6-8; *Nat.* 2688-2691, see Ibn Ezra 1485, sig. b8v: 14-17.

[270] Abraham Ibn Ezra 1485, sig. a2r-c4r.

[271] See Sela (forthcoming).

[272] See MS Oxford, BL, Bodley 472, fol. 144ra: "Abraham Iudeus de nativitatibus, qui Compilator dicitur".

CHAPTER 7
BASIC ELEMENTS OF BATE'S ASTROLOGICAL TECHNIQUE
(Steven Vanden Broecke)

7.1. The four astrological charts of the *Nativitas*

Bate's analysis in the *Nativitas* rests on four charts:

(1) Bate's natal chart (24 March 1246, 0h06 a.m.)
(2) Chart for the conjunction of Sun and Moon immediately preceding Bate's birth (19 March 1246, 3h47 a.m.)
(3) Chart for Bate's 35th revolution (23 March 1280, 5h01 a.m.)
(4) Chart for Bate's 36th revolution (23 March 1281, 10h48m30s a.m.)

Bate's central reference point is obviously his natal chart, which maps the state of the visible heavens in relation to the local horizon at the precise moment of Bate's birth. The astrological chart for the syzygy (i.e., opposition or conjunction) of Sun and Moon immediately preceding Bate's birth supplements this. Although it plays a minor role in Bate's self-analysis, it does allow him to check alternative methods for rectifying his nativity (see below).[273] Bate also draws upon the syzygy chart in assessing the qualities of his soul,[274] in his analysis of the tenth house,[275] and in his predictions of his manner of death.[276] Finally, we have the solar revolutions of Bate's nativity for his 35th and 36th year, which allow him to fine tune his analysis for these specific years of his life.

Much of what these figures can teach us about Bate's biography, self-fashioning, and attitude towards astrological meaning making, have been discussed above (see above, sections 2.3 and 4.2). In this section, we focus on some of the technical aspects of these horoscopes, particularly on the actual interpretive procedures by which Bate gradually unfolds the secrets of his astrological persona.

The approximate latitude for which Bate's four astrological horoscopes were cast can be determined through their house cusps.[277] In order to determine the boundaries or 'cusps' between different houses (for further discussion, see below, section 7.4), astrologers developed many different methods. Throughout the *Nativitas*, Bate uses what John North has called the 'standard method' of house division (also known as the 'Alcabitius method').[278]

---

[273] *Nat.* 155 and *passim*.
[274] *Nat.* 1175-1184.
[275] *Nat.* 2513.
[276] *Nat.* 2632-2634.
[277] We follow the method discussed in North 1986, pp. 17-20. For the obliquity of the ecliptic (ε), we use the standard medieval value of 23;33,30° as found, *inter alia*, in the Toledan tables.
[278] North 1986, p. 4 and *passim*.

Bate's birth chart was cast for a latitude of 51;2,15°; the chart for the preceding syzygy for a latitude of 50;24,13°; the chart for the revolution of the 35th year for a latitude of 58;16,46°; the chart for the revolution of the 36th year for a latitude of 50;54,18°. These results are considerably underdetermined by the accuracy of the stated values for the house cusps. Unfortunately, we do not know which house tables Bate used (he probably made his own for the latitude of Mechelen), since these are not present in the extant versions of the Tables of Mechelen. Nevertheless, the divergent result for the third horoscope disappears by slightly altering Bate's stated value for the longitude of the cusp of the fourth house. The results are thus sufficiently close to the Mechelen latitude of 51° to conclude that the *Nativitas*'s horoscopes were cast for the horizon of that city.

In calculating planetary and zodiac positions at each particular time (and for this particular place), Bate used his own Tables of Mechelen (see above, section 3.1.3). Each of the resulting four astrological charts are given below (see also pp. 119-121).

Paris, BnF, lat. 10270, fol. 143r

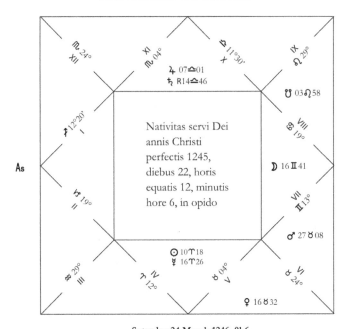

Saturday 24 March 1246, 0h6

Paris, BnF, lat. 10270, fol. 143v

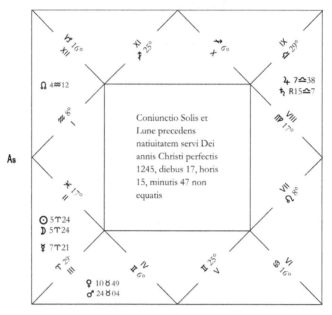

Monday 19 March 1246, 3h47

Paris, BnF, lat. 10270, fol. 170v

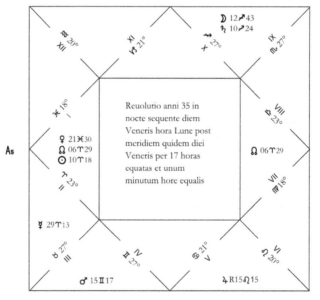

Saturday 23 March 1280, 5h01

Paris, BnF, lat. 10270, fol. 175r

Sunday 23 March 1281, 10h48m30s

7.2. Rectifying the nativity

Until at least the sixteenth century, precise knowledge of one's age was hardly common, or even considered important.[279] Accordingly, Bate considered himself lucky to have gleaned sufficient data from his mother before her death. According to her, Henry was born shortly after midnight during the night following the Friday before Palm Sunday 1245 [Easter reckoning].[280] Bate tells us that both the day and the time were confirmed by female family members who assisted during his mother's labor as well as by his own wet-nurses.[281] Bate obtained indirect confirmation of the year from the birth date of his older sister.[282] Nevertheless, Bate required more precision to accurately determine his ascendant degree: the degree of the ecliptic that was rising above the eastern horizon at his time and place of birth.[283]

Several astrological methods were available for this. On the authority of Abraham Ibn Ezra's *Sefer ha-Moladot*, Bate rejected the one proposed in Ptolemy's *Tetrabiblos* III.2.[284] Instead, he followed the so-called *trutina Hermetis* or 'Enoch's

---

[279]   Ariès 1962, pp. 15-8.
[280]   *Nat.* 36-41.
[281]   *Nat.* 44-45.
[282]   *Nat.* 53-70.
[283]   *Nat.* 81-83.
[284]   *Nat.* 83-84.

balance', as advocated and refined by Ibn Ezra.[285] This method rests on the assumption that "the position of the Moon at the time of birth is the ascendant degree at the time of conception, and vice versa".[286] Having established the position of the Moon at Gemini 17° and on the Western horizon (i.e., near the descendant degree of the ecliptic) around his approximate time of birth, Bate relies on Ibn Ezra to infer that his conception happened 259 days before his birth.[287]

This result allows Bate to cast a precise horoscope for his time of conception with Gemini 17° as the ascendant degree (following the aforementioned principle of the *trutina Hermetis*), and to determine the position of the Moon at that time, which turns out to be in Sagittarius 12°20'.[288] Bate verifies his chosen estimate for the time of pregnancy against other options offered by Ibn Ezra, but finds that the latter contradict certain basic tenets of Ibn Ezra's theory.[289] Accordingly, he settles for Sagittarius 12°20' as his true ascendant degree at birth, finding further support for this result through a close match with the —initially rejected— Ptolemaic method.[290] This in turn allows him to determine that his birth occurred on Saturday 24 March 1246 [new style], at 6 minutes past midnight.[291]

7.3. Hyleg, alcochoden, and empirical verification of the rectified nativity

Having found his true nativity, Bate's first task was to determine the *hyleg* "administering the life of the native".[292] *Hyleg* is a Latin transliteration of the Persian *haylāj*, which in turn translates the Greek ἀφέτης or "prorogator". Direction (also known as 'prorogation' or 'primary direction') or ἄφεσις is an astrological technique for determining the native's lifespan and accidents in life, whose classic (but by no means definitive) exposition is found in Ptolemy's *Tetrabiblos* III.10.[293] According to Ptolemy, individual human lifespans were represented by a specific arc of the ecliptic, situated between the place of one's personal 'prorogator' and the place of one's 'destroyer' (ἀναιρέτης). At birth, a person's life was launched at the place of the prorogator, beginning a lifelong journey (at 1° per year) to the destructive point. Specific accidents in life were symbolized by intermediate significations encountered during that journey, and herein lies one immediate benefit of knowledge of the *hyleg*: it allows Bate to pursue empirical *a posteriori* verification of his rectified

---

[285] *Nat.* 85-91. For a complete exposition of this method, see Sela 2014, pp. 42-5.

[286] See Sela 2014, p. 43.

[287] *Nat.* 124-126. See Sela 2014, p. 43.

[288] *Nat.* 127-128.

[289] *Nat.* 129-150.

[290] *Nat.* 152-158.

[291] Bate goes on to consider and reject a number of alternative methods of rectification, attributed to Messahallah, Abraham Iudeus (see chapter 6 above), Albumasar, and Hermann of Carinthia: see *Nat.* 159-217.

[292] *Nat.* 540-541; *Nat.* 650.

[293] For an excellent overview of the different uses of the doctrine of prorogation, see Sela 2014, pp. 46-57.

nativity, precisely by checking whether known accidents in life match the calculated progression of his *hyleg* along the ecliptic.[294] Bate identifies the Moon as his *hyleg*, and this for three reasons: his nativity is nocturnal, the Moon is in the seventh house, and it is in aspect to Mercury, the ruler of that house (*Nat.* 536-541).[295]

The *alcochoden* (a Latin transliteration of the Persian *kadhkhudāh*), on the other hand, is not a place but a planet.[296] It denotes the ruler of the *hyleg*, and is usually identified as the ultimate "giver of life".[297] Without specifying his methodology, Bate identifies Mercury as his *alcochoden*.[298] The underlying logic is nevertheless clear: in Bate's nativity, Mercury rules the Moon. The Moon being at Gemini 17°, he finds that Mercury is both the ruler of this sign and the planet that has the most essential dignities in the degree of the Moon. Another condition stipulated by astrological authorities is that the prospective *alcochoden* be in aspect to the *hyleg*.[299] Bate notes that both Mercury's status as *alcochoden* and the Moon's status as *hyleg* are threatened by Mercury being combust (i.e., covered over by the Sun's rays), but eliminates this possibility by drawing an extensive analogy between Mercury and the effects of the Sun's position in Aries.[300] This allows him to retain Mercury as the "giver of years" (*dator annorum*) and to project a life expectancy of 80 years for himself.[301]

7.4. A template for analysis: the twelve houses

Bate's analysis of his natal chart follows the order of the twelve astrological houses (*domus*, τόποι): a division of the local horizon into twelve parts, each of which is responsible for one specific area of human life. Bate's association of specific houses to specific areas of life is rather standardized and closely follows the description of Albumasar's *Introductorium maius* VI.26.[302]

According to Bate, the first house stands for the complexion and form of the body, as well as the qualities of the soul (i.e., mores and passions of the native).[303]

---

[294] *Nat.* 223-236. Bate traces the match between the *hyleg*'s progression and his life events from *Nat.* 241 to *Nat.* 346, and supplements this with astrological data from relevant natal revolutions (see below, section 7.6).

[295] Bate's method is attested, *inter alia*, in Alcabitius, *Introductorius* IV.4 (Burnett, Yamamoto and Yano 2004, pp. 319-20) and Johannes Hispalensis, *Epitome* (Hispalensis 1548, sig. I3r/v). For a discussion of the method laid out in Abraham Ibn Ezra's *Sefer ha-Moladot*, see Sela 2014, pp. 45-50, with additional references to Dorotheus of Sidon and Ptolemy (amongst others).

[296] North 1988, p. 216.

[297] For a number of useful medieval astrological references, see Dunlop 1949.

[298] *Nat.* 642. For other mentions of the *alcochoden*, see *Nat.* 572, 579, 585, 589, 664, 670, 675, 686, 713, 715, 724, 920, 1145, 2757, 2837, 2843.

[299] See e.g. Alcabitius, *Introductorius* IV.5 (Burnett, Yamamoto and Yano 2004, p. 323); Hispalensis 1548, sig. [I4r].

[300] *Nat.* 585-624.

[301] *Nat.* 710-712.

[302] See Albumasar 1995-1997, vol. 8, p. 121:965 to 122:1036.

[303] *Nat.* 751, 759, 814, 842.

The second house indicates material prosperity.[304] The third house refers to the native's relation to brothers and sisters (although Bate does not discuss the latter).[305] The fourth house indicates the native's parents and hidden things.[306] The fifth house determines offspring and matters pertaining to love.[307] The sixth house stands for bodily health and diseases.[308] The seventh house indicates negotiations concerning marriage, as well as other social relations.[309] The eighth house reveals the native's manner of death.[310] The ninth house stands for religion, science, and travel.[311] The tenth house shows worldly honors and dignities, particularly in relation to princes. The eleventh house manifests good fortune and friendships.[312] The twelfth house reveals the native's enemies.[313] Concerning the eight house, Bate favours the examples of Ptolemy and Ibn Ezra by relegating treatment of his manner of death to the very end of the analysis, thus minimizing his discussion of this particular house.[314]

7.5. Bate's procedure of astrological self-analysis: the example of the first house

7.5.1. Complexion and shape of the body

Among the twelve houses, Bate's analysis of the first is by far the lengthiest, comprising 46% of the total length of the judgment of his nativity. As was usual, the judgment of the first house begins with an analysis of the complexion and shape of Bate's body. It is followed by a discussion of the quality of Bate's soul (see below, section 7.5.2). The classic astrological signifiers of the complexion and shape of the body were the ascendant, its ruling planet, and the Moon. Accordingly, Bate announces that he will first consider the disposition of these.[315]

Bate's ascendant sign was Sagittarius, which is the principal house of Jupiter. Accordingly, he determines his bodily complexion to be jovial and sanguine. Saturn's sextile aspect to the ascendant, however, also suggested tinges of slowness (*tarditas*) and indolence (*pigritia*). Bate uses the authority of Albumasar and Ibn Ezra to mitigate this melancholic interpretation of his complexion.[316] Interestingly,

---

[304] *Nat.* 1424.
[305] *Nat.* 1512.
[306] *Nat.* 1533, 1587.
[307] *Nat.* 1652.
[308] *Nat.* 1706.
[309] *Nat.* 1751-1752, *Nat.* 1898-1899.
[310] *Nat.* 2125.
[311] *Nat.* 2130-2131.
[312] *Nat.* 2546-2547.
[313] *Nat.* 2589.
[314] *Nat.* 2125-2127.
[315] *Nat.* 753-756.
[316] *Nat.* 757-775.

his astrological arguments for a hot complexion are combined with astronomical and seasonal ones.[317]

The Moon's opposition to the ascendant signified bodily problems, and Bate specifically identified this as a cause of his digestive problems.[318] In Firmicus Maternus's *Mathesis*, however, Bate stumbled upon other dimensions of his natal Moon that fitted his life (*secundum quod experimenta declarauerunt*) and nativity to a tee. A waxing Moon moving away from Saturn and into aspect with Mercury (as was the case at the time of Bate's birth) announced, despite Mercury's being combust (see above), silent and secretive individuals, students of the stars, teachers, orators, or physicians.[319] Sun and Moon being both in masculine signs, Bate's bodily condition was also diagnosed as being of noble and virile form.[320]

Bate next considered the ascending face (*facies*). In the faces system, each zodiac sign was divided in three ten-degree arcs (totaling 36), each of which has its own planetary ruler. Bate's ascending degree being Sagittarius 12°, he was thus looking at the second face of Sagittarius, whose ruler is the Moon.[321] On the authority of 'Abraham Princeps' and Abraham Ibn Ezra, Bate took this to signify —among other things— a rotund face, upright posture, white color, connected eyebrows, and a quickness of motion tempered by Saturnine tardity.[322]

Finally, Bate also took in data from the so-called planetary hour: the planet ruling the specific hour in which Bate was born, which he previously determined to be Jupiter.[323] Satisfyingly, this confirmed the general predominance of Jupiter in shaping Bate's bodily form and complexion.[324]

7.5.2. *Qualities of the soul*

In investigating the qualities of his soul, Bate took the disposition of his ascending sign (Sagittarius) and of Mercury as his main basis. Emphasis on Mercury as a privileged signifier of the qualities of one's soul was standard in medieval Latin astrology; moreover, Bate had already self-identified as "mercurial in his main actions".[325] Nevertheless, the combination with the lord of the ascendant specifically echoed the instructions in chapter 5 of Albohali's *De nativitatibus*.[326]

---

[317] *Nat.* 775-783. Such combinations were recommended by Ibn Ezra. See Sela 2014, pp. 98-9.
[318] *Nat.* 783-786.
[319] *Nat.* 788-795.
[320] *Nat.* 809-811.
[321] See Alcabitius, *Introductorius* I.20 (Burnett, Yamamoto and Yano 2004, p. 237-8).
[322] *Nat.* 812-832.
[323] *Nat.* 377-378. By his own reckoning, Bate was born in the seventh hour after sunset on a Friday. See Alcabitius, *Introductorius* II.49 (Burnett, Yamamoto and Yano 2004, pp. 293-4).
[324] *Nat.* 833-837.
[325] *Nat.* 647.
[326] Albohali 1546, sig. c2r.

7.5.2.1. Jupiter

Beginning with the disposition of the ascendant, Bate first focuses on Jupiter, lord of the ascendant (see above, section 7.5.1), and more specifically on that planet's conjunction with Saturn in mid-heaven (i.e., the cusp of the tenth house, which is usually the culminating degree of the ecliptic above one's local horizon).[327] As was the case in his analysis of bodily qualities, Bate identified Jupiter as a sufficient curb on Saturn's noxiousness, despite the latter planet's retrograde motion at the time of Bate's birth. Even so, Saturn would continue to shape "labor and difficulty" in attaining jovial goods such as worldly pre-eminence, nobility, loftiness of mind, profundity or excellence of counsel.[328]

In a later passage, Bate offered a methodological gloss on this interpretation, claiming that whenever contrary significations manifest themselves in a chart, the nature of the native typically mixes and mutually tempers these; nevertheless, the stronger planet usually has the upper hand.[329] Bate also recommended the technique of revolutions as a privileged way of detailing and discerning these seemingly confused significations.[330]

Distancing the threats of Saturn even further, Bate subsequently argued that at least in his nativity, this maleficent planet was actually a beneficent influence, on account of — among other reasons — its place in exaltation in Libra, in the exalted tenth house, and its association with Jupiter.[331] More specifically, it signified a soul, curious about higher things.[332] Here too, associations with the culminating tenth house came in handy.[333]

Bate detailed the specific qualities conferred by Jupiter at a later stage of his analysis, mostly on the authority of Albumasar's *Introductorium maius*:

> "A noble soul, healthy wisdom and intellect, interpretation of visions, certainty and truth, duties, laws, temples, ceremonies, religion, honesty, fortitude, temperance, justice, grace, true faith, humility and obedience. Sometimes, after deliberation, [the native will] rashly take up an affair and run into difficulty. [Jupiter also indicates] patience, the company and co-dwelling of men, steadfastness in promises, reliable testimony. [The native will be] cheerful, happy, gentle, indulging Venus, useful in addresses, both to himself and others, fleeing the bad and seeking out the good, circumspect through counsel, serious in speech, healthy and fruitful, both in private and public affairs".[334]

---

[327] On the dominance of Jupiter as an indicator of the qualities of Bate's soul, see also *Nat.* 1015-1017.

[328] *Nat.* 846-864, 1017-1018, 1037-1040. For Bate's qualification of the supposed negative significations of Saturn's retrograde motion, see *Nat.* 903-922 and 930-948.

[329] *Nat.* 1203-1210.

[330] *Nat.* 1210-1230.

[331] *Nat.* 864-928. Also see *Nat.* 1020-1022, 1165-1167.

[332] *Nat.* 949 and 998-1000.

[333] *Nat.* 989-998.

[334] *Nat.* 1004-1014.

The third significator to enter Bate's purview was the sign of Libra, home to both Jupiter and Saturn in Bate's nativity. For Bate, Libra's significance lay with its reputation as a sign of justice, prophets, princes, and men obedient to divine matters. This reinforced the suggestion that a Saturn-Jupiter conjunction in the tenth house signified the appearance of a king or prophet.[335] Further evidence for the significance of Libra was taken from the fact that by Bate's reckoning (which placed his birth in 1245 AD, Easter style), twenty years had elapsed since the previous Saturn-Jupiter conjunction of 1225 (which occurred in Aquarius). Applying the technique of astrological profection, this yielded Libra as the sign of profection for the year of his own birth.[336]

Apparently, Bate's claim that he was born in a year with a Saturn-Jupiter conjunction[337] (one did occur on September 21, 1246, in Libra 19°) provided him with sufficient reason to apply knowledge from mundane astrology (which specializes in events pertaining to large groups, countries, regions, or even the entire world) in natal astrology (which specializes in individual events). He thus uses a passage from Albumasar's *De magnis coniunctionibus* IV.7, discussing the signification of Libra, to not only confirm his soul's special affinity with religious matters, but to add associations with public speech, trade, mathematics, and music.[338]

7.5.2.2. Mercury

Having analysed the disposition of Jupiter, Bate turns next to the second main signifier of the qualities of his soul: Mercury. Not unlike his procedure for Jupiter (in its relation to Saturn), Bate begins by considering a number of threats to Mercury's beneficent influence. First, there is the fact that Mercury was combust in Bate's horoscope (see above, section 7.3). Bate sidesteps this by adducing empirical evidence, arguing that his character and biography to date, illustrated how the planet continued to send down its benefits.[339]

Secondly, Bate acknowledges Mercury's association with Mars through the former planet's position in Aries, the house of Mars. This too suggested dubious qualities such as loquaciousness (*lingua facilis*) and hasty foresight.[340] Bate distances this second threat by focusing on Mercury's relation to the Sun, with which he considers Mercury to be in conjunction in his natal horoscope.[341] Later in his analysis, he also argued that one baneful influence could cancel out another. More specifically, the unruliness of the soul that comes from Mars's hold over Mercury through a sextile

---

[335] *Nat.* 957-968.
[336] *Nat.* 968-971. On profections, see Alcabitius, *Introductorius* IV.8-10 (Burnett, Yamamoto and Yano 2004, pp. 326-31).
[337] *Nat.* 982-983.
[338] *Nat.* 971-981.
[339] *Nat.* 1049-1063.
[340] *Nat.* 1064-1083, 1157-1158.
[341] *Nat.* 1093-1094, 1099.

aspect, is tempered and resisted by Saturn's opposition to Mercury, which "hinders sudden and rash motions while providing cause for deliberation".[342]

Mercury's association with the Sun also brings other benefits to Bate. Like Mercury, the Sun is in Aries, where it has more strength and pre-eminence than Mars.[343] Where Aries brings justice, oratory prowess, judgment and moderation,[344] the pairing of Mercury with the Sun also announces special affinity for the science of the stars (*astrologia*), and indeed an overall predisposition towards wisdom and knowledge.[345] The latter are confirmed, Bate claims, by Mercury's position in opposition to Saturn.[346] Added to this are religious contemplation and the natural company of kings and secretaries among other traits.[347]

All this allows Bate to conclude that the greater part of mercurial properties were impressed on him:

> "probable inductions, necessary syllogisms, the study of philosophy, poetry, as well as medicine, several mathematical arts such as arithmetic, geometry and astronomy, as well as music, poetry, and dance".[348]

Bate further develops these properties by considering the sextile aspect between Mercury and the Moon (both of which are also in aspect to the natal ascendant). This planetary disposition signified an intellect that consistently mastered the appetites.[349] The Moon's motion into conjunction with Mercury after the preceding New Moon of 17 March 1246 (see above, sections 7.1 and 7.5.1) signified wisdom and an aptness for handiwork.[350]

Through the intermediary of this New Moon, the sign of Aquarius also gained a role in shaping Bate's soul. Once again, this became possible by taking in material from the tradition of mundane astrology. First, Bate pointed out that the ascendant of the chart for the New Moon of 17 March 1246 was Aquarius, the same sign in which the Saturn-Jupiter conjunction of 1225 (see above) occurred. This was a so-called 'middle conjunction' involving a change of triplicity (for this specific conjunction, from the earthy to the airy triangle).[351] Secondly, Bate invokes the current *dawr*-cycle (*orbis*), which began in the year 940 according to Albumasar's *De magnis coniunctionibus*. He calculates the zodiac sign where the direction from Aries has arrived in 1255 (beginning from 940). This yields Aries 1° + 315° (at the

---

342 *Nat.* 1156-1165.
343 *Nat.* 1094-1097.
344 *Nat.* 1089-1091.
345 *Nat.* 1110-1114.
346 *Nat.* 1141-1148.
347 *Nat.* 1117, 1129-1130.
348 *Nat.* 1150-1155.
349 *Nat.* 1171-1175.
350 *Nat.* 1175-1180.
351 On the theory of Saturn-Jupiter conjunctions, see Yamamoto and Burnett 2000, vol. 1, pp. 582-7.

habitual rate for directions of 1° per year) or, once again, Aquarius: the sign of "angels and demons" and signifier of the highest goods.[352]

Next, Bate returns to Jupiter's status as lord of his natal ascendant (see above, section 7.5.2.1), pointing out that this also brings an appetite for riches and justice, while Saturn adds anxiety and tolerance of labour.[353]

7.5.2.3. Interpreting the decans

In addition to Mercury and Jupiter, planetary ruler of the ascendant, Bate also spends several pages discussing two particular decans. Decans constitute an alternative system of zodiacal division, consisting of 36 ten-degree arcs (like the aforementioned faces). As early as 1912, Aby Warburg drew attention to the importance of the decan system in medieval and Renaissance culture, which drew especially on Albumasar's *Introductorium maius* VI.1 (tr. Hermann of Carinthia) as its source. In this text, Albumasar offered an overview of three different systems for describing the zodiac: the "Persian, Chaldean and Egyptian" decans, ultimately deriving from the first-century astrologer Teukros; the "Indian" decans; and the "Greek" *sphaera* as found in Ptolemy.[354]

Bate focused first on the decan hosting the Moon in his nativity chart, and secondly on the ascendant decan rising above the horizon.[355] In Bate's nativity, the Moon was in the second decan of Gemini. The latter represents a man playing a golden reed according to the Persians, and a dark man with bow and arrow who is singing and drumming according to the Indians. According to the Greeks, Albumasar reported, this decan groups the right part of the [constellation of the] Charioteer, both of Taurus's hind legs, and the head of Orion among other things.[356] The ascendant decan is the second decan of Sagittarius, whose visual representations Bate also finds in Albumasar.[357]

Bate's relation to the decans is fascinating. On the one hand, their enigmatic iconography leads him to ascribe an occult meaning to them that smacks of prophecy, whose secrets Albumasar and Ibn Ezra sought to unveil, according to Bate. On the other hand, he finds that "the fortune and choices of this native are often similar to things covertly signified by these images".[358] The second decan of Gemini, for instance, inspires Bate to develop his stunningly detailed description of personal musical prowess (see above, section 2.3).[359]

---

[352] *Nat.* 1182-1188. On the doctrine of *dawr*, see Yamamoto and Burnett 2000, vol. 1, pp. 587-9.
[353] *Nat.* 1196-1203.
[354] For a useful recent introduction to the topic of (and vast literature on) the astrological decans, see Greenbaum 2016, pp. 213-35.
[355] *Nat.* 1232-1236.
[356] *Nat.* 1236-1254.
[357] *Nat.* 1254-1266.
[358] *Nat.* 1266-1286.
[359] *Nat.* 1286-1335.

In and of itself, the decan of the ascendant appears to play a minor role in Bate's analysis. Its representation of a human figure does allow Bate to connect with a classification of the zodiac signs in chapter I.24 of Alcabitius's *Introductorius*.[360] More specifically, he points out that the zodiac signs occupying three of the four cardinal points or pivots (namely, the ascendant or eastern angle, the mid-heaven or cusp of the 10th house, and the descendant or western angle) are all human and shaped in the images of men. The remaining cardinal point, the Imum Coeli or cusp of the seventh house, is in a so-called domestic sign.[361]

On the authority of Johannes Hispalensis's *Epitome*, Bate sees this as signifying a predilection for conversation, association in groups, banquets and feasts. Bate points out that this also entails a tendency to submit to the plans of his associates, even if these plans are displeasing to himself.[362] Concerning the latter point, Bate also recognizes something of himself in a claim of the *Liber novem iudicum*, according to which the mercurial man "while having many friends, finds very few of them to be trustworthy".[363] Ultimately, however, it is the "noble love of the sciences" that Bate sees himself attracted to beyond any other delight.[364]

7.6. Solar revolutions of the nativity

The last section of Bate's *Nativitas* (lines 2782 to 3400) is devoted to a reading of the solar revolutions of Bate's nativity for his 35th and 36th year. Revolutions are part of what David Pingree called "continuous horoscopy": the study of celestial influence in between birth and death.[365] The astrological method of solar revolutions, which modern-day astrologers call 'solar returns', is based on the assumption that the Sun's annual return to a specific point on the ecliptic marks a moment of particular celestial influences, which would remain active for one year of the native's life (i.e., until the next solar return).

In natal astrology, such revolutions were based on the position of the Sun in the ecliptic at the time of birth. Indeed, a solar revolution was nothing other than a return of the Sun to that point of the ecliptic. In Bate's case, this was Aries 10°18'. In order to cast a revolution for the 35th year, one simply drew an astrological chart for the precise moment of the Sun's 34th return to that point of the ecliptic after Bate's birth: in this case, 23 March 1280 at 5h01 a.m.

Interpreting a revolved chart was no mean feat. One of the earliest and most influential treatises on the subject, Albumasar's *De revolutionibus nativitatum*, states that:

---

[360] Burnett, Yamamoto and Yano 2004, pp. 240-1.
[361] *Nat.* 1345-1349.
[362] *Nat.* 1350-1355.
[363] *Nat.* 1356-1357.
[364] *Nat.* 1364-1376.
[365] Pingree 1997, p. 69. For a useful overview of continuous horoscopy, see Sela 2014, pp. 58-69.

"Similarly [you will set down] the place of the profection where the year arrives from the ascendant, taking one sign [for each year], and also the place where the year arrives from the Lot of Fortune in the nativity. Also [take into account] the places to which the profection from the principal houses of the [nativity] chart applies. Next you will set down in this [revolved chart] which place in the division the divisor and its partaking co-divisor have reached. Also, the ruler of the *ferdaria*, and its co-ruler. You will also note the ruler of the orb. For each of these you will especially note the zodiac signs in which they are located. And if a fixed star should occupy the mid-heaven, or be conjoined in the cardines with one of the luminaries or planets, you will mark this too".[366]

This passage introduces no less than 19 different signifiers for the adequate judgment of a revolved chart. Although Bate does not systematically follow the advice of Albumasar, many of these parameters do appear in the analysis of the *Nativitas*. Another crucial dimension of the interpretation of revolved charts, which Bate also takes into account, is the monitoring of planetary ingress into significant positions of the original birth horoscope.[367]

---

[366] Albumasar 1559, p. 214a:2-15.
[367] Albumasar 1559, p. 272a and *passim*.

Index of manuscripts

Bibliography to the Introduction

Albohali 1546. *De nativitatibus* [trans. Johannes Toletanus] (Nürnberg: Johannes Montanus & Ulricus Neuber).

Albumasar 1559. *De revolutionibus nativitatum* in: ΕΙΣ ΤΗΝ ΤΕΤΡΑΒΙΒΛΟΝ ΤΟΥ ΠΤΟΛΕΜΑΙΟΥ ΕΧΗΓΗΤΗΣ ΑΝΩΝΥΜΟΣ *(...) praeterea Hermetis Philosophi De Revolutionibus Nativitatum (...)* (Basel: Henricus Petreius), pp. 211-279.

Albumasar 1995-1997. *Liber introductorii maioris ad scientiam judiciorum astrorum*, ed. Richard Lemay, 9 vols. (Napoli: Istituto universitario orientale).

Ariès, Philippe 1962. *Centuries of Childhood. A Social History of Family Life*, trans. Robert Baldick (New York: Alfred Knopf).

Abraham Bar Ḥiyya 1924. *Sefer Megillat ha-Megalle*, eds. Adolf Poznanski and Julius Guttmann (Berlin: Verein Mekize Nirdamim).

Bataillon, Louis-Jacques 1988. "Comptes de Pierre de Limoges pour la copie de livres" in: *La production du livre universitaire au Moyen Âge. Exemplar et pecia*, eds. Louis-Jacques Bataillon, Bertrand Georges Guyot and Richard H. Rouse (Paris: Éditions du Centre national de la recherche scientifique), pp. 265-273.

Benjamin, Francis S.; Toomer, Gerald J. 1971. *Campanus of Novara and Medieval Planetary Theory: Theorica planetarum* (Madison/London: University of Wisconsin Press).

Bériou, Nicole 1986. "Pierre de Limoges et la fin des temps" in: *Mélanges de l'Ecole Française de Rome. Moyen-Age, Temps modernes*, vol. 98, pp. 65-107.

Birkenmajer, Aleksander 1949. "Pierre de Limoges commentateur de Richard de Fournival" in: *Isis*, vol. 40, pp. 18-31.

Birkenmajer, Aleksander 1970 [1923]. "Henri Bate de Malines, astronome et philosophe du XIIIe siècle", repr. and transl. in: Idem, *Etudes d'histoire des sciences et de la philosophie du Moyen Age* (Wroclaw/Warszawa/Kraków: Ossolineum), pp. 105-115.

Birkenmajer, Aleksander 1972 [1937]. "Les astronomes et les astrologues silésiens au Moyen Age", repr. and transl. in: Idem, *Etudes d'histoire des sciences en Pologne* (Wroclaw/Warszawa/Kraków: Ossolineum), pp. 437-468.

Boes, Helmut; Steel, Carlos 1990. *Henricus Bate, Speculum divinorum et quorundam naturalium, parts XI-XII, On Platonic Philosophy* (Leuven: Leuven University Press).

Bogaerts, Ambrosius M. 1979. *Het klooster Hertoginnedal der zuster Dominikanessen te Oudergem, 1262-1797* (Leuven: Dominikaans Archief).

Boudet, Jean-Patrice 1997-1999. *Le Recueil des plus célèbres astrologues de Simon de Phares*, 2 vols. (Paris: Librairie Honoré Champion).

Boudet, Jean-Patrice 2015. "La science des étoiles dans la librairie de Charles V" in: *Traduire au XIVe siècle: Evrart de Conty et la vie intellectuelle à la cour de Charles V*, eds. Joëlle Ducos and Michèle Goyens (Paris: Honoré Champion), pp. 379-401.

Boudet, Jean-Patrice; Lucken, Christopher 2018, "In Search of an Astrological Identity Chart: Richard of Fournival's *Nativitas*" in: *Richard de Fournival et les sciences au XIIIe siècle*, eds. Joëlle Ducos and Christopher Lucken (Firenze: SISMEL), pp. 283-322.

Bridges, John Henry 1897. *The Opus Maius of Roger Bacon*, vol. 1 (Oxford: Clarendon Press).

Burnett, Charles 1978. "Arabic into Latin in Twelfth Century Spain: The Works of Hermann of Carinthia" in: *Mittellateinisches Jahrbuch*, vol. 13, pp. 100-134.

Burnett, Charles; Yamamoto, Keiji; Yano, Michio 1994. *Abū Ma'shar: The Abbreviation of the Introduction to Astrology, together with the Medieval Latin Translation of Adelard of Bath [Ysagoga minor]* (Leiden/New York: Brill).

Burnett, Charles; Yamamoto, Keiji; Yano, Michio 2004. *Al-Qabīṣī (Alcabitius), The introduction to astrology* (London: Warburg Institute).

Burnett, Charles 2009. "Abū Ma'shar (A.D. 787-886) and His Major Texts on Astrology" in: *Kayd. Studies in History of Mathematics, Astronomy and Astrology in Memory of David Pingree*, eds. Gherardo Gnoli and Antonio Panaino (Roma: Istituto Italiano per l'Africa e l'Oriente), pp. 17-29.

Burnett, Charles 2014. "Stephen of Messina and the Translation of Astrological Texts from Greek in the Time of Manfred" in: *Translating at the Court. Bartholomew of Messina and Cultural Life at the Court of Manfred of Sicily*, ed. Pieter De Leemans (Leuven: Leuven University Press), pp. 155-164.

Burnett, Charles 2017. "Béziers as an Astronomical Centre for Jews and Christians in the Mid-Twelfth Century" in: *Aleph*, vol. 17, pp. 197-219.

Chabás, José; Goldstein, Bernard 2003. *The Alfonsine Tables of Toledo* (Dordrecht: Kluwer).

Croenen, Godfried 2003. *Familie en Macht. De Familie Berthout en de Brabantse Adel* (Leuven: Universitaire Pers Leuven).

D'Alverny, Marie Thérèse; Poulle, Emmanuel 1958. "Un nouveau manuscrit des Tabulae Mechlinenses d'Henri Bate de Malines" in: *Actes du VIIIe Congrès international d'histoire des sciences* (Vinci: Gruppo italiano di storia delle scienze), pp. 355-358.

Delisle, Léopold 1868-1881. *Le cabinet des manuscrits de la Bibliothèque Impériale [Nationale]*, 3 vols. (Paris: Imprimerie impériale).

Dell'Anna, Giuseppe 1999. *Dies critici. La teoria della ciclicità delle patologie nel XIV secolo*, 2 vols. (Galatina: Congedo).

Delorme, Ferdinand M. 1936. "Manuscrit du 'Computus' de Roger Bacon annoté par Guillaume de Saint-Cloud" in: *Antonianum*, vol. 11, pp. 554-562.

Dorez, Leon; Thuasne, Louis 1897. *Pic de la Mirandole en France (1485-1488)* (Paris: Ernest Leroux).

Dunlop, Douglas M. 1949. "A Note on Colcodea in Renderings from the Arabic" in: *The Jewish Quarterly Review*, vol. 39, pp. 403-406.

Edmunds, Sheila 1991. "From Schoeffer to Vérard: concerning the scribes who became printers" in: *Printing the Written Word: The Social History of Books, circa 1450-1520*, ed. Sarah Hindman (Ithaca NY: Cornell University Press), pp. 21-40.

Erens, Mattheus A. 1950. *De oorkonden der abdij Tongerloo*, vol. 2 (Tongerlo: St..-Norbertusdrukkerij).

Federici Vescovini, Graziella 1991. "Una versione latina medievale dell'opera escatologica di Abramo bar Hijja, *Megillat ha Megalleh*, il *Liber de redemptione Israhel*" in: *Filosofia e cultura. Per Eugenio Garin*, eds. Michele Ciliberto and Cesare Vasoli, vol. 1 (Roma: Editori Riuniti), pp. 5-37.

Federici Vescovini, Graziella 1992. *Pietro d'Abano, Trattati di Astronomia. 'Lucidator dubitabilium astronomiae', 'De motu octavae sphaerae' e altre opere* (Padova: Esedra).

Filangieri di Candida, Riccardo 1964. *I registri della cancelleria angioina*, vol. 19 (Napoli: L'Accademia Pontaniana).

Goetschalckx, Pieter J. 1907. "Cartularium der abdij van S. Michiels te Antwerpen" in: *Bijdragen tot de geschiedenis bijzonderlijk van het aloude hertogdom Brabant*, vol. 6., pp. 280-356.

Goldine, Nicole 1964. "Henri Bate chanoine et chantre de la Cathédrale Saint-Lambert à Liège, et théoricien" in: *Revue Belge de Musicologie*, vol. 18, pp. 10-27.

Goodman, Mordechai S. 2011. *Sefer Ha'ibbur, A Treatise on the Calendar by Rabbi Abraham Ibn Ezra* (Jerusalem: Ktav).

Grayson, Cecil 1970. "Bonincontri, Lorenzo" in: *Dizionario Biografico degli Italiani*, vol. 12 (Roma: Istituto della Enciclopedia Italiana), pp. 209-211.

Greenbaum, Dorian Gieseler 2016. *The Daimon in Hellenistic Astrology. Origins and Influence* (Leiden/Boston: Brill).

Guldentops, Guy 1997. "Een spookverhaal van Bate. Een bron voor de mediëvistiek" in: *Ons geestelijk erf*, vol. 71, pp. 193-204.

Guldentops, Guy 2001. *Henricus Bate, een filosofische 'encyclopedist' uit de late dertiende eeuw. Kritische uitgave van de delen XIII-XVI van het Speculum divinorum met doctrinele studies over Bate's metafysica en psychologie*, 3 vols. (Katholieke Universiteit Leuven: PhD dissertation).

Guldentops, Guy 2001a. "Albert's Influence on Bate's Metaphysics and Noetics" in: *Albertus Magnus. Zum Gedenken nach 800 Jahren. Neue Zugänge, Aspekte und Perspektiven*, eds. Henryk Anzulewicz, Walter Senner, Maria Burger and Ruth Meyer (Berlin: Akademie Verlag), pp. 195-206.

Guldentops, Guy 2001b. "Henry Bate's Aristocratic Eudaemonism" in: *Nach der Verurteilung von 1277*, eds. Jan A. Aertsen, Kent Emery Jr. and Andreas Speer (Berlin/New York: Walter de Gruyter), pp. 657-681.

Guldentops, Guy 2002. *Henricus Bate, Speculum divinorum et quorundam naturalium, Parts XIII-XVI: On Thinking and Happiness* (Leuven: Leuven University Press).

Guldentops, Guy 2005. *"Famosus expositor.... On Bate's (Anti-)Thomism"* in: *Recherches de théologie et philosophie médiévales*, vol. 72, pp. 191-231.

Gunther, Robert T. 1932. *The astrolabes of the world: based upon the series of instruments in the Lewis Evans Collection of the old Ashmolean Museum at Oxford, with notes on astrolabes in the collections of the British Museum, Science Museum, Sir J. Findlay, Mr S.V. Hoffman, the Mensing Collection, and in other public and private collections*, 2 vols. (Oxford: Oxford University Press).

Hackett, Jeremiah 1998. "The Hand of Roger Bacon, the Writing of the *Perspectiva* and Ms Paris Lat. 7434" in: *Roma, magistra mundi. Itineraria culturae medievalis. Mélanges offerts au père L. E. Boyle à l'occasion de son 75ᵉ anniversaire*, ed. Jacqueline Hamesse, 3 vols. (Turnhout: Brepols), vol. 1, pp. 323-336.

Harper, Richard I. 1966. *The Kalendarium Regine of Guillaume de St-Cloud* (PhD dissertation, Emory University).

Jamees, Alfred 1991. *De oorkonden van Pitsenburg. Commanderije van de Duitse Ridderorde te Mechelen (1190-1794)*, vol. 1 (Antwerpen: Provincie Antwerpen)

Johannes Hispalensis 1548. *Epitome totius astrologiae* (Nürnberg: Johannes Montanus and Ulricus Neuber).

Abraham Ibn Ezra 1485. *Liber de nativitatibus* (Venezia: Erhard Ratdolt).

Jeffreys, Catherine 2009. "Some early references to Aristotle's *Politics* in Parisian writings about music" in: *Identity and locality in early European music, 1028-1740*, ed. Jason Stoessel (Farnham: Ashgate), pp. 83-106.

Juste, David 2015. *Catalogus Codicum Astrologorum Latinorum*, vol. 2, *Les manuscrits astrologiques latins conservés à la Bibliothèque nationale de France à Paris* (Paris: CNRS Editions).

Juste, David 2015a. "A Sixteenth-Century Astrological Consultation" in: *Astrologers and Their Clients in Medieval and Early Modern Europe*, eds. Wiebke Deimann and David Juste (Köln/Weimar/Wien: Böhlau), pp. 151-204.

Juste, David 2016. "The Impact of Arabic Sources on European Astrology: Some Facts and Numbers" in: *The Impact of Arabic Sciences in Europe and Asia* (Firenze: SISMEL), pp. 173-194.

Kronk, Gary W. 1999-2017. *Cometography. A Catalog of Comets*, 6 vols. (Cambridge: Cambridge University Press).

Kupin, Jane 2014. "Aldaraia sive Soyga vocor", *Esoteric Archives*, retrieved 12 July 2017: http://www.esotericarchives.com/soyga/Book_of_Soyga_8x10.pdf.

Lanza, Lydia 2001. "Antonius de Murellis de Camerino" in: *Compendium Auctorum Latinorum Medii Aevi* [C.A.L.M.A.], vol. I/4, eds. Gian Carlo Garfagnini, Michael Lapidge, Claudio Leonardi, Lucia Lanza (Firenze: SISMEL & Edizioni del Galluzzo, 2001).

Lévy, Tony; Burnett, Charles 2006. "*Sefer ha-Middot*: A Mid-Twelfth-Century Text on Arithmetic and Geometry Attributed to Abraham ibn Ezra" in: *Aleph*, vol. 6, pp. 57-238.

Lipton, John D. 1978. *The Rational Evaluation of Astrology in the Period of Arabo-Latin Translation ca. 1126-1187 AD* (PhD dissertation, University of California in Los Angeles).

Lucken, Christopher; Boudet, Jean-Patrice (forthcoming). *Richard de Fournival astrologue. Avec une édition de la Nativitas et de son commentaire par Pierre de Limoges.*

Mabille, Madeleine 1970. "Pierre de Limoges, copiste de manuscrits" in: *Scriptorium*, vol. 24, pp. 45-47.

Mabille, Madeleine 1976. "Pierre de Limoges et ses méthodes de travail" in: *Hommages à André Boutemy*, éd. Guy Cambier (Bruxelles : Latomus), pp. 244-251.

Mancha, José Luis 1992. "Astronomical Use of Pinhole Images in William of Saint-Cloud's Almanach Planetarum (1292)" in: *Archive for History of Exact Sciences*, vol. 43, pp. 275-298.

Millás Vallicrosa, José M. 1940. "Un nuevo tratado de astrolabio de R. Abraham ibn Ezra" in: *Al-Andalus*, vol. 5, pp. 9-29.

Millás Vallicrosa, José M. 1947. *El Libro de los Fundamentos de las Tablas Astronómicas de R. Abraham Ibn Ezra* (Madrid: Instituto Arias Montano).

Nardi, Bruno 1945. *Sigieri di Brabante nel pensiero del rinascimento italiano* (Roma: Edizioni italiane).

Muñoz, Rafael 1979. "Una maqāla astrológica de al-Kindī" in: *Boletín de la Asociacion Española de Orientalistas*, vol. 15, pp. 127-139.

North, John D. 1986. *Horoscopes and History* (London: Warburg Institute).

North, John D. 1988. *Chaucer's Universe* (Oxford: Clarendon Press).

North, John D. 2003. "Winchester 1067" in: *Centaurus*, vol. 45, pp. 130-141.

Nothaft, C. Philipp E. 2014. "Climate, Astrology and the Age of the World in Thirteenth-Century Thought: Giles of Lessines and Roger Bacon on the Precession of the Solar Apogee" in: *Journal of the Warburg and Courtauld Institutes*, vol. 77, pp. 35-60.

Nothaft, C. Philipp E. 2014a, "Origen, Climate Change, and the Erosion of Mountains in Giles of Lessines's Discussion of the Eternity of the World (*c.* 1260)" in: *The Mediaeval Journal*, vol. 4, pp. 43-69.

Nothaft, C. Philipp E. 2015, "Critical Analysis of the Alfonsine Tables in the Fourteenth Century: The Parisian *Expositio Tabularum Alfonsii* of 1347" in: *Journal for the History of Astronomy*, vol. 46, pp. 76-99.

Nothaft, C. Philipp E. 2016. "*Vanitas vanitarum et super omnia vanitas*: The Astronomer Heinrich Selder and a Newly Discovered Fourteenth-Century Critique of Astrology" in: *Erudition and the Republic of Letters*, vol. 1, pp. 261-304.

Nothaft, C. Philipp E. 2017. "Criticism of Trepidation Models and Advocacy of Uniform Precession in Medieval Latin Astronomy" in: *Archive for History of Exact Sciences*, vol. 71, pp. 211-244.

Nothaft, C. Philipp E. (forthcoming). "Henry Bate's Tabule Machlinenses: The Earliest Astronomical Tables by a Latin Author" in: *Annals of Science*.

Page, Christopher 1986. *Voices and Instruments of the Middle Ages. Instrumental Practice and Songs in France, 1100-1300* (Berkeley: University of California Press).

Pedersen, Fritz S. 1983-1984. *Petri Philomenae de Dacia et Petri de S. Audomaro opera quadrivalia*, 2 vols. (København: F. Bagge).

Pedersen, Fritz S. 1984. "A Paris Astronomer of 1290" in: *Cahiers de l'Institut du Moyen-Âge Grec et Latin*, vol. 48, pp. 163-188.

Pedersen, Fritz S. 1986. *Scriptum Johannis de Sicilia super canones Azarchelis de tabulis Toletanis*, 2 vols. (København: Institut du Moyen âge grec et latin).

Pedersen, Fritz S. 2001-2002. "Anonymous Parisian Astronomer of 1290" in: *Cahiers de l'Institut du Moyen-Âge Grec et Latin*, vol. 72, pp. 169-269; Ibidem, vol. 73, pp. 61-166.

Pedersen, Fritz S. 2014. "William of Saint-Cloud: *Almanach Planetarum*. An Edition of the Canons, a Few Samples from the Tables, and a Foray into the Numbers" in: *Cahiers de l'Institut du Moyen-Âge Grec et Latin*, vol. 83, pp. 1-133.

Pingree, David E. 1986. *Picatrix: the Latin version of the Ghayat al-hakim.* Text, introduction, appendices, indices (London: The Warburg Institute).

Pingree, David E. 1997. *From Astral Omens to Astrology: From Babylon to Binaker* (Roma: Istituto italiano per l'Africa e l'Oriente).

Poulle, Emmanuel 1954. "L'astrolabe médiéval d'après les manuscrits de la Bibliothèque nationale" in: *Bibliothèque de l'École des Chartes*, vol. 112, pp. 81-103.

Poulle, Emmanuel 1963. *La Bibliothèque scientifique d'un imprimeur humaniste au XVe siècle: catalogue des manuscrits d'Arnaud de Bruxelles à la Bibliothèque Nationale de Paris* (Genève: Droz).

Poulle, Emmanuel 1964. "Astrologie et tables astronomiques au XIIIe siècle: Robert Le Febvre et les tables de Malines" in: *Bulletin philologique et historique*, pp. 793-831. Reprinted in: Idem, *Astronomie planétaire au Moyen Age latin* (Aldershot/Brookfield VT: Variorum), art. VII.

Poulle, Emmanuel 1964a. "Bernard de Verdun et le turquet" in: *Isis*, vol. 55, pp. 200-208.

Poulle, Emmanuel 1980. *Les instruments de la théorie des planètes selon Ptolémée: Équatoires et horlogerie planétaire du XIIIe au XVIe siècle*, 2 vols. Genève: Droz/Paris: H. Champion.

Poulle, Emmanuel 1999. "L'horoscope de Louis X" in: *Finances, pouvoirs et mémoire. Mélanges en l'honneur de Jean Favier* (Paris : Fayard), pp. 256-268.

Poulle, Emmanuel 2008. "Henry Bate of Malines", *Complete Dictionary of Scientific Biography*, retrieved 12 July 2017: http://www.encyclopedia.com/science/dictionaries-thesauruses-pictures-and-press-releases/henry-bate-malines

Poulle, Emmanuel 2008a. "William of Saint-Cloud", *Complete Dictionary of Scientific Biography*, retrieved 1 August 2018: https://www.encyclopedia.com/science/dictionaries-thesauruses-pictures-and-press-releases/william-saint-cloud

Reeds, Jim 2006. "John Dee and the Magic Tables in the *Book of Soyga*" in: *Interdisciplinary Studies in English Renaissance Thought*, ed. Stephen Clucas (Dordrecht: Springer), pp. 177-204.

Renardy, Christine 1981. *Les maîtres universitaires dans le diocèse de Liège. Répertoire biographique (1140-1350)* (Paris: Les Belles Lettres).

Samaran, Charles; Marichal, Robert 1974. *Catalogue des manuscrits en écriture latine portant des indications de date, de lieu ou de copiste*, vol. 3, *Bibliothèque Nationale, fonds latin (Nos 8001 à 18613)* (Paris: CNRS).

Sanderus, Antonius 1659. *Chorographia sacra Brabantiae sive celebrium aliquot in ea provincia ecclesiarum et coenobiorum descriptio*, vol. 1 (Bruxelles: Philips Vleugaert).

Sela, Shlomo 2003. *Abraham Ibn Ezra and the Rise of Medieval Hebrew Science* (Leiden/Boston: Brill).

Sela, Shlomo 2007. *Abraham Ibn Ezra. The Book of Reasons. A Parallel Hebrew-English Critical Edition of the Two Versions of the Text [Te'amim I], [Te'amim II]* (Leiden/Boston: Brill).

Sela, Shlomo 2010. *Abraham Ibn Ezra. The Book of the World. A Parallel Hebrew-English Critical Edition of the Two Versions of the Text ['Olam I], ['Olam II]* (Leiden/Boston: Brill).

Sela, Shlomo 2011. *Abraham Ibn Ezra on Elections, Interrogations, and Medical Astrology. A Parallel Hebrew-English Critical Edition of the Book of Elections (3 Versions), the Book of Interrogations (3 Versions), and the Book of the Luminaries* (Leiden/Boston: Brill).

Sela, Shlomo 2014. *Abraham Ibn Ezra on Nativities and Continuous Horoscopy: A Parallel Hebrew-English Critical Edition of the Book of Nativities and the Book of Revolution [Sefer ha-Moladot], [Sefer ha-Tequfah]* (Leiden/Boston: Brill).

Sela, Shlomo 2017. *Abraham Ibn Ezra's Introductions to Astrology. A Parallel Hebrew-English Critical Edition of the Book of the Beginning of Wisdom and the Book of the Judgments of the Zodiacal Signs [Reshit Ḥokhmah], [Mishpeṭei ha-Mazzalot]* (Leiden/Boston: Brill).

Sela Shlomo 2017a. "The Ibn Ezra-Henry Bate Astrological Connection and the Three Abrahams" in: *Mediterranea. International Journal for the Transfer of Knowledge*, vol. 2, pp. 163-186.

Sela, Shlomo (forthcoming). "Origins and Transmission of *Liber Abraham Iudei de Nativitatibus*: A New Appraisal Based on the Scrutiny of the Available Manuscripts and Other Sources" in: *Revue des études juives*.

Sela, Shlomo (forthcoming a). "The Abraham Ibn Ezra-Peter of Limoges Astrological-Exegetical Connection" in: *Aleph*.

Silan, Karen 2008. "Dance in Late Thirteenth Century Paris" in: *Dance, Spectacle, and the Body Politick, 1250-1750*, ed. Jennifer Neville (Bloomington: Indiana University Press), pp. 67-79.

Smithuis, Renate 2006, "Abraham Ibn Ezra's Astrological Works in Hebrew and Latin: New Discoveries and Exhaustive Listing" in: *Aleph*, vol. 6, pp. 239-338.

Smithuis, Renate 2006a. "Science in Normandy and England under the Angevins. The Creation of Avraham Ibn Ezra's Latin Works of Astronomy and Astrology" in: *Hebrew to Latin-Latin to Hebrew: The Mirroring of Two Cultures in the Age of Humanism*, ed. Giulio Busi (Berlin: Institut für Judaistik Freie Universität Berlin/Torino: N. Aragno), pp. 26-61.

Steel, Carlos; Guldentops, Guy 1996. *Henricus Bate, Speculum divinorum et quorundam naturalium, Parts XX-XXIII, On the Heavens, the Divine Movers, and the First Intellect* (Leuven: Leuven University Press).

Steel, Carlos 1996. "Individuation of the human intellect: Henry Bate's Platonic-nominalistic position" in: *Individuum und Individualität im Mittelalter*, eds. Jan A. Aertsen and Andreas Speer (Berlin: Walter de Gruyter), pp. 230-248.

Steel, Carlos (forthcoming). "A discussion on Ptolemy's Authority. Henry Bate's Prologue to his Translation of Ibn Ezra's Book of the World" in: *Ptolemy's Science of the Stars in the Middle Ages*, eds. David Juste, Benno van Dalen, Dag Nikolaus Hasse, Charles Burnett (Turnhout: Brepols).

Thorndike, Lynn 1923. *A History of Magic and Experimental Science*, vol. 2 (New York: Columbia University Press).

Thorndike, Lynn 1944. "The Latin Translations of the Astrological Tracts of Abraham Avenezra" in: *Isis*, vol. 35, pp. 293-302.

Thorndike, Lynn 1945. "Peter of Limoges on the Comet of 1299" in: *Isis*, vol. 36, pp. 3-6.

Thorndike, Lynn 1950. *Latin Treatises on Comets Between 1238 and 1368 A.D.* (Chicago: University of Chicago Press).

Travaglia, Pinella 1999. *Magic, Causality and Intentionality. The Doctrine of Rays in al-Kindi* (Turnhout: Brepols).

Uyttebrouck, André; Graffart, Arlette 1979. *Inventaire des archives du prieuré de Val-Duchesse à Auderghem* (Bruxelles: Archives générales du royaume).

Van der Lugt, Maaike 2004. *Le ver, le démon et la vierge. Les théories médiévales de la génération extraordinaire* (Paris: Les Belles Lettres).

Van de Vyver, Emiel 1960. *Henricus Bate, Speculum divinorum et quorundam naturalium, part I, Littera dedicatoria*, ed. E. Van de Vyver (Louvain: Publications Universitaires).

Vuillemin-Diem, Gudrun; Steel, Carlos 2015. *Ptolemy's Tetrabiblos in the Translation of William of Moerbeke: Claudii Ptolemaei Liber Iudicialium* (Leuven: Leuven University Press).

Walker Bynum, Caroline. 1982. "Did the Twelfth Century Discover the Individual?" in: Idem, *Jesus as Mother: Studies in the Spirituality of the High Middle Ages* (Berkeley/Los Angeles: The University of California Press), pp. 82-109.

Wallerand, Gaston 1931. *Henricus Bate, Speculum divinorum et quorundam naturalium, fasc. 1, Etude bio-bibliographique, Epistola ad quidonem hannoniae, Tabula, Ia et IIa pars* (Louvain: Institut Supérieur de Philosophie de l'Université).

Wallerand, Gaston 1934. "Henri Bate de Malines et Saint Thomas d'Aquin" in: *Revue néo-scolastique de philosophie*, vol. 41, pp. 387-411.

Westman, Robert S. 1980. "The Astronomer's Role in the Sixteenth Century: A Preliminary Survey" in: *History of Science*, vol. 18, pp. 105-147.

Wetzer, Ton 2017. "Ghemert, Gerlacus de", *Bossche Encyclopedie*, retrieved 12 July 2017: http://www.bossche-encyclopedie.nl/personen/ghemert,%20gerlacus%20de.htm.

Wickersheimer, Ernest 1936. *Dictionnaire biographique des médecins en France au Moyen Age*, 2 vols. (Abbeville: F. Paillart/Paris: Droz).

Yamamoto, Keiji; Burnett, Charles 2000. *Abū Maʿsar on Historical Astrology: The Book of Religions and Dynasties (On the Great Conjunctions)* [*De magnis coniunctionibus*], 2 vols. (Boston/Leiden: Brill).

determinare magis parum et convenientius ad sequencia palã q̃
fiet ex hiis que infrascribentur. sequitur cum via sensus memorie
et experiencie que principia scientiarum nobis cognita fiunt nos dirigat ad idem ascendens nativitatis ad quod superiorem philosophiam
documenta nos appulerunt ut sic ex omnimoda concordia utriusq̃ consi-
deratam pretciorum speculario sciuiram in eligacione exhibeat funda-
buntur cum dei adiutorio et firmabimus gradum ascendentem radicis
nativitatis ex unanimi quaesicionis quam veram intendebamus.
Alia vero ponendo ascitia nequaquam possunt evenire et accidencia
supranotatam disposicionem supra celestia et philosophorum doctrinam concordari
ponamus ergo in nomine dei figuram nativitatis secundum dei gloriose secundum longitudinem et latitudinem episcopi malachim infra tabulas ascensionum eiusdem loci nec non et loca planetarum super
eundem locum nec non et loca planetarum super eundem locum
ultima examinacione verificata et correcta secundum equaciones
ptolomei et super observaciones suas et nostras. placuit autem
tamen in correctione tabularum radicibus equacionum uti a
mathematicis pragmaticorum omissis que principiis philosophie
naturalis concedant cuiusmodi himur diversos in comento
super methaphisicam et alibi f. saluando apparentia eccentricoq̃
et epicicloru per quosdam motus polorum orbium secundum ipsa
core nititur alpetragius in sua astrologia in possibilis apparuit
cum illa que centrica apparent in superioribus per potentia
pluralitatis ordinis et multiplicium motuum polorum ut finiuit philosophus in
secundo methaphisice sine eccentricis et epiciclis alii saluaverim propter difficultatem tamen operis et prolixitatem eius malebam secundum
viam mathematicorum in motibus cum necesse haberem eos sequi
in iudiciis ut si in motibus errare contingat in caput ipsorum
redundet error ex quo doctrinam suam imitamur sed unde sunt
venit prius ponamus nam figura nativitatis etiam figura coniunctionis solis et lune precedentis propter maiorem operis perfectionem et consimiliter ponemus figuras revolucionum annorum
secundum q̃ necesse fuerit et alia simili modo quaq̃ indigebimus.
In hiis ergo omnibus protestor me aut parum aut nichil de meo positurum sed quantum fidelius potero philosophorum iudicia et
non mea preconizabo.

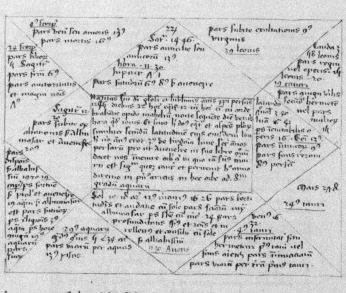

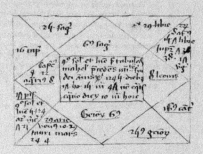

"Liber de revolutionibus nativitatum. Liber Servi Dei de Mechlinia super inquisitione et verificatione nativitatis incerte"
Bibliothèque nationale de France, Latin 10270 folio 143v.

Unc tempus est ut ad
annorum reuolutiones perueniamus natiuitatis date
Nam ut dicit alhumasar in libro reuolutionum annorum natiuita
tum si feuerimus dispositiones figurarum que sunt in natiui
tatis principio et ne feuerimus eas que sunt in reuolutione
non poterimus diligenter aut distincte distinire significationes
earum et quoniam de reuolutionibus annorum preteritorum
satis dictum est supra quantum necesse erat propter anim
dauium iudiciorum ad rebus seusatis super optimu reuoluere
annii presentem et conuenienter alios futuros Reuolationis
autem anni presentis qui est tricesimusquintus a natiuitate
hec est figura·

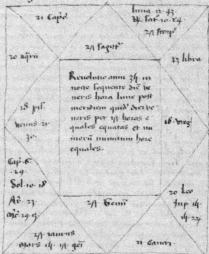

21 Cape⸳   luna·12·43·
                              ♃ ♈ 10·24·
                                 2/ scorp⸳
            2/ sagit⸳
20 aquri⸳   13 libra

       Reuolutio anni 34· in
       nocte sequente die ue
       neris hora lune post
   18 pis⸳ meridiem quid dicit ue
   ueriius 21· neris per 1/1 horas e
       30·   quales equatas et nu
            meru sumatum hore
            equales·
   Cap·6·
   ·29·
   Sol·10·18·   20 Leo
   Asc⸳ 23·   Jup 14·
   mercurius 29·15·   2/ Gemi   14·27·
       2/ taurus
    Mars 14· 1/1 qui⸳   21 Cancri⸳

Cum igitur in reuolutionibus annorum natiuitatum multa
requirantur consideranda ut patet per alhumasar et per
hispanum abraham et aueuezre et hispalensi de hiis tractatus
ponamus quidam ad presens illa cu passione ut pro indice sit

napantibus mercurio et saturno cum suis dispositionibus supradictis. Rursum requirito domum anni ex nonenariis secundum opinionem indorum hoc anno nos perducit ad venerem sic ipsa domina primi nonenarii signi libre ad quod annus applicuit ut igitur ad vivum sit dicere summa prosperitatis veneri tribuamus qua hunc annum sigillavimus.

venus 2. 2.
luna 2. 4
4° tauri
24 mc. 24. 24
Caput 4 pis
pis 21   29 Aquarii
Sol 10. 18. aries

13. Get.

Mars 22. 22
8° aquarii

figura revolutionis
anni que die solis
ante meridiem per-
nam horam equalem
et 11 aÿ hore et 30

20 Cancri

20 Cape

8 leonis

Jupi 19. 0. 2t°
21 Vginis

Sat 22. 28.
24
19. sagit.

29 leonis

4 scorpii

Deinde quidem revolutionis figura sexti anni prosperitatem significare videntur et alacritatem secundum q testantur sapientes unde bonu in fine precedentis anni insinuatum continuationem recipiet testante albumasar in prima quarta huius anni propter presentium significationem inter alias et angulum medii celi promissa namque prosperitas in radice se quidem promissionem solis et lune ac veneris in hoc tempore videntur ostendenda super prenominatas assertiones Est in luna huius nativitatis nunc vero alsius domina in loco bono fortune et amicorum locata in gradu quidem locationis sue anita lunc nunc et numero suo in coniunctione cum venere simul cum mutua receptione ambarum in domo ac exaltatione ac duodenario veneris atque cum bona dispositione utriusque

"Liber de revolutionibus nativitatum. Liber Servi Dei de Mechlinia super inquisitione et verificatione nativitatis incerte"
Bibliothèque nationale de France, Latin 10270 folio 175r.

Nativitas Magistri Henrici Baten

Edidit Carlos Steel
Auxiliantibus Steven Vanden Broecke, David Juste et Shlomo Sela

CONSPECTUS SIGLORUM

P = cod. Parisinus, Bibliothèque nationale de France, lat. 7324: saec XIV²
S = cod. Segovensis, Archivo y Biblioteca de la Catedral, B 349 (84): saec XV²
V = cod. Venetus, Biblioteca Nazionale Marciana, lat. VI.108 (2555): saec. XV²

Rarius citantur:
L = cod. Hispalensis, Biblioteca Capitular y Colombina, 5-1-38: saec XV exeunte
M = cod. Monacensis, Bayerische Staatsbibliothek, Clm 3857: saec. XIII exeunte
Par = cod. Parisinus, Bibliothèque nationale de France, lat. 10270: saec. XV exeunte

In appendice II:
Lm = cod. Lemovicensis, Bibliothèque municipale, 9 (28): saec. XV
Lp = cod. Lipsiensis, Universitätsbibliothek, 1466: saec. XIV medio

ABBREVIATIONES

add. : addidimus, -idit
codd.: codices omnes (*PSV*)
coni. : coniecimus
corr. : correximus, correxit, correctio
del. : delevimus, -vit
ed. : editio fontis allegati
exp. : expunxit
hab.: habet, -unt
inv. : invertit, -erunt
iter.: iteravit
lac.: lacuna
mg.: margine
om.: omisit, omiserunt
praem. : praemisit, -miserunt
ras. : rasura
rest. : restituit, restituerunt
scr. : scripsimus
s.l : super lineam
s.v. : super verbum
transp. : transposuit, -suerunt

< > : uncis acutis indicantur verba ab editore suppleta
[ ] : uncis quadratis indicantur verba ab editore deleta

NATIVITAS
Magistri Henrici Baten

1. \<Prooemium\>

5 | Quoniam, ut testatur **Philosophus** Politicorum 3°, P24v S1r V113r *fere quidem plurimi sunt iudices praui de propriis* ; unusquisque enim naturali amoris affectu ad se ipsum inclinatur ; *amor* autem *et odium prohibent procedere recta iudicia* iuxta **Ptolomeum** 12° uerbo Centilogii ; *non enim eadem uidentur amantibus et odientibus,*
10 secundum quod uult **Philosophus** 2° Rhetoricorum, *neque iratis et mansuete se habentibus, sed aut omnino altera aut secundum magnitudinem altera ; amanti quidem enim eum de quo facit iudicium aut non iniustum fecisse aut secundum parua iniustum fecisse, odienti autem contrarium ;* itaque *passionibus commoti differunt ad iudicia ;* unde
15 *medici egrotantes inducunt ad se ipsos alios medicos tamquam non potentes iudicare quod uerum, quia iudicant de propriis, et in passionibus existentes ;* eapropter memetipsum iudicaturus de propriis inquam accidentibus et euentibus timeo ne prauus iudex inueniar et iniustus ; quocirca inducam ad meipsum alios
20 iudices, puta philosophos ueritatis amatores cum sententiis suis et iudiciis scripto commendatis. Iudiciis quidem enim et *legibus que secundum litteras non adest quod passionale omnino,* sicut testatur **Philosophus** 3° Politicorum. Hac igitur conditione infor-

---

1   NATIVITAS...Baten] natiuitas magistri Henrici [...] Macliensis cum quibusdam reuolutionibus *mg. P²* liber Henrici Baten cantoris Leodiensis de natiuitate propria *mg. S titulum non hab. V* liber serui Dei de Mechlinia de ducatu Brabantie super inquisitione et uerificatione natiuitatis incerte ex indiciis ac subsequentibus nato post natiuitatem *Par. De titulo vide introductionem 1.2.3*   7 naturali] naturalis *P*   8 12°] 33° *PV*   10 neque] uidelicet *V* | neque...habentibus] *om. S*   13 non] *om. S* | iniustum¹] iniuste *PV*   14 differunt...egrotantes] *mg. P* 15 potentes] pretereuntes *P*   16 quod] quid *V* | uerum] est *add. P*   19 quocirca inducam] quo certa iudicia *S*   21 enim] autem *P om. V*   23 igitur] *om. V*

---

6 fere...propriis] Arist., *Polit.* III 9, trans. Guilelmi, 1280a15-16 | 7 amor...9 Centilogii] Ps.-Ptol., *Cent.*, trans. graeco-latina, v. 12 | 9 non...14 contrarium] Arist., *Rhet.* II 1, trans. Guilelmi, 1377b31-1378a3 | 14 passionibus...iudicia] Arist., *Rhet.* II 1, trans. Guilelmi, 1378a20-21 | 15 medici...17 existentes] Arist., *Polit.* III 16, trans. Guilelmi, 1287a41-b3 | 21 legibus ...23 Politicorum] Arist., *Polit.* III 15, trans. Guilelmi, 1286a15 et 17-18

matus astrologie pretorium aggredi temptabo, natiuitatis proprie et reuolutionum eius negotium alterius extranei fore repu-   25
tando ; officium uero iudicis, nec amore nec odio nec propter
aliquam passionem declinantis a recto, philosophorum sibi
assumat auctoritas, in quorum uestigia, quanto fidelius potero,
pedes collocare curabo, si deus uoluerit.

2. <Inventio ascendentis nati>

Et quia presentis negotii tota uis radicatur in habenda   30
cum certitudine hora natiuitatis proposite serui inquam Dei
gloriosi et sublimis, principaliter hoc uenari intendens nutu Dei
examinaui caram matrem, cuius anima nunc et in perpetuum
uiuat cum beatis, que omni occasione circumscripta passionem
inducente horam natiuitatis euenisse affirmauit cum discretione   35
circa mediam noctem, immo potius post mediam noctem
sequentem diem Veneris septimane sequentis mediam quadra-
gesimam, hoc est nocte diei Veneris precedentis <domini-
cam>, que erat ante dominicam in ramis palmarum secundum
modum uerborum eius, anno Domini 1245 secundum compu-   40
tationem ecclesie usualem, que datum annorum non innouat
antequam in cereo pascali innouetur secundum consuetudinem
patrie nostre. Consimilem quoque examinationem et inquisitionem feci ab illis que partui interfuerunt mulieribus de nostro
sanguine necnon et a nutricibus meis quibus per multa signa   45
credendum erat, que omnes in die conuenerunt et hora, quod
circa mediam noctem accidisset et post mediam noctem potius
quam ante, parum tamen ualde.

De anno etiam concordate sunt omnes pariter, quod post
illum siue citra non poterat accidisse, quod et ego ipse propter   50
S1v | multa que longum esset enarrare certum habeo. At uero

---

24 aggredi] ingredi *S*   25 reuolutionum] reuolutionem *P* | extranei] *om. PV*
reputando] deputando *P*   27 recto] ratione *S*   31 serui] summi *PV* | Dei
gloriosi] *inv. S*   34 circumscripta] conscripta *S* | passionem] -ne *PV*   35 indu-
cente] iudicante *PV* | euenisse] inuenisse *PV*   36 mediam²] *om. S*   37 mediam]
noctem mediam *add. S*   38   dominicam] *add.* Guldentops (dominica ante
dominicam in Palmis, i.e. dominica 'Iudica')   41 datum] datam *PV* | innouat]
innouauit *S*   43 quoque] que *S*   44 que] qui *S*   45 et] *om. P*   46 conuenerunt]
conueniunt *V*   47 mediam¹] *om. S.*   49 omnes] *ante* concordate *trsp. S* pariter
s.l. add. sed del. S | quod] *om. S*   50 citra] circa *PV* | et] *om. PV*

quod ante predictum annum non euenerit hec natiuitas nec
possibile fuerit ipsam euenisse, palam est per natiuitatem sororis ex eadem matre, que nata fuit in festo beati Martini hiemali
55   post mortem illustris uiri Wal. Bertoldi domini Machlinie apud
fratres minores sepulti in Machlinia, in qua et proposita natiuitas euenit quasi circa medium ipsius opidi. Obiit autem predictus uir nobilis in ramis palmarum 4° idus Aprilis, ut patet in
epitaphio tumbe sue, anno Domini 1243 secundum computa-
60   tionem ecclesie supra tactam. Et quod natiuitas sororis fuerit
tempore nominato, probauit uxor auunculi, que uix per duos
menses nupta iam fuerat eidem, cum mortem subiit nobilis uir
prenominatus, que postea in festo sancti Martini hiemali ma-
trina sororis effecta, ipsam de sacro fonte leuauerat, matre hoc
65   idem ueraciter confirmante et absque omni dubio cum uni-
formi testimonio aliarum et multorum credendi fide dignorum.
Cum igitur impossibile sit a tempore natiuitatis sororis infra 5
menses immediate sequentes partum uite aptum eandem
matrem   edidisse,   de   necessitate   sequitur   natiuitatem
70   propositam post annum reuolutum accidisse et hoc est tempus
ante positum. Insuper adiecit dilecta mater bone memorie
quod in gestatione nati propositi | uterus eius uix in tantum   V113v
intumescebat quod notaretur fuisse grauida. Vnde quidam
amicus suus, qui secum in uespere precedente noctem partus
75   confabulatus fuerat, cognito puerperio stupefactus fuit, cum
ipsam grauidam fuisse non notasset. Mensem autem et diem
natiuitatis quam pre manibus habemus reuoluendo tabulas
compotistarum deprehendimus fuisse Martium, decimo uideli-
cet Kalendas Aprilis. Hec ergo sunt | illa in quibus radicem   P25r
80   negotii presentis inserere dignum duxi.

Hiis uero prelibatis ad artem inueniendi cum precisione
natiuitatis date gradum ascendentis ex hora estimationis ueritati

---

54 beati] *om. PV*   55   Wal *scr.*] aval *S* W. *PV* | Machlinie *scr.*] michlinie *S*
mahcl'm *P* mahelium *V*   56 Machlinia] *scr.*] mehlia *S* mahclinia *P* mahelima *V*
et] *om. PV*   57 quasi] *om. S* | ipsius] *om. S*   60 fuerit] fuit *S*   61 nominato] *om.*
PV   62 mortem] iam *add. V*   63 sancti] *om. PV*   65 cum] *om. P*   66 credendi]
certitudine *S*   67 igitur] ergo *V*   68 partum…aptum] *om. S*   73 notaretur]
uocaretur *PV*   74 noctem] nocte *P*   76 notasset] uocasset *PV*   77 reuoluen-
do…compotistarum] *om. S*   78 deprehendimus] comprehendimus *S* | uidelicet]
scilicet *V om. P*   82 date] dicte *PV* | ascendentis] -tem *S*

propinqua accessimus in hunc modum. Dimisso annimodar
Ptolomei ab auctoritatibus improbato, licet ueritati ex parte
consonum per nos aliquando sit inuentum, ad trutinam **Her-**   85
metis, qui et **Enoch,** confugimus iuxta consilium **Abrahe**
cognomine **Principis** et **Ptolomei** in CENTILOGIO 51 propositione et **Albumasar** in SADAN necnon et reliquorum et precipue **Abrahe Auenezre** in suo LIBRO DE NATIVITATE corri-
gentis ibidem et uerificantis pretactam trutinam siue annimodar   90
Hermetis. Hec igitur trutina siue annimodar, cui nullus philosophorum contradicit, talis est quod *gradus Lune in hora concep-*
tionis est ascendens in hora natiuitatis, et e contrario gradus Lune in hora
natiuitatis erat ascendens in conceptione. Et huic correspondent
diuerse more fetus in utero materno secundum diuersam   95
situationem Lune in hiis duobus temporibus. Nam, ut testantur
philosophi supra nominati cum aliis non nominatis hic, si in
conceptione Luna fuerit supra terram, in natiuitate eiusdem
sub terra erit et e conuerso non fuit in ascendente, quia tunc ad
eundem locum | regreditur. Vnde ex hiis contingit mora media,   100
maxima et minima et alie que sunt inter istas, secundum quod
auctores in suis tractatibus sufficienter explanauerunt et in hoc
omnes concordati sunt. Hee autem more correctionem et
uerificationem recipiunt interdum sub aliquo equipollenti iuxta
testimonium **Auenezre** in libro supra tacto necnon et alterius 105
Abrahe cognomine **Principis** in suo DE ELECTIONIBVS tractatu. Potest enim tempus harum morarum anticipari propter
Venerem et Mercurium, ut scilicet alter illorum sit in gradu illo,
in quem ingressura est Luna hora natiuitatis, habens utique in

S2v (margin, next to line 100)

---

86   qui] Hermetis qui *S* | Abrahe] et *add. S*   89   Libro] *post* Natiuitate *trsp. S*
90   ibidem et] *inv. S*   91   igitur] ergo *V*   94   erat] est *P* | correspondent] -det *S*
99   erit] *om. S* | non] nisi *PV* | fuit] fuerit *PV*   100   contingit] constat *S* | media]
et *add. P*   104   equipollenti] equiuallenti *S*   105   in…suo] *om. S*   107   enim] a' *V*
harum] istarum *P* | morarum] horarum *S*   108   illorum] ipsorum *S* | illo…110
gradu] *om. S*   109   quem] quo *P*

---

83 annimodar…84 Ptolomei] Ptol., *Quad.* III.2, sig. c8vb-d1ra | 85
ad…86 Enoch] De fontibus dictae trutinae Hermetis vide Sela 2014, pp. 42-43
| 86 iuxta…87 Principis] Ibn Ezra, *Liber Electionum*, fol. 41v:17-42r:4 | 87
Ptolomei…propositione] Ps.-Ptol., *Cent.*, v. 51 | 88 Albumasar…Sadan]
Sadan, *Excerpta* 23, p. 317 | precipue…91 Hermetis] Ibn Ezra, *Moladot*, II 4, 5,
pp. 92-93. De trutina Hermetis vide Sela 2017a | 91 Hec…94 conceptione]
Ibn Ezra, *Moladot*, II 5, 1, pp. 92-93 | 103 Hee…104 equipollenti] Ibn Ezra,
Moladot, II 6, 3-6, pp. 94-95 | 106 Abrahe…117 exaltatione] Ibn Ezra, *Liber*
Electionum, fol. 42r:6-14. Vide Sela, "Trutina Hermetis"

110 eodem gradu dignitatem aliquam, et Luna ipsum gradum aspiciat aspectu quarto sinistro, ita uidelicet quod post 7 dies uel circiter Luna peruenire debet ad eundem gradum, cum hoc quod tunc mora integraliter debeat compleri, quia tunc antici-patur mora illa per 7 dies uel circiter propter Venerem uel
115 Mercurium supplentes Lune uices. Consimili quoque modo facit Mars cum fuerit in aliqua domorum suarum aut in exaltatione.

Hee sunt equationes annimodar **Hermetis** quas ponunt **Auenezre** et magister suus **Princeps Abraham**. Sed cum in
120 natiuitate data nec Venus nec Mercurius nec similiter Mars in tali fuerint habitudine, necesse erat trutinam ipsam assumi secundum quod ab **Hermete** posita est. Equauimus ergo Lunam ad horam estimatam, scilicet ad mediam noctem predictam, et inuenimus cum Dei adiutorio Lunam supra terram
125 circa angulum occidentalem in 17 gr. Geminorum, ratione cuius moram accipiendo minimam, scilicet 259 dierum, retro-cessimus ad horam conceptionis posito ascendente in 17 gr. Geminorum, et reperimus locum Lune 12 gr. 20 min. Sagittarii. Et quoniam in natiuitate supposita Luna circa angulum occi-
130 dentis reperta est, ubi predicte more maximam diuersitatem recipiunt in tempore modico, ut de inuentione gradus ascen-dentis maiorem fiduciam acquireremus, temptauimus quid nobis emergeret si mora maxima uteremur. Cui cum intende-remus, emersit nobis contrarium illius quod supponit hic
135 **Hermetis** trutina. Hac enim uia incedentes inuenimus in conceptione locum Lune 18 gr. 9 min. Sagittarii et latitudinem eius meridianam quasi 5 gr. ; quapropter sub terra tunc erat ratione latitudinis, ut patet intuenti, 17° gr. Geminorum tunc ascendente. In mora autem maxima secundum auctores Luna
140 ponitur in conceptione super terram et in natiuitate subtus, cuius contrarium hic accideret secundum hanc uiam. Qua de

---

110 aspiciat] aspic' *PV*   111 uidelicet] *om. S*   113 debeat] gradus *add. P*   114 uel Mercurium] et Mercurium *mg. P*   116 fuerit] fuit *S* | suarum] *om. S*   120 nec³] neque *S*   121   fuerint] sunt *PV* | habitudine] habitatione *S*   122 secundum…est] scilicet ab hermete composita *S* | Equauimus] equabimus *S* | ergo] igitur *P*   124   inuenimus] eam *add. P* | Lunam] *om. P*   125 occidentalem] occidentali et *S*   126 scilicet] *om. PV*   127 in] *om. PV* | gr] *om. P*   133 cum] *om. S*   135 incedentes] intendentes *S* | inuenimus in] *om. S*   136 locum Lune] *om. S*   137 eius] *om. P*   138 tunc] *om. PV*   139 auctores] doctores autores *S*

causa pertransito huius scrupulo ulterius hanc examinaui
moram subtrahendo diem unum ab hac maxima ad sciendum
si fortassis hora natiuitatis | fuerit post mediam noctem per
horam integram et amplius ; per quem modum in conceptione   145
inueni locum Lune 1 gr. 38 min. Capricorni. Quo posito pro
ascendente accidentia nati et euentus eufortuniorum et infortuniorum nullatenus concordare poteram huic stellarum dispositioni. Quamobrem dimissis moris maioribus duabus securius
esse uidetur ut mora minima contenti sumus. Nam hac con-   150
cessa ita quod secundum ipsam ascendens natiuitatis radicetur
et sit cum omni equatione 12 gr. 20 min. Sagittarii, non erit in
hoc magna differentia ab annimodar **Ptolomei**. Secundum
Ptolomeum enim deberet Sol esse in gradu anguli terre, cum
in coniunctione precedente hanc natiuitatem Sol fuerit prepo-   155
tentior in ipso gradu coniunctionis Lune cum Sole. Vnde
differentia inter **Hermetem** et **Ptolomeum** in hoc proposito |
uix ascenderet ad 8 min. hore.

Rursum iuxta artem **Messehallah** quam refert **Auenezre**
in secunda parte LIBRI RATIONUM : cum in natiuitate *masculi*   160
tempus esse debeat *in hora impari* totaque parte illius hore im-
paris, quota est *dies natiuitatis* eiusdem *a die coniunctionis seu*
preuentionis precedentis faciendo proportionem de numero
illorum dierum ad numerum dierum qui sunt inter coniunctionem et oppositionem, quod est 15 aut circiter, erit differen-   165
tia hore per supra dictam moram minimam inuente a tempore
arti **Messehallah** correspondenti uix 12 minutorum hore aut
parum plus, ita quod tempus nostrum secundum annimodar
Hermetis inuentum per moram minimam quasi in medio erit

V114r (margin, line 144)
S2v (margin, line 157)

---

142 ulterius] alterius *S*   143 sciendum] studendum *S*   144 mediam] *om. PV*
145 et] *om. S*   146 1…min] 1.38 V   148 huic *scr.*] huius *codd.* | stellarum] *om. V*
dispositioni *scr.*] dispositionem *codd.*   150 uidetur] uidentur *PV* | Nam] nati *PV*
153 magna differentia] *iter. S*   154 gradu anguli] angulo *S*   155 coniunctione]
precedente *praem. P*   161 imparis] *om. PV*   164 illorum dierum] illarum partium
V   167 arti *scr.*] artis *PSV*   169 erit inter] et intra *S*

---

153 ab…156 Sole] Cf. Ptol., *Quad.* III 3 | 159 Rursum…165 circiter] Ibn
Ezra, *Ṭeʿamim II*, §6.1:1, pp. 234-235, quod Bate sic interpretatus est: "Inquit
sapiens qui uocatus est Messehallach quod semper nascetur masculus in hora
impari et femella in hora pari. (…) Dicit eciam quod secundum distanciam diei
natiuitatis a die coniunctionis aut opposicionis que erat in principio ante
natiuitatem erit numerus minutorum hore" (MS Leipzig 1466, fol. 57vb:18-24).
Forte Bate etiam usus est tractatu ab ipso Messahallah facto

170 inter tempus quod annimodar **Ptolomei** correspondet et arti
Messehallah, que tamen ars, licet aliquando uera reperiatur,
aliquando etiam erronea est et defectiua, ut habetur | in LIBRO P25v
RATIONUM. Possibile est enim in eadem hora siue pari siue
impari ab una matre partum edi masculum et ab altera femel-
175 lam. Quapropter in arte **Messehallah** non est prorsus confidendum. Annimodar uero **Ptolomei** adheret **Auicenna** in suo
LIBRO NATIVITATUM. Vidi autem in quodam libro NATIVITA-
TUM relato ad quendam **Iudeum Abraham** scriptum sic :
consentio Hermeti in hoc quod locus Lune in conceptione erit oriens in
180 *natiuitate semper ; contingit uero si prope natiuitatem, scilicet 7 uel 5 dies*
ante natiuitatem, alius planeta quam Saturnus obtinuerit gradum orien-
tem in conceptione ibique potestatem habens Lunam uel ex quadrato uel
ex opposito respexerit, exhibit partus citius tempore prefinito.

Sed hiis dictis non uidetur esse omnino fides adhibenda,
185 tum quia utrique **Abrahe** superius nominatis, quos auctor illius
libri nititur imitari, aliter uisum erat, et rationabilius, nec est
huiusmodi sententia per omnia concors auctoritati et rationi
illorum ex quibus iste sua dicta extraxit, tum quia inconside-
ratus est sermo eius et incautus. Luna enim gradum aspiciens
190 ex opposito infra 5 dies uel 7 attingere non potest eundem,
immo infra 14 dies ad minus. Est igitur ille contrarius sibi ipsi,
unde de dicto eius non est multum curandum. Et dato quod
uerum diceret, nihil tamen propositum nostrum impediret.
Denique uero dicit **Albumasar** in SADAN quod *in omni natiui-*
195 *tate ubi est Luna in* tempore *conceptionis, ibi est ascendens gradualiter*
in tempore partus uel differentia usque ad gradus 5 plus aut minus. Si
autem equas horoscopum per artem conceptionis, et discordet Luna

---

170 quod] *om. S*   171 tamen] cum *P* | ars] arti *P* artis *S* | reperiatur] reperiam *P*
173 siue[1]] seu *S* | siue[2]] seu *S*   174 masculum] masculinum *S*   178 relato]
relatum *S*   182 ibique] ubique *V*   183 ex] *om. S* | respexerit] despexit *S*
respexit *V* | citius] prius *P*   184 esse omnino] *inv. PV* | adhibenda] habenda *P*
185 tum] tamen *P* | nominatis] nominati *P*   187 rationi] rationem *P*
188 quibus] quo *S*   191 immo] *om. S* | igitur] ergo *V*   194 uero] non *S*
195 est[2]] in *S*   197 artem] gradum *ed.* (*sed* artem *VM*) | Luna] locus *ed.* (*sed* luna
VM)

---

172 ut…173 rationum Vide supra ad l. 159-165 | 176 Annimodar…177
Nativitatum] In Nativitate 'Avicenna' semper designat Albohali, *De nativitatibus*,
sed in illo libro non disputatur de annimodar | 179 consentio…183 prefinito]
Ibn Ezra, *De nativitatibus*, sig. a2v: 21-25 | 194 in[2]…198 errasti] Sadan,
Excerpta 19, p. 312

conceptionis ab oriente *partus* siue horoscopo, *scias quod errasti.*
Vnde non immerito uocata est Luna a poetis Diana seu Phebe,
dea partus et Lucina. Ipsius enim influentia et quadam singulari   200
uirtutis prerogatiua regulantur fetuum gestationes et partus
secundum quod testatur **Philosophus** 4° DE GENERATIONE
ANIMALIUM. Quod autem dicit **Albumasar** 5 graduum differentiam plus aut minus in hoc documento posse contingere,
hoc dicit propter motum Lune diuersum tum ratione equatio-   205
nis nunc addende, nunc subtrahende, tum etiam ratione latitudinis ipsius Lune. Trutina namque **Hermetis** tradita est sub
motu Lune medio, ut per ipsum uerus motus inueniatur, quemadmodum facit **Albumasar** in LIBRO CONIUNCTIONUM differentia prima tractatus primi de inuentione coniunctionum   210
Saturni et Iouis. Hoc enim modo docet **Hermannus** in fine
LIBRI COGITATIONUM ET RERUM ABSCONDITARUM inuenire
oriens conceptionis et partus per statum rectum et non rectum,
ut per non rectum, idest medium, ad rectum, idest equatum,
deueniamus. Et quia huiusmodi negotium hoc nostrum trans-   215
cendit propositum, alibi forsan conabimur hoc cum diligentia
declarare. Hoc autem nobis ad presens sufficiat quod supra
dictis documentis coacti philosophicis moram minimam |
accipiendo secundum uerum motum Lune, necesse uidemur
habere ut ponamus ascendens natiuitatis cum omni precisione   220
12 gr. 20 min. Sagittarii. Nam, posito loco Lune | in natiuitate,
qui est 17 gr. Geminorum, pro ascendente conceptionis, erat
locus Lune in conceptione 12 gr. 20 min. Sagittarii precise. Sed
quoniam experientia ueritatis exigit ut conueniat rebus sensatis,
considerauimus accidentia serui Dei gloriosi et euentus   225
eufortuniorum eius et infortuniorum, que nulla tergiuersatione

S3r (margin, line 218)

V114v (margin, line 221)

198 partus] partus est *add. S*   201 uirtutis prerogatiua] *inv. S*   202 4°] 5° *PV*
203 5...differentiam] differentiam 5 graduum *S* | graduum] gradus *P*   205 dicit]
om. P | tum] *s.l. S* cum *PV*   206 nunc[1]] *om. S* | tum *scr.*] tunc *S* cum *PV*
208 motus *scr. cum Par.*] locus *PSV*   211 modo] *om. S*   213 non] per non *P*
214 idest equatum] *om. S*   215 huiusmodi...propositum] *om. V*   216 hoc] licet
S   217 quod] ut *S*   219 necesse...223 Lune] *iter. V*   223 precise] *om. PV*
224 ueritatis] necessitatis *P*   225 accidentia] ad *praem. PV*

199 uocata...200 Lucina] Conradus de Mure, *Fabularius*, p. 368:474 et 490 |
200 Ipsius...203 animalium] Arist., *De gen. an.* IV 10, trans. Guilelmi, 777b24-27
| 203 Albumasar...204 contingere] Sadan, *Excerpta* 19, p. 312 | 209
Albumasar...211 Iouis] Albumasar, *De magnis coniunctionibus*, I.1 (vol. 2, p. 9:106-
107) | 211 Hermannus...215 deueniamus] non invenimus

celari possunt aut dissimulari, ut sic ueritas magis comprobetur. Hec est enim uia uocata a posteriori, que innata est nobis iuxta **Philosophum**, ut per effectus nobis notos de causis magis
230 certificemur inter ipsa conuenientiam reperientes euidentem. Et hoc est documentum nobis traditum ab antiquis super electione facienda illi cuius natiuitas ignoratur, secundum quod refert **Haly** in ELECTIONIBVS suis, cui etiam consentit **Abraham** in LIBRO REVOLUTIONVM ANNORUM MUNDI loquens de
235 inuentione constellationum ciuitatum. Consimiliter quoque faciunt alii sapientes. Primum igitur occurrit illud dictum care matris de modica uentris intumescentia et uix notabili, per quod mora minor fetus in utero materno rationabilius probari uidetur et concludi quam maior uel maxima. Arbitrandum est
240 enim fetum minoris temporis minorem esse quam maioris ceteris paribus accidentibusque extraneis circumscriptis. Item 21° etatis anno infirmatus est hic seruus Dei gloriosi graui dissinteria. Supposito autem ascendente more minime, secundum quod positum est, si a loco hyleg, prout inferius liquide
245 patebit, retrorsum fiat directio, ut docent auctores, peruenit hoc anno ad Martem, qui latitudinem habet septentrionalem in natiuitate peruenitque signum profectionis ad domum Martis. Et eodem anno percurrebat Saturnus ipsum gradum hyleg in signo Geminorum, quod egritudinem sanguineam significare
250 habet, ut dicit **Auenezre** in INITIO SAPIENTIE. Saturnus etiam dissinteriam significat, secundum quod testatur **Ptolomeus** 3°

---

227 sic] sit *V*   228 Hec] *om. V* | est enim] *inv. V* | uocata] nota *S* | innata] inuenta *in ras. P*   232 electione] electionem P | illi cuius] alicuius *P*   235 ciuitatum] ciuitatem *S* | quoque] autem P   236 igitur] ergo *V* | illud dictum] *inv. P* 238 mora minor] *inv. P*   239 uel] seu *S*   240 enim] *om. P*   241 Item] iterum *S* 245 auctores] doc (*del.*) actores *V* | peruenit] peruenitur *P*   247 profectionis] perfectionis *V* | ad] id S   251 3°] in 3° *P*

---

228 Hec…230 euidentem] Cf. Arist., *An. post.* II 15 | 231 Et…233 suis] Haly Embrani, *De electionibus horarum*, p. 329: "omnes astrologi concordati sunt nemini sit eligendum cuius natiuitas ignota sit, quod mihi non uidetur congruum. | 233 Abraham…235 ciuitatum] Cf. Ibn Ezra, ʿ*Olam I*, §38:1-24, pp. 76-79, ubi inueniuntur tabulae constellationum ciuitatum. Vide etiam ʿ*Olam II*, §15:24-25, pp. 166-167, sed textus ille non fuit translatus ab Henrico | 249 signo…250 Sapientie] Ibn Ezra, *Reshit Ḥokhmah*, §2.3:23, pp. 74-75. Ibn Ezra, *Commencement*, p. 39: "Et ses maladies si sont la maladie de quoi on chiet en desoute de quoi en ne se prent garde", quod Bate sic interpretatus est: "egritudines eius sunt omnes ex sanguine" (MS Leipzig 1466, fol. 5ra:6-7) | 250 Saturnus…252 14] Ptol., *Quad.* III 14, trans. Guilelmi, p. 262:816-817

QUADRIPARTITI capitulo 14. In Geminis quoque Saturnus infirmitates uentris causare habet, nec est Martis significatio ab huiusmodi malo diuersa.

Item in reuolutione eiusdem anni fuit Luna in uia com- 255
busta in gradu ascendentis qui abscidit super Lunam cum est
hyleg. Vnde **Albumasar** : *si in ascendente reuolutionis fuerit Luna,
languebit periculoso languore* ; et iterum : *quoniam Saturnus fuit in
opposito augis sui ecentrici, causabat huiusmodi egritudinem per solutio-*
P26r *nem uentris*, secundum quod testatur **Auenezre** et alii. | Rursum 260
cum perueniret directio supra dicta ad Aldebaran, oculum
scilicet Tauri, qui est de natura Martis, et signum profectionis
ad partem mortis in Scorpione, infirmatus est iterum natus iste
consimili dissinteria, sed non tam periculosa, 24° etatis anno,
tempore scilicet quo Mars partem mortis percurreret. Adhuc, 265
cum perueniret directio supra tacta ad locum Pleyadum in
Tauro, que oculorum infirmitates significant, et Mars hoc
anno, scilicet 30°, ad ascendens perueniret, ad locum Sagittarii,
qui consimiliter oculorum passiones significat, passus est natus
egritudinem oculorum grauissimam, obtalmiam. Amplius 270
secundum directionem a gradu medii celi factam ad sciendum
promotiones nati ad dignitates, cum perueniret directio a termino quidem Mercurii ad principium 12^i gradus Scorpionis, in
quo etiam incipit terminus Mercurii, qui dominus est triplicitatis lunaris, cuius est auctoritas, anno scilicet nati 28°, in 275
cuius reuolutione Mercurius, qui prepotentiam in figura natiuitatis habebat, in angulo medii celi locatus erat, tempore equidem quo Iupiter, dominus ascendentis, qui in radice natiuitatis
angulum medii celi consimiliter amplectabatur, in termino
Mercurii existens, nunc partem fortune sibi associaret, collatum 280

---

253 Martis significatio] *inu.* S   255   in^1] *om.* V   257   reuolutionis] *om.* PV
258   quoniam] quando V   259   huiusmodi] hanc P hic V   260   alii] alibi S
263   mortis]] Martis V | infirmatus] infortunatus V   264 consimili dissinteria]
inu. P   265 tempore scilicet] temporis PV | mortis] Martis V | Adhuc] ad hoc
PV   266 cum] omni P | tacta] dicta PV   267 que] qui P | significant] signant S
268 ad^2 *scr.*] ut S ubi PV | Sagittarii] sagitte PV   269 qui] que S | consimiliter]
cum similiter P | passiones...oculorum] *iter.* V | significat] inuenit *add.* S
273 quidem] quodam PV   277 habebat...natiuitatis] *om.* S   279 consimiliter]
post natiuitatis *trsp.* P

---

257 si...258 languore] Albumasar, *De revol.*, p. 274a:43-45 | 258
quoniam...260 Auenezre] Ibn Ezra, *Moladot*, III II 5, 1, pp. 124-125

| est primum beneficium huic nato seruo Dei ab illustri prin-
cipe Martiali propter Scorpionem. Est enim natus hic Martia-
libus familiaris. Nam Scorpio sibi est domus amicorum. Signa
autem dominorum suorum significationes gerunt, ut uolunt
285   philosophi. Adhuc autem 30° etatis anno est colloquium habitum super secundo beneficio et pinguiori et collatio eius confirmata ab eodem principe. Nam potestatem suam super hoc,
ad opus scilicet serui Dei, tradidit specialiter cuidam uiro Martiali, puta militi, a quo idem collatum est beneficium eidem
290   seruo Dei anno sequenti in fine Maii. Consimiliter quoque in
reuolutione 30^i anni redibat idem ascendens cum reliquis domibus quod in radice natiuitatis. Vnde in CAPITULIS ALMANSORIS
fortunabitur eritque boni esse ille cuius annus reuolutionis similis fuerit
radici etc. Item **Albumasar** in LIBRO REVOLUTIONUM AN-
295   NORUM NATIVITATUM: *intensibiliores autem operationes fiunt quando*
concordabuntur figure reuolutionis *figuris initii natiuitatis.* Et resti-
tutus est Saturnus in angulo medii celi, quemadmodum in
natiuitate, quod secundum **Albumasar** in LIBRO REVOLUTIO-
V115r   NUM NATIVITATUM ipsum natum *a dignitate producit ad*
dignitatem. Restitutio etiam Solis in signum exaltationis sue huic
non contradicit, sed in reuolutione sequentis anni, cum signum
profectionis egrederetur domum sextam et intraret septimam
natiuitatis fieretque dominus anni Mercurius, qui prerogatiuam
in natiuitate habuit, et adhuc staret directio a gradu medii celi
305   facta secundum circulum directum a termino quidem Mercurii
iterato in termino eiusdem, item et directio a parte fortune
attingeret gradum Solis in natiuitate et reuolutione et peruenisset Iupiter ad ascendens reuolutionis anni diametrizans
Saturnum angularem in signo exaltationis sue, complementum
310   recepit promotionis huius negotium hora qua peruenit Mercurius ad signum profectionis. Hii autem euentus huiusmodi
constellationum ex dictis **Albumasar** in libro suo DE REVOLU-

---

283 sibi est] *inv. S*   285 philosophi] plurimi P | Adhuc] ad hoc P*V*   286 secun-
do] secundario *S* | cius] quasi *S*   287 potestatem] potentiam P   288 tradidit
specialiter] *inv. S*   290 Dei] *om. S*   291 idem] eidem P*V*   292 Almansoris *scr.*]
Amansor PS*V*   293 fuerit] fuit *S*   295 intensibiliores] sublimiores P   297 est]
om. S   300 etiam] enim *S*   302 intraret] incurerent *S*   304 staret] statim *V*
305 quidem…termino] *om. S*   307 gradum] gradus P

---

293 fortunabitur…294 etc] *Capitula Almansoris*, c. 64, sig. 121rb | 295
intensibiliores…296 natiuitas] Albumasar, *De revol.*, p. 258a:6-9 | 299 a…300
dignitatem] Albumasar, *De revol.*, p. 273b:25-26

TIONIBVS ANNORUM NATIVITATUM et ex dictis aliorum liquide
comprobantur. Turbationes autem uarie et difficultates in hac
promotione inciderunt, quod satis innuebatur per retrograda-   315
tionem Saturni et Iouis in radice natiuitatis et per oppositum
Iouis aspectum et Saturni in reuolutione. Porro significata sunt
impedimenta aliqua in 35° nati huius anno nunc instante et
ingresso, in cuius reuolutione peruenit Saturnus ad gradum
ascendentem in natiuitate fere Luna complete ipsum gradum   320
attingente. Iupiter autem, quia in hac reuolutione Saturnum
aspicit et Lunam aspectu trino secundum gradus equales, licet
cadat ab angulo, uidetur impedimenta ista per hoc aliqualiter
alleuiare. Hoc tamen anno iam ingresso passus est natus apostema in maxilla et faucibus satis nociuum cum estu febrili.   325
Ascendens enim super ea que sunt capitis significationem
habet, Luna autem inimica ascendenti est et Saturnus etiam
ledit ipsum, ut testantur philosophi. Nam Saturnus egritudi-
nosus est, et quod *ascendens super caput significationem habeat*, dicit
Auenezre in LIBRO NATIVITATUM cum auctoritate **Messehal-**   330
lah se expertum esse. **Albumasar** quoque dicit idem in SA-
DAN, et similiter **Hermes** teste **Abraham Compilatore** in
LIBRO NATIVITATUM, adhuc et in libro DE IVDICIO VRINE NON
VISE idem affirmatur. Sed de hiis et aliis supra tactis cum
sufficientia determinare magis pertinet et conuenientius ad   335
sequentia palamque fiet ex hiis que infra scribentur. Igitur, cum
uia sensus, memorie et experientie, qua principia scientiarum
nobis cognita fiunt, nos dirigat ad idem ascendens natiuitatis,
ad quod supra tacta philosophica documenta nos compulerunt,

---

314 comprobantur] comprobatur *P* | hac promotione] hanc promotionem *PV*
315 inciderunt] incidunt *V* | innuebatur] inueniebatur *PV*   317 Saturni] Sa-
turno *P*   318 aliqua] *om. S* | 35° *scr.*]25° *S* 31° *PV* | anno] anis *ante* nati *trsp. S*
nunc] unde *V om. P*   319 peruenit Saturnus] per Saturnum *S*   322 aspectu
trino] *inv. S*   323 uidetur] uidentur *V*   324 apostema] ap'a *V*   325 nociuum
cum] nocumentum *V*   327 etiam] *om. S*   329 habeat] habet *S*   330 cum...333
natiuitatum] *om. S*   333 adhuc] ad hoc *SV* | et] quod *S*   334 Sed...hiis] *sup. l. S*
et] etiam de *S* | tactis] dictis *PV* 335 determinare magis] *inv. S*   336 palamque]
palam *S*   337 scientiarum] scientie *S*   338 dirigat] dirigant *S*

---

328 Nam...331 esse]] Ibn Ezra, *Moladot*, III VI 10, 3, pp. 154-155 | 331
Albumasar...Sadan] Bate 'Arietem' pro 'Saturnum' accipit: vide Sadan, *Excerpta*
5, p. 301 | 332 et...333 natiuitatum] Ibn Ezra, *De nativitatibus*, sig. b6a:8-9 |
333 et...334 affirmatur] Guillelmus Anglicus, *De urina non visa*, c.4, p. 148 |
337 uia...338 fiunt] Cf. Arist., *An. post.* II 15

340 ut sic ex omnimoda concordia omniquaque considerata preteritorum speculatio futurorum inuestigationem exhibeat, funda-
bimus cum Dei adiutorio et firmabimus gradum ascendentem
radicis natiuitatis ex unanimi conuenientia, quam uenari inten-
debamus. | Alia enim ponendo ascendentia nequaquam pos-   P26v
345 sunt euentus et accidentia supra notata dispositioni supracelesti
et philosophorum doctrine concordari.

3. <Figura nativitatis>

Ponamus igitur in nomine Domini figuram natiuitatis | s4r
serui Dei gloriosi secundum longitudinem et latitudinem opidi
Machliniensis iuxta tabulas ascensionum eiusdem loci necnon
350 et loca planetarum super eundem locum ultima examinatione
uerificata et correcta secundum equationes **Ptolomei** et super
obseruationes suas et nostras. Placuit autem mihi in correctione tabularum radicibus equationum uti a mathematicis
imaginatarum, omissis illis que principiis philosophie naturalis
355 concordant, cuiusmodi innuit **Auerroes** in COMMENTO SVPER
METAPHYSICAM et alibi, scilicet saluando apparentiam ecentri-
corum et epiciclorum per quosdam motus polorum orbium,
secundum quod facere nititur **Alpetragius** in sua ASTROLOGIA.
Nam licet huiusmodi astrologia mihi possibilis apparuerit, cum
360 ea que magis extranea apparent in superioribus per positionem
pluralitatis orbium et multiplicium motuum polorum, ut innuit
Philosophus in 12° METAPHYSICE, sine ecentricis et epiciclis
aliquando saluauerim, propter difficultatem tamen operis et
prolixitatem eius malebam sequi uiam mathematicorum in
365 motibus, cum necesse haberem eos sequi in iudiciis, ut, si in

---

340 omniquaque] omniaque *S* omnisque *p. corr. P*   341 speculatio] speculo *S*
342 gradum ascendentem] gradus ascendente *P*   344 ponendo] ponenda *S*
345 notata] dicta *S* | dispositioni] disponi *P* disponunt *S*   347 Ponamus]
notamus *S* | igitur] ergo *V*   349 Machliniensis] mach'niensis *P* mechchilini *S*
mahelm' *V* | necnon…locum] *iter. V*   352 autem] *om. S* | mihi] tamen *V*
354 naturalis] *om. S*   355 cuiusmodi] cuius *S*   356 Metaphysicam]
mathematicam *PS* | ecentricorum] centricorum *S*   359 Nam…astrologia] *om.*
SV   360 magis] *om. PV*   361 multiplicium motuum] mult'em motum *S*
362 ecentricis] centris *S*

---

355 Auerroes…356 Metaphysicam] Averroes, *In Metaph.* XII, c. 45, 329H-M |
358 Alpetragius…Astrologia] Cf. Alpetragius, *De motibus celorum* | 360 per…-
362 Metaphysice] Cf. Arist., *Metaph.* XII 8, 1073b1 sqq

motibus errare contingat, in caput ipsorum redundet error, ex quo doctrinam suam imitamur. Sed unde sermo uenit, prius ponamus cum figura natiuitatis etiam figuram conunctionis Solis et Lune precedentis propter maiorem operis perfectionem, et consimiliter ponemus figuras reuolutionum annorum, secundum quod necesse fuerit, et alia simili modo quorum indigebimus. In hiis ergo omnibus protestor me aut parum aut nihil de meo positurum, sed quanto fidelius potero, philosophorum iudicia, et non mea, preconizabo. |

370

V115v

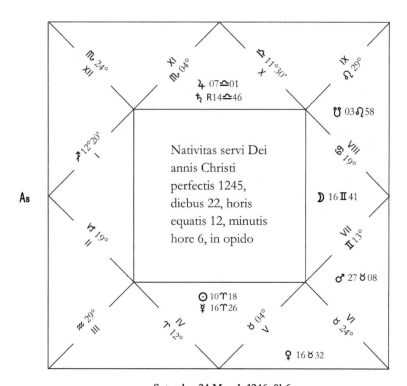

Saturday 24 March 1246, 0h6

Natiuitas serui Dei gloriosi et sublimis annis Christi perfectis 1245, diebus 22, horis equatis 12, minutis hore 6, in corde Brabantie opido Machliniensi, nocte sequente diem

375

---

367 prius] primo S   370 consimiliter] cum similiter P   372 ergo] igitur P | aut] ut P   376 equatis] equalibus LMP   377 corde] om. S | Machliniensi] scr. Melchini S Machn' LMP Mahelin' VPar | horis] om. S

Veneris, hora quidem Iouis. Et sunt hic domus equate et aspectus planetarum similiter secundum latitudinem eiusdem
380 loci. Hic uero annus erat 3us de firdaria Lune secundum annos Persarum, prout **Auenezre** in suo LIBRO CONIUNCTIONUM docet eos inuenire ; orbis autem in quo iam sumus Mercurii est, signum quoque Cancri, et peruenit hoc anno directio a principio Arietis in hoc orbe ad 8um gradum Aquarii.

385 **I.** Sagittarii 12.20 ; pars subite exaltationis secundum **Albumasar** et **Auenezre** 20us.

II. Capricorni 19 ; pars desponsationis secundum **Alkabitium** 19.20 ; pars fortune secundum **Ptolomeum** et **Auenezre** 19 Aquarii ; secundum **Albumasar** est pars futurorum ; pars
390 religionis 13 Aquarii ; pars hore coniugii 19 Aquarii ; pars seruorum.

III. Aquarii 29 ; Sol 10.18 ; gradus coniunctionis Solis 5.34 Arietis ; pars uiarum per aquas 13 Piscium.

IV. Sol 10.18 ; Arietis 12 ; Mercurius 16.26 ; pars
395 fortitudinis et audacie cum Sole ; pars scientiarum iuxta **Albumasar** ; pars substantie cum Mercurio 24 ; pars

---

379 eiusdem] eius *praem. Par* 380 uero] autem *S* | annus] *iter. S* | firdaria] firidaria *S et sic semper* 382 eos] nos *Par* | iam] *s.l. S* | Mercurii] iam *add. sed del. S* 383 Cancri] orbis *praem. S* | hoc] in *praem. M* | a] in *Par* 384 Aquarii] natiuitas nocturna *add. a. m. S* 387 desponsationis] dispositionis *LMPParV* Alkabitium] Alcabicium *P* Alkabissium *ParV* Alkarabitium *S (et sic etim in l. 398)* 389 secundum] uero *add. P* | pars^2...Aquarii] *ante* pars fortune *trsp. S* 390 13] tertius *LMPParV* | pars seruorum] *om. S* pars seruorum 19 15 *mg. P* seruorum *om. L* 392 Aquarii 29] 19 Aquarii *M* | Solis] *om. LMPParV* 393 5.34] 5.24 *P* Piscium] piscis *LPParV* 394 Sol 1018] *del. L expectes in fine domus tertiae* pars...Sole] *om. S* | pars...396 24] *om. L* 396 pars^1...Mercurio] *post* 16.26 *S* cum Mercurio] *om. M* | cum...pars] et *M*

---

380 firdaria...382 inuenire] Ibn Ezra, ʿOlam I, §23:1, pp. 66-67, quod Bate sic interpretatus est: "Dicunt autem Persarum sapientes quod semper aduertendum est ad partes firidarie" (MS Leipzig 1466, fol. 26vb35-36) | 385 pars...386 Auenezre] Albumasar, *Introductorium maius*, VIII.4 (vol. 8, p. 163: 528-529); Ibn Ezra, *Reshit Ḥokhmah*, §9.13:6, pp. 250-252: see Sela, 2017, appendix 5 | 387 pars...Alkabitium] Cf. Alcabitius, *Introd.*, V.10, p. 354 : "Septima domus. Pars desponsationis virorum accipitur in die et nocte a Sole in Venerem, et proicitur ab ascendente" | 388 pars...Auenezre] Ptol., *Quad.* IV 2, trans. Guilelmi, pp. 278:25-26; Ibn Ezra, *Reshit Ḥokhmah*, §9.1:2-7, pp. 234-235 | 389 secundum...futurorum] Albumasar, *Introductorium maius*, VIII.3 (vol. 8, p. 153:155-172) | 395 pars...396 Albumasar] Albumasar, *Introductorium maius*, VIII.4 (vol. 8, p. 162:493-498) | 396 pars^2...398 Alkabitium] Cf. Alcabitius, *Introd.*, V.16, p. 357: " Pars rationis et profunditatis sensus accipitur in die a Saturno in Lunam, et in nocte e converso, et proicitur ab ascendente"

profunditatis sensus et rationis et intellectus et consilii cum
Sole secundum **Alkabitium**.

V. Tauri 4 ; Venus 16.32 ; pars infirmitatum secundum
Hermetem primus Tauri uel finis Arietis; pars inimicitiarum ;   400
pars uiarum per terram primus Tauri.

VI. Tauri 24 ; Mars 27.8.

VII. Geminorum 13 ; latitudo septentrionalis 3.40 ; Luna
16.41 ; pars ineuitabilis operis 16 ; pars inimicorum 9 ; pars
finis rerum 8 perfecti.   405

VIII. Cancri 19 ; Cauda 3.58 Leonis ; pars regni uel operis
15 Leonis ; pars coniugii uirilis secundum **Hermetem** uel pars
mulierum 15.

IX. Leonis 29 ; pars subite exaltationis 9us Virginis.

X. Libre 11.30 ; Saturnus 14.46 retrogradus; pars amicitie   410
seu amicorum 13 ; Iupiter 7.1 retrogradus ; pars futurorum
gradus 8us secundum **Auenezre**.

XI. Scorpionis 4 ; pars Veneris seu amoris 13 ; pars mortis
16.

XII. Scorpionis 24 ; pars filiorum 5 Sagittarii ; pars   415
fratrum 6 ; pars auctoritatis et magni nominis 7.

397 et[1]] *om. S* | rationis…Alkabitium] intellectus 24 *M* (s*ed infra figuram add.* pars
rationis et intellectus et et consilii cum Sole secundum Alkabitium)
398 Alkabitium] 11 Arietis *add. Par* 399 Venus 1632] *ante* Tauri *LMPParV*
1632] 16.31 *P* 61.32 *L* | infirmitatum] -tatis *LMP* -tat' *ParV* 400 pars
inimicitiarum] *om. M* 402 27.8] 27 *LMP* 403 latitudo…3.40] *post* Luna 16.41
(*more solito) transp. LP om. M* 404 16.41] 16.42 *S* 406 19] 20 *superscr. SV post*
Leonis[2] *add. M* | Leonis] *om. LP* | uel] seu *P* | operis] pars *praem. S* 407 15
Leonis] *om. P perperam ut longitudinem posuit S post* Leonis *add.* 20 (*pro* 15 ?)
MSParV | uirilis] uniuersi *L* 408 mulierum] mulieris *S* in Cancro *add. L*
410 retrogradus] *om. M* | amicitie seu] *om. P* 411 7.1]7 *P* | retrogradus] *om.*
MParV 412 gradus 8us] 6us gradus *LP* 413 seu] siue *S* 414 16] 6 *S*
415 Sagittarii] *om. S*

399 pars…400 Hermetem] Albumasar, *Introductorium maius*, VIII.4 (vol. 8, p.
159:388-391) "secundum Hermetem" | 406 pars…operis] cf. Albumasar,
Introductorium maius, VIII.4 (vol. 8, p. 163:536-538): "pars regis atque operis nati"
| 407 pars[1]…Hermetem] Albumasar, *Introductorium maius*, VIII.4 (vol. 8, p.
160:407-409) "secundum Hermetem" | 411 pars…412 Auenezre] Ibn Ezra,
Reshit Ḥokhmah, §9.2:1-4, pp. 234-235.

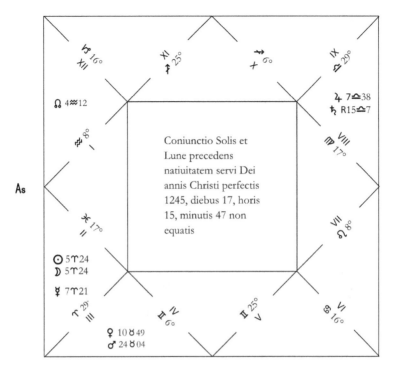

Coniunctio Solis et Lune precedens natiuitatem servi Dei annis Christi perfectis 1245, diebus 17, horis 15, minutis 47 non equatis

Monday 19 March 1246, 3h47

Coniunctio Solis et Lune secundum tabulas Machlinienses precedens natiuitatem serui Dei annis Christi perfectis 1245, diebus 17, horis 15, minutis 47 non equatis. Equatio dierum 10 min. hore. Ascensiones 338.47.

I. 8 Aquarii ; Caput (Draconis) 4.12

II. 17 Piscium ; coniunctio Solis et Lune 5.24 Arietis ; Mercurius 7.21

III. 29 Arietis ; Venus 10.49 Tauri ; Mars 24.4

IV. 6 Geminorum

V. 25 Geminorum

VI 16 Cancri

420

425

417 Machlinienses *scr.*] Marchialenses *P* Machel' *L* Malch' *M* Mahel' *VPar* Mechli' *S* 420 Ascensiones 338.47] *add. S deest in ceteris codd.* 421 I...7.21] *domus I et II vacuae in S* | Caput *scr.*] cap' *LParV* cap^r *M* capricorni *P* | 4.12] 4 *P om. M* 422 5.24] 5.34 *M* 2.24 *L* | Arietis] *om. P* 423 7.21] 21 *P* 424 29 Arietis] *om. S* 10.49] 10.40 *M* | Tauri] in Tauro *post* Venus *P* | 24.4] 24.40 *L* 24 *P* 425 Geminorum...428 Leonis] *domus IV-V-VI-VII vacuae in S*

VII. 8 Leonis
VIII. 17 Virginis ; Saturnus retrogradus 15.7 Libre ;
Iupiter 7.38   430
   IX. 29 Libre
   X. 6 Sagittarii
   XI. 25 Sagittarii
   XII. 16 Capricorni

   <Tabulae>

   Latitudo Saturni septentrionalis 2 gr. 54 min. 56   435
   latitudo Iouis septentrionalis 2 gr. 6.52
   latitudo Martis septentrionalis 0.26.40
   latitudo Veneris septentrionalis 0.27.30
   latitudo Mercurii meridiana 0.52.7
   latitudo Lune septentrionalis 3 gr. 40 min.   440
   [Ascensiones gradus ascendentis 280 gr. 44 min.
correspondentes 12 gr. 20 min. Sagittarii
   Equatio dierum 12 min. hore]

V116r | Aspectus Solis equati:
   sextilis 23 Tauri (ante 19 Capricorni)   445
   quartus 11 Geminorum (ante 11 Sagittarii)
   trinus 19 Cancri (ante 23 Scorpionis)

   Aspectus Lune equate:
   sextilis 3 Virginis (ante 6 Tauri)
   quartus 15 Libre (ante 15 Arietis)   450
   trinus 6 Scorpionis (ante 3 Piscium)

   Aspectus Saturni equati:
   sextilis 25 Scorpionis (ante 24 Cancri)
   quartus 16 Sagittarii (ante 6 Geminorum)
   trinus 24 Capricorni (ante 25 Tauri))   455

429 17] 27 *M* | 17 Virginis] *om. S* | 15.7] 15 *S*   432 6…434 Capricorni] *domus*
X-XI-XII vacuae in S   435 gr] et *add. M* | 56] secunda *add. LMP*   436 6.52] 6
min. 52 secunda *LMP*   437 0.26.40] *an erronee pro* 0.56.40 ?   438 0.27.30] *an*
erronee pro 0.57.30?   439 meridiana] meridionalis *S*   441 Ascensiones…443
hore] *haec additio sola invenitur in codd. L(partim legibili) P et M* | 44 min] *inv. M*
442 gr] et *add. M*   445 23] 26.49 *S* | ante…Capricorni] *in serie aspectuum gradus*
constellationis quae directionem ante indicat solum invenitur in LPParV et sic deinceps ; ante
seriem aspectuum "post" *pos. M*   446 ante] 2us *S*   448 equate] *om. M et sic deinceps*

Aspectus Iouis equati :
sextilis 22 Scorpionis (ante 16 Cancri)
quartus 11 Sagittarii (ante 11 Geminorum
trinus 16 Capricorni (ante 22 Tauri)

460 Aspectus Martis equati:
sextilis 27 Cancri (ante 17 Arietis)
quartus 6 Virginis (ante 6 Piscium)
trinus 17 Libre. (ante 27 Capricorni)

Aspectus Veneris equati:
465 sextilis 6 Cancri (ante 22 Piscium)
quartus 14 Leonis (ante 14 Aquarii)
trinus 12 Virginis (ante 6 Capricorni)

Aspectus Mercurii equati:
sextilis 26 Tauri (ante 26 Capricorni)
470 quartus 15 Geminorum (ante 15 Sagittarii)
trinus 26 Cancri (ante 26 Scorpionis)

In duodenario Martis:
principium domus 2^e Solis
principium domus 3^e Saturni
475 principium domus 4^e Solis
principium domus 6^e Mercurii
principium domus 7^e Veneris
principium domus 5^e Lune
principium domus 6^e Saturni
480 principium domus 8^e Saturni
principium domus 10^e Saturni
principium domus 12^e Solis

Saturnus in duodenario Iouis
Iupiter in duodenario proprio
485 Mars in duodenario Iouis
Sol in duodenario proprio
Venus in duodenario Martis
Mercurius in duodenario Veneris
Luna in duodenario Iouis

458 11^1] 29 *S*   459 Tauri *scr.*] Cancri *LPParV*   472 In duodenario] duodenarie
S post 2^e Solis *LPParV Hoc titulum et omnia quae sequuntur usque ad* "12^e Solis"
(482) *desunt in M*

Ad tempus natiuitatis huius hii auges et centra et media et　490
argumenta
 Aux Saturni 8.11.47.9
 aux Iouis 5.24.2.9
 aux Martis 4.14.53.9
 aux Solis et Veneris 2.28.50.9　　　　　　　　　　　　495
 aux Mercurii 6.26.45.9
 Centrum Saturni 9.26.34.10
 centrum Iouis 0.14.29.39
 centrum Martis 10.2.52.47
 centrum Veneris 9.9.31.9　　　　　　　　　　　　　500
 centrum Mercurii 5.11.36.9
 Argumentum Saturni 5.29.59.59
 argumentum Iouis 5.29.49.30
 argumentum Martis 9.22.35.22
 argumentum Veneris 3.3.44.7　　　　　　　　　　　　505
 argumentum Mercurii 1.1.25.33
 argumentum Lune 7.25.56.22
 Medius Saturni 6.8.21.19
 medius Iouis 6.8.31.48
 medius Martis 2.15.45.56　　　　　　　　　　　　　510
 medius Solis 0.8.21.18
 medius Lune 2.9.55.48
 medius Capitis 1.26.2.16
 medius Mercurii et Veneris idem cum Sole.
 Centrum 9.27.52.7　　　　　　　　　　　　　　　515
 centrum non equatum 0.13.0.25
 minuta proportionalia 5.9
 argumentum equatum 5.1.18.44
 equatio argumenti min. 0.0.19.22
 equatio argumenti : addere 00.51.30　　　　　　　　520

---

490 Ad tempus] *omnia quae sequntur usque ad* "argumentum Mercurii" (506) *desunt*
in M Saturnus retrogradus, Iupiter retrogradus, Mars directus, Venus directa,
Mercurius directus, Luna tarda cursu *hab.* M | hii auges] *om. LPParV* | et[2]] *om.*
LPParV　493　5.24.2.9] 9.24.2.9 *S*　494　4.14.53.9] 4.12.53.9 *P* 4.29.53.9 *S*
502　Saturni] *om. S*　507　argumentum...7255622] *om.* L | Lune] *om. S*
7.25.56.22] 7.27.56.22 L　508　6.8.21.19] Medius Saturni 6.9.29.16 *add. S*
509　6.8.31.48] Medius Iouis 6.8.17.3 *add. S*　510　medius...2.15.45.56] *om.*
LPParV　511　medius] motus *add.* M | 0.8.21.18] 0.8.0.21 M　512　medius]
motus *add.* M　514　medius...Sole] *om.* M　515　Centrum] *quae sequuntur abhinc*
usque ad l. 529 solum in S inveniuntur

pars longioris min. 0.0.59
pars longioris : addere 2.8
uerus Saturni 6.16.10.26
uerus Iouis 6.6.24.11
525   equatio centri : addere 0.59.39.32
centrum equatum 10.3.23.4.30
omne 9.14.14.54
equatio circa meridianum 0.1.14.29

uerus locus Solis 0.10.22.45 (sign., gr., min., sec.)

4. <Iudicium nativitatis>

4.1. <Introductio ad vitam nati>

530 | Supposita quidem igitur celestium armonia natiuitatis S5r proposite, prout superius est uenata, afferamus nunc secundum ipsam philosophorum iudicia, per que huiusmodi constellationis nati accidentia et euentus nobis innotescant. Verum quia natus hic iam est adultus, superfluum uideretur si testimonia
535   nutritionis ad presens inquireremus. Omissis illis igitur uideamus quid dicant philosophi super uita natiuitatis huius. Et quoniam nocturna fuit hec presens natiuitas, primo respeximus Lunam, que, cum fuerit in angulo occidentali in domo Mercurii, aspecta ab eodem, et secundum equationem domorum et
540   secundum gradus equales apta fuit ut esset hyleg administrans nato uitam. Preterea dicit **Hermes** in FLORIBVS suis et similiter **Albumasar** in SADAN quod *Sol et Luna post Deum omnium uiuentium uita sunt ; multorum quidem natiuitates hyleg non habent, sed quia Sol et Luna ascendens* | *eorum ex dilectione aspiciunt eodem libero* V116v
545   *existente eorum uita diutius elongatur.* In natiuitate autem proposita Sol angularis est et cum hoc ex dilectione ascendens aspicit, nec est hoc inconueniens. Licet enim huiusmodi aspectus secundum equationes domorum sit quartus, secundum gradus tamen equales est trinus. Vnde **Auenezre** in LIBRO NATIVI-

---

530 igitur] *om. S* 532 per] *om. S* | huiusmodi] huiuscemodi *V* 535 illis igitur] ergo illis *V* 538 fuerit] fuerat *P* fuit *S* 539 aspecta] respecta *S* 543 uita] uitam *S* 544 libero] libro *P* 546 ascendens aspicit] *inv. P*

---

542 Sol...545 elongatur] Hermes, *Cent.*, v. 1., sig. 117ra; Sadan, *Excerpta* 1, p. 297

TATUM, capitulo de domo tertia uersus finem, loquitur de *do-*   550
mino tertie domus, secundum quod fuerit *in aliquo angulorum ascen-*
densque aspexerit aspectu amicitie. Sol igitur in proposito gradum
ascendentem aspiciens uitam confirmat. Vnde **Ptolomeus**, 2°
QUADRIPARTITI, capitulo 9°, *Sol quidem enim et Luna ordinatores et*
quasi presides sunt aliorum, cum sint ipsi causa eius quod secundum   555
actum totius et dominationis astrorum et adhuc fortitudinis et debilitatis
dominantium. Item **Albumasar**, 4° INTRODVCTORII, capitulo 5°,
summa mundi fortuna Sol est, post hunc Luna.

Item ex quo luminaria tante uirtutis sunt in administrando
uitam, ut testantur auctores, mutuus aspectus ipsorum ad   560
inuicem, ut est in proposito, tanto magis ipsam corroborat.
Dicit enim **Auenezre** in suo LIBRO ELECTIONUM quod *omnes*
aspectus Solis ad Lunam boni sunt quia lumen suum a Sole recipit.
Idem quoque ait in LIBRO NATIVITATUM : *scito quod aspectus Solis*
ad Lunam siue sextilis siue trinus aut quartus melior est quam aspectus   565
Iouis et Veneris. Quamuis enim ambe infortunate coniuncte essent Lune,
fortitudo aspectus Solis impedimenta repelleret ambarum. Rursum in 9
IVDICUM : firmissimum itaque *receptionis genus inter Solem et Lu-*
nam deprehenditur. Vndelibet enim et de omnibus signis tamquam coniugem et sororem eam recipit et benignitatis sue   570
gaudio illustrat. Preterea si Luna non esset hic hyleg, Sol tamen
P28v   aspectus esset adhuc, ut cum hoc esset alkocoden, etiam si |
non aspiceretur ab aliquo, cum sit in exaltatione sua, aspicitur
tamen hic a dominis triplicitatis et consimiliter a Marte domino
domus in qua est Sol aspectu sextili secundum distinctionem   575

---

551   aliquo angulorum] *inv. V*   553   ascendentem] ascendens *P* as. *V*
confirmat] afirmat *S*   555 eius] et *add. S*   556 et²] *om. S*   564 scito] sucita *S*
565 siue sextilis] *om. S*   567 repelleret] repellet *P*   568 receptionis] recessionis *P*
569 Vndelibet] unum *S* | et] *om. S*   570 eam] cum *S*   571 Preterea...hyleg] *om.*
S | tamen] cum *P*   572 aspectus] aptus *S* | adhuc *scr.*] ad h' *codd.*   574 tamen]
cum *P* | hic] hoc *PV* | dominis] domino *P* | consimiliter] *om. S* | a Marte]
amare *S* | Marte] et *add. P*

---

550 domino...552 amicitie] Ibn Ezra, *Moladot*, III III 4, 9, pp. 134-135 | 554
Sol...557 dominantium] Ptol., *Quad.* II 9, trans. Guilelmi, pp. 217:520-218:523
| 558 summa...Luna] Albumasar, *Introductorium maius*, IV.5 (vol. 8, p. 64:327) |
562 omnes...563 recipit] Ibn Ezra, *Mivharim II*, §1.5:3, pp. 152-153: "The same
applies if the Lord of the third place is in one of the cardines, has its power, and
is in trine with the Lord of the ascendant sign" | 564 scito...567 ambarum]
Ibn Ezra, *Moladot*, III VI 11, 4, pp. 154-155 | 568 receptionis...569
deprehenditur] *Liber novem iudicum*, A.98: "Amplius receptionis genus inter
Solem et Lunam deprehentitur [sic]" (MS Vat. lat. 6766, fol. 6ra:34-35).

domorum ; propter quod non modicum confert Sol ad uitam in proposito. Vnde **Abraham Princeps** et **Iohannes Hispalensis** in suis tractatibus NATIVITATUM : *quanto plures fuerint significatores uite, hyleg scilicet et alkocoden, tanto diuturnior erit uita* et
580 natus magis sospes erit et incolumis in corpore et animo. Item in CAPITULIS ALMANSORIS : *ex multis uite significatoribus in alhyleg significatur uita longa et purus intellectus maximeque uigor.*

Quoniam uero supra dictum est Lunam esse aptam hyleg, ratione pretacta consideremus an eius hylegia annullari debeat
585 propter sui alkocoden combustionem. Mercurius enim nondum egressus est hic complete terminum combustionis secundum equationes nostras. Consentit autem in hoc tota cohors astrologorum unanimiter quod planeta combustus, tamquam uirtute et dominatione priuatus, alkocoden seu predominator
590 esse non potest. Aut intelligendum hoc ubique uerum esse preterquam in Leone et Ariete : ibi enim receptio impedimentum combustionis restaurat et recompensat. Nam ut uult **Auenezre** in LIBRO RATIONUM, 2ª particula, *ob hoc quod operatio stelle non | apparet, cum fuerit Sol supra terram, ideo dixerunt astrologi*
595 *fortitudinem non habere stellam que est coniuncta Soli. Hebetat enim Sol* hoc modo *effectus astrorum*, ut dicit **Albumasar** in SADAN : *si non extiterit Sol in Leone uel Ariete*, et licet Sol per coniunctionem *omnino* sit *maleficus, quando* tamen *est in Leone et Ariete, non nocet, quia Sol* lumine suo *dominatur reliquis astris et assimilatur regi.*
600 *Quando igitur* rex *fuerit in sua regione aut in proprio palatio, predominatur omnibus,* et congaudens eis confortat omnes qui secum

S5v

576 propter…proposito] *om., sed mg. rest.* P¹   578 fuerint] fuerunt S
579 diuturnior] diuturnorum P -iorum V   581 significatoribus] signatoribus S
in²] et in S   582 significatur] significator S | maximeque] maximusque *ed.*
584 debeat] debe't S 586 egressus] ingressus V | est hic] *ante* egressus P
589 predominator] dominator S   590 Aut] ad S | ubique] *om.* V
592 combustionis] *om.* S   600 igitur] ergo S | in²] *om.* V 601 omnibus] *om.* S
confortat *scr.*] confortantur *codd.*

577 Iohannes Hispalensis] Cf. Iohannes Hispalensis, *Epitome*, sig. H4v:16-21 |
578 quanto…580 animo] Ibn Ezra, *Liber nativitatum*, fol. 58v:28-29 | 581
ex…582 uigor] *Capitula Almansoris*, c. 10, sig. 120va | 593 ob…595 Soli] Ibn
Ezra, *Te'amim II*, §4.1:3, pp. 206-207, quod Bate sic interpretatus est: "Sane
quod stellarum non apparet virtus seu fortitudo quam diu sol est supra terram
ideo posuerunt quod non est illi fortitudo qui in coniunctione est cum sole"
(MS Leipzig 1466, fol. 53va:9-13) | 595 Hebetat…602 sunt] Sadan, *Excerpta*
15, p. 308

sunt. Vnde **Abraham Princeps** et alter **Abraham Auenezre** in suis LIBRIS NATIVITATUM et consimiliter in LIBRO ELECTIONUM **Abrahe Principis**, capitulo domus septime, et **Auenezre** in LIBRO INTERROGATIONUM et in LIBRO ELECTIONUM similiter : 605 combustio cum receptione in Leone uel Ariete non exterminat uirtutem combusti. Rursum in LIBRO 9 IVDICUM, capitulo de receptione testimoniorum eligendorum, et alibi plurisque locis, habetur quod *Solis adustio* cum receptione *non obest*. Idem quoque uult **Messehallah** in LIBRO INTERROGATIONUM : quousque 610 autem et ubicumque ledat combustio, *inter omnes* tamen *Mercurio ut consueto ac familiari Solis adustio minus grauis minimeque dum directus sit*, secundum quod testatur **Albumasar**, 7° sui IN-

V117r TRODVCTORII, capitulo 4°. | Vnde ab Hebreis uocatus est Mercurius stella Solis ; quamobrem dixit **Auenezre** in SAPIEN- 615 TIE INITIO quod *Mercurius propter copiam motuum eius et propter consuetam propinquitatem eius ad Solem iugem et naturalem, minimum ledi potest a combustione Solis. Vnde sub testimoniis antiquorum dicit quod si Mercurius fuerit Soli copulatus, duo Mercurii sunt in celo.* Idem

---

602 Auenezre] *om. S* 606 exterminat] extimat *S* 608 et alibi] *om. S* 611 ledat] ledit *S* 612 dum] cum *S* 616 motuum] motus *S* | et propter] *om. PV* 617 ad Solem] cum sole *S* 618 testimoniis] testimonio *PV* testimoniorum *add., sed del. V*

---

602 Vnde...Princeps] Ibn Ezra, *Liber nativitatum*, fol. 57r:3-6 | Abraham[2]...603 nativitatum] Ibn Ezra, *Moladot*, III X 2, 4, pp. 172-173 | 603 consimiliter...604 septime] Ibn Ezra, *Liber Electionum*, fol. 45r:9-13 | 604 Auenezre...605 interrogationum] Ibn Ezra, *She'elot II*, §10.1:1-2, pp. 383-384 | 605 Libro[2]...607 combusti] Ibn Ezra, *Mivharim II*, §10.2:1-2, pp. 172-173 | 609 Solis...obest] *Liber novem iudicum*, A.112: "Malivola item stellarum recipiens vel ab eodem recepta non obest, idem quoque nec Solis adustio nec oppositio" (MS Vat. lat. 6766, fol. 9ra:5-7) | Idem...610 interrogationum] Messahallah, *De receptione*, sig. N1v:6-8 | 611 inter...613 sit] Albumasar, *Introductorium maius*, VII.4 (vol. 8, p. 134:275-6) | 616 propter[1]...619 celo] Ibn Ezra, *Reshit Hokhmah*, §7.4:8-9, pp. 198-201. Ibn Ezra, *Commencement*, p. 101: "Et mercure, pur la plenté de ses mouvemens et que il est pres du soleil tos jors, petit le damachera quant il est desous le soleil ou desous la termine de l'arson; et quant est l'estoile enpressee avec le soleil, selonc le sens as anciens, il a grant force jusques qu'il ont dit, s'il est ainsinc en mercure, 2 mercures sont ou ciel" , quod Bate sic interpretatus est: "Mercurius uero, propter multitudinem motuum suorum et mobilitatem et quia semper propinquus est soli modicum ledi potest quando sub radiis solis est aut sub termino combustionis. Cum autem precise coniunctus est soli secundum antiquorum sententiam fortitudinem habet magnam in tantum quod dixerunt quando sic se habet Mercurius, duo Mercurii sunt in celo" (MS Leipzig 1466, sig. 17r:a39-b2)

620 quoque dicit in LIBRO RATIONUM, capitulo 6°, prima particula :
Vidi, inquit, *in libris Dorothii, qui princeps est* inter iudices, nempe
experimentatus fuerat *sermones Indorum,* qui dixit *si fuerit Mercurius
coniunctus Soli, tunc erit secundus in celo Mercurius, hoc est quia uirtus
eius duplicata est.* Amplius concordati sunt omnes quod con-
625 iunctio planete cuiuslibet cum corde Solis, quam uocant zamin,
fortunata est et fortis ; tunc autem est stella in medio combustionis. Vnde necessarium est quod stelle in corde Solis
existentis combustio, que tunc fortissima est, uirtutem eidem
non tollat. Quinimmo Sol in hac dispositione quasi receptor
630 stelle effectus uim eius aut sibi assumit aut, quod uerisimilius
est, magis corroborat et intendit. Sed postquam ita se habet res,
quid est ergo arbitrandum de Solis secretario familiarissimoque
eius camerario, cuius proprietas est et natura radios Solis frequentius et quasi iugiter peruagari? acsi ex hoc sustentamentum
635 sibi destinatum sit, uelut alteri cuidam salamandre, refocil-
lationem prebet ignis et fomentum, cum in proposita combustione sit receptus, tum ratione exaltationis, tum ratione
triplicitatis et faciei ; insuper et reministret Mercurius ipse
uirtutem termini sui, in quo ipse est, amplius et propter exitum
640 putei et ingressum eius in gradum lucidum, ut patebit infra.
Rationabile igitur uisum est et tolerabile hiis de causis Mercurium esse alkocoden et dominum uigoris, cum in proximo,
uidelicet infra diem unum, combustionem egressurus fuerit,
que tamen ipsum ibidem precipue ledere non poterat. Et re
645 uera experientia confirmat hoc quod Mercurius huiusmodi
obtineat dominium super uitam nati propositi. Nam hic natus
in principalioribus actionibus suis Mercurialis est. Accidentia

---

620 dicit] ait *S* | capitulo 6°] 6. capitulo *S* | prima particula] prime particule
PV 621 Dorothii] Doram *S* | nempe] tempore *S* 623 Mercurius] *post*
secundus *trsp. P* 628 existentis] existenti *SV* 630 stelle] *om. PV* 631 intendit]
attendit *P* incendit *S* 632 est ergo] *inv. S* 633 natura] *om. S* 638 Mercurius
ipse] *inv. S* 639 uirtutem termini] terminum *PV* 640 ut...infra] *om. PV*
642 dominum] dignum *S* 643 egressurus] ingressurus *P* 644 tamen] cum *P*

---

621 Vidi...624 est] Ibn Ezra, *Teʿamim I,* §6.2:4, pp. 86-87, quod Bate sic
interpretatus est: "Ego tamen uidi in libris Doronii qui aput nos quidem est
princeps iudicum quod ipse sermones indorum expertus erat et sic ait in libro
suo: si fuerit Mercurius coniunctus soli, tunc in celo secundus erit Mercurius
siue duplex, et hoc est dictum quia [quod *L*] duplicatur virtus eius seu forti-
tudo" (MS Leipzig 1466, fol. 70va:4-12) | 635 salamandre] De imagine
salamandrae vide *Physiologum* (versio B), c. XXX, p. 52

quoque eius et euentus ab hoc non discordant, secundum quod
superius aliqualiter tactum est et inferius palam fiet ex dicendis.
Rationabiliter quidem autem accepimus Lunam hyleg, secun-　650
dum quod supra terram est et non subtus. Omne enim quod
sub terra merito | repudiandum est ad tantum dominium
exceptis solis prodeuntibus in lucem penes ipsam eleuationem,
ut dicit **Ptolomeus,** cui consentit **Auenezre** affirmans etiam se
hoc idem expertum esse. **Dorothius** quoque uult hoc idem. Et　655
postquam gradus hyleg in quarta occidentali repertus fuerit,
necessarium est ut directio, que ab ipso fieri debet ad sciendum
esse uite, retrorsum fiat, secundum quod uoluit **Ptolomeus** et
Aomar et uterque **Abraham** cum tertio uocato **Compilatore.**
Iohannes quoque **Hispalensis** uult hoc idem in suis YSAGO-　660
GIS. Et hoc est | quod supra innuebam, cum mentionem face-
rem de directionibus ad concordandum nati accidentia cum
celesti armonia.

S6r (margin, left of line 652)

P29r (margin, left of line 661)

4.2. <Longevitas ex alkocoden>

Supposito igitur alkocoden Mercurio, datore scilicet annorum, considerauimus numerum annorum uite, quos secundum　665
dispositionem suam et habitudinem possit elargiri. Quamquam
autem dator annorum in maxima existeret dignitate sua et cum
hoc in angulo, non conferret ultra annos suos maiores, ut
uolunt omnes astrologi. Vnde **Auicenna** in suo LIBRO NATIVI-
TATUM : alkocoden in angulo existente quantum sibi defuerit de　670

648 secundum] *om. S*　653 penes] ponere *PV*　655 Dorothius] Doronius S
hoc[2]] *om. PV* | Et] *om. S*　656 repertus] receptus *PV*　658 esse] *om. P* | fiat] *om.*
PV | uoluit] uolunt P　659 uocato] notato P　664 alkocoden Mercurio] *inv. S*
665 considerauimus] considerationis P | numerum] *om. PV*　666 possit] -set
PV　667 sua] *om. PV*

651 Omne...654 Ptolomeus] Ptol., *Quad.* III.10, 4, p. 205:575-577　|
Omne...655 idem[1]] Ibn Ezra, *Moladot,* III I 8, 10, pp. 108-109　|　655
Dorothius...idem[2]] Dorothius apud Ibn Ezram in loco citato.　|　658
secundum...Ptolomeus] Ptol., *Quad.* III.10, 9, p. 209:623-625　|　659 Aomar]
Aomar, *De nativitatibus,* p. 124:10-12 | uterque Abraham] Ibn Ezra, *Moladot,* III
I 11, 1-4, pp. 114-115; Ibn Ezra, *Liber nativitatum,* fol. 59r:21-24　|
cum...Compilatore] Ibn Ezra, *De nativitatibus,* sig. a8r:26-28　|　660
Iohannes...Ysagogis] Iohannes Hispalensis, *Epitome,* sig. E2v, in margine:
"Planetae qui sunt in parte occidentali coeli, quae est a quartae usque ad
decimae initium dirigantur, secundum et contra successionem signorum".　|
669 Auicenna...672 annorum] Albohali, *De nativitatibus,* c.2, sig. b4v:24-27

aliis dignitatibus, tantum auferendum est proportionaliter a
datione annorum. Et huic uidetur consentire **Aomar. Iohannes** tamen **Hispalensis** et **Abraham Princeps** et quidam
Iudeus Abraham, non **Auenezre**, sed alter **compilator** qui-
675   dam, dicunt simpliciter quod alkocoden in angulo constitutus
dat annos maiores nisi fuerit sub luce Solis ; sed hoc est intelligendum eo modo quo supra dictum est. **Albumasar** uero in
SADAN adiudicat cuidam nato terminum uite in comparatione
| ad uitam patris et matris et aui. In LIBRO etiam REVOLU-   V117v
680   TIONUM NATIVITATUM, qui dicitur **Albumasar,** habetur consi-
mile. Et hoc idem confirmatur per utrumque **Abraham** in
principiis suorum librorum DE NATIVITATIBUS, scilicet quod
iudicia natorum debent fieri in comparatione ad parentum
conditiones. Hinc quoque est quod **Albumasar** in SADAN, cum
685   adiudicaret natiuitatem *filii regis Indorum* ponendo Saturnum
alkocoden qui erat in domo secunda in *summo retrogradationis,*
dixit ipsum dare *annos medios* propter longeuitatem Indorum,
non propter esse sui ipsius in quo erat. Dixit etiam retrogradationem Saturni ibidem *a datione annorum* nihil auferre propter
690   exitum Saturni de gradu puteali. Cum ergo parentes nati propositi satis fuerint longeui Mercuriusque sit in angulo in termino
proprio nec obsit ei combustio, ut premonstratum est, insuper
quoque egressurus sit in proximo combustionem aut iam forsan egressus secundum testimonium **Abrahe Principis** dicen-
695   tis quod Mercurius tendens ad occidentalitatem, cum distiterit a

---

671   auferendum] conferendum *V* | proportionaliter] -nabiliter *V a.corr. S*
679   uitam] uite *add. S* | aui…etiam] Auicenna etiam in libro *S*   680   habetur]
dicitur *P*   681   confirmatur] affirmatur *P*   682   scilicet] *om. V* quod *praep. S*
683   iudicia] uita *S*   684   quod] *om. S*   685   adiudicaret] iudicarent *PV*
686   retrogradationis] interrogationis *V*   687   Indorum] uite *add. mg. S*   691   lon-
geui] longe uite *P*

---

672   Aomar] Aomar, *De nativitatibus,* p. 125:44-45 | Iohannes…673
Hispalensis] Cf. Iohannes Hispalensis, *Epitome,* sig. I4r: 12 *et passi*m | 673
Abraham Princeps] Ibn Ezra, *Liber nativitatum,* fol. 58r:19-22 | 674 Iudeus
Abraham] Ibn Ezra, *De nativitatibus,* sig. a7v:25-27 | 677 Albumasar…679 aui]
Sadan, *Excerpta* 20, p. 314 | 679 In…681 consimile] Albumasar, *De revol.,* p.
217b:51-54: "scit autem e reuolutione mortui filiorum euentus. Fit enim quasi
secunda relatio post obitum patris ad filium, sicut cognoscuntur accidentia
patris ex natiuitate filli etsiamsi mortuus est" | 681 Et…684 conditiones] Ibn
Ezra, *Moladot,* II 8, 1, pp. 96-97; Ibn Ezra, *Liber nativitatum,* fol. 55r:21 | 684
Hinc…690 puteali] Sadan, *Excerpta* 21, p. 315 | 694 Abrahe…697 terminum]
Cf. Ibn Ezra, *Mishpetei ha-Mazzalot,* §29:1, pp. 512-513.

Sole 6 gradibus, ut facit in proposito, iam exiuit combustionis
terminum. Et merito! Nam ob hoc quod directus est, citius
relinquit Solem et ad maiorem tendit dignitatem quam si orientalis fieri deberet. Vnde idem **Abraham** : et semper est fortitudo duorum inferiorum, Mercurii scilicet et Veneris, maior   700
quando fuerit motus eorum uelocior motu Solis : sic autem est
in proposito. Adhuc, cum Mercurius iam exiuerit puteum et
ingressus sit gradum lucidum, si uerum est quod dicit **Albuma-**
sar in SADAN et **Auenezre** in LIBRO RATIONUM, uidelicet quod
huiusmodi gradus sunt accipiendi in octaua sphera cum stellis   705
fixis, debent autem cum motu octaue sphere rectificari, non
irrationabile uisum est ut Mercurius largiatur annos suos maiores qui sunt 76, quibus si addantur anni nutritionis 4 secundum
modum **Auenezre** in quodam exemplo natiuitatis cuiusdam ab
S6v   ipso iudicate, fiunt anni | 80. Pauciores autem annis mediis qui   710
sunt 48 dare non potest Mercurius ad presens, qui cum annis
nutritionis fiunt 52, rationabilius tamen est 80. Porro dicit
Iudeus ille *Abraham* **Compilator** : *si planeta sit alkocoden, qui*
inferior existens superiori planete alicui uim suam dederit, superior erit
alkocoden uitaque erit secundum esse eius. Est autem Mercurius sub 715
Sole secundum sententiam omnium astrologorum, quamuis
secundum **Platonem** et **Aristotelem** et suos contemporaneos

---

697 Nam] non *S* | est] *om. V*   701 est] et *PV*   702 Adhuc] ad hoc *S* | cum]
tum *S*   704 et] *om. S* | uidelicet] scilicet *S*   705 sunt] sint *P*   706 rectificari]
ratificari *S*   710 iudicate] -to *S* | anni 80] *inv. P*   711 annis] annus *V*   712 52]
quinquaginta duo *V* que *? S* | tamen est] tamen est de *P* de *V*   713 Abraham]
om. PV   715 uitaque] eius *add. P* | esse eius] esse illius *P* eius esse *S*

---

699 et…701 Solis] Cf. Ibn Ezra, *Reshit Ḥokhmah*, §6.7:1-3, pp. 194-195. Ibn
Ezra, *Commencement*, p. 97: "et s'il est plus, adonc sont il hastif", quod Bate sic
interpretatus est: "et si maior fuit tunc sunt veloces" (MS Leipzig 1466, fol.
16ra:13) | 703 Albumasar…704 Sadan] Cf. Sadan, *Excerpta* 21, p. 315: "Et dixi
Albumazar: Quid sunt qui dicuntur putei? Respondit quod stelle fixe
fortificantes maleficos et conservantes beneficorum effectum" | 704
Auenezre…706 rectificari] Ibn Ezra, *Te'amim II*, §8.7:4, pp. 254-255, quod Bate
sic interpretatus est: "Si igitur scire uolueris loca horum graduum quia quolibet
anno mutantur minime a locis luminarium ac etiam a locis planetarum in hoc
parte (tempore *mg.*) 8. gr. 24. minuta" (MS Leipzig 1466, fol. 60va:18-22) | 707
ut…710 80] Videtur hoc loco Henricus referre ad iudicium nativitatis cuiusdam
nati anno 1135 ab Ibn Ezra factum, quod invenitur in MS Erfurt O. 89: "et sic
erunt 68 et cum annis nutritionis 72" (fol. 37v:5) | 713 si…715 eius] Ibn Ezra,
De nativitatibus, sig. a8r:12-14 | 717 Platonem…Aristotelem] Cf. Plato, *Timaeus*
38 D1-2; Arist., *Metaph.* XII 8, 1073b32 sqq

supra Solem ordinatus fore estimetur ; dat quoque uim suam
Soli propter rationes supra tactas. Vnde **Iohannes Hispalen-**
720 **sis** in LIBRO DE NATIVITATIBUS : *et si dominus uite est unus planeta*
leuium et dat uim suam planete qui sibi preest et suscipit uim ab eo,
iudicium annorum est superioris planete et hoc compertum est, inquit, *ad*
inueniendum annos uite secundum uicinitatem ueritatis. Si igitur hec
uera sunt et stabilienda, tunc esset Sol alkocoden dans annos
725 suos maiores 120 preter annos nutritionis. Sol enim est in
angulo in exaltatione sua, triplicitate et facie, necnon et duodenario, aspectus autem Saturni oppositus non potest hic auferre
aliquid ab annis Solis propter coniunctionem Iouis cum ipso,
que impedimenta eius refrenare habet, ut uolunt philosophi. Et
730 si dictum illius **Abrahe** et **Iohannis Hispalensis** intelligendum sit de planeta superiori, supra Solem uidelicet, ut uidetur
sonare alia littera eiusdem **Iohannis** sic dicentis *quod si planeta*
habens posse in loco Solis de subsolaris fuerit et dat uim supersolato et sit
receptus, iudicium transportabitur *ab ipso secundum quod existit,*
735 cuius etiam simile uult **Abraham Princeps** in LIBRO
NATIVITATUM, capitulo de testimoniis. Saltem remanebit
Mercurius dator annorum et dominus uigoris, cum hoc modo
superioribus non det uim suam. Est enim infra terminos | V118r
coniunctionis cum Sole, licet ab aliis aspiciatur, coniunctio
740 autem aspectu preualet et est ipso fortior, ut testatur **Zael** et
alii. At uero expresse dicit **Auenezre** in fine LIBRI NATIVITATUM
quod *planeta principans in 5 locis uite*, hoc est in loco hyleg, *si fuerit*

---

718 estimetur] extimetur *S* 719 propter] per *S* | tactas] dictas *PV* 720 Libro]
om. S | dominus…est] dominus ut *scrips. V et del.* | est] *iter. S* | planeta]
planetarum *ed.* 721 suscipit uim] suscipitur *ed.* suam *add. V* 722 compertum]
apertum *P* 724 et] *om. P* | esset] est *S* 726 duodenario] -ria *PV* 727 aspectus]
aspiciens *P* 728 aliquid] aliquod *P* aliud *S* 729 Et] quod *PV* 733 Solis] et *add.*
PV | fuerit] *om. S* | sit] sit *P* 734 secundum] *om. V* 735 Abraham Princeps]
inv. S 736 capitulo] in *praem. S* 737 Mercurius dator] *inv. P* 738 det] debet *PV*
739 cum…preualet] *om., sed mg. rest. P* | aspiciatur] inspiciatur *V* 740 aspectu]
aspectuum *PV* | testatur] est attestatur *V* 742 principans] -pians *S*

---

720 et…723 ueritatis] Iohannes Hispalensis, *Epitome*, sig. I4v:8-12 | 730
dictum…Hispalensis] Vide supra, 713 et 719 | 732 alia…734 existit] "alia
littera" est alia versio *Epitome* Hispalensis, ut inuenitur in Vat. Reg. lat. 1452,
fols. 65rb-va. | 735 Abraham…736 testimoniis] Ibn Ezra, *Liber nativitatum*,
fols. 57r:2-30 et 57v:1-2 | 739 coniunctio…741 alii] Zael, *Introductorium*, sig.
123rb:31-32 et 124va:17-18; Iohannes Hispalensis, *Epitome*, E1r: "et dicunt
astrologi quod coniunctio destruit omnem aspectum" | 742 planeta…745
uigoris] Ibn Ezra, *Moladot*, IV 29, 2, pp. 202-203

in coniunctione aut in aspectu cum planeta sibi superiori, ille superior qui fortitudinem alterius recipit, | est principans super natum seu dominus uigoris. Hec ergo dicta de numero annorum uite nati quem pre   745
manibus habemus sapientum iudicia sequendo sufficiant. Fina-
lis uero determinatio annorum et uite terminus cum precisione
successusque euentuum cum specificatione singulari ex directionibus et annorum reuolutionibus super radicem natiuitatis
posterius declarabuntur.   750

4.3. <Domus prima>

Nunc autem mores nati et passiones eius et accidentia
eufortuniorum et infortuniorum ex subiecta supracelestium
armonia corporum speculemur. Et quia complexio naturalis et
qualitas animi ab ascendente et Luna dominoque ascendentis et
Mercurio habent dinosci, primo ad dispositionem horum   755
consideremus.

4.3.1. <Complexio et forma corporis>

Est autem ascendens signum regale Sagittarius domus
Iouis. Cum igitur signa uirtutem suorum gerant dominorum, ut
uolunt omnes astrologi unanimiter, erit complexio nati Iouialis
sanguinea. Sed quoniam Saturnus partem habet in ascendente,   760
uidetur quod aliqua nota Saturnina nato debeat inesse, puta
tarditas quedam et pigritia. Vnde **Albumasar** in SADAN : *si
inueniatur aliquis habens horoscopum Arietem et si in cadente fuerit*
*dominus ipsius, | aut Sol, dominus exaltationis ipsius, et nullum sit
bonum in figura, tamen erit boni moris et bone fidei et dilectus ab omnibus*   765
*et habens mores regales. Est enim signorum significatio mansiua, astrorum
autem uariatur.* Vnde **Auenezre** in 1° RATIONUM, capitulo 9°,

---

743 superiori ille] *om. S*   744 est] erit *S* | super] supra *S*   748 euentuum]
euentum *S*   752 eufortuniorum] et fortuniorum *P*   755 Mercurio] Mercurii *S*
758 suorum gerant] *inu. P*   759 astrologi] astronomi *S*   761 nota Saturnina] *om.
P*   762 Sadan] est *add. P*   764 dominus[1]] Mars *praem. ed.* | aut…ipsius] *om., sed
mg. rest.* (aut *om.*) *P*   765 tamen] et *praem. S* | fidei] faciei *ed.* | omnibus]
hominibus *S (cf. L in ed.)*   766 regales] regulares *PV* | mansiua] iuxta *ed. Sadan,
sed* mansiua *hab. EL, quae lectio melior est*   767 1°] principio *S*

---

762 si…767 uariatur] Sadan, *Excerpta* 5, p. 302

dicit quod *signum ascendens in natiuitate naturam sui domini influit nato, quamquam dominus eius in malo loco foret.* Et quia potiorem
770 partem ascendentis obtinet Sagittarius quam Capricornus iuxta mentem **Albumasar** 7° CONIUNCTIONUM, differentia prima (in LIBRO quoque 9 IUDICUM, capitulo de receptione testimoniorum eligendorum, consimile habetur), idcirco magis declinare debet complexio nati ad sanguineam | Iouialem quam ad Saturninam
775 melancolicam. Saturnus tamen in proposito calidam acquirit complexionem tum ratione signi in quo est tum ratione locorum in ecentrico et epiciclo, secundum quod uult **Auenezre** in LIBRO NATIVITATUM, et alii sapientes hoc idem uolunt. Item natiuitas uernalis est, de qua **Ptolomeus** in QUADRIPARTITO :
780 *quarta que a uernali equinoctio ad estiuam uersionem facit boni coloris, bone magnitudinis, bone habitudinis, bonorum oculorum, quod plurimum habentes in humido et calido,* cuiusmodi complexio apparet in hoc nato. Luna quoque, que consimiliter super corpus significationem habet, ascendens aspicit contrario aspectu difficultatem
785 portendente, ratione cuius difficultas et tedium in nutritione causabantur. Iterum et retrogradatio dominorum ascendentis, que contradictionem et difficultatem innuit, ad hoc forsan cooperabatur. Item Luna aucta lumine et numero in domo Mercurii est separata quidem a Saturno et iuncta Mercurio

V119r

768 ascendens] as. *V* | naturam] nocturna *P*   773 declinare] declarare *primo scrips. sed exp. S* | debet] habet *S*   775 melancolicam] melencolicam *P* malencolicam *S* | tamen] cum *P*   780 boni] bone *P*   781 bone[1] et *praem. S* habitudinis] habitationis *PV* | bonorum] et *praem. S*   782 habentes] homines *PV* | hoc nato] *inv. S*   783 que] in *S* | consimiliter] consimili *S* similiter *V* super] supra *P*   784 contrario] contrarie *S*   785 portendente *scr.*] protendente *PV* procedente *S*   786 causabantur] _-batur *PV*   787 ad hoc] aduc *S*

768 signum…769 foret] Ibn Ezra, *Ṭeʿamim I*, §9.1:6, pp. 92-93, quod Bate sic interpretatus est: "Et hic quidem sermo qui propinquus est ueritati est quod quocunque signo in orientali angulo ascendente in hora natiuitatis semper erit natus de natura domini signi, quamuis etiam de genere non sic conueniente ad talem gradum puta dominandi" (MS Leipzig 1466, fol. 71rb:31-37) | 769 Et…771 prima] Albumasar, *De magnis coniunctionibus*, VII,1.5 (vol. 2, p. 270) | 771 in…773 habetur] Bate referre videtur ad *Librum novem iudicum* I.1, p. 418: "Consequenter vero signorum testimonia discernenda erunt. Vtile enim et necessarium existimo ut oriens sit firmum, uel saltem debipartitis quodlibet et cardines recti" | 775 Saturnus…778 nativitatum] Ibn Ezra, *Moladot*, III II 5, 4-5, pp. 124-127 | 780 quarta…782 calido] Ptol., *Quad*. III.13, trans. Guilelmi, p. 258:701-703

aspectu duplici de quo **Firmicus Iulius** asserit quod *facit obscu-*   790
ros seu absconsos et tacitos secretarum litterarum conscios aut celestibus
regionibus occupatos aut peritis computationibus interpretantes siderum
cursus. Facit etiam negotiationibus prepositos et liberalium artium publi-
cos magistros, facit oratores eloquentie splendore fulgentes aut medicos
cunctorum testimoniis adornatos. Et nota quod hec applicatio Lune   795
ad Mercurium frustrari non potest per redditionem, ut infra
melius apparebit, et ex supra dictis etiam satis est manifestum.
Non est enim Mercurius in hoc loco tantum debilitatus per
combustionem, ut supra ostensum est, quod ob hoc cogatur
reddere Lune applicationem suam, immo satis est adhuc fortis   800
in proposito, secundum quod experimenta declarauerunt.
Quod autem Lune dispositiones corporis obediant conditiones,
testatur **Ptolomeus** in Centilogio 61 propositione dicens
quod *Luna significat ea que corporis tamquam assimilata sibi secundum*
motum. Vnde **Iulius** : *omnis enim substantia humani corporis ad istius*   805
pertinet numinis potestatem. Nam postea quam perfectum hominem
uitalis aura susceperit, et postea quam se spiritus diuine mentis corpori
infuderit compositi corporis formam pro qualitate cursus sui Luna
sustentat. Preterea cum *luminaria* sint *in signis masculinis, significatur*
natus uirilis forme et magnanimus, iuxta quod dicit **Ptolomeus**   810
et sui **expositores** 71ª propositione Centilogii.

   Preterea dixerunt antiqui, ut testatur **Abraham Princeps**
et alii, quod dominus faciei signi ascendentis significat super

---

790 quo] Mercurius *add. P* | Firmicus Iulius] *inv. S*   791 et] *om. P* | secretarum]
secretos *P* scientie (?) *V* et illicitarum *add. ed.* | litterarum] lunarum *V*
792   computationibus] interpretationibus *p. corr. S*   797   etiam] *om. P*
798   tantum] *post* Mercurius *trsp. P*   799   ob] ab *S* | cogatur] cogitatur *S*
800 adhuc] ad hoc *SV*   801 secundum] sed etiam *PV*   802 dispositiones] -nem
PV   804 ea que] illa *P*   806 pertinet] partium *V* | postea quam] postquam *S*
807 susceperit] suscepit *S* | postea quam] postquam *S*   809 significatur] agatur
S   810 forme] fore *PV*   812 ut] et *S*

---

790 facit…795 adornatos] Firmicus Maternus, *Math.* IV 9, 8, p. 211:1-8 | 803
Ptolomeus…805 motum] Ps.-Ptol., *Cent.*, trans. graeco-latina, v. 61 | 805
omnis…809 sustentat] Firmicus Maternus, *Math.* IV 1, 1, p. 197:4-9 | 809
cum…811 Centilogii] cf. Ps.-Ptol., *Cent.*, v. 71; 'expositores' sunt 'Haly et
Abuifar Hamet' (cf. Nat. 1027-1030); vide transl. 'Mundanorum': "In
nativitatibus virorum quando fuerint luminaria in signis masculinis eorum opera
current super cursum naturalem… [expositio] Quando luminaria in nativitate
viri alicuius in signis masculinis fuerint, natus erit valde virilis." | 812
Abraham…814 aspiciens] Ibn Ezra, *Liber nativitatum*, fol. 59v:25-28: "Antiqui
dixerunt quod potentes facierum significant super formam; et verum dixerunt si
aspiciat ascendens"

formam hominis, precipue cum est aspiciens. In proposito
815 autem domina faciei Luna est, que etiam aspicit suam faciem.
Quapropter quantum in se est, significat faciem rotundam, ut
uult uterque **Abraham**, et staturam rectam cum albedine,
precipue cum sit in augmento luminis, | et supercilia quasi   S7v
coniuncta et motus nati et ambulationes ueloces, sed hoc
820 ratione tarditatis et pigritie Saturni obtemperatur. Dicit quoque
Auenezre in LIBRO INITII SAPIENTIE quod *qui natus fuerit sub*
Sagittario *erit eius statura recta et ipse clarus et tibie eius grosse et ipse*
hilaris et fortis et liberalis et sapiens in mensuris et ingeniosus et non
tenens se super uiam | unam et uox eius humilis siue submissa et filii eius   P30r
825 *parum uiuent.* | Item et in eodem : *et qui natus fuerit in facie Sagitta-*   V119v
rii secunda, ut est hic, *erit corpus eius placidum et facies aliquantulum*
crocea et supercilia eius coniuncta et habebit signum in pectore. Et uniuer-
salitas significationis huius signi secundum **Auenezre** *significat*

---

815 autem] aut *S* | que etiam] et *S*   818 supercilia] super alia *PV*   819 motus]
ueloces *praem. S* | ueloces] uelocis *P*   821 fuerit] fuit *S*   822 eius statura] *inv. S*
ipse²] homo *add. PV*   824 siue] uel *PV*   825 Item et] idem *S*

---

821 qui…825 uiuent] Ibn Ezra, *Reshit Ḥokhmah*, §2.9:26, pp. 112-113. Ibn Ezra,
Commencement, p. 64: "Et celi qui est né en li d'enfans d'ome il sera s'estande
droit et il cler, et sen vit et si coullion sont lons et ses jambes espesses, et il
home goieus et fort et volentif, et son front aguisié et ausinc sa barbe, et son
poil menu et son ventre grant, et il ert legier a saillir et amans les chevaus, et
sages en mesures, et sires d'engingnement, et ne se tient mie sur une voie, et sa
vois basse et non croistront ses enfans", quod Bate sic interpretatus est: "At
uero qui natus fuerit ex hominibus in hoc signo erit statura rectus et ipse
splendidus, ueretrum eius et testiculi longi, tybie eius grosse, et ipse homo
gaudiosus et fortis seu robustus et placidus, frons eius acuta et similiter barba
eius et capelli minuti, uenter eius magnus, et ipse agilis erit ad saliendum, equos
amabit, et sapiens erit in mensuris atque cauillosus, secundum unam uiam non
se tenebit, et uox eius humilis seu grauis, et filii eius pauci" (MS Leipzig 1466,
fol. 8vb:32-41) | 825 et²…827 pectore] Ibn Ezra, *Reshit Ḥokhmah*, §2.9:28, pp.
112-113. Ibn Ezra, *Commencement,* p. 64: "Et celi qui sera né es faces secondes
sera son cors avenant, mes ses faces seront safrenaces et ses sourcis empressés
et ara enseigne sur son pis", quod Bate sic interpretatus est: "et qui in secunda
facie natus fuerit, erit corpus eius placidum et facies eius crocea, supercilia eius
coniuncta et signum habebit supra pectus" (MS Leipzig 1466, fols. 8vb44-45-
9ra1) | 827 Et…829 iustum] Ibn Ezra, *Reshit Ḥokhmah*, §2.9:30, pp. 112-113.
Ibn Ezra, *Commencement,* p. 65: "Et la communauté de ce signe enseigne sur
home juste", quod Bate sic interpretatus est: "communiter autem significat
signum hoc super hominem iustum" (MS Leipzig 1466, fol. 9ra:7-8)

hominem iustum. Idem quoque dicit quod *de filiis hominum significat
iudices et illos qui Deo seruiunt et liberales ac homines misericordie et*   830
somniorum explanatores. Item **Hispalensis** asserit Sagittarium
esse *signum prophetarum et contemplantium* regum et potentum.
Preterea idem dicit quod dominus hore colorem proprium
significat. Iupiter autem est hic dominus hore ; quocirca
commiscenda sunt hec omnia de forma nati et complexione   835
eius recitata, in quibus Iupiter uidetur predominari, non tamen
absque adminiculo reliquorum. Hoc ergo modo complexionem
nati inuestigauimus ex dispositione Lune corpus gubernantis
secundum philosophos et ex dispositione ascendentis seu
horoscopi in quo *uita hominum et spiritus continetur,* ut testatur   840
Iulius Firmicus.

4.3.2. <Qualitas animae>

Anime uero qualitas, que a dispositione signi ascendentis
et a dispositione Mercurii dependet, talem se nobis offert
inuestigandam. Dominus quidem ascendentis primus et principalis Iupiter in medio celi existens coniungitur Saturno, consi-   845
militer ascendentis domino pro parte minus principali. Vnde
Saturni austeritas noxia refrenatur a Ioue, secundum quod
uolunt omnes astrologi et precipue diuus **Hermes** in FLORIBUS

---

829   significat] signat *S*   830   iudices] homines *praem. S* | et[2]] ac *S*
832   potentum] potestatum *S*   833   Preterea] *post* dicit *P* | idem dicit] dicit
Ioannes Ispalensis *S* | proprium *scr.*] piū *PSV*   836 eius] nati *P* | predominari]
dominari *S*   837   adminiculo] masculino *praem. S, sed del.* | ergo] autem *S*
838 inuestigauimus] inuestigamus *S*   839 ex] *om. S*   842 a dispositione] ad
dispositionem *P* | signi] domini *praem. PV*   843   talem] tal' *V*
844 inuestigandam] -da *V* 845 consimiliter] similiter *PV* 847 noxia] *om. S*
848 omnes] *om. PV*

---

829 Idem…831 explanatores] Ibn Ezra, *Reshit Ḥokhmah,* §2.9:33, pp. 112-113.
Ibn Ezra, *Commencement,* p. 65: "Et en sa partie d'enfans d'ome les jugeurs, et
ceus qui servent Dieu, et les volentis, et les homes de misericorde, et les espla-
neurs de songes, et les archiers et les marcheans", quod Bate sic interpretatus
est: "de hominibus autem in parte eius sunt iudices et illi qui deo seruiunt et pii
atque misericordes et sompniorum interpre<te>s et sagitarii et mercatores"(MS
Leipzig 1466, fol. 9ra:15-18). | 831 Sagittarium…832 potentum] Iohannes
Hispalensis, *Epitome,* sig. C1r:14-15: "Sagittarius signum prophetarum
contemplatiuorum et magnatum" | 833 dominus…834 significat] Iohannes
Hispalensis, *Epitome,* sig. I2r:26-27 | 840 uita…continetur] Firmicus Maternus,
Math. II 19, 2, p. 61:12-13

suis dicens quod *Iupiter soluit Saturni malitiam.* Sunt enim infra
850 terminum coniunctionis, licet nondum coniuncti, de quo in
CAPITULIS ALMANSORIS : *meliores coniunctiones due sunt quarum una*
est coniunctio luminarium, altera uero duorum planetarum ponderosorum.
Vnde in LIBRO RATIONUM : coniunctio Iouis *cum Saturno significat*
magnum sapientem. Est autem Iupiter summe beneficus. Vnde
855 **Iulius Firmicus** bonitatem eius excellentem uolens innuere dicit quod homines *immortales essent si numquam in genituris hominum*
Iouis benignitas uinceretur. Beneficientia igitur Iouis, secundum
quod concordati sunt omnes philosophi, seueritatem Saturni et
duritiam placat. Non est autem opinandum quod in hac dispo-
860 sitione Iupiter a Saturno per retrogradationem separetur, ut sic
uirtus coniunctionis depereat Iouiane, cum in tota retrogradatione subsequente infra terminos coniunctionis permaneant
quousque directi redeuntes ad ultimam applicent coniunctionem. At uero *neque est Saturnus omniquaque maleficus,* ut testatur
865 **Albumasar** in SADAN sub affirmatione Indorum. Item in eodem: habent planete malefici donationes magnas, sed perfi-
ciuntur per *laborem et dolorem et timorem* multum et austeritatem.
Vnde **Auenezre** in INITIO SAPIENTIE loquens de Saturno ait
quod *cum fuerit ipse almutas seu principans in natiuitate alicuius, confe-*
870 *ret eidem quidquid boni conferre habet, si bene fuerit dispositus secundum*

---

852 duorum] coniunctio *praem. S*   853 significat] signat *S*   856 genituris] genitu
P   857 Iouis benignitas] *inv. P*   858 seueritatem] sanitatem *S*   859 duritiam] -
tiem *PV* | Non...864 coniunctionem] *om. PV*   864 uero] nec *S*   867 multum]
post dolorem *S*   869 fuerit] fuit *S* | almutas seu] *om. S*   870 boni] *om. PV*
bene...dispositus] bone fuerit dispositionis *PV* | fuerit] fuit *S*

---

849 Iupiter...malitiam]] Hermes, *Cent.,* v. 27, sig. 117rb | 851 meliores...852
ponderosorum] *Capitula Almansoris,* c. 128, sig. 122ra | 853 coniunctio...854
sapientem]] Ibn Ezra, *Te'amim II,* §5.4:10, pp. 228-229, quod Bate sic interpretatus est: "Cum Saturno autem super magnum sapientem significat" (MS
Leipzig 1466, fol. 56va:36-37) | 856 immortales...857 uinceretur] Firmicus
Maternus, *Math.* II 13, 6, pp. 56:30-57:1 | 864 neque...maleficus] Sadan,
Excerpta 17, pp. 310-311 | 866 habent...867 austeritatem] Sadan, *Excerpta* 15,
p. 308 | 869 cum...876 eorum] Ibn Ezra, *Reshit Hokhma,* §4.1:22, pp. 152-153.
Ibn Ezra, *Commencement,* p. 83: "Et s'il est en la nativité d'un home princoiant
sur li, il li donra de la nature tout le bien qui i sera s'il est en bon lieu de par le
soleil, des parties du soleil, et des parties de l'orbe et les parties de l'eure ausi
com j'esplanerai", quod Bate sic interpretatus est: "Et si in hominis natiuitate
principans fuerit super ipsum dabit ei de natura sua quidquid boni habuerit, si in
bono loco fuerit ex parte solis et ex parte orbis signorum, et ex parte hore seu
horarum, secundum quod explanabo" (MS Leipzig 1466, fol. 12vb:5-9)

habitudinem eius ad Solem, ratione scilicet orientalitatis et directionis *et aliorum secundum habitudinem etiam eius in orbe signorum*,
ratione uidelicet domus et exaltationis et ceterorum huiusmodi,
s8r tertio etiam secundum habitudinem eius in figura | hore
natiuitatis respectu ascendentis, scilicet ratione angulorum et 875
succedentium eorum. Vnde idem in suo LIBRO NATIVITATUM :
secundum quod deficit planeta ab hiis tribus fortitudinibus,
secundum hoc iudicandum erit de planeta, uerbi gratia ut si
tantum unus modus deficit, deerit consimiliter et una tertia
V120r eufortunii. Tamen erit planeta | magis fortunatus quam infor- 880
tunatus propter duplicationem duarum tertiarum fortitudinis
supra unam debilitatis et infortunii. Sic autem est in proposito.
Saturnus enim et Iupiter retrogradi sunt, ratione cuius sibi
deest una tertia summe fortitudinis et complete, sed quia sunt
in angulo honorato secundum equationes domorum et in 885
domo undecima secundum gradus equales, quod fortitudinem
angularem augmentat, ut testatur **Haly** in suo LIBRO ELEC-
TIONUM et **Aomar** in LIBRO NATIVITATUM. Amplius et Saturnus
in signo exaltationis sue recipiens Iouem, qui cum moderatus
sit natura, in moderatis gaudet locis secundum **Albumasar** in 890
SADAN. Moderata autem loca sunt equinoctialia. Adhuc in
triplicitate sua sunt ambo et quilibet in sua nouenaria et sunt
ambo in duodenario Iouis estque Saturnus in propria facie et
gradu lucido aspiciturque a Luna aucta lumine et secundum
equationes domorum et per gradus equales, per quod malitia 895
Saturni etiam reprimitur secundum astrologos ; insuper etiam
in termino Iouis secum infra terminos coniuctionis associati,
per quod malitia Saturni *mitigatur* etiam secundum **Iulium
Firmicum**. Sunt etiam ambo in signo masculino et gradibus
masculinis. Hec igitur omnia dignitates amborum, scilicet 900

---

871 scilicet] *om. P*   874 hore] hora *P et add. S*   876 eorum] eorundem *S*
879 deficit] desit *PV* | et] *om. S* | tertia] *om. P*   880 eufortunii] infortunium (in-
ex eu-) *P*   890 natura in] naturam *P*   893 duodenario *scr.*]-naria *S* -nariis *PV*
estque] que *S* | et] est *S*   896 etiam[1]] *post* quod *P post* malitia *sed corr. S*
898 malitia] mala *P* | mitigatur] -antur *PV* | etiam] et *S*   899 etiam] quoque *S*
900 scilicet Saturni] *inv. S*

---

876 Vnde…880 eufortunii] Ibn Ezra, *Moladot*, III I 3, 1-5, pp. 100-101 | 886
quod…888 electionum] Bate referre videtur ad Haly Embrani, *De electionibus
horarum*, p. 335 | 888 Aomar…nativitatum] Bate referre videtur ad Aomar, *De
nativitatibus*, p. 121:42-44 | Amplius…891 Sadan] Sadan, *Excerpta* 8, p. 303 |
898 per…899 Firmicum] Firmicus Maternus, *Math.* III 2, 19, p. 102:10-11

Saturni et Iouis, accumulantia maiorem habent fortitudinem secundum doctrinam sapientum ad meliorandum effectus ipsorum quam sola retrogradatio ad impediendum. Retrogradatio enim superiorum non est perfecta debilitas, ut uult **Aue-**
905 **nezre** in suo LIBRO INTERROGATIONUM. Item *Aomar* in LIBRO NATIVITATUM dicit quod retrogradatio non tantum nocet superioribus quantum inferioribus. Rursum **Messehallah** in LIBRO REVOLUTIONUM MUNDI asserit retrogradationem *in domo fortune,* secundum quod hic est, adhuc et in termine fortune, minus
910 nocere. Nec est etiam ipsa retrogradatio, quantum in se est, impedimentum negatiuum simpliciter, quamuis | contradic- P30v
tionem et difficultatem et laborem et tarditatem cum prolixitate significet, secundum quod in LIBRO 9 IUDICUM habetur, in quo consimiliter omnes conueniunt sapientes. Vnde **Iohannes**
915 **Hispalensis** : *planeta retrogradus, quod innuit, non fit sine magno labore.* **Zael** quoque dicit quod planeta retrogradus tardus est in omnibus rebus. Quod autem retrogradatio non sit impedimentum simpliciter negatiuum, satis patet per **Albuma-**
sar in SADAN et per **Auenezre** in LIBRO NATIVITATUM, qui
920 ponunt planetas retrogrados alkocoden in natiuitatibus subtrahentes modicam particulam a datione annorum propter retrogradationem. Hiis ergo de causis uidetur Saturnus in proposito iudicandus fortunatus magis quam infortunatus, licet cum difficultate et contradictione et quasi post desperationem
925 aliquas de suis bonis donationibus conferat non speratis. Vnde in SADAN : quando fuerit Saturnus *coniunctus beneficis* in propria

---

905 interrogationum] retrogradationum *S*   909 adhuc] ad hoc *P* | minus] nimis *S* non posse *mg. add. a.m. post* nocere   910 Nec] neque *PV*   911 negatiuum] negatum *PV*   914 consimiliter] similiter *PV* | Vnde…Hispalensis] *om. S* 916 tardus est] *inv. S*   918 simpliciter] in omnibus *praem. S* | Albumasar] Albumasarem *S*   920 alkocoden] *post* natiuitatibus *S*   923 magis…infortunatus] *om. PV*   924 desperationem] -nes *P*   925 speratis] separatis *PV*

---

903 Retrogradatio…905 interrogationum] Ibn Ezra, *She'elot II,* §7.1:4, pp. 368-369 | 905 Aomar…907 inferioribus] Aomar, *De nativitatibus,* p. 125:39-40 | 907 Messehallah…908 fortune] Messehallah, *De revolutione annorum mundi,* sig. C4r:15-17 | 911 contradictionem…913 habetur] non inuenimus | 915 planeta…916 labore] est altera uersio *Epitome* Hispalensis, ut inuenitur in Vat. Reg. lat. 1452, fol. 66ra | 916 Zael…917 rebus] Zael, *Quinquaginta Praecepta,* c. 48, sig. 127rb:8-10 | 918 Albumasar…922 retrogradationem] Sadan, *Excerpta* 17, p. 310 | 919 Auenezre…922 retrogradationem] Ibn Ezra, *Moladot,* III 1 9, 6-7, pp. 112-113 | 926 quando…927 exaltatione] Sadan, *Excerpta* 17, p. 311

domo aut *exaltatione*, bene fortunatus erit natus et firmiter
permanebit fortuna ipsius quamdiu uita ipsius. Sepe autem
pertingit usque ad pueros et parentes, sed in hac bona fortu-
nitate forsan subintelligitur quod Saturnus sit directus. Retro-   930
gradatio enim eius partem unam fortitudinis sue sincopat, ut
predictum est. Propter quod aduertendum est quod motus
retrogradationis assimilatur motui nobiliori, | qui est primi
mobilis. Motus uero planete uocatus | directus, qui est secun-
dum successionem signorum in obliquo circulo causans gene-   935
rationem et corruptionem, est illi motui quasi contrarius. Ob
hoc rationi consonum est ut ille motus qui est secundum
successionem signorum in obliquo circulo, qui est causa transmutationis in entibus, prerogatiuam obtineat super res corporis
susceptiuas transmutationis, ille uero motus, qui primo magis   940
assimilatur, uocatus retrogradatio, super res nobiliores, que,
quantum in se est, transmutationi non subiacent, ut sint res
anime, propter maiorem eius affinitatem cum rebus nobilio-
ribus diuinis, quemadmodum a nobis latius est expositum
super LIBRO RATIONUM **Auenezre**, ubi mentio fit de materia   945
consimili. Quamquam igitur retrogradatio partem fortitudinis
diminuat in rebus corporalibus, in rebus tamen anime fauora-
bilis uidetur iudicanda. Quod si uerum est, uidebitur forsan
anima nati sublimia curiose appetitura cum hoc quod ambo,
Saturnus scilicet et Iupiter, circa terminos sint augium suarum,   950
quod anime sublimitatem insinuat, ut habetur in LIBRO RA-
TIONUM et alibi in plerisque locis. Libra quoque ratione sue
complexionis rectificat Saturnum. Amplius dicit **Albumasar** in
SADAN quod *coniunctiones Saturni et Iouis habent secreta magna*. Item
ait **Messehallah** in suo LIBRO CONIUNCTIONUM quod Saturnus   955

V120v

S8v

---

927 natus] *om. S* | firmiter] frequenter *S*   928 quamdiu] erit *add. p. corr. Par.*
931 sue] *om. P*   933 primi] motus *praem. S*   934 uocatus] uocatur *PV* | qui est]
om. PV   939 res] *om. P*   940 susceptiuas] suscepturas *S*   941 uocatus] uocatur
PV   942 subiacent] subiaceret *P*   943 eius] *om. PV*   945 Libro] librum *PV*
949 curiose appetitura] *inv. S*   950 augium] augmentum *S*   952 in] *om. PV*
954 quod] *om. S*   955 Libro] libello *V*

---

934 Motus…936 contrarius] Vide textum Avenezrae in appendice II | 944
a…946 consimili] Vide digressionem translatoris ad librum Avenezrae *Te'amim
I*, §6.2:5-8 in codice Lipsiensi 1466, fols. 69v-70r (vide appendicem II) | 951
quod…rationum] Vide supra 943-4 | 954 coniunctiones…magna] Sadan,
Excerpta 3, p. 298 | 955 Saturnus…957 miraculorum] Messahallah, *Epistola*,
sig. G2r:25-28

et Iupiter, cum iuncti *fuerint in exaltationibus suis, significabunt bonum et demonstrationem miraculorum.* Et infra dicit quod coniunctio ipsorum *in angulo medii celi* significat *apparitionem regis uel prophete ex parte eiusdem signi.* Hoc autem dictum **Messehallah**

960 non est super natiuitatibus, sed super reuolutionibus mundanis. Posui tamen ipsum propter magnitudinem significationis talis coniunctionis in angulo medii celi in signoque exaltationis Saturni. Est enim Libra signum iustitie et *prophetarum* et principum *diuinique obsequii,* ut uult **Iohannes Hispalensis** in suis

965 YSAGOGIS et **Albumasar** in SADAN. Item **Auenezre** in LIBRO RATIONUM. Vnde **Ptolomeus** in QUADRIPARTITO, capitulo 8° secundi : *equinoctialia quidem signa sacris et religionibus circa deos significationes insinuant.* Amplius etiam Libra signum profectionis a loco coniunctionis que fuit in Aquario per mutationem

970 triplicitatis que fuit anno domini 1225 precedente hanc natiuitatem. Vnde **Albumasar** 4° CONIUNCTIONUM, differentia 7ª, asserit hoc significare *leges prophetarum et decreta eorum et fidem et sermonem in eis et fabricare ecclesias et domos orationis et seruientes earum et custodes earum cum bonitate facierum et pulchritudine que erit in eis et*

975 *largitate et iustitia et equitate et ueritate* | *in sermone et explanatione et*   V121r
acceptione et donatione et uenditione et emptione et arismetica et geometria in diuersis scientiis ex compositione cantuum et modulationum et aliorum preter hoc et esse sponsalicii et gaudii et tripudiorum et delectationis et multiplicationem pecunie in manibus hominum et edificationem ciuitatum

980 *et aularum et uiridariorum et locorum amenorum et permutationes rerum*

957 infra] ita *S*   958 ipsorum] eorum *S* | angulo] angulis *PV*   961 tamen ipsum] *inv. P* | magnitudinem] talis *add. S*   965 Item] etiam *add. S*   966 8°] 6° *S*   967 quidem signa] *inv. P*   968 etiam] *om. P*   970 que fuit] *iter. S om. P* que *V* 972 asserit] *om. S* | hoc] hic *SV* | decreta] secreta *S*   974 erit] cum *S*   976 arismetica] arismetrica *V*   977 in] et *PV* | ex] in *S* | modulationum] -nis *S* 978 esse] *om. V* | sponsalicii] *sic codd.* solacii *ed.* | delectationis] -nem *P* 979 multiplicationem] -num *V* | edificationem] -num *V* -nibus *S*   980 aularum] uillarum *P*

957 coniunctio…959 signi] Messahallah, *Epistola,* sig. G2v:29-30 | 963 Est…- 964 obsequii] Iohannes Hispalensis, *Epitome,* sig. B4r | 965 Albumasar…- Sadan] Sadan, *Excerpta* 3, p. 300 | Auenezre…966 rationum] Ibn Ezra, *Ṭeʿamim II,* §2.4:13, pp. 192-193, quod Bate sic interpretatus est: "Quoniam Aries et Libra signa sunt equalitatis plus quam reliqua omnia quia in eis sequitur dies nocti ideo significant super res iusticie" (MS Leipzig 1466, fol. 51rb:38-42) | 966 Ptolomeus…968 insinuant] Ptol., *Quad.* II.8, trans. Guilelmi, p. 217:498-499 | 972 leges…981 infortunia] Albumasar, *De magnis coniunctionibus,* IV.7 (vol. 2, p. 131)

cum uelocitate de esse ad esse et incurrere infortunia et reliqua. Iterum est et Libra signum coniunctionis presentis, que scilicet erat in anno natiuitatis huius quam pre manibus habemus. Secundum autem quod uult **Auenezre** in INITIO SAPIENTIE, Libra est signum *hominum fori et iudicum, arismeticorum quoque et omnium* 985 *eorum qui ludunt instrumentis* melicis seu musicis, *mercatorum etiam et conuiuia exercentium.* Cum ergo domini domus uite ambo, scilicet superiores, in huiusmodi signo sint infra terminos coniunctionum circa medii celi angulum, qui dignior est aliis et excellentior, iuxta quod uult **Auenezre** in LIBRO RATIONUM et 990 consimiliter in LIBRO NATIVITATUM, de quo **Ptolomeus** secundo QUADRIPARTITI in fine sic ait : *attingentes quidem enim uel* S9r *accedentes | ad medium celi maxime uirtuosi sunt, secundo autem quando in ipso orizonte fuerint etc.,* et **Iulius Firmicus** dicens quod *hic locus principalis est et omnium cardinum potestate sublimior,* et infra: 995 P31r medium celum *semper principatum* obtinet *in omnibus | genituris,* rationabile uisum est ex hiis et aliis supra dictis animam nati et mentem eius circa sublimia uersaturam. *Saturnus* namque, prout uult **Albumasar**, *occulta profundorum atque inexhaustam sapientiam significat,* 7° sui INTRODUCTORII. **Auerroes** quoque super secun- 1000

---

981 infortunia] -nium *P* 983 huius] eius *P* | Secundum] uerum *S* 986 eorum] illorum *P* | etiam et] *om. P* 987 ergo] igitur *P* 988 sint] sunt *S* | infra] extra *sed* in. s.l. *V* 989 coniunctionum] -nis *P om. S* 990 iuxta] *om. PV* 992 secundo] *rectius* primo | enim uel] *inv. V* 993 sunt] *om. S* 994 orizonte] oriente *P* fuerint] fuerunt *S* 995 et[1]] *om. S* | sublimior] -ius *S* 996 semper] *om. P* 997 ex...eius] *om. PV* 998 namque] autem *S* 999 occulta] per *praem. S* inexhaustam] mox haustam *P* 1000 Auerroes] Auenezre *P* | quoque] *om. PV* super] supra *S*

---

984 Libra...987 exercentium] Ibn Ezra, *Reshit Ḥokhmah,* §2.7:33, pp. 100-101. Ibn Ezra, *Commencement,* pp. 58-59: "Et en sa partie des enfans d'ome les homes du marchié, et les jugeurs, et les sires de nombre, et tous ceus qui chantent es estrumens, et les marcheans, et les entremetans en mengier et en boivre", quod Bate sic interpretatus est: "De hominibus in parte eius sunt mercatores, iudices et arismetici ac omnes instrumentis cantantes et commestionibus et potacionibus se inmiscentes" (MS Leipzig 1466, fol. 7vb:7-10) | 990 Auenezre...991 Nativitatum] cf. Ibn Ezra, *Ṭeʿamim* II, §6.2:1-11, pp. 236-239 et *Moladot* III I 3, 1-5, pp. 100-101 | 991 Ptolomeus...994 etc] Ptol., *Quad.* I.24, trans. Guilelmi, p. 196:962-964 | 994 hic...995 sublimior] Firmicus Maternus, *Math.* II 19, 11, p. 64:10-12 | 996 semper...genituris] Firmicus Maternus, *Math.* III 1, 18, p. 96:25-26 | 998 Saturnus...1000 Introductorii] Albumasar, *Introductorium maius,* VII.9 (vol. 8, p. 144:622-3) | 1000 Auerroes...1002 Babiloniorum] Averroes, *In De Caelo* II, c. 68, 144G-H: "dant consyderationem ei et bonitatem in finibus rerum"

dum CELI ET MUNDI in commento attestatur ipsam *bonam conside-rationem in finibus rerum* significare sub assertione Babiloniorum. Item **Zafo** in YSAGOGIS suis : *et* cum *sensum prebet* Saturnus, *multum prebet*. Insuper et iuxta **Albumasar** *animi nobilitatem*

1005 *tribuit et sanam sapientiam et intellectum, uisionum interpretationem, certitudinem et ueritatem, tum iura, leges, templa, ceremonias, religionem, honestatem, fortitudinem, temperantiam, iustitiam, gratiam, ueram fidem, humilitatem et obedientiam, accidentaliter aliquando post deliberationem, inconsultum rerum aggressum ac difficultatum incursum, tum patientiam,*

1010 *hominum societates et cohabitationes et contubernia, promissionem stabi-lem, depositionem fidelem, hilarem, iocundum, placidum, indulgentem Veneri, lingue officio et sibi et suis utilem, malum fugientem, bonum appetentem, prouidum consilio, graui sermone et priuatis et publicis salubrem et fructuosum.*

1015 Et ut ad unum sit dicere, ex commixtione Iouis cum Saturno qualitas anime nati trahenda est, quantum est ex hac parte, principalius autem a Ioue. Verumtamen labor et difficul-tas cum aduersitatibus ratione retrogradationis insinuantur, ut predictum est, et hoc in exterioribus bonis. Quod autem hoc

1020 uerum sit, satis patet ex supra dictis, cum ex donationibus Sa-turni natus iste beneficia notabilia fuerit consecutus, licet cum aliqua difficultate, ut dictum est, ubi de euentibus nati fecimus mentionem. Nisi enim in radice natiuitatis magis fortunatus fuisset Saturnus quam infortunatus, non contulisset nato de

---

1001 in commento] *om.* P*V*   1002 significare] considerare *praem.* P | assertione] ascensione P   1003   cum sensum] consensum P   1004   Insuper] Iupiter P*V* nobilitatem] mobilitatem P   1005   sanam] *om.* P*V* | uisionum] -nem P 1006   certitudinem] -num P | tum] cum P tamen *S* | leges templa] *inv. S* religionem] *om. V*   1007   honestatem *scr. cum ed.*] honestam *codd.* 1008 accidentaliter] accidentis *S*   1009 inconsultum] -tam P*V* | difficultatum] -tem P | tum patientiam *scr. cum ed.*] cum patientia *codd.*   1010 cohabitationes] hominum *add. S* | contubernia] concubina P*V*   1011   indulgentem] -te P*V* 1012 Veneri] uerum *V*   1013 graui] grauidum *S* | et²] *om.* P*V*   1014 et] ac *S* 1017 parte] per *add.* P*V*   1018 ratione] *om.* P*V*   1020 supra dictis] predictis *S* ex²] *om.* P*V*   1021   natus] *om.* P*V* | fuerit] fuit *S*   1022   de] in *S* 1024 fuisset…infortunatus] *om. S*

1003 et…1004 prebet] Albumasar, *Ysagoga minor*, V.4, p. 124 | 1004 Albumasar…1014 fructuosum] Albumasar, *Introductorium maius*, VII.9 (vol. 8, p. 144:628-640) | 1023 Nisi…1026 sapientie] Ibn Ezra, *Reshit Ḥokhmah*, §4.1:22, pp. 152-153. Ibn Ezra, *Commencement*, p. 83: "et se est a rebours, il donra toute chose despite", quod Bate sic interpretatus est: "quod si fuerit e contrario, dabit omne despectum" (MS Leipzig 1466, fol. 12vb:8-9)

suis bonis donationibus, sed de uilibus et despectis, ut testatur   1025
Auenezre in INITIO SAPIENTIE, cui etiam concordat tota cohors
astrologorum. Nihil autem confert planeta aut parum nisi *in*
natiuitate promiserit, ut habetur in LIBRO ARBORIS 78° uerbo, quod
et manifestius affirmant eius expositores **Haly** et **Abuiafar**
Hamet filius Ioseph filii Abrahe. In LIBRO quoque DE REVOLU-   1030
TIONIBUS ANNORUM NATIVITATUM, qui dicitur **Albumasar**,
uersatur principalis intentio circa hoc idem ; et **Auenezre**
consimiliter quoque in fine LIBRI NATIVITATUM loquens de
reuolutionibus hoc idem affirmat, in quo etiam consentiunt
astrologi omnes unanimiter. *Iupiter* ergo *dominus ascendentis in*   1035
bono loco constitutus et *liber a malis* significat iuxta **Albohali**, qui
et **Auicenna**, *principatum et nobilitatem ac sublimitatem animi.*
Saturnus quoque consimili modo *significat* magnam ualentiam et
nobilitatem animi ac *profunditatem et singularitatem consilii et pauci-*
tatem interrogationis, prout testatur idem. Sic ergo domini domus   1040
prime animam nati afficiunt, quemadmodum ipsa domus cum
Luna complexionem corporis. Vnde **Zael** in FATIDICA : *profun-*
dissimum autem id in omni hominum conceptione, quoniam planete
signorum tantam uim gerunt ut spiritus eorum astronomice dicantur. Et
iterum in CAPITULIS ALMANSORIS : *signa significant corpora, planete*   1045
uero significant ea que mouent corpora.

1025 ut] unde *PV*   1028 78°] 76 ? *S*   1029 Abuiafar] Albu'asar *P* Aluiafar *S*
1032 uersatur] nescitur *P*   1033 quoque] et *S om. P*   1035 astrologi omnes] *inu.*
P | ergo] igitur *P*   1036 Albohali] Albuhaly *P* Albulahi *V*   1037 ac] et *PV*
sublimitatem] subtilitatem *S*   1038   consimili modo] consimiliter *S*
1039 nobilitatem] ac subtilitatem *add. S* | et¹] ac *S*   1043 autem id] *inu. S*
1044 gerunt] generant *PV* | astronomice] astrologice *S*   1045 iterum] *om. S*
significant] signant *S*   1046 significant] signant *S* | corpora] corpus *S* cor' *V*

1027 Nihil…1028 uerbo] Ps.-Ptol., *Cent.*, trans. Platonis, v. 78, sig. 114rb "de
significatione planete quando peruenit ad locum in quo promiserit aliquid in
natiuitate: Nil operatur planeta.in quo nil promiserit" | 1028 quod…1030
Abrahe] *Liber centum uerborum Ptholemei cum commento Haly*, sig. 114rb-114va |
1030 In…1032 idem] Cf. Albumasar, *De reuol.*, p. 216a:38-41 "quilibet planeta
suam operationem ostendit secundum dispositionem quam habet in natiuitatis
initio" | 1032 Auenezre…1034 affirmat] Cf. Ibn Ezra, *Moladot*, IV 12, 17, pp.
192-193 | 1035 Iupiter…1037 animi] Albohali, *De natiuitatibus*, sig. c3r:9-11 |
1038 Saturnus…1040 interrogationis] Albohali, *De natiuitatibus*, sig. c3r:4-6 |
1042 profundissimum…1044 dicantur] Zael, *Fatidica*, p. 234:4-6 | 1045
signa…1046 corpora] *Capitula Almansoris*, c. 113, sig. 121vb

Esse uero Mercurii animam nati condisponentis supra
tactum est in parte. Nunc autem residuum influentie sue decla-
remus. Est igitur Mercurius in Ariete | nondum complete   S9v
1050 egressus terminum combustionis, qui uirtutem eius non abigit,   V121v
ut preostensum est, cum eo scilicet quod experientia hoc idem
comprobat. Nam si combustio beneficientiam sibi abstulisset,
ea que de beneficiis suis natus hic adeptus est, nequaquam fuisset consecutus, secundum quod supra memini. Vnde **Abraham**
1055 **Princeps** in LIBRO NATIVITATUM : regula quidem generalis est :
si fuerit Mercurius sub radiis Solis fueritque almutas, erit scientia nati uirtusque Mercurialis abscondita. Item **Albumasar** 3°
CONIUNCTIONUM differentia quarta : *et quando coniungitur Soli*
Mercurius, significat occultationem rerum et secretum earum et tegumen-
1060 *tum scientie et sapientie et libros tegere uel subterrare et rumores tegere.* Et
re uera tali affectu afficitur hic natus. Receptio namque impedimentum combustionis dissoluit forsan non ex toto, secundum
quod uidetur innuere **Zael** in LIBRO 9 IUDICUM, ubi de bello fit
sermo. Dicit igitur **Albumasar** in SADAN : *Mercurius quando fuerit*
1065 *in domibus Martis est secundus Mars.* Et **Ptolomeus** in CENTILO-
GIO, 38 uerbo, quod *si* Mercurius *fuerit in duobus signis Martis, da-*
bit fortitudinem perfidie et stultitie; et fortior duobus locis est Aries. Et
hoc quidem secundum unam translationem. Alia uero transla-
tio sic habet: *et si fuerit* Mercurius *in domibus Martis dabit ei acuita-*
1070 *tem ingenii in astutia et maxime in Ariete.* Item alia translatio : *cum*

1047 condisponentis *scr.*] condisponentes *S* cum disponentis *V* cum dispositis *P*
1049] nundum *V* mundi *S*   1050   egressus] cum *praem. PV* | qui] que *P*
uirtutem] uirtute *PV* | eius] *om. S* | abigit] ambigit *P*   1051 scilicet] similiter *S*
1052 comprobat] probauit *PV* | si] et si *P* | sibi] suam *praem. S*   1053 benefi-
ciis] -cis *S* | natus] *om. P*   1054 supra] super *V*   1056 fuerit Mercurius] *inv. P*
fueritque] quod *S*   1057   uirtusque] uirtus *S*   1058   et] *del. V*
1060   tegere[1]...subterrare] legere uel scribere *ed.* | uel] et *S* | subterrare]
subtrahere *S*   1062 dissoluit] dissolui *S*   1066   38] 30 *S* | Martis] Mars *S*
1067   perfidie] perfidies *PV* | et[1]] *om. PV*   1068   unam] bonam *S*
1069 domibus] domo *S*   1070 alia] illa *PV*

1054 Abraham...1057 abscondita] Ibn Ezra, *Liber nativitatum*, fol. 60b:2-3: "Et
regula generalis est si Mercurius fuerit sub radiis Solis, ipse erit dominus,
secundum verba sua in absconditis" | 1058 et...1060 tegere[2]] Albumasar, *De*
magnis coniunctionibus, III.4 (vol. 2, p. 114) | 1061 Receptio...1064 sermo] *Liber*
novem iudicum VII.160, p. 516a | 1064 Mercurius...1065 Mars] Sadan, *Excerpta*
22, p. 317 | 1066 si...1067 Aries] Ps.-Ptol., *Cent.*, trans. Platonis, v. 38, sig.
110rb | 1069 et...1070 Ariete] Ps.-Ptol.., *Cent.*, trans. 'Mundanorum 1', v. 38
| 1070 cum...1072 Aries] Ps.-Ptol., *Cent.*, trans. Adelardi, v. 38

uero fuerit in signo Martis, super primitias et fortunam ; potentior autem horum duorum locorum est Aries. Et iterum alia translatio : *et cum in uno signorum Martis fuerit, significat hominem qui cito respondet interrogationi; et Aries melius est Scorpione.* Translatio denique de Greco talis est : *in domo autem Martis dabit facilem linguam et maxime in Ariete.* Huic uero sententie ultime translationis concordant commentatores. Vnde prima translatio impropria est. At uero in CAPITULIS ALMANSORIS habetur : *cuicumque fuerit Mercurius in radice natiuitatis in domo Martis, erit male suspicionis et festinus in suis negotiis.* Dicitur enim infra in eisdem CAPITULIS quod *omnis res que festinanter | fit, et festinanter destruitur et que reiteratur in significatione Martis est.* Quantum igitur est ex hac parte, significatur nato facilitas lingue et circumspectio festina. Sed aliud est quod reformat pactum. Nam licet Aries, ratione qua domus Martis est, in circumspectionem portendere debeat, ratione tamen qua talis exaltatio Solis est, mores regales insinuat, ut habetur in LIBRO RATIONUM. Et hoc est etiam quod dicit **Albumasar** in SADAN quod significatio Arietis mansiua est in *bonis moribus,* ut supra memini. Est enim signum iustitie et domorum orationis et iudicum et totius moderationis propter

1075

1080

1085

1090

P31v

1071 uero] *om. PV* 1073 fuerit] *om. S* | respondet] -dit *P* 1074 Aries] anime *V* 1075 est] *om. S* | dabit] dat *S* 1076 ultime] huius *praem. S* 1077 commentatores] expositores *praem. S* 1078 est] et ma' secunde ? *S* | At] et incirconspectio festina. quantum igitur ex hac parte significatur nato facilitas (*ex* felicitas) lingue *praem. S* (cf. l. 1082) | in Capitulis] *s. l. ante* uero *S* cuicumque] cuique *P* cuicque *V* 1079 suspicionis] suspectionis *S* 1081 quod] *om. PV* 1082 Quantum] quando tamen *P* | Quantum...festina] *trsp. ante* At (ll. 1078) *S* | ex] in *P* 1085 portendere *scr.*] protendere *PSV* 1086 ratione tamen] tam *S* | talis] *om. PV* | est] *om. PV* 1087 est] *om. S* 1088 mansiua] mansura *P* est] sit *S*

1072 et...1074 Scorpione] Ps.-Ptol., *Cent.*, trans. 'Mundanorum 2', v. 38 | 1075 in...1076 Ariete] Ps.-Ptol., *Cent.*, trans graeco-latina, v. 38 | 1076 Huic...1077 commentatores] cf. Haly: "cuius nature prefuerit Mercurius erit acutus et addet ei subitam eloquentiam super cogitationem eius" | 1078 cuicumque...1082 est[1]] *Capitula Almansoris*, c. 11, sig. 120va et *Idem*, c. 56, sig. 121ra | 1084 Nam...1087 insinuat] Cf. Ibn Ezra, *Ṭeʿamim II*, §2.7:1, pp. 198-199, quod Bate sic interpretatus est: "Ait Ptolomeus rex quod totum signum Arietis honor Solis est, cuius racio est quod ibi apparet eius fortitudo sicut fortitudo regis" (MS Leipzig 1466, fol. 52ra:24-27) | 1088 significatio...1089 moribus] Sadan, *Excerpta* 5, p. 302 | 1089 signum...1091 equalitatem] Ibn Ezra, *Ṭeʿamim II*, §2.4:13, pp. 192-193, quod Bate sic interpretatus est: "Quoniam Aries et Libra signa sunt equalitatis plus quam reliqua omnia quia in eis sequuntur dies nocti, ideo significant super res iusticie " (MS Leipzig 1466, fol. 51rb:38-42)

equalitatem, ut habetur in LIBRO RATIONUM. Videtur quidem igitur Mercurius in proposito naturam Martialem amittere propter maiorem eius affinitatem ad Solem, cui corporaliter est coniunctus in loco, in quo maiorem fortitudinem et plures
1095 dignitates habet Sol quam Mars, licet domus eius sit. Habet enim Sol in hoc loco dignitates, scilicet ratione exaltationis, triplicitatis et faciei, Mars autem nonnisi tantum ratione domus. Et quamquam secundum partitionem domorum Mars aspiciat Mercurium aspectu sextili, coniunctio tamen corporalis cum
1100 Sole magis potest secundum doctrinam sapientum. Vnde **Zael** in FATIDICA : *maior autem omnium planetarum uirtus est Sol. Hic ergo de quocumque signo exit quodam modo spiritum eius auferens uires ipsius extinguit. In quo autem intrat, quasi uiuificans naturam eius excitat, eruntque possessiones | signi sub consilio Solis donec inde exeat.* Preterea
1105 quod dominus exaltationis in maiori affinitate existens cum signo proportionatur aliquando domino domus eiusdem signi, satis innuit **Auenezre** in suis INTERROGATIONIBUS et **Albumasar** in LIBRO EXPERIMENTORUM. Dicit autem **Auenezre** in LIBRO RATIONUM quod *cum Mercurius* fortitudinem *suam* Soli
1110 pulsauerit aut cum ipso fuerit, significat hoc *scientiam astrologie. Nam siderum rex Sol est.* Mercurius etiam de se astrologiam significat necnon et omnem sapientiam et scientiam. Et iterum in eodem, prima parte, capitulo de Sole: *anima* autem *humana a Sole* dependet et per consequens *sapientia et intelligentia* propter
1115 uirtutem anime, et significat super leges et consuetudines, secundum quod et Iupiter de significatione etiam Solis est

S10r

1091 equalitatem] equinoctietatem *? S*   1092 igitur] ergo *S* | amittere] uidetur *add. P*   1097 autem] habet *add. Par* | nonnisi] .5. *add. PV* | tantum] *s.l. P* ratione] scilicet *add. V*   1099 tamen] *om. P*   1104 possessiones] *ex corr. L* posesores *S* passiones *PV* | donec inde] deinde donec *S*   1106 signo] sole *S* 1110 pulsauerit] pulsauit *P*   1111 Sol est] est sol et *P* | de se] *om. PV*   1112 et¹] *om. PV*   1114 intelligentia] intellectiua *PV*   1116 et] *om. P*

1101 maior...1104 exeat] Zael, *Fatidica*, p. 234:6-10 | 1104 Preterea...1107 Interrogationibus] Ibn Ezra, *She'elot II*, §8:1-3, pp. 354-355 | 1109 cum...1110 astrologie] Ibn Ezra, *Ṭe'amim II*, §5.4:9, pp. 226-227, quod Bate sic interpretatus est: "Cum vero Mercurius donans est uirtutem suam ei, tunc omnis eius sciencia in legibus erit et iudicijs ad iuste iudicandum. Et si cum sole astrologus erit ; rex enim stellarum sol est" (MS Leipzig 1466, fol. 56va:30-34) | 1112 Et...1116 Solis] Ibn Ezra, *Ṭe'amim I*, §4.5:4-5, pp. 76-77, quod Bate sic interpretatus est: "quod humana anima a uirtute Solis est quod significat super sapientiam et intellectum ac super honorem qui est tamquam similitudo regis" (MS Leipzig 1466, fol. 54vb:27-30)

summa diuinitatis contemplatio, prout asserit **Albumasar**. Amplius
ait **Iulius** quod *Sol cum* Mercurio *geniture domino* associatus *facit
homines plenos fidei, sed inflatos superbie spiritu, sapientes et omnia
spiritu equitatis moderatione compositos, humanos, religiosos, et qui patres*   1120
*suos integro semper amore colunt ; facit etiam corpulentos et quorum caput
flauo capillorum crine lucescat ; facit etiam agricolas patrimonia propria
uirtute querentes, efficaces, cordatos et qui semper aquosa regionum delectatione letentur ; facit etiam tales qui omnes actus cum maxima honestate*
perficiant. | *Sed hii ab uxore et a filiorum erunt affectibus separati ; uitia*   1125
*uero et ualitudines circa oculos et ceteras corporis partes frequenti faciet
igne comburi ; mortis uero exitus in peregrinis locis uiolentos publicosque
decernit.* **Auicenna** uero dicit quod *si Mercurius* fuerit *cum Sole,
significat* commixtionem *regum et principum ac* scribarum; hoc est
secundum aliam translationem *quod associabitur regibus et scribis.*   1130
Idem quoque dicit quod *si fuerit in signo mobili,* ut est hic, *significat
subtilitatem* ac perfectionem *et pulchritudinem ac amorem scientiarum
atque religionem* (secundum aliam uero translationem : *festinum
atque clarum intellectum diuinumque timorem*). Vnde **Ptolomeus** 3°
QUADRIPARTITI, capitulo de qualitate anime : *signa quidem igitur*   1135
tropica Mercurium continentia *communiores faciunt animas, popula-
rium et ciuilium rerum concupiscitiuas, adhuc autem amatrices glorie et
Deo supplices bene aptasque et boni motus inquisitatiuasque et inuentiuas,
bene coniecturatiuas et astrologicas et diuinatiuas.* Hoc quoque idem

---

1117 diuinitatis] deitatis *PV*   1119 spiritu] a *praem. s.l. P* | spiritu…omnia] *om.*
V | omnia] *sic P cum ed.* o's *S*   1120 equitatis moderatione] *iter. P*   1123 uirtute]
om. PV   1124 actus] artes *S*   1125 perficiant] proficiant *PV* | uxore] uxoribus *S*
uxoris *ed.* | et] aut *ex* et *corr.V*   1126 ualitudines] -dine *PV* | circa] curas *PV*
oculos et] omnes *S* | ceteras] certas *V*   1127 igne] igni *P* | mortis] martis *S*
peregrinis] peregrinationis *S*   1131 mobili] nobili *PV*   1132 subtilitatem]
sublimitatem *ed.* | perfectionem] perceptionem *PV* | ac²] et *P*   1133 atque] ac
S   1134 diuinumque] diuinum per *S*   1135 igitur] ergo *S*   1138 bene] unde *S*
inquisitatiuasque] -uas quoque *S* | inquisitatiuasque…coniecturatiuas] quesitiuas
PV   1139 astrologicas] astrologias *V a.corr. P* | diuinatiuas] dominatiuas *PV*

1117 summa…contemplatio] Albumasar, *Introductorium maius,* VII.9 (vol. 8, p.
145:672-3) | 1118 ait…1128 decernit] Firmicus Maternus, *Math.* IV 19, 32-33,
pp. 254:16-255:3 | 1128 si…1129 scribarum] Albohali, *De natiuitatibus,* c.5, sig.
c3v:20-22: "ubi inuenitur cum Sole, natus se regibus, principibus ac doctis
admiscebit et adiunget" | 1130 quod…scribis] Albohali, *De natiuitatibus,* trans.
Platonis, c. 5 (MS Oxford Digby 51, fol. 116vb) | 1131 si…1133 religionem]
Albohali, *De natiuitatibus,* c.5, sig. c2r.:21-24 | 1133 festinum…1134 timorem]
Albohali, *De natiuitatibus,* trans. Platonis, c. 5 (MS Oxford Digby 51, fol. 116rb)
| 1134 Ptolomeus…1139 diuinatiuas] Ptol.., *Quad.* III.15, trans. Guilelmi, p.
264:873-876

1140 uult uterque *Abraham*. Preterea dicit **Auenezre** iuxta auctori-
tatem Indorum quod *si fuerit Mercurius in aspectu opposito cum*
Saturno, secundum quod hic est, *significat hominem sapientem ex*
corde suo trahentem sapientiam et intelligentiam, et eo melius si alter
eorum fuerit almutas siue dux. Est autem in proposito Mercu-
1145 rius dominus uigoris seu alkocoden, Saturnus uero alter dominus ascendentis. Item **Abraham Compilator**: *si* Mercurius
Saturnum ex opposito, ubicumque fuerit, respiciat, aliquam philosophiam
predicat, altorum et diuinorum indagatricem. Et ut ad omne dicatur,
maior pars proprietatum Mercurii et conditionum eius huic
1150 nato est impressa, ut sunt *probabiles inductiones, necessarii sillogismi,*
philosophie ac poetrie studium necnon et medicine plurimumque in mathe-
maticis, arismetice, geometrie et astronomie, nec sine melica, metrica et
rhytmica, tum libri commenta, scribe eorumque officii acuta et prompta
artificia, diligens omnium scientiarum usus et exercitatio cum nouitatis
1155 *inuentione ac secretorum intellectu soli diuinitati patentium* et cetera que
de hac materia philosophi scribunt. Quamquam igitur Mars per
aspectum eius sextilem ad locum Mercurii facilem linguam aut
indiscretionem causare nitatur, ponderositas tamen Saturni et
eius inquisitiua perscrutatio per immissionem seu influentiam
1160 sui aspectus oppositi, qui iuxta omnes philosophos omnium
aspectuum fortissimus est, precipue | quidem cum Saturnus sit   P32r
in angulo medii celi, | Mars autem cadens in domo sexta,   S10v
procacitati nature Martialis resistit eamque exterminat, incon-
stantiam obtemperans, repentinos motus et inconsultos retar-
1165 dans deliberationique locum administrans. Insuper quoque
Saturni conditiones in hoc proposito per bonitatem Iouis sibi
associati multum nobilitantur, ut supra monstratum est. Am-

1142 significat] hic *add.* S   1144 eorum] ipsorum S | almutas siue] *om.* S
Mercurius] *ante* in proposito P   1147 ex] de PV   1148 indagatricem] indigatio-
nem PV   1150 sunt] sint S | inductiones *scr.*] indiciones PV *om.* S | necessarii]
necnon S   1151 ac] aut PV | plurimumque] pluriumque S   1152 nec] necnon
S | et²] *om.* P   1153 rhytmica] reginica ? S | tum] t'n S | scribe eorumque]
scribereque eorum S   1154 et] *om.* S   1155 intellectu] intellectum V | cetera
que] etiam qui S   1157 sextilem] subtilem S   1158 nitatur *scr.*] nitctur S
nitteretur P *p.corr.* V   1159 inquisitiua] mansiti'a S | immissionem]
immixtionem P missionem V   1161 est] *om.* PV | cum] tamen P
1165 deliberationique] debilitationique P -oni V   1166 hoc proposito] *om.* PV

1141 si...1143 intelligentiam] Ibn Ezra, *Moladot*, III I 7, 8, pp. 106-107 | 1146
si...1148 indagatricem] Ibn Ezra, *De nativitatibus*, sig. a6r:8-11 | 1150
probabiles...1155 patentium] Albumasar, *Introductorium maius*, VII.9 (vol. 8, p.
146:699-706)

plius *cum Mercurius et Luna colligati sint utroque aspectu,* scilicet illo
qui secundum domorum distinctionem et illo qui per gradus
equales, *amboque aspiciant ascendens,* significat hoc iuxta **Ptolo-**   1170
meum et **Auenezre** et alios quod *anima nati perfecta erit et preerit*
ratio appetitui neque faciet res nisi cum discretione et equitate nec aleuia-
bitur a discretione dum in egritudinibus fuit. Vnde in CAPITULIS
ALMANSORIS : *non amittet sensum in cuius natiuitate Luna inerit ad*
Mercurium. Adhuc in coniunctione luminarium precedente   1175
natiuitatem hanc, cum separetur Luna a Sole, coniuncta est
corporaliter Mercurio, et iterum in hora natiuitatis reiuncta est
eidem per aspectum cum receptione, quod quidem secundum
Hispalensem significat hominem *sapientem* et *bonas manus*
habentem ad opera. Item in eadem coniunctione luminarium erat   1180
ascendens Aquarius, signum uidelicet magne coniunctionis, in
mutatione triplicitatis, gradus autem ad quem peruenit directio
ab Ariete iuxta inceptionem orbis in quo nunc sumus erat in
ascendente. Et hoc forsan cum aliis notabile aliquod insinuat.
Aquarius enim est *signum angelorum et demoniorum,* ut dicit   1185
Hispalensis in YSAGOGIS suis, quod et manifestum est ex 11°
capitulo libri **Hispalensis.** Item in libro SOYGA scriptum est
quod Aquarius est *optimum bonorum.* Vnde in eodem sic
habetur : *et Aquarius suscipit o. s. m., quod quamuis uocetur fixum,*
hoc est manifeste ratio, quia descriptio o. potest assimilari homini et per   1190
V122v   *illum | intelligimus Iesum qui est fixura nostre saluationis uel quia*
Adam fuit primus homo et nos debemus esse eiusdem fixionis, et cetera.
Secundum mentem etiam **Iulii Firmici** *geniture dominus* in
proposito *Mercurius* est faciens *cordatos,* ut dicit, *ingeniosos cuncta*

1168 illo] primo *S*   1172 neque] nec *S* | aleuiabitur] alienabitur *V*   1173 a] ab
ipso *PV* | fuit *scr.*] suis *codd.*   1174 amittet] -tit *S*   1177 natiuitatis] cum se *add.*
S | est] *om. P*   1178 eidem] *post* aspectum *S*   1181 ascendens] aspectus *S*
1182   mutatione] imitatione *S*   1185   demoniorum] demonum *PV*
demoniacorum *ed.* | dicit] ait *P*   1186 Hispalensis] alb' *S* | et] *om. V*
1187 Soyga] soiga *P* sorga *S*   1189 suscipit] recipit *PV* | o...m] o. s. in *S*
1190 o] *om. S* | per] *om. S*   1192 homo] *om. PV* | fixionis] religionis *praem. V*

1168 cum...1173 fuit] Ibn Ezra, *Moladot,* III 1 7, 7, pp. 106-7 | 1174
non...1175 Mercurium] *Capitula Almansoris,* c. 16, sig. 120va | 1179
significat...1180 opera] Iohannes Hispalensis, *Epitome,* sig. I2v:23-24 | 1185
Aquarius...demoniorum] Iohannes Hispalensis, *Epitome,* sig. C1v:31-C2r:1 |
1186 quod...1187 Hispalensis] Hispalensis de Aquario loquitur in 11 capitulo
introductionis | 1187 in...1188 bonorum] *Liber soyga* 22, p. 251 | 1189
et...1192 cetera] *Liber soyga* 16, p. 172. | 1193 geniture...1195 cupientes]
Firmicus Maternus, *Math.* IV 19, 24, p. 251:27-29

1195 *discentes modestos omnium artium secreta discere cupientes.* Porro dicit
Princeps et **Hispalensis** cum ipso quod cum in natiuitate
fuerit ascendens domus Iouis, significat hoc natum querere
pecuniam et diuitias, et quia Capricornus partem habet in
ascendente, significat hoc partem tribulationum et aduersi-
1200 tatum. Confert igitur Iupiter iuxta hec uirtutem firmam et
appetitum diuitiarum et iustitie et reliqua sue nature, Saturnus
uero sollicitudinem et tolerantiam laboris, secundum quod
uolunt philosophi. Notandum est autem propter hoc et huiusmodi iudicia diuersos effectus et contrarios significantia in
1205 eodem quod, ubicumque hoc acciderit, commiscenda et temperanda est natura significati, ut quasi quoddam medium per
commixtionem generetur, quemadmodum ex contrariis qualita-
tibus ad inuicem alteratis fit mixtum ; magis tamen declinan-
dum est ad latus prepotentis et fortioris, et hoc uolunt omnes
1210 philosophi. Iterum cum in natiuitate sunt significatores contrarii, et quantum ad hoc iudicium eius redditur confusum et
inuolutum, reuolutiones annorum ac eorumdem partium,
mensium uidelicet, dierum et horarum, confusa sequestrantes
contraria iuxta fortitudines et debilitates eorum in natiuitate et
1215 consimiliter in reuolutionibus, nunc hoc nunc illud explicant
dearticulantes nunc prospera nunc aduersa. Et hoc est quod
habetur in LIBRO DE IUDICIO URINE NON VISE capitulo 1°, cui
unanimiter consentiunt astrologorum precipui ob dictam
causam de reuolutionibus natiuitatum annualibus tractantes.
1220 Vnde **Albumasar** : *Si enim significauerit in natiuitate aliquis planeta*
uel locus bonum uel malum, tunc apparet significatio quando dominabitur

1197 fuerit] fuit *S* | hoc] hic *S* 1198 pecuniam] - as *S* 1199 hoc] hic *S*
aduersitatum] -tem *P* 1200 uirtutem] ueritatem *P* | et] ei *add P* ey *add. V*
1202 laboris] laborum *PV* 1203 huiusmodi iudicia] *inv. S* 1210 Iterum] item
V | in] *om. S* 1211 eius] *om. P* | redditur] reddatur *P* 1212 ac] et *S* | eorum-
dem] earundem *S* 1213 mensium] *om. V* 1214 eorum] earum *S* 1215 illud]
hoc *S* 1216 prospera] propria *S* 1219 annualibus] animalibu*s P* 1220 aliquis
planeta] *ante* in natiuitate *trsp. PV* 1221 dominabitur] -natur *S*

1196 Princeps...1200 aduersitatum] Ibn Ezra, *Liber nativitatum*, fol. 60a:28-30 |
cum[1]...1198 diuitias] Iohannes Hispalensis, *Epitome*, sig. K1v:30 | 1198
Capricornus...1200 aduersitatum] Iohannes Hispalensis, *Epitome*, sig. M4v:13-
14: "cuius in nativitate ascendit Cancer uel Capricornus, is inimicitiam gerit cum
fratribus" | 1201 Saturnus...1203 philosophi] cf. Iohannes Hispalensis,
Epitome, sig. I2v:17-18: "si Saturno nodet, natus aptus erit ad multos labores
tollerandos" | 1217 Libro...1°] Guillelmus Anglicus, *De urina non visa*, c.1, p.
137-140 | 1220 Si...1224 maliuolos] Albumasar, *De revol.*, p. 246b9-16

planeta diuisionis per aliquos annorum circuitus, et quando gubernabit per
S11r   *corpus | siue per iactum radiorum uel applicuerit ad beniuolos uel mali-*
uolos. Vnde hec consideratio usque ad menses et dies et horas
extenditur. Sed quia difficile esset aut impossibile omnes reuo-   1225
lutiones et constellationes singulas ad inuicem comparando
cum omnibus aliis que ad complementum causarum faciunt
respectu suorum effectuum considerari, idcirco possibilibus
contenti et facilioribus ultra reuolutiones annorum raro pro-
cedimus aut ultra mensium significationes. Sed ad inceptum   1230
sermonem redeamus.

Dicit quidem **Hispalensis** quod *considerandum est que imago*
de 36 ascendat cum gradu ascendente et que sit cum Luna. **Ptolomeus**
quoque dicit in LIBRO FRUCTUS uerbo 95: *que cooriuntur*
unicuique decano fore significant electionem nati et fortunam quam   1235
percurret. Est autem Luna *in secundo Geminorum decano,* cui *iuxta*
Persas cooritur *uir aureo canens calamo, Persica lingua Teruueles, Greca*
Hercules dictus, idemque nixus genu pariterque et Coluber arborem
ascendens fugiendo Teruuelem mediumque Cerastis, cum quo lupus manu
signata. Iuxta Indos uir forma Ethiopi similis, colore grisus, caput   1240
plumbea uicta ligatus, armis indutus, ferrea tectus galea, desuper ostro
cirritus, idest corona cerica uel aurifrigia, *manu tenens arcum et*
P32v   *sagittas, iocos ac saltus parans, cantans, timpanum percutiens, poma | ex*
horto rapiens, qui simul oritur cum eo multi odoriferi ligni. Post Grecos
dextra aurige manus atque alter posteriorum Tauri pedum simulque   1245
Orionis caput, humerus, manus, pectus Baltheus genu cum pede Leporis

---

1222 aliquos] alios *S*   1223 uel maliuolos] *om. PV*   1224 hec] *om. P* | et²] *om. P*
1225 quia] *om. PV* | omnes] *om. S*   1227 omnibus] *om. S* | complementum] -ta
PV   1228 respectu] respectum *S*   1229 contenti] contempti *P* | procedimus
scr.] proceditur *SV* -detur *P*   1231 redeamus] ueniamus *PV*   1233 ascendente]
ascendentis *ex* ascendente *corr. V*   1234   que] quo *V*   1235   fore] fere *S*
1236 percurret] procurret *V*   1237 cooritur] cooriuntur *V* | lingua] signa *PV*
Teruueles *scr. cum ed.*] t'uelos *P* terauelos *S* tucolos ? (-e- *sup.* -co *V*) *V* | Greca]
gratia *V*   1238 dictus] decus *V* | Coluber] colubri *S*   1239 ascendens] signans
S | Teruuelem *scr. cum ed.*] t'uelon *P* terboelem *S* tucoleon *V*   1241 uicta] nuta
SV | ostro] astro *S*   1242 cirritus] orritus S corritus *V* | idest] hec est *S*
aurifrigia *scr. cum ed.*]-gio *codd.*   1244   multi] multi *S*   1245   posteriorum]
posterior *S*   1246 Baltheus…pectus] *om. PV*

1232 considerandum…1233 Luna] Iohannes Hispalensis, *Epitome,* sig. I2r:23-24
| 1233 Ptolomeus…1236 percurret] Ps.-Ptol., *Cent.,* trans. graeco-latina, v. 95
| 1236 Est…1247 clunis] Albumasar, *Introductorium maius,* VI.1 (vol. 8, pp.
98:177-99:186)

quoque pectus et clunis. Hee autem imagines **Ptolomei** mutant locum, secundum quod octaua sphera, licet alie imagines, Persarum scilicet et Indorum, fixe sint, secundum quod testa-
1250 tur **Albumasar.** Qualitercumque autem hoc sit, tertia tamen facies Geminorum cum imaginibus suis non multum differt a secunda. Dicit quoque **Zael** in suis INTERROGATIONIBUS quod *in secunda facie Geminorum ascendit uir in cuius manu est fistula et alter curuus.* Et iterum *secundo Sagittarii decano,* qui est ascendens, co-
1255 oritur *iuxta Persas Keakasius cepheus* (alia littera habet *thimeus*) |
sinistra manu canis fauces obtundens, dextra capricorni cornua premens, pede dextro fero cani resistens in canis capite lepus caputque leonis pariter et dimidium corpus naute dimidiumque nauis cum dimidio delphine medioque asturcone. Iuxta Indos mulier supra *camelum sedens pilosa*
1260 *pannis induta cum cartan, idest ueste pilea, inter manus eius cistella redimicula continens* et ornamenta. *Post Grecos* uero *pectus urse minoris cum parte Draconis et genu alchide, tum uultures due tum anguitenentis caput cum humero et manu sinistra parsque anguis finisque nerui arcus cum parte qua manus sagittam tenet atque ferro sagitte ac pars certi*
1265 *australis.* **Zael** quoque dicit quod *in secunda facie* Sagittarii *ascendit mulier supra quam sunt panni.* Et re uera mirabilis est nimiumque stupenda uirtus harum imaginum et mysterium earum, quod a sapientibus sic occultatum est et sepultum, ut sit quasi res prophetica, secundum quod testantur **Albumasar** et **Aue-**
1270 **nezre,** qui secretum hoc reuelare uoluerunt, licet quidam philo-

---

1247   Hee] hec *SV*   1250   sit] fit *P om. V*   1251   imaginibus suis] *inv. S*
1254 curuus] caruus *V* | secundo] duo *S* tertio *ed.* | decano] *om. S* | est] *om. S*
1255   thimeus] timens *del. et* Thimeus *scr. S*   1256   canis fauces] *inv. P*
1257 caputque] caput quoque *S*   1260   induta] inducta *P* | cistella] phistela *S*
1262 due] duo *S* | tum² scr. *cum ed.*]cum *S* tum cum *PV* | anguitenentis] eguitenentis *S*   1263 parsque] pars S | nerui *scr. cum ed.*] mu' *PV* ueru *S*   1266 supra] super S   1267   mysterium] misteria S   1269   secundum quod] ut S
1270 hoc] *om. P* | uoluerunt] noluerunt *S* uolunt *V*

1247 Hee…1248 locum] Bate ad praecessionem aequinoctiorum referre videtur
| 1248 licet…1250 Albumasar] Albumasar, *Introductorium maius,* VI.1 (vol. 8, p. 96:94-96) | 1253 in¹…1254 curuus] Zael, *De interrogationibus,* sig. 132rb:64-65
| 1254 iterum…1265 australis] Albumasar, *Introductorium maius,* VI.1 (vol. 8, p. 104:365-374) | 1265 in…1266 panni] Zael, *De interrogationibus,* sig. 132va:12-13
| 1269 secundum…1270 uoluerunt] vide Albumasar, *Introductorium maius,* VI.1 (vol. 8, p. 96:76-77): "celique secreta adumbrato sermone et minus peritis occultarent, et sapienti ingenio pleno intellectu designarent" | 1270 licet…1273 Compilatoris] Ibn Ezra, *De nativitatibus,* sig. a3r:18-21

sophi Iudeorum non sint reueriti ipsarum contradicere uirtuti et ueritati, secundum quod apparet in LIBRO NATIVITATUM **Abrahe Compilatoris**. Sed uisum est mihi hoc accidisse precipue propter imaginem crucifixi inter huiusmodi imagines figurati, ut est cepheus et mulier que non nouit uirum et alie, 1275 secundum quod alias palam est. Nolunt enim Iudei aliquod testimonium ueritatis honorande aut signum auctoritatis concedere talibus imaginibus propter odium crucifixi, et hoc satis uidetur innuere **Auenezre** in LIBRO RATIONUM uersus finem

S11v   loquens de huiusmodi imaginibus, ubi dicit quod *non est* | *hoc* 1280 *fas in lege Iudeorum :* nam alique imagines sunt ad *similitudinem ritus* alieni (secundum alium uero translatorem : *nam quedam imago est ad similitudinem crucis*). *Amor* enim *et odium prohibent recta iudicia.* Quidquid autem dicant Iudei aut alii quicumque, fortuna tamen nati huius et electio in multis assimilata est hiis que per 1285 imagines innuebantur integumentis. Hic enim seruus Dei a pueritia calamis canentes et fistulis omneque genus instrumentorum musicorum libenter audiuit et in tantum delectatus est in eis, ut quasi de qualibet artium huiusmodi partem sit adeptus. Etenim flatum in tibiis et calamis diuersoque fistularum genere 1290 artificiose modulari nouit, organis quoque et chordis clauos pellendo melos elicere. Sed postquam philosophie limites ingressus est et effectus alumnus eius animumque magis colens, intellectui factus obedientior, actum fistularum amplius exercere non curauit, iuxta illud **Philosophi** in 8° POLITI- 1295 CORUM : *Aiunt enim Palladem, cum inuenisset fistulas, abiecisse ; non*

1271   uirtuti…ueritati] ueritati et uirtuti *S*   1273   accidisse] apparere *V* 1274 imagines] -nem *S*   1275 que…nouit] non habens *S*   1276 Nolunt] uolunt P | aliquod] ad *PV*   1277 aut] ut P   1278 imaginibus] *om. PV*   1280 hoc] *om. PV*   1281 ad] in *S*   1282 uero] *s.l. S post* secundum P   1283 ad] in *S*   1284 dicant] dicunt *S* | alii] aliqui *S*   1286 Dei] domini *V*   1287 canentes] canens P 1290 tibiis…calamis] *inv. S*   1291 artificiose *scr.*] artificio se *codd.* | quoque] -que *S* | chordis *scr.*] choris *codd.* | clauos] claues *S*   1293 animumque] animique P animumque…colens] *iter. S*   1294   intellectui] intellectus *PV* | fistularum] fistulationum *S*   1295 in] *om. S*

1280 non…1283 crucis] Ibn Ezra, *Te'amim II*, §8.3:-2, pp. 250-251, quod Bate sic interpretatus est: "Et hoc quidem faciendum est non in lege iudeorum quod ibi est ymago crucis, vel secundum aliam lecturam quod in similitudine est ritus siue cultus extranei" (MS Leipzig 1466, fol. 60ra:34-37). | 1283 Amor…1284 iudicia] Ps.-Ptol., *Cent.*, v. 12 | 1296 Aiunt…1298 artem] Arist., *Polit.* VIII 6, 1341b3-4 et 6-8 (transl. Guilelmi)

male enim habet dicere, quia ad intellectum nihil est eruditio fistulationis,
Palladi autem scientiam attribuimus et artem. Item *cistella redimicula*
continens et huiusmodi mulier quoque equitans et non equitans
1300 frequenter locum habuerunt circa hunc natum necnon et circa
harum imaginum integumenta, que magis arbitror sub silentio
pertransire quam recitare tum propter prolixitatem, tum propter secretum occultandum. *Qui* enim *occulta detegit et arcana reuelat*
ipsum in proximo multa infortunia consequntur, ut habetur in libro
1305 DE REGIMINE PRINCIPUM. Vt autem ad omne dicatur, pauca
restant imaginum integumenta, que aut re aut nomine aut
similitudinis interpretatione fortunam nati uel id quod habet in
animo non percurrerunt. Nouit equidem natus iste uiellam
baiulare melodiosam tactum cordarum eius et tractum arcus
1310 proportionaliter conducendo, cistri quoque fides digitis et
plectro docte tangere atque dulcisoni psalterii dulce melos
penna duplici concorditer euocare necnon et delectabile mur-
mur tubisoni Licii penne plectro replicare ictibus timpanizando
uicissim replicatis. Amplius omne genus musici cantus sibi
1315 notum est et magistralis, adhuc | et diuerse species cantionum V123v
uulgarium in diuersis linguis ipseque cantans libentius. Rithmo-
rum quoque inuentor et cantionum hilaris, iocosus, amatiuus,
corearum ductor et dux tripudiorum in uirgultis, ludos,
conuiuia et iocos parari affectans, ludum quoque saltationis
1320 aliis interponens. Hec autem et huiusmodi non sunt operatio-
nibus studiosis inimica, maxime in iuuenibus, secundum quod
uult **Philosophus** 8° POLITICORUM dicens : *ponunt autem et*

1297 nihil] nulla *S* autem in hoc P | eruditio] *om. S* 1299 huiusmodi] huius *V*
huius et P 1302 tum¹] *om. V* 1303 occultandum] ocultationum S | occulta]
secreta P*V* 1304 infortunia] fortunia S (*sed* in- *s.l.*) 1306 que] *om. S*
1307 habet] habebit S 1308 percurrerunt] -rerent *S* | Nouit equidem] nouiter
quidem *S* | uiellam] uielleam *V* | uiellam…melodiosam] baiulare uiellam *S*
1309 arcus] artis *V* 1311 psalterii] psaltii *V* 1313 Licii *scr.*] licui P*SV* | repli-
care] replicare producere *S* 1314 replicatis] refricatis P refricans *V*
1315 magistralis] magistral' P*V an* magistraliter *scrib.* ? | adhuc] ad h' P*V*
cantionum…1317 et] *om. S* 1316 Rithmorum] bachinorum *V* 1317 iocosus]
iocundus PV | amatiuus] clinatiuus *V* 1318 in] et *S* 1319 affectans] affectum
S 1320 aliis] *om. S* | sunt] aut *add. S* | operationibus] operibus *S* 1322 8°] 6°
S | dicens] scilicet *S*

1303 Qui…1304 consequntur] Ps.-Arist., *Secretum secretorum*, pars I, c. 4, p.
41:17-19 | 1322 ponunt…1326 prudentiam] Arist., *Polit.* VIII 5, 1339a21-26
(transl. Guilelmi)

P33r saltationem in | hiis aut magis ad uirtutem tendere secundum aliquid
extimandum musicam tamquam potentem sicut exercitatiua quale aliquod
corpus efficere et musicam morem qualem quendam facere assuescentem 1325
gaudere recte ad deductionem aut aliquid confert et ad prudentiam.
Quomodo autem ad prudentiam ad illum locum spectat declarandum. Museus ait enim, ut ibidem habetur, hominibus delectabillis-
simum cantare : propter quod in conuentus et deductiones rationabiliter
assumunt ipsam tamquam potentem letificare, quare et hinc extimabit 1330
utique aliquis oportere musicam erudiri iuniores. Vacare autem, inquit,
ipsum uidetur habere delectationem et felicitatem et uiuere beate. Quare
manifestum quod oportet et ad eam que in deductione uacationem ad-
discere quedam et erudiri et has eruditiones. Habet enim musica delectationem naturalem propter quod omnibus etatibus, ut ibidem habetur, et 1335
omnibus moribus usus ipsius est amicus. Non immanifestum autem quod
multam habet differentiam ad fieri quales quosdam, si quis ipse communi-
S12r cet operibus: unum enim | aliquid impossibilium aut difficilium est eos,
qui non communicauerunt operibus, iudices fieri studiosos. Quoniam igitur
gratia iudicii oportet participare operibus propter hoc oportet iuuenes 1340
quidem existentes in operibus, seniores autem factos opera quidem dimit-
tere, posse autem bona iudicare et gaudere recte propter eruditionem factam
in iuuentute. Recte enim gaudere et delectari rationi a uirtute est, ut
patet 10° ETHICORUM et 4° similiter. Sed hec hactenus.

Pars quidem ascendentis signi humana est et angulus 1345
medii celi consimiliter, in quo dominus ascendentis, angulus

1323 aut] autem PS | tendere] scr. cum Arist.] tandem PV tn' S 1324 tamquam]
aliquid add. PV | sicut] om. S 1325 corpus] om. P mg. add. | efficere...quendam]
om. V | assuescentem] ascuescentis V 1326 aut] autem PS
1327 Quomodo...prudentiam] om. PV 1328 ait enim] etiam ait PV 1329 et]
om. S 1330 ipsam] ipsa p. corr. P | hinc] huic P 1331 utique] utrum V
iuniores] minores PV 1332 ipsum uidetur] inv. PV 1333 manifestum] est add.
s.l. P 1334 quedam scr. cum Arist. quidem PS quid V 1335 etatibus] errantibus
PV 1336 moribus] moris P | autem] est P 1337 habet] om. PV | ad] om. PV
1338 unum...operibus] om. PV | est eos] inv. S 1339 iudices] iudice P
1343 Recte] ratione S | rationi] secundum rationem S | ut] om. S
1345 ascendentis] post signi S | signi scr.] autem signi PV asigni S

1328 Museus...1331 iuniores] Arist., Polit. VIII 5, 1339b21-25 (transl. Guilelmi)
| 1331 Vacare...1332 beate] Arist., Polit. VIII 3, 1338a1-3 (transl. Guilelmi) |
1332 Quare...1334 eruditiones] Arist., Polit. VIII 3, 1338 a9-11 (transl.
Guilelmi) | 1334 Habet...1336 amicus] Arist., Polit. VIII 5, 1340a3-5 (transl.
Guilelmi) | 1336 Non...1339 studiosos] Arist., Polit. VIII 6, trans. Guilelmi,
1340b22-25 | 1339 Quoniam...1343 iuuentute] Arist., Polit. VIII 6, trans.
Guilelmi, 1340b35-39 | 1343 ut...1344 similiter] Cf. Arist., Eth. Nic. IV 2,
1121a3-4 et X 1, 1171b22

quoque occidentis, in quo Luna est, est talis necnon et angulus terre, in quo Mercurius dominus uigoris est, de signis domesticis et mansuetis, que omnia, iuxta **Hispalensem** et alios,
1350 natum faciunt cum hominibus conuersari, sodalitates diligere et conuiuiis interesse et commessationibus. Est enim hic natus omnibus promiscuus et conuertibilis ad omnia que consortibus placent attemptari, etiam si displicerent sibi ipsi, quemadmodum et dominus suus Mercurius ei cui coniungitur assimi-
1355 latur. Impressa quoque est huic nato illa natura Mercurii, quam refert **Aristoteles** in LIBRO 9 IUDICUM, scilicet quod, *quamuis multos acquirat amicos, nullos tamen aut paucos fideles inuenit.* Verum, quomodocumque uariis occupationibus diuersimodisque negligentiis inuoluatur seu curis quibuslibet, immaterialis tamen
1360 luminis radius quidam internos sensus illustrando mentem eius supertrahit ad diuina, iubens ut Palladi de cerebro Iouis procreate hospitium preparet, in quo nuptie Mercurii et Philologie queant digne celebrari iuxta poeticam **Martiani Capelle** insinuationem. In mente quidem enim nati propositi preeminet
1365 omnibus aliis delectationibus ille nobilis amor scientiarum, sermocinalium uidelicet, moralium et reliquarum, puta, secundum tres philosophie theorias, mathematicam, physicam siue naturalem et theologicam. | In hiis enim et que ad hec referun- V124r
tur, pregustatur delectatio, que aliis delectationibus incompara-
1370 bilis merito iudicatur, de qua dicit **Philosophus** 10° ETHI-
CORUM quod *admirabiles delectationes affert philosophia puritate et firmitate, puritate* quidem quia alie contrarium habent admixtum, puta tristitiam aliquam, ista non, *firmitate* uero, quia alie durabiles non sunt propter mutabilitatem subiectorum, ista propter

1347 est¹] est *add. S* | est²] *om. PV* 1350 et] *om. PS* 1353 displicerent] -cent *V* | ipsi] *om. S* 1355 Impressa] impremissa *V* 1358 diuersimodisque] diuersis modisque *S* 1359 seu] *om. PV* | immaterialis] in malis *S* 1360 quidam] quidem *P* quid' *S* | internos] inter honores *praem. S* honorus (honor' P) *praem. PV* 1361 procreate] procreare *PV* 1362 preparet] imparet per quod *PV* Philologie] *mg. Par.* ph'e *PSV* 1364 In…enim] quod enim in mente *S* propositi] *om. PV* 1366 uidelicet] et *add. S* 1367 theorias] tehoricas *P* 1368 enim] *om. S* 1373 non] uero *P* | uero] non *P*

1349 Hispalensem…1351 commessationibus] Cf. Iohannes Hispalensis, *Epitome*, sig. I2v:11-13; Ibn Ezra, *Reshit Ḥokhmah*, §2.7:33, pp. 100-101 | 1362 in…1364 insinuationem] Martianus Caplla, *De nuptiis Philologiae et Mercurii* II 214 | 1371 admirabiles…1372 firmitate] Arist., *Eth. Nic.* X 7, 1177a25-26

durabilem et firmam sue perfectionis excellentiam felicitatem   1375
concludit speculatiuam. Hec igitur dicta sunt ob concordiam
effectuum cum suis causis.

Reuertamur autem ad propositum principale et compleamus sermonem de domo prima. Dicit igitur **Alendruzagar**
quod *domini triplicitatis signi ascendentis successum uite significant,*   1380
aliqui uero sapientes dicunt se hoc expertos fore. Primus autem
dominus triplicitatis Sagittarii Iupiter est, cum natiuitas nocturna fuerit. Secundum dispositionem ergo Iouis dictam et
dicendam disposita est prima uite tertia. Et hoc modo iudicanda est secunda per Solem, ultima uero per Saturnum. De   1385
prima igitur domo dicta sint tot et tanta. Nam *magis erit planum
quod per plura dictum,* ut dicit **Philosophus** 1° RHETORICORUM.
In reliquis uero domibus breuius procedemus. Maxime enim
difficultates huic proposito incidentes pertractate sunt iam in
maiori parte.   1390

4.4. <Domus secunda>

Nunc autem domus secunde, que *domus spei* a **Iulio Fir-
mico** nuncupatur, significationem edisseramus. Dicit quidem
enim **Albumasar** *quod mysteria secundi loci sunt multa et non potest
aliquis hoc scire si non sit perfectus sapiens. Obseruaui enim,* inquit, *in
multis natiuitatibus quod quando maleficiatus est locus secundus et domi-*   1395
S12v   *nus ipsius, numquam proficiet natus.* | Dominus autem huius loci in
proposito Saturnus est, cuius dispositio supra dicta est in parte.
Vnde in CAPITULIS ALMANSORIS : *ualde diuites et quilibet habunda-
bunt diuitiis magnique nominis sunt quibus dominus secunde domus fuerit*

1375 felicitatem] felicitatis *V*   1381 aliqui *scr.*] reliqui *S* qui *PV* | autem] igitur *P*
1384 iudicanda] dicenda *V*   1386 erit *scr. cum Arist.*] exit codd.   1387 quod]
dicitur *add. S*   1388 enim] autem *P*   1389 iam] *om. S*   1391 que domus] *om. S*
1392 edisseramus] disseramus *P*   1393 mysteria] in scientia *S*   1394 aliquis hoc]
inv. PV | hoc] hec *S*   1396 numquam] umquam *P* | proficiet] -cit *P*
1397 Saturnus est] *inv. S* | in parte] imparte *S*   1398 Vnde…1400 ascendentis]
post debilitati retrogradationis (l. 1408) *trsp. PV* | quilibet] quibus *PV*
1399 diuitiis] diuitie *PS* | domus] *om. P*

1379 Dicit…1381 fore] apud Ibn Ezra, *Moladot,* III III 6, 3, pp. 104-105 | 1386
Nam…1387 dictum] Arist., *Rhet.* I 2, trans. Guilelmi, 1358a9-10 | 1391
domus[1]…1392 nuncupatur] Firmicus Maternus, *Math.* II 14, 3, pp. 57:31-58:2
| 1392 Dicit…1396 natus] Sadan, *Excerpta* 28, p. 321 | 1398 ualde…1400
ascendentis] *Capitula Almansoris,* c. 103, sig. 121vb

1400 *in exaltatione sua iens ad dominum ascendentis*. Quamquam igitur,
ratione qua maleficus est et retrogradus et dominum ascendentis similiter retrogradum recipiens, laborem et angustiam et
timorem cum desperatione significet in fortuna possessoria,
ratione tamen angularitatis medii celi et exaltationis sue impedi-
1405 menta Saturni remittuntur, ut dignitas exaltationis malignitatem
nature sue temperet iuxta illud **Hermetis** : *maliuolus abstinet se a*
malitia cum fuerit in domo sua uel exaltatione, et ut fortitudo
angularitatis medii celi preponderet debilitati | retrogradationis.   P33v
Vnde **Zael** : *mali cum fuerint in domibus suis* aut *in exaltationibus aut*
1410 *triplicitatibus aut terminis suis et in angulis uel in* sequentibus *angulo-*
rum, erit fortitudo eorum sicut fortitudo fortunatarum. Iterum idem :
et omnis planeta fortunatus aut malus cum fuerit in domo sua aut exalta-
tione aut triplicitate sua, conuertitur quidquid in eis est ex malo in
bonum. Vnde **Hermes** : *in propria domo uel in exaltatione si fuerit*
1415 *maliuolus, licet cum tarditate, tamen exhibet bonum finem.* Item: dominus secundi cum *domino ascendentis* in medio celi existens *signifi-*
cat multitudinem substantie, ut uult **Auicenna**, et consecutionem
fortune possessorie *a rege et ex causis eius* (secundum aliam translationem: *et erit uita eius ab eis*). Et quia est *in undecimo* secundum
1420 gradus equales, significat hoc *substantiam* inueniri *ab amicis et*
negotiationibus et accommodationibus ac *messibus*, sed non erit hoc
sine timore et angustia propter | retrogradationem Saturni.   V124v
Quod autem retrogradatio Saturni non neget consecutionem
substantie et fortune possessorie et prosperitatis, satis patet per

---

1401 et²] *om. S* | dominum] -que *s l. add. S*   1405 Saturni] *om. S* | ut] *om. V*
dignitas] *ex corr.* Pᵉ dignitates *PV* | malignitatem] -tatis *V*   1408 debilitati] debi-
litas *S*   1409 aut¹…suis] *om. S*   1410 triplicitatibus] in triplicitate *V* | in¹] *om. S*
1411 fortunatarum] forᵃʳᵘᵐ P fortunarum *SV*   1412 fortunatus fortunatus *scr.*
cum Zael.] fortu'a *S* fortuna et *V* | aut²] in *add. V*   1413 aut] in *add. SV* | sua] et
add. S etcetera *add. PV* | in¹…est] est in eis *S*   1414 Vnde Hermes] *om. S* | in²]
om. S   1416 secundi…domino] etiam dominus *S*   1417 substantie] et *add.* P
1419 in] *om. S*   1421 negotiationibus] negociatoribus *ed.* | accommodationibus]
datoribus *ed.* | messibus] mercibus *ed.*   1423 consecutionem] consecutioni *V*

1406 maliuolus…1408 retrogradationis] Hermes, *Cent.*, c. 59, sig. 117va et c. 86,
sig. 118ra | 1409 mali…1411 fortunatarum] Zael, *Iudicia*, c. 26, sig. 126va:41-
45 | 1412 et…1414 bonum] Zael, *Iudicia*, c. 30, sig. 126va:67-126vb:3 | 1414
in¹…1415 finem] Hermes, *Cent.*, c. 99, sig. 118ra | 1415 dominus…1417 sub-
stantie] Albohali, *De nativitatibus*, c.11, sig. f2v:8-10 et f4r:4 | 1419 et…eis]
Albohali, *De nativitatibus*, c. 11, trans. Platonis (MS Oxford, Digby 51, fol. 120ra)
| in…1421 messibus] Albohali, *De nativitatibus*, c.11, sig. f4r:5-7

Auicennam in quodam exemplo natiuitatis in quo Saturnus in   1425
summo retrogradationis sue erat in Libra, secundum quod hic
est. Dicit tamen ipsum taliter in angulo terre existentem *signifi-
casse prosperitatem* et exaltationem *in fine uite sue,* cum esset dominus triplicitatis tertius luminaris cuius erat auctoritas. Concordati sunt enim omnes astrologi quod domini triplicitatis lumi-   1430
naris cuius est auctoritas super prosperitatem nati significant
secundum ordinem dominorum et tertiarum uite. In proposito
autem domini triplicitatis Lune sunt Mercurius, Saturnus et
Iupiter. Mercurius quidem uim suam Soli committens per
receptionem coniunctiuam primam tertiam disposuit faciendo   1435
natum nobilem, acceptabilem et gratiosum, Saturnus autem in
medio celi recipiens Iouem secundam tertiam disponere habet
secundum esse suum quod supra declarauimus, uidelicet, quod
Saturnus in proposito magis est fortunatus quam infortunatus.
Vnde **Stephanus** in SADAN : *sciendum quod si fuerit bonus in domo*   1440
corruptoris uel in exaltatione ipsius, recipit maleficus bonum et minuit
malitiam ipsius. Iupiter quoque dominus triplicitatis tertius
luminaris cuius est auctoritas consimiliter est in angulo secundum equationes domorum, quemadmodum et alii duo, quod
quidem prosperitatem significat secundum **Auicennam** per   1445
totam uitam non obstante retrogradatione, ut dictum est. Item
dominus ascendentis Iupiter est planeta diuitiarum qui receptus
est a Saturno in cuius coniunctione est in angulo medii celi
signo exaltationis sue. Estque Saturnus dominus partis fortune
secundum **Ptolomeum** et suos sequaces. Secundum uero   1450
Albumasar est pars fortune in domu Iouis. Est quoque Iupiter
dominus hore et pars fortune in domo substantie, in signo
uidelicet coniunctionis magne aspecta a domino suo per gradus

1427 existentem] *ante* in angulo *trsp. S* existente *P*   1429 cuius…luminaris] *om. S*
1430 enim] autem *P*   1436 nobilem] nobilibus *P*   1437 secundam] suam *PV*
disponere] dispositionem *V*   1439   quam infortunatus] *om. S*   1440   fuerit
bonus] fuit locus *S*   1444   et…1446 non] *om. S*   1446   obstante] stante *S*
1449 sue] *om. PV*   1451 domu] loco *P* gradu *V*

1425 in¹…1428 sue] Albohali, *De nativitatibus*, sig. e2v:13-23 | 1440 scien-
dum…1442 ipsius] Sadan, *Excerpta* 30, p. 324 | 1442 Iupiter…1446 uitam]
Albohali, *De nativitatibus*, c.7, sig. d1v:21-25 | 1450 secundum Ptolomeum]
Ptol., *Quad.* III.12, trans. Guilelmi, p. 248:448-450 et IV.2, trans.Guilelmi, p.
278:25-26 | 1451 Albumasar] Albumasar, *Introductorium maius*, VIII.3 (vol. 8, p.
152:131-142)

equales. Item est et Luna aucta lumine et numero in angulo *sui*
1455 *honoris*, ut dicit **Princeps**, dispositionem suam et uirtutem
pulsans planete qui ipsam recipit et cum quo est pars substantie. Et hec omnia significant magnitudinem fortune et prosperitatis secundum dicta sapientum, preter quod retrogradatio
Saturni et Iouis difficultatem et timorem in acquisitione por-
1460 tendit. Attamen in 9 IUDICUM habetur *quod si hec applicatio in*
retrogradatione accidat, ex improuiso diuitias aggregat. Preterea presen-
tia domini ascendentis in 10° secundum equationes |domo-   S13r
rum, quamquam angulum transiuerit modicum, significat iuxta
Auicennam *quod* natus *semper erit cum regibus et cum eis uiuet* et
1465 quod secundum gradus equales est *in 11°* significat *quod erit* bene morigenatus *et habebit plures amicos* et *raros filios.* In omnibus
autem hiis est particeps retrogradationis difficultas. Rursum
dicit **Auicenna** quod pars fortune in domo Saturni aspecta ab
ipso, ut est hic, significat *fortunam nati in commixtione seruorum et*
1470 *ancillarum* et hominum etate mediocrium (alia littera habet
senum), presentia autem eius in medio celi nobilitat conditiones
eius, et consimiliter Iupiter, qui est dominus termini nouenarie
et triplicitatis partis fortune; hic enim secundum eundem
significat *fortunam in commixtione nobilium et magnorum hominum ac*
1475 *religiosorum.* Adhuc Venus, domina termini ascendentis in domo
sua existens in quinta domo secundum equationes domorum, a
nullo impedita, *infallibiliter bonam fortunam significat* secundum
Albumasar in SADAN. | Item dicit **Auenezre** quod presentia   V125r
Veneris *in domo quinta, que est domus gaudii sui, significat bonam*
1480 *fortunam sine angustia et timore, sed in gaudio et leto animo, et secundum*

1456   quo] qua *S*   1459   portendit *scr.*] protendit *codd.*   1460   in²] ex *S*
1461 improuiso] impulso *PV*   1464 quod] *om. S* | uiuet] uixerit *S*   1465 11°]
septimo *S* | significat] signatur *S* | bene morigenatus] bonis moribus preditus
ed.   1469 commixtione] coniunctione *ed.* | et ancillarum] *om. S*   1471 senum]
senium *P* | presentia] principum *S* | autem] aut *S* | nobilitat] nobilitas *S*
1472   qui...dominus] *om. S*   1473   hic] hoc *PV*   1474   commixtione]
coniunctione *ed.* | hominum] *om. PV* | ac] et *S*   1477 infallibiliter] inefabiliter *S*
1479 sui] *om. S*

1454 Luna...1455 Princeps] Ibn Ezra, *Liber nativitatum*, fol. 64v:17-18 ; cf. infra
1787-1788 | 1460 quod...1461 aggregat] *Liber novem iudicum*, II.3, p. 422a |
1462 in...1466 filios] Albohali, *De nativitatibus*, c.10, sig. f1v:25-28 | 1469
fortunam...1471 senum] Albohali, *De nativitatibus*, c.9, sig. e4v:2-3 | 1474
fortunam...1475 religiosorum] Albohali, *De nativitatibus*, c.9, sig. e4r:15-17 |
1477 infallibiliter...significat] Sadan, *Excerpta* 28, p. 321 | 1479 in...1481 boni]
Ibn Ezra, *Moladot*, III II 6, 5, pp. 126-127

fortitudinem eius erit quantitas boni. Infra uero palam erit quantam fortitudinem Venus habeat in proposito specialiter. Hic autem cadit pars fortune sub aspectu Veneris duplici uia. At uero quia pars fortune cadit in domo tertia secundum gradus equales, paululum diminuit hoc de bonitate sua. Presentia quoque eius 1485 in domo secunda cum conditionibus ante positis *bona exauget honestamque uitam regum de causa inducit*, secundum quod habetur in LIBRO DE PARTIUM LOCORUMQUE IUDICIIS. Amplius pars pecunie siue substantie in eodem gradu est cum Mercurio existente in proprio termino in domo quarta, quod etiam bo- 1490 num augmentat in fortuna possessoria secundum proprietatem Mercurii et domus quarte, ut patebit infra. Item dicit **Albuma-sar** in LIBRO REVOLUTIONUM NATIVITATUM quod *si fuerit* in radice natiuitatis Caput Draconis *in secundo*, ut est hic, *ditabitur* natus. Preterea domini triplicitatis huius domus secunde pro 1495 prima parte bene se habent preter Martem, pro secunda uero parte, | in qua est pars fortune, omnes sunt angulares, ut dic-tum est. Denique Luna *in domo Mercurii* et in aspectu eius *signifi-cat natum calidum, ingeniosum, sapientem in contentionibus et consequi fortunam et bonum ex eis*, ut uult **Auicenna**. Item aspectus Solis 1500 ad ipsam *significat natum consequi bonum ex regibus et altis hominibus* secundum quod dicit idem. Vt igitur ad omne dicatur, secun-dum iudicia sapientum prosperitas et bona fortuna satis nota-bilis huic nato significata est ex proposita dispositione celesti, non tamen absque angustia et difficultate. 1505

P34r

4.5. <Domus tertia>

Tertie uero domus significatio talis est : cum dominus ascendentis infra terminum coniunctionis sit cum domino huius domus secundum gradus equales accepte, maxime pro

---

1481 erit[1]] et *S* 1482 specialiter] particulariter *S* | Hic *scr. cum Par*] hec *PSV* 1486 cum] *om. PV* | ante] autem 1487 honestamque] honestam P 1491 possessoria] possessoris *S* 1494 est hic] *inv. S* | ditabitur] dictabitur *SV* 1496 uero] *om. S* 1499 contentionibus] contemptionibus *PS* | et] *om. S* 1503 notabilis] nobilis *V* 1504 est] *om. S* 1508 accepte] accepto P

1486 bona...1487 inducit] Ps.-Ptol.., *De iudiciis partium*, fol. 44ra | 1493 si...1495 natus] Albumasar, *De revol.*, p. 278a:34-35 | 1498 Luna...1500 eis] Albohali, *De nativitatibus*, c.9, sig. e4v:23-27 | 1500 aspectus...1501 hominibus] Albohali, *De nativitatibus*, c.9, sig. f1r:7-9

prima parte, et pro secunda idem sit dominus ascendentis et
1510 tertie, secundum equationes quoque domorum potior sit hec
uirtus, *significat* hoc iuxta **Auicennam** et **Auenezre** et reliquos
stabilitatem amicitie fratrum. Pars quoque fratrum *in sextili* cadit
aspectu Iouis domini ascendentis, quod etiam *amicitiam confirmat.* Verum quia in fine domus duodecime cadit ipsa, ob hoc
1515 aliqualis discordiola significatur. Quoniam autem hic natus non
erat de primogenitis, sed penultimus, idcirco natiuitas eius
super significationibus parentum et fratrum magnam certitudinem habere non poterat, secundum quod dicunt astrologi.
Virtus autem huius domus super uias propinquas, ut sunt
1520 diurne et consimiles, iudicanda est secundum dispositionem
Saturni et Iouis supra dictam, et dicenda inferius cum maiori
complemento ; et ut in summa tangatur, aliquid magnum
significare uidetur et notabile, licet cum labore et anxietate.

4.6. <Domus quarta>

|Domus quoque quarte uirtus super significationem   S13v
1525 parentum huius nati certitudinem magnam habere non potest,
ut dictum est, quod etiam attestatur **Hermes** in FLORIBUS suis
dicens hoc dependere | a primogenitis. In CAPITULIS quoque   V125v
ALMANSORIS idem habetur, propter quod alias mentio facta est
de uita et morte parentum eiusdem nati in iudicio natiuitatis
1530 fratris antiquioris. Hiis igitur dimissis dicamus de reliquis huius
domus significatis. Et quoniam idem est dominus ascendentis
et quarte domus secundum gradus equales, significat hoc amicitiam parentum cum filio, prout innuunt sapientes ; secundum
equationes uero domorum idem est dominus quarte et unde-
1535 cime, quod idem significare habet. Item dicit **Hispalensis**: *si*

1509 pro] *om. P* | idem sit] *inv. PV* 1510 equationes] ascensiones *praem. PV*
1512 amicitie] *om. S* 1513 etiam] et *S* 1515 autem hic] ad' *S* 1518 habere]
continere *S* 1519 domus] *om. V* | ut] et *S* 1520 dispositionem] uirtutem
praem. V 1521 dicenda] dicendam *PV* 1524 uirtus] *om. S* 1526 etiam] *om. S*
1530 dimissis] missis *S* 1531 significatis] signatis *S* 1534 equationes] *inv. S*
1535 idem] et *praem. V* quidem *S*

1512 stabilitatem…1514 confirmat] Albohali, *De nativitatibus*, c.15, sig. g3r:15-18
et 20-21 | 1526 Hermes…1527 primogenitis] Hermes, *Cent.*, c. 20, sig. 117rb
| 1527 Capitulis…1528 habetur] *Capitula Almansoris*, c. 95, sig. 121va | 1535
si…1537 filium] Iohannes Hispalensis, *Epitome*, sig. K4r:24-27

*dominus ascendentis fuerit cum Saturno in natali noctis et fuerit ab eo
receptus*, ut est in proposito, *pater semper diliget filium*. Preterea
dicit **Abraham Compilator** : *si oriens sit Sagittarius, ex (repo-
sitione) negotiatione comparatorum ditabitur, quia dominus orientis et
quarte idem est*. Idem quoque dicit **Auenezre**. Vnde in CAPITU-   1540
LIS ALMANSORIS : *non congregabit pecuniam nec thesaurizabit nisi ille
cuius dominus ascendentis et dominus quarte fuerit idem planeta*. Item
ait **Compilator** : *si planetam fortune in quarta domo existentem
dominus secunde quocumque modo respexerit, nisi alteruter eorum combustus uel retrogradus fuerit, nascens pecuniam absconditam inueniet*. Est   1545
autem hec domus quarta secundum equationes domorum Aries
signum regale. Exaltatio quidem | Solis, in quo Sol est tenens
angulum aspiciturque a Saturno et Ioue aspectu opposito, a
Ioue quidem separatus et Saturno applicans, qui consimiliter in
sua consistit exaltatione, quamquam ante ratione huius applica-   1550
tionis Solis cum Saturno a casu suo pena laboris et anxietatis
nimis portendatur, ut habetur in 9 IUDICUM, assimileturque illi
qui hosti proprio quem abhorret et negligit, minus offert inimi-
cabilem et timendum ipsiusque nature contrarium, ut ibidem
habetur. Et iterum iuxta **Messehallah** : si *fuerit Sol in Ariete et*   1555
Saturnus in Libra, erunt inimicitie et contrarietates et ignorationes *et
denegationes*. Consortium tamen Iouis cum Saturno infra terminos coniunctionis una cum reliquis conditionibus supra memoratis impedimenta Saturni mitigat et emendat, ut dictum est

V126r (margin)

1537 Preterea] ppa' (= propterea) *S et sic passim*   1538 ex] *om. V* | repositione]
depositione *P om. S*   1539 ditabitur] dictabitur *S* dubitatur *V*   1540 est] *om. PV*
Capitulis] capitulo *P*   1541   congregabit] -auit S | thesaurizabit] -auit *S*
1542 dominus[1]] *om. S* | fuerit] fuit *S*   1544 respexerit] aspexerit *P* | alteruter]
alterutrum *P*   1546 autem hec] aduc *S* | hec] hic *P*   1547 quo] in *add. S* | est
tenens] *inv. S*   1549 separatus] -tur *P* | consimiliter] similiter *S*   1550 consistit]
post consimiliter *trsp. P* | ante] autem *P* aut *V*   1551   pena *scr.*] pene *PSV*
1552   nimis] manus *S* minis *V* | portendatur] *scr.* pretendatur *PSV* | 9]
commento *V* | assimileturque] assimiletur *S* | illi qui] *an* illinc *scrib. ?*   1553 et
negligit] *om. PV* | minus] unus *P* | offert] afert *S*   1555 et...Libra] *om. S*
1557 Saturno] *om. PV* | terminos coniunctionis] *om. V*   1559 et emendat] *om. S*

1538 si...1540 est] Ibn Ezra, *De nativitatibus*, sig. b6v:33-35 | 1540
Idem...Auenezre]   Ibn Ezra, *Moladot*, III III 1, 5, pp. 130-131 | 1541
non...1542 planeta] *Capitula Almansoris*, c. 20, sig. 120va-b | 1543 si...1545
inueniet] Ibn Ezra, *De nativitatibus*, sig. b4r:17-20 | 1550 quamquam...1552
Iudicum] cf. *Liber novem iudicum*, XII.4B, p. 575a "quidquid tandem poenae et
anxietatis Martis rabies significat, ferrio erit et flagellis" | 1555 si...1557
denegationes] Messahallah, *De receptione*, sig. M1r:31-Mv:1

1560   supra. Concordati quidem enim sunt philosophi quod aspectus
coniunctionem non frustrat neque soluit, licet radius aspicientis
propior sit, neque similiter est ibi prohibitio luminis ex toto,
cum Sol per aspectum propinquior sit Saturno quam Iupiter
per coniunctionem. Est tamen huiusmodi coniunctio fortior
1565   aspectu, ut testatur **Zael.** Perficitur enim coniunctio Iouis cum
Saturno corporaliter antequam Sol ad Saturnum poterit corporaliter peruenire. Quapropter difficultas et angustia tribulationum, que per oppositionem Solis cum Saturno significate sunt,
ratione bonitatis Iouis et signi in quo Saturnus est in melius
1570   conuertentur. Si igitur natus pecuniam absconditam aut aliud
sibi simile inuenire debeat seu acquirere, per hunc modum erit.
Amplius presentia Mercurii in eadem domo, cuius dispositionem ante diximus, ad idem cooperari uidetur, cum sit receptus
a Sole. Nam receptio, ut dicit **Messehallah**, res efficit et *nullo*
1575   *modo* potest fieri *quin fiat siue* prolongata *fuerit* eadem *siue* abre-
uiata, idest siue longum fuerit eius tempus an breue. Item in
NOVEM IUDICUM : receptio *est sine obstaculo et impedimento rerum*
confirmatio. Et iterum **Alkindus** : *receptio acceptationem significat.*
Habet quidem enim Mercurius partem in domo substantie,
1580   cum sit dominus triplicitatis eius pro secunda parte aspiciatque
partem fortune aspectu sextili dupliciter. Item et pars
substantie in gradu eius est que omnem possessionem uel
absconditam uel a parentibus prouenientem nato insinuat.

1560 quidem enim] *inu. S*   1561 coniunctionem] conditionem *S* | neque] nec *S*
1562   neque] nec *S* | est ibi] est hic *P* ibidem est *S*   1564   tamen] enim *P*
1565   Perficitur enim] perficieturque *PV*   1566   antequam] au' *S*
1568 significate] signate *S*   1570 conuertentur] -titur *S* | natus] *om. P* | aut]
addit *S* 1571 debeat] *post* acquirere *trsp. S* 1572 Amplius] a- *P sed exp.* 1574 ut
dicit] inquit *S* | et] in *S*   1575 prolongata] per- *S* | eadem] *om. S* | siue^2] seu
PS | abreuiata] breuia *PV*   1576 longum] *post* tempus *trsp. P* | an] aut *P* in *S*
1580   secunda] sua *V* | aspiciatque] acipiatque *S*   1582   gradu] gradum *V*
omnem] omnia *PV* | possessionem] eius *add. S*   1583 insinuat] *scr.* insinuant
codd.

1564 Est...1565 Zael] Zael, *Introductorium*, sig. 123rb:31-32 et 124va:17-18 |
1574 Nam...1576 breue] Messahallah, *De receptione*, sig. O1r:3-5 | 1577
receptio...1578 confirmatio] *Liber novem iudicum* A.98 (Vat. lat. 6766, fol. 7va:15-
16: "fortitudo stellarum est sine obstaculo et impedimento rerum confirmatio"
| 1578 Alkindus ...significat] *Liber novem iudicum* A125 (Vat. lat. 6766, fol. 11vb:
13-14 "receptio adoptionem, renuitio neglectum adducet"; cf. infra 1825-1826

Dicit enim **Princeps** : *si planeta bonus fuerit in domo quarta habens partem in domo secunda siue per gradus equales siue secundum equationes domorum, inueniet natus res absconditas.* Quarta namque domus, ut testantur philosophi, res absconditas et | *loca subterranea* | occultasque facultates significat. Mercurius quoque parti substantie coniunctus per artem Mercurialem acquiri substantiam innuit, presertim sub aspectu Saturni occulta significantis, cum difficultate tamen et quasi post desperationem propter aspectum oppositum cum retrogradatione. Rursum eadem domus *finem* euentuum significat siue *rerum.* Vnde **Hispalensis** : si hec domus de signis fuerit obliqua, ascendentibus finem rerum significat illaudabilem. **Abraham** uero **Princeps** dicit hoc uerum esse *nisi fuerit ibidem planeta fortunatus.* Est autem in hac domo Sol dominus exaltationis eius ; que quidem exaltatio significationem magis notam et magis famosam habet quam domus, secundum quod testatur **Iulius Firmicus** et **Auicenna** et alii plerique, licet significatio domus et uirtus eius sit magis realis et necessaria. Dicit igitur **Auicenna** quod si in Ariete Sol fuerit, fortunitatem atque *exaltationem omni tempore uite sue portendit, sed si fuerit in natiuitatibus nocturnis,* erit infra hec. Nam Sol planeta diurnus est et habet uim maiorem et magis notabilem super terram quam subtus. Item pars profunditatis sensus siue rationis et intellectus et consilii est coniuncta Soli, per quod regularitas morum intellectusque nobilitas magis corroboratur

1585

1590

1595

1600

1605

P34v
|S14r

1585   siue[2]…equationes] *om. S*   1588   significat] -cant *PV*   1589   acquiri]
acquiret *PV*   1590   significantis] signantis *S*   1593   finem] finis *S*
1595   significat] set *add. S*   1596   planeta] *om. P* | fortunatus] fortuna *PV*
1599 Firmicus] *om. S*   1600 plerique] plurimique *P*   1601 si] *om. S*   1602 uite
sue] *inu. S* | portendit] pro- *PS*   1603 in] *om. V* | hec] hoc *S*   1605 super] supra
S | pars] per *P*   1606 et[1]] siue *S* | quod] quam *V*   1607 regularitas] regalitas
PV

1584 si…1586 absconditas] Ibn Ezra, *Liber nativitatum*, fol. 61v:9-11: "Et si
fuerit stella bona in domo quarta et si sic ei pars secunda in divisione
ascensionum vel in gradibus equalibus, inveniet absconditum" | 1586
Quarta…1588 significat] Cf. Albumasar, *Introductorium maius*, VI.26 (vol. 8, p.
121:971-972) | 1592 eadem…1593 rerum] cf. Albumasar, *Introductorium maius*,
VI.26 (vol. 8, p. 121:972) | 1593 Vnde…1595 illaudabilem] cf. Iohannes
Hispalensis, *Isagoge*, sig. K4v:15-16: "si planeta fortunatus fuerit in domo quarta,
erit finis eius honorabilis; si infortunatus ibi fuerit, erit contarium" | 1595
Abraham…1596 fortunatus] Ibn Ezra, *Liber nativitatum*, fol. 63a:19 | 1597
que…1599 Firmicus] Firmicus Maternus, *Math.* II 3, 4, p. 44:3-6 | 1602
exaltationem…1603 nocturnis] Albohali, *De nativitatibus*, c.42, sig. o2v:17-19;
vide supra 1602-1603 | 1605 pars…1606 consilii] vide supra 397-398

hiis que predicta sunt hoc addendo. Adhuc pars fortitudinis et audacie consimiliter Soli copulatur, quapropter dispositionem
1610 eius induit. Preterea dicit **Iergis** in 9 IUDICUM quod *Sol in quarto thesauros significat et quod furto sublatum fuerat apparet, sed etiam gloriam et prouentum habet iudicare.* Item in libello DE SIGNIFICATIONIBUS PLANETARUM IN DOMIBUS *Sol in quarto thesauros significat | et apparitionem rei* furate *et laudem et sublimitatem inter* V126v
1615 *homines.* Et iterum **Iulius** *Sol in quarto bonam senectutem faciet ita ut in hac etate constituto lucra maxima conferantur.* Adhuc pars finis rerum, licet casum minetur ab angulo occidentali, non tamen complete cecidit et cum hoc aspicitur a Ioue aspectu duplici, trino scilicet secundum gradus equales et quarto secundum
1620 domorum partitionem. Insuper et a Sole consimiliter aspicitur uia duplici, ratione quorum finis euentuum et exitus rerum seu negotiorum post dolorosas huius seculi erumnas et inuolutiones feliciori significatur concludi termino conclusiuo. *Ait quoque* **Albumasar**, ut refert **Auenezre**, *quod dominus domus Lune ·*
1625 *finem rerum significat.* Est autem ille ad presens Mercurius, cuius significatio iam tacta est supra. Cum enim sit dominus uigoris a Sole receptus in signo exaltationis sue infra terminos coniunctionis et cum hoc in angulo, significat hunc natum cum principibus conuersantem, ut dictum est supra, nec impeditur ab
1630 oppositione Saturni, tum quia infra terminos coniunctionis est cum Sole, tum quia Saturnus sibi non inimicatur, ut dicit **Alkabitius**, sed est amicus presertim cum reministret Saturno uirtutem triplicitatis, in qua est iuxta illud **Aomar** in 9 IUDICUM

1608 addendo] -da *S* | Adhuc] ad hoc *PV* | fortitudinis…audacie] audacie et fortitudinis *V* 1609 consimiliter] *om. S* 1610 induit] innuit *PV* | Iergis] Gergis *S* | 9] libro *add. S* | Sol] *om. PV* 1611 fuerat] fuerit *S* | apparet] aperit *V* 1612 libello] bello *S* 1613 planetarum] *om. S* 1614 furate] future *ed.* 1615 Et] dicit *S* | faciet] significat *P* | ut] quod *P* 1616 lucra] lucta *P* | Adhuc] ad hoc *PV* | pars] *om. V* 1618 cecidit] accidit *P* | et] *om. S* | aspicitur] -ietur *P* -iatur *V* 1623 significatur] significant *S* 1624 ut] et *S* 1627 receptus…signo] *iter. S* sue] *om. S* 1628 hunc] h' *P* hic *V* 1630 coniunctionis] eius *P* | coniunctionis est] *inv. S* 1631 non] *om. V*

1608 pars…1609 audacie] vide supra 394-395 | 1610 Sol…1612 iudicare] *Liber novem iudicum*, A.119 (MS Vat. lat. 6766, fol. 10rb) | 1613 Sol…1615 homines] Gergis, *De significatione*, sig. F1v | 1615 Sol…1616 conferantur] Firmicus Maternus, *Math.* III 5, 17, pp. 132:27-133:7 | 1623 Ait…1625 significat] Ibn Ezra, *Moladot*, III IV 5, 2, pp. 142-143 | 1629 nec…1632 Alkabitius] cf.Alcabitius, *Introd.*, III.30, p. 313: "Mercurii amici sunt Iupiter et Venus et Saturnus"

de hiis que ad septimam domum pertinent in fine : *Mercurius a
Saturno respectus, dum quid readministret, nequaquam ipsius leditur*   1635
consortio. Vnde domus Mercurii eiusdem sunt triplicitatis cum
domibus Saturni. Et iterum proportionales sunt ad inuicem
Saturnus et Mercurius, ut patet in LIBRO RATIONUM et ex
Hispalensi. Nam Saturnus ad corpus terre se habet sub
proportione 32, Mercurius uero sub 16, que est proportio dupli   1640
ad subduplum, et hoc modo se habet aspectus eorum oppositus. Item **Alendruzagar** : *dominus triplicitatis domus quarte non
secundum gradus equales, sed equate primus patrem significat* - in
proposito quidem Iupiter -, *secundus* uero Sol, cuius dispositio
dicta est possessiones *terre* portendere, demum autem *tertius,*   1645
uidelicet Saturnus, cuius esse tactum est supra, sed completius
infra pertractabitur, *finem rerum nati* conclusurus est iuxta dispositionem eius. Et hec de quarta domo dicta sufficiant.

4.7. <Domus quinta>

Eorum uero que ad quintam domum pertinent significatio
talis est. Cum Sol et Mercurius sint in domo quinta secundum   1650
gradus equales, secundum equationes uero domorum Venus
quintam | obtineat, uidetur hoc prolis generationem signifi-
care. Verum quoniam Mercurius, qui est dominus hore quinte
prolis esse significantis, nondum combustionem egressus est
consistensque sub aspecto opposito sterilis Saturni, et Iupiter,   1655

S14v

1634   septimam] aliam *S*   1635   respectus] aspectus *PV* | quid] quidem *S*
1637   iterum] cum *add. PV*   1638   Saturnus…Mercurius] *inv. S*   1641   ad
subduplum] *om.* P | aspectus eorum] ipsorum aspectus *S*   1642 Alendruzagar] -
du- *P* | domus] primus *P*   1643 patrem *scr. cum Par.*] pr'em *PSV* | in] im *PS*
1645   possessiones] -nis *S* | portendere *scr.*] protendere *S* portendit *PV*
demum] dominus *P*   1646   uidelicet] scilicet *P*   1649   significatio] sermo *S*
1652 uidetur] uidentur *V* | hoc] hec *S*   1653 quoniam] quia *P*   1654 esse *scr.*]
esset *PV* est *S* | est] *om. PV*   1655 sterilis] sterili *P* steril' *V*

1634 Mercurius…1636 consortio] *Liber novem iudicum,* VII.203, p. 530b | 1637
Et…1640 16] Ibn Ezra, *Te'amim I,* §4.1:2, pp. 68-69, quod Bate sic interpretatus
est: "Invenerunt enim Saturnum secundum numerum 32 et hoc quidem
sumptum erat ex proportione circuli sui ad terre circulum, et dixerunt etiam
quod Iupiter est secundum numerum 34 et Sol secundum numerum 18, Venus
autem et Mercurius seundum numerum 16, Luna uero" (MS Leipzig 1466, fol.
67ra:28-34). | 1638 et[2]…1639 Hispalensi] Iohannes Hispalensis, *Epitome,* sig.
Q2r:33-Q2v:2 | 1642 dominus…1648 eius] Vide apud Ibn Ezra, *Moladot,* III
IV, 5, 3, pp. 142-143

qui specialis est prolis generator, sit in signo sterili retrogradus, domus quoque quinta graduum equalium et equationis domorum sit pauce prolis necnon et pars prolis in signo pauce prolis, similiter uidentur planetarum testimonia paucitatem prolis
1660 significare aut uite eius breuitatem, si plurificentur. Reuolutiones autem annorum hec et huiusmodi habent certificare. Vnde **Auicenna** : quando peruenerit annus *ad signum in quo fuerit Iupiter uel Venus in natiuitate, significat filios in ipso anno.* Et hoc quidem uerum est nisi aliud sit prohibens. Sane propter
1665 presentiam Veneris in hac domo significatur *gaudium in prole*, si natus ipsam habeat, ut uult **Auenezre**. Dignitates enim Veneris in hoc loco plurime concurrunt. Nam Venus in domo propria est et triplicitatis nouenaria et gradu lucido egressa puteum. Amplius et in suo gaudio gradusque trium angulorum, ascen-
1670 dentis scilicet et terre anguli et domus septime, in terminis sunt Veneris - unde **Hermes** in FLORIBUS : *donat felicitatem | immen-* ^P35r *sam planeta beniuolus, cum fuerit in propria domo receptus* - nec est Venus a quoquam impedita nisi quod secundum gradus equales cadit in domo sexta, per quod bonitas significationis eius
1675 paululum diminuitur. Significat tamen eius dispositio secundum conditiones supra tactas natum hilarem et iocundum conuiuiis interesse frequentius et gaudiis deliciarum quoque non expertem, ut uolunt philosophi. Et reuera sic est natus, incidit tamen nonnumquam in aduersitates et tribulationes
1680 multimodas presertim de Veneris significatione. Vnde **Albu-** **masar** : *Veneris fortunam animi passiones | consequi solent.* Item ^V127r **Compilator Abraham** : *Venus 12e domui similis de labore et peni-*

1659   uidentur] *ante* testimonia *trsp. S* uidetur *PV* | planetarum] *post corr. Par.* planeta *SV* plura *P*   1660 plurificentur] -cetur *V* prolificetur *P*   1661 habent] sunt *P*   1663 fuerit] fuit *S* | ipso] illo *P*   1666 enim] *om. S*   1668 triplicitatis] temporalis *V* et *add. P* | et²] in *P*   1670 et¹] *om. S* | anguli] *om. PV*   1672 receptus] *om. PV*   1675 paululum] paulum *PV*   1676 supra tactas] subtractas *V*   1677 gaudiis] gaudium *P*   1678 natus] nato *PS*   1680 multimodas] multitudinis *S*   1681 passiones] possesiones *S*   1682 similis] est *add. S*

1662 quando…1663 anno] Albohali, *De nativitatibus*, c.21, sig. i1r:16-18 | 1663 Et…1666 Auenezre] Ibn Ezra, *Moladot*, III v 7, 2, pp. 148-149 | 1671 donat…1672 receptus] Hermes, *Cent.*, c. 59, sig. 117va | 1681 Veneris…solent] Albumasar, *Introductorium maius*, VI.27 (vol. 8, p. 123:1038) | 1682 Venus…1683 indicat] Ibn Ezra, *De nativitatibus*, sig. b2v:13-14

tentia uoluptatis precedentis indicat. Et iterum *Auenezre* in LIBRO RATIONUM et **Princeps** magister eius loquentes de Venere dicunt quod finis deliciarum et gaudii meror est et tribulatio et   1685 tendit in uituperium et uilitatem. Vnde hoc est quod dicitur *extrema gaudii luctus occupat.* Dicit quidem igitur **Auicenna** quod Venere *in domo sua reperta gaudii multitudinem* et dilectionem cum mulieribus insinuat de quo mala opera dicentur a pluribus. Ipse tamen erit fortunatus et consequetur bonum in omnibus operi-   1690 bus suis. Item **Iulius** : *in quinto loco Venus ab horoscopo constituta faciet bonos et benignos et qui quod uolunt facile impetrent et quibus a mulieribus patrimonia conferantur maxima uel qui presidio aut patrocinio mulierum ad maximos ueniant dignitatis gradus.* Rursus in 9 IUDI-CUM : *Venus in quinto filiorum naturam portendit, gaudia etiam affec-*   1695 *tus, sed denique non modica anxietate afficit.* Insuper, ut habetur in CAPITULIS ALMANSORIS, *Venus in Tauro cantum tribuit,* cuius causam ponit **Ptolomeus** in LIBRO 100 VERBORUM dicens quod *Venus efficit nato delectationem in membro cui dominatur signum in quo est.* Vocalis autem siringa pars colli est, cui Taurus   1700 dominatur. Hinc est cur natus uocum modulamina nouit. Tot igitur dicta sunt de quinta domo.

4.8. <Domus sexta>

Domus autem sexte uirtus talem se offert. Cum secundum gradus equales distinctis domibus Venus cadat in sexta

---

1683 Et…de] *om. S*   1686 uituperium] uituperationem *S* | hoc] hic *V* | est] *om. S*   1687 extrema] extremum *P* | quidem igitur] *inv. S*   1690 consequetur] consecutus *P*   1691 suis] *om. PV* | loco] *om. S*   1692 et[1]] *om. S*   1693 patrimonia] patrocinia *S* | conferantur maxima] *inv. S*   1694 ueniant *scr.*] perueniat *P* ueniat *S* uenient *V*   1695 portendit] protendit *P* pretendit *V* | etiam] et *add. S* 1697 cantum] tamen *S*   1698 ponit] *om. V*   1699 delectationem] di (-e- *P*)lectionem *PV*   1700 autem] *om. P* | Taurus] cantus *P*   1701 Hinc] hic *S* huic *P* | uocum] uotum *PV*   1703 Cum] *om. S*   1704 cadat] cadit *S*

1683 Et…1686 uilitatem] Ibn Ezra, *Te'amim II*, §5.4:6, pp. 226-227, quod Bate sic interpretatus est: "Et Venus super delicias propter eius convenienciam cum domo quinta" (MS Leipzig 1466, fol. 56rb:43-44). | 1684 Princeps…eius] Ibn Ezra, *Liber nativitatum*, fol. 64v:25-27 et passim | 1687 extrema…occupat] *Prov.* 14,13 | 1688 Venere…1689 pluribus] Albohali, *De nativitatibus*, c.43, sig. o3v:21-25 | 1691 in…1694 gradus] Firmicus Maternus, *Math.* III 6, 10, pp. 145:20-146:3 | 1695 Venus…1696 afficit] *Liber novem iudicum*, A.120 (MS Vat. lat. 6766, fol. 10va) | 1697 Venus…tribuit] *Capitula Almansoris*, c. 33, sig. 120vb | 1699 Venus…1700 est[1]] Ps.-Ptol., *Cent.*, trans. graeco-latina, v. 27

1705 concurrentibus ibidem fortitudinibus supra memoratis, uidetur
ob hoc sanitas nati multum roborari et bona corporis habitudo
ad resistendum morborum incursibus et ualitudinum. Adhuc
ascendens et Luna impedimentis non subduntur, propter quod
inseparabilibus subiacere passionibus non debet hic natus. Item
1710 principium huius domus equate finis Tauri est, cuius domina
Venus salua salutem significat infirmitatum. Mars autem in hoc
loco, ut dicit **Auicenna**, *significat multitudinem infirmitatum calida-*
rum nati, a quibus cito liberabitur uel cito morietur, sed *Luna et* Mercurius *dominus* domus *eius* et domus sexte pro maiori parte
1715 *signumque*, in quo est Mercurius, satis *liberi a malis salutem nati*
significant. Cauendum tamen est in collo et brachiis propter
Taurum et Geminos, capiti etiam timendum est propter Arietem, in quo Mercurius, secundum quod dicit **Auenali**. Secundum autem quod dicit **Auenezre**, egritudo *Mercurii est super*
1720 *excrescentias*. Vnde hec forsitan | est causa quare in capite nati   S15r
aliqui noduli excreuerunt, quos per cirurgicum erui seu extrahi
fecit natus. Adhuc Sagittarius, secundum quod dicit **Auenezre**,
excrescentias significat, ascendens quoque caput. Item timendum est tibiis. Nam infirmitas Mercurii in Ariete tibiis appro-
1725 priatur. Plures quidem infirmitates nati prouenire significantur
ex sanguine propter Geminos, qui maiorem partem sexte
domus continent, ratione cuius priorificantur in significatione,
ut habetur in 9 IUDICUM. Gemini autem sanguinem
gubernant, iuxta quod uolunt astrologi. **Iergis** adhuc in 9

1707 incursibus] recursibus *S* | et ualitudinum] respectu altitudinum *V*
Adhuc] ad hoc *V* 1710 principium] presentia *S* | est] *om. S* 1711 salutem] *om.*
P | Mars…infirmitatum] *om. PV* 1713 sed] si *S* 1714 dominus…et] domina *S*
1715 quo] *om. S* 1716 significant] -cat *P* 1717 capiti…timendum] caput et
caudam *P* | est] *om. S* 1718 secundum…Auenali] *om. S* 1719 autem] *om. S*
1720 hec] *om. PV* | forsitan] forsam *S* 1722 Adhuc] ad hoc *V* | Sagittarius]
sagitas *S* 1723 quoque] autem *P* 1724 est] *om. PV* | appropriatur] approbatur
S 1725 quidem] igitur *P* igitur *add. S* | prouenire] peruenire *S* | significantur]
significat *P* 1726 qui] que *PV* 1727 continent] obtinent *P* 1729 Iergis]
Gergis *S* | Iergis adhuc] *inu. P*

1711 Mars…1716 significant] Albohali, *De nativitatibus*, c24, sig. i4r:12-18 |
1716 Cauendum…1718 Auenali] Ibn Ezra, *Moladot*, III VI 10, 2, pp. 154-155 |
1719 Auenezre…1720 excrescentias] Ibn Ezra, *Moladot*, III VI 11, 3, pp.
154-155 | 1722 Sagittarius…1723 caput] Cf. Ibn Ezra, *Te'amim I*, §2.3:2, pp.
40-41, quod Bate sic interpretatus est: "Sagittarius super femora seu coxas" (MS
Leipzig 1466, fol. 62vb:43). De ascendente vide Ibn Ezra, *Moladot*, III VI 10, 3,
pp. 154-155. | 1725 Plures…1728 Iudicum] non invenimus

IUDICUM : *Mars in sexto morbos et febres calidas et siccas exauget,*   1730
sanguinis indicat feruorem, causa seruorum et itineris efficit anxium.
Cauendum igitur uidetur ratione Tauri, in quo Mars est, a febre
per adustionem siue incinerationem colere generata, cum anni
reuolutio concors fuerit huic significationi, et hoc post medium
uite propter occidentalitatem Martis. Iterum Saturnus Martem   1735
aspiciens trino aspectu secundum domorum partitionem, nisi
Iouis beneficio mitigaretur, morbos graues insinuaret. Preterea
cauendum est nato a casu equorum et consimilium propter
ascendens et propter Taurum in quo Mars iuxta consilium
Principis Abrahe. Item dicit **Hispalensis** quod Mars in domo   1740
Veneris innuit laborem et nomen malum causa mulierum.
Amplius fortitudo Veneris in loco in quo est, cum sit domina
prime partis domus sexte, et dispositio Mercurii supra dicta
natum faciunt satis fortunatum in seruis. Amplius et pars
seruorum, que in eodem gradu coincidit cum parte fortune, ad   1745
idem cooperatur, quapropter fortunatus iudicandus est in
seruis et uernaculis. Verumtamen presentia Martis in hac domo
conditionem | seruorum reddit aliquantulum irascibilem. Si-
mile quoque est iudicium de pecudibus nati et armentis quod
de seruis. Et hec de domo sexta ad presens sufficiant.   1750

V127v (margin)

4.9. <Domus septima et octaua>

Septime quidem autem domus negotium nunc occurrit
considerandum. Et primo *de coniugio,* hoc est *de conuictu uiri et*
mulieris secundum leges, ut dicit **Ptolomeus**, qui | *Lunam*

P35v (margin)

1730 et siccas] *om.* P   1731 indicat feruorem] *inv.* S | et] atque S   1733 siue] seu
S | colere] *i.e. cholerae* collere S   1734 reuolutio] reuolutione S   1735 uite] *om.* S
1741 mulierum] mulieris S   1743 dicta] dictum S   1744 Amplius] adhuc S
1745 coincidit] concidit PV   1746 cooperatur] comparatur PV   1748 reddit
aliquantulum] *inv.* S   1749 nati] *om.* S | armentis] iudicio *add.* S   1751 autem]
om. P | nunc occurrit] *inv.* S | occurrit] concurrit V   1752 conuictu] coniunctu
P coniunctione S   1753 ut] et S | Lunam principaliter] Luna principatur S

1730 Mars...1731 anxium] *Liber novem iudicum,* A.118 (MS Vat. lat. 6766, fol.
10rb) | 1737 Preterea...1740 Abrahe] Ibn Ezra, *Liber nativitatum,* fol. 68r3-4:
"Mars dampnum faciet; si fuerit in Tauro Leone et Sagittario, cadet de bestia".
| 1740 dicit...1741 mulierum] cf. Iohannes Hispalensis, *Epitome,* sig. N4v:17-
19: "Si vero [Venus] est infortunata in natiuitate a Marte, angustabitur et
diffamabitur ex fornicatione incommuni quam habet cum Marte" | 1752
de[1]...1754 precepit] Ptol., *Quad.* IV.5, trans. Guilelmi, p. 283:177-179

principaliter in hoc negocio *considerare* precepit. **Auicenna** uero
1755   dicit quod in *rebus desposationum* accipiendum est a *signo septimo et
domino eius et* a *planeta* qui fuerit in domo *septima* et *a Luna et
Venere necnon et a parte desponsationum et domino* eius. **Enoch**
quoque, qui et **Hermes**, hoc idem uoluit, necnon et ceteri
sapientes. Venus quoque in quinta significat natum gaudere
1760   cum mulieribus, secundum quod uult **Abraham Princeps**.
Item iuxta **Auicennam** significat ratione loci in quo est *bonam
et optimam desponsationem*. Adhuc dicit idem quod Venus
secundum dispositionem in qua hic est *significat desponsationem
nati propinquarum mulierum* (alia translatio *cum consanguinea*). Dicit
1765   etiam quod significat citam et leuem desponsationem et bonum
esse ipsius. Adhuc **Auenezre** : *cum fuerit dominus septime in angulo,
significat hoc natum desponsaturum mulierem sue stirpis*, precipue si
Venus huic significationi concors fuerit. Hoc autem de despon-
satione consanguinearum intelligendum est suo modo. Item
1770   **Hispalensis** : Venus *in quinta* significat quod natus erit leta-
bundus cum *mulieribus sue stirpis et* habebit *mulierem nobiliorem se*.
Idem quoque affirmat **Auenezre**. Et iterum **Hispalensis** :
Venus in domo sua, secundum quod hic est, significat natum
multa bona habere ex parte mulieris. Idem quoque dicit **Princeps** :
1775   Verum quamuis *domini triplicitatis* domus Veneris *primus et*

1754 negocio] precipue *add. S* | uero] *om. S*   1755 accipiendum] aspicientium *V*
| accipiendum est] *om. P*   1756 et³] a *add. P*   1757 et¹] *om. S*   1758 idem] *om. S*
1759 quoque] igitur *PV* | quinta] quinto *SV*   1760 cum] *om. S*   1762 Adhuc]
ad hoc *PV*   1763   desponsationem] -num *P*   1764   cum consanguinea]
consanguinearum *P*   1765 et¹] siue *S* | et²...ipsius] *om. S*   1766 Adhuc] ad hoc
V | septime] -mi *PS*   1767 hoc] hic *PV*   1768 significationi] -nem *P* | Hoc] hic
S | de desponsatione] desponsationem *S*   1769 consanguinearum] -eorum *PV*
1770 Venus...1772 Hispalensis] *om. S*   1774 mulieris] mulierum *PV*

1755 in...1757 eius] Albohali, *De nativitatibus,* c.25, sig. k1r:1-5 | 1757
Enoch...1758 Hermes] Henricus interpretationem nominis Enoch ut Hermetis
recipit ab Ibn Ezra. Vide Sela, 2014, p. 228. | 1759 Venus...1760 Princeps]
Ibn Ezra, *Liber nativitatum,* fol. 64v:25-27 et passim | 1761 iuxta...1762
desponsationem] Albohali, *De nativitatibus,* c.26, sig. k2v:11-12 | 1763
dicit...1764 mulierum] Albohali, *De nativitatibus,* c.26, sig. k2v:22-23 | 1766
Adhuc...1768 fuerit] Ibn Ezra, *Moladot,* III vii 1, 13, pp. 158-159. | 1770
Venus...1771 se] Iohannes Hispalensis, *Epitome,* sig. L3r:23-25 | 1772
Idem...Auenezre] Ibn Ezra, *Moladot,* III ii 6, 5, pp. 126-127 | 1773
Venus...1774 mulieris] Iohannes Hispalensis, *Epitome,* sig. L3v:5-7 | 1774
Idem...1776 habeant] Ibn Ezra, *Liber nativitatum,* fol. 64v:19-22

secundus, Luna scilicet et *Venus,* bene se habeant, tertius tamen, Mars, cadens ab angulo in domo sui detrimenti de Veneris eufortunio aliquantulum subripit, secundum quod innuit **Aui-cenna,** nisi radii splendoris Veneris Martis lucem percutientes ipsi succurrant propter compassionem siue largitionem. Hoc 1780 autem uidetur futurum esse uersus finem uite ratione ultimi domini triplicitatis. Preterea pars desponsationis finem subin-trans domus septime in sextili cadit aspectu Veneris domine triplicitatis signi in quo est. Item et Luna domina partis in angulo iuxta **Auicennam** s*ignificat desponsationem nati optimarum* 1785 *mulierum* (alia translatio *castarum*) atque *pulchrarum* et sine uitio aliquo. Est autem hic Luna in angulo *sui honoris,* ut testatur **Princeps** in domo septima. Vnde in 9 IUDICUM : *Luna in septima coniugium laudat et omnem mulierum de causa predicat hones-*

S15v   *tatem.* Item *in domo Mercurii existens* significat | iuxta **Auicen-** 1790 **nam** natum *bone uite et magne intelligentie in omni re diligentem paruas puellas.* Item Luna Mercurio applicata, domino inquam domus in qua est, significat iuxta **Ptolomeum** mulieres *perspicaces et acutas* siue boni intellectus. Et quia Luna est domina domus septime pro secunda parte aspicitque partem hore coniugii 1795 coniunctam parti fortune aspectu trino secundum gradus equales, pro tanto in signo coniugii magis ratificari, secundum enim quod habetur in 9 IUDICUM de hiis que ad domum septimam pertinent : *Luna in septimo matrimonia confirmat hyme-neumque optatis inducit thalamis.* Et huic consentiunt reliqui sapi- 1800

1777   ab angulo] *om. S*   1779   nisi...Martis] *om. S*   1781   ultimi] *om. V*
1785   optimarum] optimam *ex corr. P*   1786   mulierum...castarum] *om. PV*
uitio] mentio *P* | uitio aliquo] *inv. S*   1788 Vnde...Luna] *om. P, sed mg. rest. post*
Princeps | in septima] *om. P*   1791   magne] maxime *S*   1797 pro...hiis] *om. S*
1798   que] *om. PV s.v. Par.* qui *S*   1799   septimam] *om. S sed* 7. *s.l. ante* domum
confirmat] affertur *S*

1776 tamen...1778 subripit] Cf. Albohali, *De nativitatibus,* c.26, sig. k2v:7-9 et
c.43, o3v:12-14 | 1784 Luna...1787 aliquo] Albohali, *De nativitatibus,* c.26, sig.
k2r:3-8 | 1787 Est...1788 septima] Ibn Ezra, *Liber nativitatum,* fol. 64v:17-18;
cf. infra 1454-1455 | 1788 Luna...1790 honestatem] *Liber novem iudicum,* A.122
(MS Vat. lat. 6766, fols. 10va-10vb) | 1790 Item...1792 puellas] Albohali, *De
nativitatibus,* MS Leipzig 1466, fol. 76va:16-18: "In domo vero Mercurii si
existent, erit, bone vite magneque intelligentie in omni re ac parvas puellas
diligens". Cf. Albohali, *De nativitatibus,* c.45, sig. p1r:4-6: "Eadem in domo
Mercurij conuersans, significat amorem erga   iuuenculas paruasque puellas" |
1793 mulieres...1794 intellectus] Ptol.., *Quad.* IV.5, trans. Guilelmi, p. 284:192
| 1800 optatis...thalamis] *Liber novem iudicum,* VII.1, p. 467b

entes interrogationum. Item **Ptolomeus :** Luna in angulo
occidentali significat natum *tarde nubere.* **Dorothius** uero dicit
quod Luna crescens lumine significat natum nubere in iuuentute. Temperanda sunt igitur hec amborum dicta. Et quamuis
1805   presentia Lune in signo communi et Mercurius in signo tropico
pluralitatem mulierum significant, Venus tamen in fixo seu
firmo significat unam inter ceteras eligi predilectam iuxta
mentem **Auicenne**.

Postquam igitur significatores uxorie conditionis in nego-
1810   tio coniugii taliter se habuerint, consideremus ipsorum habitudinem ad significatores masculinos, si forsan ex utrorumque
armonia, qualitercumque significata sit, desponsatio aliqua
consummationem legalem receptura. Quemadmodum autem
testantur **Aomar** et **Auicenna** et reliqui sapientes, ex applica-
1815   tione dominorum et ascendentis et septimi ad inuicem aut ex
equipollenti huiusmodi negotium | legitimum recipit comple-   V128r
mentum ac in proposito Mercurius septimi dominus neque
Ioui applicat neque Saturno, qui sunt domini ascendentis,
quinimmo separatur ab oppositione Saturni, cui propinquior
1820   est quam Ioui, principali domino ascendentis, cuius lumen Sol
prohibet et abscidit a Mercurio, cum hoc quod separatus est a
Ioue, per quod huius rei complementum impeditur. Saturnus
quoque renuens aspectum Mercurii propter impedimentum
renuitionis, ut habetur in 9 IUDICUM et alibi, idem negotium

1802 Dorothius] Ptholomeus *V* | Dorothius…nubere] *om. S*   1804 hec] hic
PV   1805 communi…Mercurius] Mercurii et communi *S* | tropico] tepido *P*
1806 mulierum] rerum *S* | fixo…firmo] firmo seu fixo *S*   1807 eligi predilec-
tam] *inv. S*   1810 habuerint] -unt *P*   1811 forsan] forte *S* | utrorumque] utro-
que *S*   1812 qualitercumque] qualicumque *PV* | significata] signata *S* | aliqua]
om. P   1813 receptura] receptam *S* | Quemadmodum] quod *P*   1814 et¹] *om. S*
1815   et¹] *om. S*   1817   ac] aut *V* | neque] nec *S*   1818   neque] nec *S*
1820 lumen Sol] *inv. P*   1821   abscidit] -cendit *P* -cindit *V*   1822   rei] *om. P*
Saturnus] -no *P*   1823 quoque] *om. P*

1801 Luna…1802 nubere] Ptol.., *Quad.* IV.5, trans. Guilelmi, p. 283:182 |
1802 Dorothius…1804 iuuentute] cf. Ibn Ezra, *Liber Nativitatum* fol. 65r:2-3 :
"Et Doroneus dicit quod si fuerit Luna in medietate mensis prima accipiet
uxorem et gignet pueros in medietate suorum dierum primorum" | 1804
Et…1807 predilectam] Albohali, *De nativitatibus*, c.25, sig. k1v:8-10 et c.26,
k3r:7-9 | 1810 consideremus…1814 sapientes] Albohali, *De nativitatibus*, c.25,
sig. i4v-k1v et Aomar, *De nativitatibus*, p. 134:42-47 | 1822 Saturnus…1825
imperfectum] Bate referre videtur ad *Librum novem iudicum*, A.99-100 (MS Vat.
lat. 6766, fol. 6rb)

relinquit imperfectum. *Renuitio namque neglectum significat*, ut dicit   1825
Alkindus. Item separatio, ut dicit **Hispalensis**, non effectum
rei, sed tantum cogitationes et uerba portendit. Verum quia
Luna a dominis ascendentis defluens Mercurio applicata est per
translationem luminis, significatur haberi tractatus aliquis aut
desiderium seu affectus circa huiusmodi negotium, sed   1830
preualentia fortitudinis aspectus oppositi qui ad expressam
ducit diuersitatem et inimicitiam, impedimentum quoque
renuitionis, hec omnia destruunt et corrumpunt ; quamobrem
desponsationis perfectio ea que secundum legem prepeditur.
Dicit tamen **Ptolomeus** et **Zael** et alii in LIBRIS   1835
INTERROGATIONUM quia Luna in septimo matrimonium confirmat. Etsi Mercurius redderet sibi uirtutem applicationis,
tanto esset Luna potentior in hoc negotio, cum sit in angulo
recepta existensque domina septime pro 2ª parte ac in aspectu
amicabiliori cum Saturno, nisi quod ab ipso separatur per quod   1840
quidem spes cassatur. Redditio tamen non competit in propo-
P36r   sito, quamuis Mercurius nondum terminos combustionis | sit
egressus propter fortitudinem receptionis eius, ut prius declaratum est ; quapropter potens est aspectum recipere sine reddi-
tione. Preterea quamuis Mercurius uirtutem suam Soli com-   1845
mitteret, non tamen Sol uidetur posse in proposito negotium
coniugii ad effectum perducere, tum propter separationem eius
a Ioue, tum propter renuitionem que Soli magis contrariatur in
proposito quam Mercurio. Notandum quoque est quod bonitas
Iouis in re proposita non potest impedimenta ex toto mitigare   1850
seu reformare quemadmodum in aliis accidentibus nati. Nam

1826 Alkindus] -dius *S*   1827 cogitationes] -nem *S* | portendit] protendit
separatio *S*   1831   preualentia] -lescentia *S*   1832   quoque] *om. S*
1835 Ptolomeus…Zael] *inv. S* | et alii] aliique *S*   1836 quia…confirmat] *om. V*
1837 redderet sibi] *inv. S*   1839 aspectu] eius *add. S*   1841 competit] conuenit *S*
1844 est[1]] *om. V ante* declaratum *P* | sine] absque *S*   1846 Sol] *om. S* | uidetur
posse] *inv. S*   1847 perducere] producere *PS* | propter] *om. S*   1849 Mercurio]
Mercurius *PV*

1825 Renuitio…1826 Alkindus] *Liber novem iudicum* A125 (MS Vat. lat. 6766, fol.
11vb: 13-14 "receptio adoptionem, renuitio neglectum adducet"vide supra 1578
| 1826 separatio…1827 portendit] Cf. Iohannes Hispalensis, *Epitome* sig.
E1r:21-14: "et cum separantur (superantur ed.) stelle a coniunctione,
superveniunt somnia et cogitationes secundum naturam ipsorum planetarum et
secundum naturam domorum in quibus fuerint in cuiusque natali" | 1835
Ptolomeus] cf. 1752-1754 | Zael…1837 confirmat] Zael, *De interrogationibus*,
sig. 130ra:37-39

tota uis huius negotii specialiter consistit in applicationibus et receptionibus a quibus significatores hic priuantur. In dispositione igitur domini ascendentis est maxima impedimenti causa,

1855 presertim iuxta **Haly** in ELECTIONIBUS suis dicentem quod *medium celi*, in quo hii sunt significatores retrogradi, *indicat quod futurum est in re nuptiarum*. Verumtamen dispositio Lune, que partim est domina septimi habensque | partem operis ineuita- S16r bilis sibi copulatam ac, prout dictum est, Mercurio applicata in

1860 re coniugii, quantum potest nititur esse paranimpha. Et quoniam Luna communis est significatrix populi, ut dicunt sapientes, ob hoc saltem more hominum necessarium est formam desponsationis huius nati celebrari. Sane non est oportunum omnia que consideranti occurrunt scripto commendare. Nam

1865 ut dicit **Albumasar** in SADAN, *sapiens si omnia quecumque nouit conscripserit, facit se ipsum ut uas uacuum et nullus indigebit ipso*. Vnde **Salomon** in PROVERBIIS : *sapientes abscondunt scientiam*. Amplius dato quod ex configuratione significatorum natus legitime uxorari portendatur, non tamen sequitur necessario ipsum

1870 subire iugum femineum iuxta illud **Ptolomei** in CENTILO-QUIO : *potest qui scit multas auertere operationes astrorum quando fuerit sciens naturam ipsorum*, cui concordat **Ptolomeus** in tertio capitulo primi QUADRIPARTITI et **Albumasar** in primo sui INTRODUCTORII. Vnde **Auenezre** hoc ipsum confirmans dicit in

1875 principio sui LIBRI NATIVITATUM, quod sapiens in astrorum scientia mutare potest superuentura propter dignitatem intellectus. *Similiter quidem*, inquit, *qui confidit in Deo ex toto corde suo, Deus illi uertet uersiones et ante ipsum parate sunt cause et occasiones ad protegendum eum et preseruandum a iactura ex natiuitate propria sibi*

1880 *significata. Dubium enim non est quin homo iustus custoditus sit melius quam sapiens in astrologia ; nam frequentius inuoluuntur super ipsum*

1855 suis] *om. S* 1856 hii *scr.*] hic *PSV* | retrogradi indicat] *inv. V* | indicat] - cant *PV* 1857 in re] *om. P* 1860 quoniam] quia *V* 1863 oportunum] optimum *PV* 1865 sapiens] sapientem *V* 1866 et] *om. S* 1869 portendatur] pretendatur *S* 1870 Centiloquio] -logio *P* 1874 ipsum] commune V *om. P* 1877 suo] *om. V* 1878 uertet] uertit *P* 1880 custoditus sit] *inv. S*

1856 medium…1857 nuptiarum] Haly Embrani, *De electionibus horarum* (MS BNF lat. 16204, p. 532a-b) | 1865 sapiens…1866 ipso] Sadan, *Excerpta* 28, p. 322 | 1867 sapientes…scientiam] *Prov.* 10,14 | 1871 potest…1872 ipsorum] Ps.-Ptol.., *Cent.*, trans. graeco-latina, v. 5 | 1872 Ptolomeus…1873 Quadripartiti] Ptol.., *Quad.* I.3, p. 18:314-316 | 1874 Vnde…1883 Deo] Ibn Ezra, *Moladot*, I 9, 1-5, pp. 88-90

confusa iudicia, secundum quod dictum est, et diuinator inuoluit et permis-
cetur ; beatus autem ille qui totum cor suum unitum habuerit suo Deo. Et

hoc est etiam quod in primo | MATHESEOS libro **Iulius** innuit
dicens *inuocemus suppliciter deos et religiose promissa numinibus uota*　　1885
reddamus ut confirmata animi nostri diuinitate ex aliqua parte stellarum
uiolenti decreto et earum potestatibus resistamus. Vnde hoc debere nos
facere uir uidelicet diuine sapientie Socrates docuit. Nam cum quidam ei
de moribus suis cupiditatibusque dixissit quas ille simili ratione collegerat,
sunt, inquit, ut dicis, agnosco et confiteor, sed hec omnia a me prudentie ac　　1890
uirtutum auctoritate superata sunt, et quidquid uitii ex praua concretione
corpus habuerit, animi sibi bene conscia diuinitas temperauit. Hic intelligi
datur, ut ait Iulius, *stellarum quidem esse quod patimur et que nos*
incentiuis quibusdam ignibus stimulant, diuinitatis uero esse animi quod
repugnamus. Sed hec et huiusmodi magis ad alium pertinent　　1895
sapientem.

　　Redeamus autem ad propositum et dicamus de residuis
huius domus, hoc est de aduersariis et conparticipantibus seu
consortibus. Et quia domini ascendentis in oppositione sunt et
renuitione cum domino domus septime, Mercurio uidelicet,　　1900
significat hoc distensiones et aduersitates precipue *cum uiris*
litteratis et mercatoribus propter Mercurium, ut uult **Auenezre**.
Luna quoque secundum dispositionem eius aliquam aduersitatem insinuat cum popularibus secundum proprietatem suam.
Sed quoniam dominus ascendentis est de superioribus, quorum　　1905
dispositio predicta est, et habet latitudinem septentrionalem et
est Iupiter in auge sui deferentis, Saturnus quoque non multum
remotus ab auge sua, Mercurius autem sub radiis et meridianus,

---

1882 secundum] qui *S* | et[1]] *om. S*　1883 suo Deo] *inv. S*　1884 etiam] *om. PV*
1885 uota] *ex corr. Par.* uoci *PV* uoti *S*　1887 debere *scr.*] deberemus *S* deberet
PV | nos] *om. PV*　1888 uir] iure *V* | uidelicet] *om. PV* | cum] *om. S*
1889 moribus] et *add. s.l. S* | cupiditatibusque] cupiditatibus *PV* | dixissit] dixit
V　1890 inquit] *om. PV* | dicis] dictis *V* | agnosco] cognosco *S* | a me] *post*
prudentie *S*　1891 superata] separata *S* | concretione] concreatione *PV*
1892 diuinitas] diuinitatis *V* | temperauit] temperat *S* | Hic] hoc *PV*
1893 patimur] patiuntur *PV*　1894 quibusdam] quibus *S* | uero] non *P*
1895 Sed] et *add. PV*　1898 hoc] *om. P* | conparticipantibus] participantibus *P*
1901 hoc] hic *V*　1903 dispositionem eius] *inv. V*　1904 popularibus] pl'ribus
S | suam] *om. S*　1905 de] in *V*　1906 predicta] dicta *S* | habet] habent *S*
1908 meridianus] -nis *V*

1885 inuocemus…1895 repugnamus] Firmicus Maternus, *Math.* I 6, 2, p. 18:10-
24 | 1899 Et…1902 Auenezre] Ibn Ezra, *Moladot*, III VII 3, 3, pp. 160-161

insuper et in opposito augis, significat hoc iuxta philosophos
1910 uictoriam nati super aduersarios suos. Vnde **Auenezre** in
LIBRO INTERROGATIONUM : *et si planeta inferior fuerit fortis, mul-*
tum superior autem mediocris, non tamen uincetur superior, et omnis
planeta siue superior siue inferior, si combustus fuerit, non erit ei fortitudo,
sed uincetur. Similiter quoque retrogradus significat debilitatem
1915 preterquam si fuerit de superioribus, non erit eius debilitas
perfecta. In proposito autem superiores sunt retrogradi, | S16v
ratione cuius difficultatem ad minus significant et tolerantiam
radiorum, sed quia Mercurius receptus est a Sole, cui naturam
suam commisit, uidetur secundum **principem Abraham**
1920 iudicium aduersariorum a Sole dependere, quod, si sic, tunc
aduersarii ab hiis qui sunt de significatione Solis, puta potentibus seu parentibus aut consimilibus, auxilium expectabunt. Ob
hoc tamen natus non significatur uincendus | fore, quoniam P36v
duo superiores pro parte sua sunt mutuo se respicientes in
1925 signo exaltationis Saturni et cum hoc in angulo honorabiliori,
angulo scilicet medii celi, supra Solem quoque eleuati, nec
potest sola ipsorum retrogradatio superioritatem ipsorum
abigere prorsus aut subicere, quamquam tribulationes adducat
et iacturas, neque hoc graue ferat natus. *Qui enim in mundo perma-*
1930 *nere uoluerit, cor patiens aduersitatibus preparet* secundum consilium
famosi atque admirabilis **Ptolomei** in prologo ALMAGESTI. Et
re uera conueniens est utique et tranquillificum uirtuosa ornari
patientia ubi nulla prorsus ualere potest recalcitratio nec resis-
tentia locum habet. Sic autem est in proposito. Tanta namque
1935 est detrahentium multitudo ac inuidorum seruo Dei obloquen-
tium cum effectu infamandi quod necessitate coactus clamare

1911 fortis] *om.* V   1913 ei] *om.* P   1916 proposito] opposito V   1923 signifi-
catur] censetur V | fore] *om.* S   1926 angulo] *om.* S   1928 subicere] subigere V
tribulationes] terribiliores S   1929 neque] nec S   1931 atque] *om.* S   1933 po-
test] posset S   1934 habet] haberet S | autem] *om.* S   1935 detrahentium] dis-
trahentium V   1936 effectu] affectu PV | infamandi] informandi P

1910 Vnde…1914 uincetur] Ibn Ezra, *She'elot II*, §7.1:2, pp. 368-369. Nota quod
Ibn Ezra in *libro Nativitatum* supra citato ad hunc librum refert: "I shall explain
this in the *Book of Interrogations*" (Ibn Ezra, *Moladot*, III VII 4, 11, pp. 162-163) |
1919 uidetur…1920 dependere] Ibn Ezra, *Liber Electionum*, fol. 44b:31-45a:1:
"Secundum quod temptaui pluries dampnum accidet ambobus bellatoribus
secundum fortitudinem Martis et Veneris a Sole" | 1928 tribulationes…1929
iacturas] Albumasar, *De revol.*, p. 220b:30 | 1929 Qui…1930 preparet] Ptol.,
Alm., sig. 1r:38

compellitur : *Domine libera animam meam a labiis iniquis et a lingua dolosa.* Non enim per se sufficit emulorum ora concludere malignantium ; studiosius itaque est et melius ineuitabilia patienter sufferendo et uiriliter locum prebere uirtuti quam 1940 eadem pusillanimiter et egre tolerando nedum per impatientiam in quoquam minorata, immo adaucta, potius priuari uirtutibus, que aduersitatum medele sunt, ac dolorem super dolorem coaugendo uitiorum turpitudine | deformari. Proinde ineuitabilem mortem expectanti prudenter consultum est 1945 Socrati in FEDONE et signanter quatenus ineuitabilia quam faciliter pati disceret et magnanimiter sufferre. Propter quod in directo mentalis oculi statuendum est illud notabile quidem uocabulum, scilicet : *fortiter indurans patientia uincit inermis armatosque uiros uincere sepe solet.* Sed horum satis. 1950

Aduersitates quidem igitur magnas et multifarias hunc natum sustinere oportebit propter habitudinem significatorum ascendentis ad significatores domus septime presertim propter renuitionem que est inter Solem a quarta domo et Iouem et Saturnum a decima in qua retrogradantur ambo, ratione quo- 1955 rum maliuolentia inuolui significatur cum rancore et prolongari iuxta mentem philosophorum, *timore* quoque ac *imbecillitate* nati *partem affici* propter retrogradationem. **Aomar** autem dicit quod *Iupiter in signo quolibet mitigando transformatur in melius* ; nec

V129r

1937 Domine] o *praem. PV* | a²...dolosa] cetera *S* 1938 sufficit] -ceret *S*
1939 studiosius...melius] melius itaque est *S* 1940 sufferendo] substinendo *S*
1941 pusillanimiter...tolerando] pusillanimitate ferendo *S* | nedum] diminuta
add. S | per] propter *V* 1942 in...priuari] carere *S* 1943 super dolorem] *om. S*
1944 uitiorum] uitiis *S* | turpitudine] -nem *P om. S* | deformari] formari *P*
1945 expectanti] -ndi *P* 1946 quatenus] ut *S* 1947 sufferre] sufic'e *ante*
magnanimiter *S* 1948 mentalis oculi] oculorum mentis *S* 1949 uocabulum]
prouerbium *S* | scilicet] *om. PV* 1952 habitudinem] multitudinem *sed exp.*
habitudinem *mg. V* 1953 significatores] signatores *V* 1955 a] in *V* | in] a *V*
1956 significatur] signatur *V* | cum rancore] cum ratione *ante* inuolui *S*
1957 ac] et *S* 1958 partem] perfecte *S om. V* | autem] aut *V*

1937 Domine...1938 dolosa] Ps. 119,2 | 1949 fortiter...1950 solet] *Proverbia*
sententiaeque Latinitatis, 14513 "Maxima virtutum patientia vincit inermis, *armatas*
vires vincere sepe solet" (vol. 2, p. 839 ed. Walther); cf. Guillelmus Peraldus, *De*
eruditione principum V.34, p. 448:30: "maxima uirtutum patientia, pugnat inermis,
armatos qui solet uincere sepe *viros*" | 1957 timore...1958 retrogradationem]
Liber novem iudicum, VII.42, p. 477b "timore et ignauia ac imbecillitate suam
afficit partem et conculcat" | 1958 Aomar...1959 melius] *Liber novem iudicum,*
VII.49, p. 480a

1960 mirum. Tanta enim est bonitas eius quod iracundiam prorsus abigit, ut habetur in LIBRO RATIONUM : dulcedinem diligens ueritatem querit et iustitiam et pacem super omnia. Item quoniam in decima domo locatus est, significatur pars nati principum fulciri auxilio. Vnde **Aomar** in 9 IUDICUM : *regia* 1965 *quidem amminicula ex stella propria, que decimum occupat, deprehendas.* Saturnus etiam per dispositionem Lune melioratus et per propriam eidem cooperatur. Presentia quoque amborum in domo *undecima* secundum gradus equales consimiliter *regios notat adiutores*, ut uult **Aomar**. Porro ut testantur **Dorothius** qui et 1970 **Doronius**, item **Alkindus**, **Albenaiach** et ceteri sapientes : quemadmodum dominus ascendentis et septimi aduersantes significant, sic et Luna secundum recessum siue separationem eius a planeta quolibet et applicationem eius alteri aduersantes moderatur. Conueniens est autem in tali materia diuersorum 1975 auctoritates adducere et plurium sententias ponderando iudicia propalare digesta et perscrutata ne nobis improperari possit illud **Philosophi** : *Ad pauca respicientes de facili enuntiare* non uerentur. Dicamus ergo quod Saturnus | a quo Luna separatur et Mercurius, cui applicat propter configurationem ipsorum 1980 supra dictam, inter natum et aduersarios maliuolentiam confirmant radicalem nisi quantum benignitas Iouis rem emendat. Verum modus translationis luminis, quem facit Luna recedens a Saturno sub aspectu trino secundum gradus equales et applicans Mercurio aspectu sextili, aduersarios placat,

S17r

1960 est] *om. S* 1964 principum] -pium *V* | fulciri] fulcirique *P* 1966 etiam] quoque *S* 1968 notat] uocat *PS* mostrat *ed.* 1969 testantur] testatur *S* 1970 Albenaiach] Albenarach *S* 1971 et septimi] *om. PV* 1972 significant] -cat *V* | et] *om. PV* 1973 et] *om. PV* | applicationem] -one *S* 1974 moderatur] -antur *S* | moderatur…2020 est] *totum textum om. P, sed alia manus supplevit dimidio folio addito* | est] *om. S* 1975 plurium] plurimum *PS* 1976 improperari] imp(e)rari *PV* 1978 quod] *om. S* | Luna separatur] *om. S* 1981 quantum] in *praem. V* 1982 emendat] -det *S* | quem] quam *S* 1984 aduersarios] -rio *V*

1961 ut…1962 omnia] Bate referre videtur ad *Te'amim II*, §5.4, pp. 226-229 | 1964 Vnde…1965 deprehendas] *Liber novem iudicum* VII.49, p. 480a | 1967 in…1969 adiutores] *Liber novem iudicum*, VII.49, p. 480a | 1969 Dorothius…1970 Doronius] *Liber novem iudicum* VII.41, p. 476b | 1970 Alkindus] *Liber novem iudicum* VII.39, p. 476a | Albenaiach] *Liber novem iudicum* VII.40, p. 476a | 1977 Ad…enuntiare] Arist., *De gen. et corr.* I 2, 316a9-10 | 1982 Luna…1986 odio] *Liber novem iudicum* VII.148, p. 514a

secundum quod innuit **Aomar** in 9 IUDICUM, ubi loquitur de   1985
amore et odio. Luna uero hoc agens officium secundum
Zaelem significat uirum uenientem inter eos cum bonitate et
iustitia. Insuper dicit **Albenaiach** : qui uero de hiis, ducibus
scilicet aduersariorum, *in cardine* fuerit *et receptus*, profecto
superat *nisi forte in adustionis sit ingressu* aut octaui dominus eidem   1990
applicet. In proposito autem Mercurius aduersariorum dux,
licet in cardine sit receptus a Sole, adustionem tamen non est
egressus totaliter. Iterum et Luna octaui domina ab ipso
recepta sibi applicat, Sol quoque Mercurium recipiens dominus
est secunde partis octaue domus. Idem tamen **Albenaiach** et   1995
alii sapientes dicunt quod *altero luminarium alteri ducum applicante*
aut si in eiusdem domo commoretur eundem extollit et fauet eidem ac
meliorem innuit. Iterum contestantur omnes quod ab octauo
auxiliatores aduerse partis considerantur, sicut a secundo
actoris. Luminaria autem in proposito dominantur octauo loco,   2000
que omnia fauent aduerse parti et fortificant eandem,
secundum quod significationes sue portendunt. Sane
concordati sunt omnes philosophi, ut dictum est supra, quod
in huiusmodi *negotio* non est habenda omnino *fiducia in* planetis
inferioribus respectu superiorum, etiam quantumcumque inferiores   2005
per se fortes fuerint sine adminiculo superiorum ; et, licet
aduersariorum fautores, luminaria scilicet, prerogatiuam
habeant magis apparentem et famosiorem apud uulgum,
duorum tamen superiorum uirtus substantialior constantie

1986 et] uel *S*   1987 uirum] unum *P*   1988 Albenaiach] Albenauit *S* | uero]
enim *V*   1989 scilicet] solet V solus *mg. Par*   1990 adustionis *scr.*] adul'tionis *S*
adustione *PV* | sit] sed *P* sed *praem. V* | eidem] ei *V*   1995 octaue domus] *inu.*
P | Albenaiach] Albenaiat *P.S*   1996 applicante] -nde *V*   1997 in] *om. P exp. V*
1998 contestantur omnes] *inu. S*   2000 actoris] auctoris *PV*   2002 portendunt]
prot- *SV*   2005 respectu] -tum *S* | etiam] et *P*   2006 adminiculo] -culis S
2007 scilicet] uidelicet *S*   2008 uulgum] uulgus *Par.*

1985 secundum…1986 odio] Bate referre videtur ad *Librum novem iudicum*,
VII.38, p. 475b: "lunae utrum sit applicatio uel recessus aeque notare memento.
Stella etiam a qua separatur Luna accusatoris, cui applicat defensoris" | 1987
Zaelem…1988 iustitia] Bate referre videtur ad *Librum novem iudicum*,VII.37, p.
475b: "inter ipsos etiam duces luminis facta translatio per internuncios pacis
foedus constituunt" | 1988 qui…1990 ingressu] *Liber novem iudicum*, VII.160,
p. 516b: "dux iste quem de superioribus stellis in cardine et receptum fore
contingeret ut uictoria potietur, nisi forte in adustionis sit ingressu" | 1996
altero…1998 innuit] *Liber novem iudicum* VII.45, p. 478a | 2002 Sane…2005
superiorum] *Liber novem iudicum*, VII.160, p. 516b: "quantum enim ad hoc
negotium attinet, nulli in inferioribus respectu superiorum habeatur fiducia"

2010 magis est effectiua et perseuerantie, ut benignitas | et iustitia V129v
cetereque conditiones Iouiane ac Saturnina patientia tantam
nato constantiam influant et perseuerantiam quatenus
aduersariorum maliuolentia ipsum omnino pessundare nequeat
et conculcare. Prudentia quidem igitur ex concursu Iouis et
2015 Saturni significata natum hortatur, cum *nobile uincendi genus sit*
patientia, si uelit uincere, discat pati precipue propter
retrogradationem significatorum sue partis et propter
fortitudinem luminarium, que subsidium influunt parti aduerse.
Non tamen significatur natus aduersariis succumbere, ut pre-
2020 monstratum est. Nam testimonia aduersariorum non superant
in fortitudine testimonia nati. Vnde **Alkindus :** *ascendentis et*
septimi dominorum omnimoda equalitas pacem generat. Item
Aristoteles in 9 IUDICUM : *utraque pars fortis neutra speratam*
assequitur uictoriam. **Alkindus** autem dicit quod *utriusque equalitas*
2025 *spem pacis inducit, si eorum domini alterno et amico fruantur respectu.*
Sed qualiter hoc sit, dictum est supra. Preterea dicit **Dorothius**
quod *pars fortune in secundo actorem prefert* ; dominus quoque,
inquit, partis idem quod pars ipsa significat. In proposito
autem dominus secundi, qui auxiliatores nati significat,
2030 Saturnus est, qui in domo existens regia magnates sibi facit
auxiliatores estque dominus partis fortune in secundo locate.
Item significatores aduersariorum sunt in signo obediente,
actoris uero significatores in signo imperante, ut testantur
philosophi, propter magnas ascensiones et paruas, et hec
2035 quidem nati fouent partem. Adhuc in huiusmodi materia,
controuersie uidelicet et rixarum et consimilium, Mars specia-

---

2010 effectiua] afectiua *S*   2011 patientia] -tiam *P*   2012 influant] inflant *V*
2015 significata] *om. V*   2016 uincere] discere *praem. S*   2020 aduersariorum]
aduersitatis *S*   2023 speratam] superatam *PV*   2024 autem] tamen *S*
2025 eorum] eodem *S* | alterno] alterna *V a. corr. P* | respectu] aspectu *V*
2026 sit] est *S* | dictum est] actum *P*   2027 actorem] auctorem *PV* accusatorem
ed.   2028 inquit partis] *inv. P* | In…significat] *om. V*   2029 qui] quod *S*
2030 existens regia] *inv. S*   2032 significatores] signatores *V*   2033 actoris]
auctoris *PV* | significatores] signatores *V*   2034 hec] hic *PV*   2035 Adhuc] ad
hoc *PS*   2036 et¹] *om. P* | rixarum] rixa *S*

2015 nobile…2016 pati] Vide *Proverbia sententiaeque Latinitatis*, 16974 ed. H.
Walther | 2021 Vnde…2022 generat] *Liber novem iudicum*, VII.178, p. 583b |
2023 utraque…2024 uictoriam] *Liber novem iudicum*, VII.47, p. 479a | 2024
utriusque…2025 respectu] *Liber novem iudicum* VII.171, p. 522b | 2027
pars…prefert] *Liber novem iudicum* VII.46, p. 478b

liter considerandus est. Vnde **Dorothius** : *Mars in oriente et ipsum respiciens* actoris *dedecus et ignominiam exauget.* Sicut autem
S17v est | de oriente, sic de septimo iudicandum uidetur suo modo. Dicit enim **Alkindus** quod *Mars, si alterum eorum aut ipsius* 2040 *dominum precipue ex aduerso corrumpat aspectu, mortem minatur.* Est autem Mars in proposito dominus domus in quo Sol est et Mercurius aspicitque ipsos secundum domorum partitionem aspectu sextili. Quapropter Sol dispositionem sibi committit et naturam, Mars uero receptor huius rei, licet sit in gaudio suo, 2045 debilis tamen est, cum sit in detrimento suo, insuper et cadens ab angulo, nec impedit ascendens nec eius dominum, et cum hiis est occidentalis, ratione quorum conditiones partis deprauantur aduerse. Occidentalitas quidem Martis maiorem innuit tribulationem et timorem quam lesionem, ut testatur 2050 **Auenezre** in LIBRO CONIUNCTIONUM. Et quoniam hoc negotium conuenientiam habet cum eo quod de inimicis, idcirco Martialis significatio usque ad illum differatur locum. Preterea Venus domina decimi, in quo significatores orientis et secundi, orienti fauet et parti fortune magis quam septimo. 2055

Perfectis igitur cum omni inquisitione et pensatis hinc inde significatoribus, meliores sunt conditiones nati huius et saniores in aduersitatibus et controuersiis quam que aduerse
P39r partis. Insuper et diuersitas | latitudinum significatarum in aspectibus inimicantium, cum hoc quod Mercurius a Saturno 2060 separatur, magis iuxta assertionem philosophorum significare uidetur cogitationes et uerba quam alium effectum realem.

2037 et] aut *S* 2038 actoris] auctoris *PV* 2040 Mars] quod *add. P* 2041 dominum] dum *P* si *V* 2047 nec²] aut *S* 2048 est] *om. S* 2049 quidem] aut *add. PV* 2050 innuit] innuunt *PV* | tribulationem] turbationem *S* | timorem] dolorem *V* 2054 orientis] *om. PV* | et] scilicet *P* 2055 secundi] et *s.l. add. P* | orienti] orientis *post corr. P* 2056 igitur] ergo *V* | inquisitione] exquisitione *PV* 2058 saniores] seniores *S* | et] *om. P* 2059 significatarum] *om. S* 2061 iuxta...philosophorum] *post* uidetur *et* sententiam *pro* assertionem *S* assertionem philosophorum] *inv. P* 2062 alium] *om. S*

2037 Mars...2038 exauget] *Liber novem iudicum* VII.46, p. 478a | 2040 Mars...2041 minatur] *Liber novem iudicum* VII.171, p. 522b | 2049 Occidentalitas...2051 Coniunctionum] Ibn Ezra, '*Olam* I, §22:1, pp. 66-67, quod Bate sic interpretatus est: "Si (Mars) orientalis (fuerit), erit metus et tribulatio maior quam occisio"(MS Leipzig 1466, fols. 26vb:24-25)

Vnde **Hispalensis** ac **Hermannus** in libro DE REBUS ABS-
CONDITIS : separatio cogitationes tantum et uerba significat et
2065 nil preter metum. Quapropter in pressuris non conturbetur
indiscrete seruus Dei, sed patiens mansuetus et constans in
equanimitate perseueret. Sic enim diuina fauente gratia inueniet
requiem anime sue et aduersariorum insultibus resistere poterit
confidenter. Nam et iustorum etiam multe tribulationes sunt,
2070 sicut apparere potest per exempla infinita, ex quibus reuelamen
consurgit in pressuris et solatium multiforme. Non contristent
ergo nimis hunc seruum Dei tribulationes et pressure. Claris-
simis enim uiris et excellentissimis iacture horribiles solent
euenire, ut patet de Pythagora, Socrate, Platone et Aristotele,
2075 qui Athenienses in ipsum machinantes fugiens ipsos *in philoso-*
phia bis peccare non consentit. Nec erat irrationabile hos passu-
ros talia. Nam *nihil omni parte beatum* presertim in rebus ex
conflictu contrariorum constitutis, cuius declaratio ad presens
talis est. Cum enim studiosis praui contrarii semper fuerint,
2080 quanto habundantior fuerit uirtutum moralium et intellectua-
lium | omniumque bonorum affluentia, tanto magis patet   V130r
inuidie locus materiaque liuoris et odii amplior succrescit inui-
dis et prauis. Nam, ut testatur **Philosophus** 2° RHETORICO-
RUM : *inuidia* quidem est *tristitia quedam super bona actione apparente*
2085 *bonorum* aut super bonorum eufortuniis. Et quia *prauorum*
numerus maior est et habundantior multitudo, studiosos affligunt

---

2063 Vnde] ut *PV* | ac] et *S* | in] *om. S*   2064 separatio] separata *S*
2066 seruus Dei] *om. PV* | patiens] passiones *S*   2067 perseueret] *om. PV*
2068 anime] *om. P*   2069 etiam] et *P*   2073 enim] quidem *S*   2076 consentit] -
sensit *S* | irrationabile] rationabile *S*   2077 nihil] nil *S* | omni] cum *S*
2078 constitutis] *om. PV*   2079 talis est] *inv. S* | semper] *om. PV*   2081 affluen-
tia] exfluentia *V*   2082 amplior] amplius *S* | inuidis] -dia *S*   2083 2° Rhetorico-
rum] Rhetoricorum 7° *V*   2085 eufortuniis] -nio *PV* | prauorum] et cetera (?)
et *add. S*   2086 numerus maior] *inv. V* | multitudo] et *praem. S*

2063 Hispalensis] vide supra 1826-1827 | Hermannus…2065 metum]
Hermannus, *De occultis*, pp. 316:25-317:1 | 2074 Aristotele…2076 consentit]
Liber de Vita et Genere Aristotelis §43: "Insurgentibus autem ipsi Atheniensibus
discessit Calchidiam, hoc dicens: non concedam Atheniensibus bis peccare in
philosophiam" (p. 157) | 2077 nihil…beatum] proverbium, cf. Horatius, *Carm.*
II, 16, 27-28: "nil est ab omni parte beatum" | 2084 inuidia…2085 bonorum[1]]
Arist., *Rhet.* II 10, trans. Guilelmi, 1387b23-24 | 2085 prauorum…2086 est]
proverbium; vide Turrinium,   1230: "pravorum numerus maior nunc vivit in
orbe"

pro libito et turpiori condemnant opprobrio et quod *finis* est *terribilium* aliquando *mori.* Sed quid mirum si boni sunt inuidiosi, cum *sola miseria careat inuidia.* Postquam igitur *prauis displicere sit laus uera,* ut testatur **Seneca**, necessarium est studiosos existentes multa pati propter prauorum importunitatem. Et hoc est quod dicit **Philosophus** in ETHICIS quod *accidentia tribulant et conturbant beatum. Tristitias enim inferunt et impediunt multis operationibus. Verumtamen et in hiis refulget bonum, cum utique ferat quis faciliter multa et magna infortunia non propter doloris insensibilitatem, sed uirilis existens et magnanimus.* Ex principiis quoque huius scientie confirmari potest idem quod dictum est ex morali philosophia. Significatores enim sublimitatis rerum anime aduersitates rerum corporalium plerumque portendunt, secundum quod supra tactum est. Et iterum ex quo significatores harum rerum uel illarum bene se habuerunt, necessarium est reliquarum | duces aduersos fore. *Impossibile est* enim, ut uult **Haly** sub assertione **Albumasar,** *omnes domos duodecim* bene disponi. *Mali* namque, inquit, *a celo remoueri* non possunt. Et hec de aduersitatibus nati huius suisque aduersariis sufficiant.

De consortibus uero eius simile iudicium est quod de aduersariis quantum ad afflictiones et tribulationes in consortio superuenientes et similiter quantum ad conditiones nati que meliores sunt quam comparticipantium, nisi quod Lune hic

2090

2095

2100

2105

S18r

2087 opprobrio] -riorum *P*   2088 mori *scr.*] morti *PSV* | sunt] sint *PV* 2089 igitur] *om. P*   2090 testatur] dicit *PV*   2091 importunitatem] inoportunitatem *PV*   2094 et] *om. S*   2095 ferat] querat *V* | faciliter] *om. S* multa] *om. PV*   2096 quoque] quorum *P*   2099 anime] *om. PV* | corporalium] incorporalium *V* | plerumque] plurimum *P* plurium *V* | portendunt] pro- *SV* 2100 tactum] dictum *PV*   2101 harum] istarum *V* | habuerunt] -int *PV* 2102 est^2] *om. PV*   2103 sub assertione] sub *P* et *V*   2104 Mali] male *S* namque] *om. PV* | hec] hoc *V*   2105 nati] nam *PV* (*sed exp. et* nati *mg. P*) huius] huiusmodi *S*   2106 eius] ipsius *V* | quod] *om. P*   2109 hic] sit *V*

2087 finis...2088 mori] Cf. Arist., *Eth. Nic.* III 8, 1115a26 | 2089 sola...inuidia] Vide *Proverbia sententiaeque Latinitatis*, 29931 (vol. 5, p. 55 ed. H. Walther). Cf. Isidorus Hispalensis, *Sententiae* 3, c.25.4 : "nulla est uirtus quae non habet contrarium inuidiae malum ; sola miseria caret inuidia" | prauis...2090 uera] Cf. Publilius Syrus, *Sententiae* [quae Senecae attribuuntur]: "Opinantur de te homines male, sed mali: displicere enim malis laudabile est" (p. 94:29) | 2092 accidentia...2096 magnanimus] Arist., *Eth. Nic.* I 11, 1100b28-33 | 2103 Haly...2104 possunt] Haly Embrani, *De electionibus horarum*, p. 333: "Dixit Albumasar: Impossibile est nobis omnes XII domos aptare, planete et enim mali ipsi sunt a celo remouendi" | 2109 nisi...2111 alias] *Liber novem iudicum* VII.147, p. 514b

2110 maior uis incumbit quam in negotio aduersariorum, secundum
quod patet ex LIBRO 9 IUDICUM et alias. Domini igitur ascendentis et septimi in signis tropicis constituti preter alias significationes eorum turbationem in consortio significant et permix-
tionem, ut testantur philosophi. Cauendum est etiam de fraude

2115 et proditione conparticipantium propter Mercurium septimi
dominum sub radiis existentem et sub aspectu Martis et in
oppositione cum domino ascendentis recedentemque ab aspectu. *Luna* uero recepta et *applicans domino* domus consortii in
qua est cum translatione luminis inter dominum ascendentis et

2120 dominum septimi, sub aspectu amico secundum gradus equales
finem cum dilatione et lucro inuenit, secundum quod testantur **Zael**,
Aomar, **Albenaiach** et ceteri sapientes. De dominis quoque
triplicitatis huius domus est supra declaratum et cum hoc
terminetur totum negotium domus septime.

2125   Octaua uero domus significationem, quoniam de fine uite
est, usque ad finem principalis negotii differamus, secundum
quod fecit **Ptolomeus** et **Auicenna**.

4.10. <Domus nona>

     Nonus autem locus a **Iulio Firmico** uocatus est deus,
quemadmodum et tertius dea ob hoc quod hec loca super res

2130 diuinas significationem gerunt principaliter, ut sunt fides et
religio, scientie et peregrinationes. Et quoniam in hiis rebus
superat uirtus none domus et preualet loco tertio, idcirco
nonus uocatur deus, tertius uero dea. Est autem principium

2113 turbationem] conturbationem *P* cum turbatione *V*   2115 conparticipan-
tium] cum participantium *PV*   2117 ascendentis] ascensionis *V* | recedentemq-
ue] -teque *S* -tem *V*   2120 amico secundum] amicorum *S* | gradus…secun-
dum] *om. S*   2121 dilatione *scr. cum ed.*] dil'cione *P* dilectione *V* | inuenit *scr. cum
ed.*] inuehit *PV*   2122 Albenaiach] Albenaiat *P*   2129 hec] hic *V*   2130 fides…-
religio] religio fides *S*   2131 et] *om. S* | Et] quorum *praem. V*   2132 superat] *om.
P*

2118 Luna…2122 Albenaiach] *Liber novem iudicum* VII.149, p. 514b | 2121
Zael] *Liber novem iudicum* VII.147, p. 513b | 2122 Aomar] *Liber novem iudicum*
VII.153, p. 515a | 2126 secundum…2127 Auicenna] Cf. Albohali, *De
nativitatibus,* qui de qualitate mortis tractat in cap. 27 post domum duodecimam.
Sic etiam Ptolemaeus in *Quadripartito* IV 8 ("in qualitate mortis nati" transl.
Platonis), 9 (translatio Guillelmi) | 2128 Nonus…2129 dea] Firmicus
Maternus, *Math.* II 16, 2, p. 59:22-25

none domus proposite in Leone, secundum quidem gradus
equales in 13° gradu eius, secundum equationem uero   2135
domorum maiorem domus partem obtinet Virgo. Quare
necessarium est Soli et Mercurio hoc incumbere negotium.
Dispositiones autem horum amborum satis sunt tacte supra in
domo prima et quarta et septima similiter, inter que hoc
notandum occurrit quod in omni iudicio plures personas   2140
respiciente, ut in iudiciis nati cum fratribus, parentibus, filiis,

P39v uxore, aduersariis, consortibus, amicis | et inimicis, oportune
et necessarie sunt considerationes precise applicationum
proprie acceptarum et separationum, renuitionum quoque et
translationum et redditionum, que in iudicio tantum unam   2145
personam comprehendente locum non habent, ut in iudicio

V130v uite, substantie, infirmitatum, mortis, fidei, scientiarum, |
peregrinationis et exaltationis necnon et operis seu
professionis, secundum quod apparere potest aduertenti. Cum
igitur domini domus deo dicate sint illi hiidem, quibus   2150
dominium uigoris nati ascriptum est supra, ratione
dispositionis sue in se ipsis et in respectu ad ascendens, uidentur huius serui Dei conditiones trahi ad res diuinas saltem post
magnam duritiam et remorsum appetitus sensitiui eiusque
recalcitrationem propter habitudinem dominorum ascendentis   2155
cum dominis domus diuine, ut dictum est in domo quarta.

Qualiter autem sentiendum est in proposito de scientiis
nati satis est declaratum in hiis que de domo prima. Mercurius
enim, ut dicunt philosophi, omnes partes philosophie genera-
liter comprehendit, *Sol* uero *astrologiam*, ut dicit **Hispalensis** ;   2160
et **Auenezre** in Libro Rationum dicit cum hoc Solem signifi-

---

2134   quidem gradus] *inv. S*   2135   in] *om. S* | equationem] -nes *S* -ne *V*
2138 autem horum] *inv. P*   2142 oportune] optime *V*   2143 sunt] *post* oportune
S | applicationum] -nem *P*   2144 et separationum] *om. V* | separationum] -nem
P | et²] *om. S*   2146 comprehendente] -tem *S*   2147 infirmitatum] -tem *P*
2149 professionis] confessionis *S*   2150 dicate] dedicate *post corr. P* | illi hiidem]
illiidem *S*   2151 dominium] dominum *SV* | ascriptum] scriptum *P*   2152 et]
om. S | ad ascendens] acendentis *P* ad sc'ns *V*   2153 huius] huiusmodi *S* | Dei]
om. PV | saltem] sol item *P*   2154   duritiam] -tiem *S*   2158   nati] *om. S*
2159 generaliter] *om. P*   2161 cum hoc] tamen *S*

2160 Sol...astrologiam] Iohannes Hispalensis, *Epitome*, sig. M1r:8 | 2161
Auenezre...2163 none] Ibn Ezra, *Te'amim I*, §4.9:1, pp. 82-83, quod Bate sic
interpretatus est: "Sol in domo nona eo quod ambo super itinera significant
longinqua et fidem seu leges" (MS Leipzig 1466, fol. 69ra:25-27)

care scientiam fidei seu legum et iudiciorum secundum proprietatem domus none. Item aduertendum est quod Sol Christiane legis planeta est. Christus enim, *Sol iustitie, in Sole posuit*
2165 *tabernaculum suum,* et hoc affirmant astrologi. Nam mutatio
triplicitatis significans natiuitatem Christi et legem eius fuit in
Leone cuius dominus Sol est. Vnde diem Solis Christiani cele-
brem habent. Sol autem in proposito nonam domum aspicit
terno aspectu secundum gradus equales et est etiam nona
2170 domus locus gaudii et est ipsemet in exaltatione sua in angulo,
in aspectu quoque Iouis, ut supra dictum est, per que | aliquod   S18v
singulare misterium fidei Christiane huic nato portenditur.
Dicit quidem enim **Aomar** in 9 IUDICUM quod *in nono nulla*
existente stella *terre cardo* respiciatur *et si que ibi consistunt stelle*
2175 *intueri necesse est ut idem quod de nono iudicium consequatur. In nono*
autem Sol legem Christi consolidat, ut dicit **Compilator Abraham**
una cum **Hispalensi**. Verum quia Sol est sub terra, per hoc
magnitudo sue significationis in oculis hominum aliquantulum
obscurari significatur iuxta illud **Auicenne** dictum in domo
2180 quarta de Sole in natiuitatibus nocturnis. Amplius quartus
aspectus Martis ad domum nonam a loco in quo est scientiam
nati et fidem eius infamare nititur et deturpare per detractiones
et mendacia, per inuidiam quoque et proditionem secundum
Martis proprietatem et naturam. Sed propter debilitatem sue
2185 dispositionis, cum sit in detrimento suo et cadens ab angulo
nec aspicit ascendens aut eius dominum, repellitur detractor ab
intento nec potest suam adimplere maliuolentiam cum effectu,
licet affectu infamandi non priuetur. Secundum enim quod uult
Zael et **Auenezre** : malus *impediens cum fuerit* in detrimento suo

---

2163 Item] itaque *S*   2165 mutatio] inmutatio *V*   2167 dominus Sol] do' sol' *P*
Christiani] *om. P*   2169   et] *om. PV*   2172   misterium] ministerium *V*
portenditur] pro- *PS*   2173   enim] *om. S*   2174   respiciatur] inspiciatur *S*
consistunt stelle] consistit stella *S*   2175   idem] id *V* | iudicium] iudicum *S*
2178 magnitudo] *om. S*   2179 significatur] signatur *V*   2183 proditionem] per-
S   2187 effectu] afectu *S*   2188 non] *om. PV*   2189 impediens] impeditus *P*

2164 Sol iustitie] *Mal.* 4,2 | in…2165 suum] *Ps.* 18,5 | 2173 in^2…2175 est]
Liber novem iudicum IX.36, p. 548a | 2175 In…2176 consolidat] Ibn Ezra, *De*
nativitatibus, sig. c1v:22 | 2177 una…Hispalensi] Iohannes Hispalensis, *Epitome*,
sig. L4v:28 | Verum…2180 Sole] Albohali, c.43, *De nativitatibus*, sig. o3r:15 |
2189 Auenezre…2191 Auenezre] Ibn Ezra, *Reshit Ḥokhmah* §8:8-9, pp. 212-213.
| malus…2190 impedit] Zael, *Iudicia*, c. 4, sig. 126ra:44-45

et *cadens ab* angulo immittit *timorem et non impedit*. Et si impediat,   2190
hoc erit modicum iuxta mentem **Auenezre**. Insuper testimonia
bonitatis huius negotii incomparabiliter meliora sunt et multo
pulchriora quam sola Martis maliuolentia ualeat impedire. Non
computatis enim aliis testimoniis melioribus, solius tamen
Veneris | aspectus amicabilis a loco supra exposito illustrans   2195
diuinam domum sue magne beniuolentie radiis Martialem
noxiam placat et curat lesionem. Hec est enim proprietas
Veneris et familiaritas eius cum Marte, ut testantur sapientes, ut
radii Martis peremptiui dulcibus radiis amorose Veneris conin-
cidentes et permixti a sua malitia reuocentur. In CAPITULIS   2200
enim ALMANSORIS habetur quod *dominus quinti circuli*, idest
Venus, dissoluit quod ligat dominus tertii circuli, qui *est Mars*. Vnde
non sine ratione dictum est a poetis quod Martem et Venerem
coeuntes Vulcanus deprehendens catena inuisibili ad inuicem
colligauit. Aspectus igitur Veneris secundum dispositionem   2205
suam ad domum nonam significat amorem misterii fidei secundum proprietatem Venerianam. Preterea pensandum est quod
dominus orbis in quo sumus hiis diebus Mercurius est qui
maiorem partem huius diuine domus moderatur, de quo dicit
Auicenna : scito quod *Mercurius habet proprietatem in re fidei et*   2210
somniorum quam non habent *ceteri* planete. Mercurius igitur
dominus none domus *significat quod natus astronomicus*, sapiens
diuinationum ac futurorum annuntiator ; quod si fuerit *in aspectu*

2190   ab angulo] *om. S*   2191   mentem] *om. S*   2192   incomparabiliter]
incorporabiliter *V*   2193   pulchriora] pl'a *PSV*   2194   computatis] putatis *P*
2197   est] *om. PV*   2198   et] *om. V*   2199   conincidentes] conc- *V*
2200   permixti] -ta *V*   2202   Venus] Veneris *S*   2203   a poetis] apotis *PV*
2205   colligauit] colligante *V*   2206   misterii] ministerii *V*   2207   est] *ante*
pensandum *P om. V*   2208   diebus] *om. PV*   2209   diuine] diuitie *V* | moderatur]
ueneratur *S*   2210   Auicenna] quod *add. S*   2211   ceteri planete] *inv. V*
2212 sapiens] peritus *ed.*   2213 ac] atque *S* | futurorum…quod] *om. S*

2201 dominus…2202 Mars] *Capitula Almansoris*, c. [35bis], sig. 120vb | 2203
a…2205 colligauit] Hyginus, *Fabulae* CXLVIII, 1: "Vulcanus cum resciit
Venerem cum Marte clam concumbere et se uirtuti eius obsistere non posse,
catenam ex adamante fecit et circum lectum posuit, ut Martem astutia
deciperet" (p. 129:2-4) | 2210 Mercurius…2211 planete] Albohali, *De
nativitatibus*, c.29, sig. 11r:20-22 | 2211 Mercurius…2213 annuntiator] Albohali,
De nativitatibus, c.29, sig. 12r:5-7 | 2213 quod…2219 patietur] Albohali, *De
nativitatibus*, c.29, sig. 11r:24-11v:4: "si Mercurius fuerit in domo Saturni aut in
aspectu eius, significat profunditatem scientiae nati et erit durabilis et occultator
cogitationum suarum, habebit odio gaudium, risus, ludos, existens humilis et
sustinens angustias ac labores"

Saturni, prout est in proposito, significat quod natus celabit
2215   quidquid in animo suo erit et profunde diliget etiam ea que
sunt alterius seculi et multum circa ea uersabitur eius cogitatio
et ea rebus presentibus huius seculi preponet, omnes etiam
ludos abhorrebit et terrena postponet gaudia ; et in eo erit
humilitas aduersaque patietur. Adhuc dicit idem quod coniun-
2220   ctio eius cum Sole, secundum quod hic est, significat quod
natus erit patiens, *humilis, fidelis* sue legis obseruator, doctus
etiam in *librorum* ac *iudiciorum* sententia, deum diliget et collau-
dationem ex hoc habebit, maxime cum Iupiter Solem taliter se
habentem aspiciat. Significat enim *Iupiter,* ut dicit **Albumasar,**
2225 | futuri *seculi beatitudinem,* que *non nisi lege, prudentia, iustitia,*   P40r
fortitudine, temperantia ac celestium speculatione consequenda est. Quod
si hec auctorum dicta uera sint, quid mirum si inter multimodas
uanitatum occupationes exercitiaque lasciuie multifaria a suis
impressa   significatoribus   animus   nati   suorum   uirtute
2230   significatorum trahatur ad diuina? Sed quoniam hec cum illis se
non compatiuntur commode, idcirco necessarium est annorum
reuolutiones   horum   discrepantium   ab   inuicem   sequestrare.
Insuper pars fidei seu religionis in Aquario cadit, in 13° scilicet
gradu eius, sub aspectu omnium planetarum preterquam
2235   Martis. Vnde ratione Saturni significat iuxta **Auicennam** quod
natus erit *inquisitor rerum* et grauis in sermone, ratione Iouis
quod *erit bone fidei pulchrique sermonis,* ratione Solis | quod *erit*   S19r
sapiens nomenque et *famam bonam diligens,* ratione Veneris quod *erit*
beniuolus ludi ac gaudii amator, propter quod etiam fidei sue ac
2240   religioni amorem immiscebit - Veneris enim aspectus ad ipsam
partem fortior est aliis -, ratione Mercurii quod sciet artem

---

2214 prout] ut *PV* 2215 etiam] *om. PV* 2216 circa] contra *V* 2217 etiam] et
V 2218 postponet] preponet *V* 2219 patietur] patientur *P* | Adhuc] ad hoc
PV | dicit idem] *inv. S* 2221 patiens] grauis *ed.* 2226 Quod] et *S* 2227 sint]
sunt *S* | mirum] mecum *V* 2228 uanitatum] -tes *V* 2229 significatoribus]
signatoribus *SV* 2231 compatiuntur] patiuntur *V* 2232 reuolutiones] -nis *S*
discrepantium] -tiam *S* 2233 13°] decimo tertio *PV* 14° *S* 2234 aspectu] 4°
add. S 2236 erit] *om. PV* | inquisitor] inquesitorum *V* 2238 et] *om. V*
2239 ac²] et *S* 2240 Veneris…aliis] *om. PV* 2241 sciet] sciat *S*

2219 coniunctio…2223 habebit] Albohali, *De nativitatibus,* sig. l1v:13-15 | 2224
Iupiter…2226 est] Albumasar, *Introductorium maius,* VI.26 (vol. 8, p. 123:1029-
1031) | 2235 Vnde…2242 negotiationis] Albohali, *De nativitatibus,* c.12, sig.
l2v:15-25

arismetice et *negotiationis*. Dicit etiam **Auenezre** quod Mercurius dominus domus none significat *intellectum nati esse maiorem et altiorem lege sua*, hoc est quod intellectus nati ingeniabitur subtilius in hiis que sunt legis et fidei quam communiter ferat   2245

V131v   usus. Item dicit **Aomar** quod | Mercurius dominus domus none, si congruit *domino ascendentis*, significat quod natus erit *contendens in fide et disputator habens disciplinam in uerbis*. Sed quoniam Mercurius est sub radiis Solis, ob id occultatur uirtus eius, quemadmodum supra diximus. Amplius dicit **Princeps**   2250 quod huic negotio associari debet pars futurorum siue pars celati animi, que quidem in SADAN *pars demonis* appellatur ob hoc, quia significat *abscondita rerum et secreta et precognitiones futurorum et prophetias et ueras reuelationes*. Hec igitur pars medii celi cardinem amplectens corporaliter coniuncta est Ioui,   2255 propter quod Iouis bonitates induit supra dictas nisi quantum pro retrogradatione aliquali inobedientia et contradictione exteriori turbatur. Sicut enim dictum est supra, licet retrogradatio impedimentum quoddam sit in rebus corporis, eufortunium tamen est in rebus anime propter conuenientiam ipsorum.   2260 Significat ergo hec pars ad presens, secundum quod habetur in LIBRO PARTIUM, *eum qui nascitur in sua lege stabilem et firmum et omnem huiusmodi scrupulum remoueri portendit*. Preterea domini domus none Sol et Mercurius sunt in quarta domo, ratione cuius, ut uult **Aomar** in 9 IUDICUM, significatur somnia nati   2265 fore de natura Solis et Mercurii. *Sol* quidem secundum eundem significat *quodlibet inter celum et terram uolans aut regem precipuum aut lumen aliquod et que de solari prodeunt natura* ; *Mercurio autem libri,*

2243 et] *om. P*   2245 subtilius] *om. V*   2248 et] *om. S*   2249 quoniam] quando *S* 2254 ueras *scr. cum ed.*] ua's ? *P* uarias *V om. S* | reuelationes *scr. cum ed.*] reuolutiones *PSV* | igitur] est *S*   2256 propter...Iouis] *om. P*   2257 aliquali] aliqua *P* et] *om. P* | contradictione] retrogradatione *S*   2258 enim] *om. P*   2259 quoddam] quod *P*   2262 eum] etiam *P*   2263 omnem] omne *S* | portendit] pro- *PS* 2265 significatur] -cantur *S*   2266 fore] *om. PV*   2267 precipuum] principem *S* 2268 Mercurio] a *praem. PV* | autem] ante *V*

2242 Auenezre...2244 sua] Ibn Ezra, *Moladot*, III IX 2, 2, pp. 170-171 | 2246 Item...2248 uerbis] Aomar, *De nativitatibus*, p. 137:24-25 | 2250 Princeps...2252 animi] Ibn Ezra, *Liber nativitatum*, fol. 66v:4: "et tu debes associare in hac re partem absconditionis" | 2252 pars...2254 reuelationes] Sadan, *Excerpta* 28, p. 322 | 2262 eum...2263 portendit] Ps.-Ptol., *De iudiciis partium*, fol. 44a | 2265 significatur...2270 designantur] *Liber novem iudicum* IX.36, p. 547b

templa orationi dedita, picture atque imaginis officia, plebs discurrens et
2270 *laborans et seditiosus et que ad Mercurium pertinent designantur.* **Zael**
quoque dicit Solem portendere uisiones *inter celum et terram*
uolantes, aut uidere lumen aut ignem aut regem et que sunt similia nature
Solis. Et reuera hic natus somniat frequentius se uolare per aera.

De peregrinationibus uero ac itineribus simile est iudi-
2275 cium suo modo quod de aliis. Vnde proficuum significatur
nato ex peregrinationibus secundum naturam Solis et Mercurii,
hoc est per nobiles et principes et reges et per consimiles. Item
per scientias et per philosophos et uiros litteratos. Venus quoque domum nonam aspiciens proficuum innuit ex mulieribus
2280 personis. Quartus autem aspectus Martis peregrinanti timorem
incutit in itineribus que per terram, sed quantum ualeat hoc
impedimentum et qualiter dissoluatur dictum est. Item receptio
Lune in loco in quo est significat iuxta **Aomar** quod *exercitium*
nati et eius uictus non *sit in alienis* regionibus. De parte uero itine-
2285 ris non est curandum ad presens, quia a nullo planeta aspicitur ;
et hoc est documentum **Auenezre** in LIBRO RATIONUM
necnon et **Abrahe Compilatoris**. Denique in uiis que per
aquas non apparet hic periclitatio, quantum ex hac celestium
dispositione perpendere possumus ad presens, immo potius
2290 uidetur ex ipsis proficuum significari et bonum aliquod propter
presentiam partis uiarum que per aquas in domo tertia, domo
inquam Iouis, | de quo supra tactum est et adhuc infra tange-   V132r
tur. Item et propter dispositionem Veneris, que domina est
exaltationis loci partis uiarum que per aquas, aspiciens quidem
2295 eandem partem aspectu sextili, nec est a quoquam infortuniorum hec pars impedita. Et hec de nona domo dicta sufficiant.

2269 orationi] orationum *PV* | picture] pictura *S* 2271 portendere] pro- *S*
2272 aut regem] *om. S* 2274 ac] atque *S* | est] erit *S* 2276 et] *om. P* 2277 et¹]
om. V 2278 per²] *s.v. S om. V* 2279 domum nonam] *inv. S* 2281 in] *om. V*
quantum] per *praem. V* 2283 in¹] *om. V* 2284 uero] *om. P* 2286 est] *om. P*
2287 et] *om. P* | in uiis] nimis *V* 2288 non] paret *praem. V* 2291 domo in-
quam] uidelicet *S* 2292 de] *om. S* 2293 propter] per *PV* | est] cum *V*
2294 loci] *s.v. S* | que] *om. S* | quidem] quod *V* 2295 nec] ut *S* 2296 dicta] *om.*
PV

2271 Solem…2273 Solis] Zael, *De interrogationibus*, sig. 134vb:21-23 | 2283
exercitium…2284 regionibus] Aomar, *De nativitatibus*, p. 137:17-19 | 2285
quia…2286 Rationum] Cf. Ibn Ezra, *Te'amim II*, §7.2:24-25, pp. 246-249 |
2287 necnon…Compilatoris] Cf. Ibn Ezra, *De nativitatibus*, sig. c1r:10-13

4.11. <Domus decima>

Decime uero domus secundum gradus equales accepte
prima portio cadit in Virgine, cuius domini dispositio, Mercurii
uidelicet, satis est declarata superius, | quatenus opus nati et
professio necnon et eius exaltatio secundum hoc iudicetur.   2300
Verum hec domus secundum equationes accepta principium
capit a 12° gradu Libre in quo quidem stella fixa notabilis,
Spica uidelicet, que iuxta arabicum idioma Alchimech alaazel
nominatur, est hiis diebus constituta. Vnde **Albumasar** CON-
IUNCTIONUM 2° : *quando fuerint stelle fixe habentes quantitatem*   2305
primam et secundam in gradu medii celi significat natiuitates regales illis
presertim quorum conditioni talis status competit, ut testantur
| sapientes, aliis uero significat exaltationes magnas et honores.
Vnde in CAPITULIS ALMANSORIS : *stelle fixe dant dona grandia et*
ex paupertate subleuant ad sublimitatem quod *non faciunt* septem   2310
planete. Dicit autem **Ptolomeus** in CENTILOGIO quod *stelle fixe*
exhibent eufortunia insperata et inopinata sed ut ad plurimum inuoluunt
hec infortuniis. Vnde **Hispalensis** : *ante omnia considerandum est si*
in gradu ascendentis uel domus decime sit aliquod de sideribus primi
honoris, quod, si fuerit, honorabitur super omnes suos ; fiant alii   2315
planete, quomodocumque uis, *tamen turpiter finiet.* Huius autem
turpis finis rationem ad presens non uideo, nisi hoc accidat ex
infortunata planetarum dispositione, cum stelle fixe dona
dederint immensa. Qualitercumque tamen hoc sit, non oberit
nato, si preuisione utens circa fines rerum sit cautus. Alia   2320
autem littera **Iohannis Hispalensis** sic habet : *si in gradu*
ascendentis uel medii celi *inueneris aliquod sidus firmamenti, quod sit*

S19v

P40v

2299 satis] ut *praem. S* | est] *om. P* | declarata] -tum *S*   2303 alaazel] alace *P*
alaze *V*   2305   2°] 7° *V*   2306   primam] *om. S* | natiuitates] nauitas *V*
2307 talis status] testatur *P* 2309 et] *om. P* 2311 autem] *om. P* 2313 hec] hoc
P 2314 sit] *om. V* 2315 honoris] fuerit *add. V* | suos…quomodocumque] *om.*
V 2317 rationem] rationi *V* | ex] ab *P* 2320 sit] sicut *P* 2321 autem] *om. V*
2322 inueneris] inuenies *P*

2305 quando…2306 regales] Albumasar, *De magnis coniunctionibus*, II.4 (vol. 2,
pp. 45-46) | 2309 stelle…2311 planete] *Capitula Almansoris*, c. 27, sig. 120vb |
2311 Ptolomeus…2313 infortuniis] Ps.-Ptol., *Cent.*, trans. graeco-latina, v. 29 |
2313 ante…2316 finiet] Iohannes Hispalensis, *Epitome*, sig. M2r:11-15 (ultima
pars differens in editione "sed tamen turpiter finiet, nisi prohibeant benefici
planetae") | 2321 si…2327 honorabitur] Iohannes Hispalensis, *Epitome*, sig.
M3r:3-12

primi honoris, et plus si sidus quod habet paruam latitudinem a cinctura,
ut est hic, etsi *inueneris omnes planetas in domibus lapsis uel in eorum*
2325 *dedecore uel in signo occasus eorum uel infortunatos, tamen pertinget*
natus *ad honorem ad quem non ascendit suus consanguineus. Si autem*
fortunati sunt planete, magis ac magis honorabitur. Porro dicit **Albu-**
masar in SADAN quod *in natiuitate prophete Spica* fuit *in ascendente,*
quemadmodum hic est in angulo medii celi. Angulus autem
2330 medii celi maiorem habet fortitudinem precipue in rerum
famositatibus quam ascendens, secundum testimonium
Auenezre in LIBRO RATIONUM commendantis ex hoc **Ptolo-**
meum et reprehendentis **Messehallah** qui dixit oppositum.
Licet enim ascendens maiorem habeat uirtutem realiter, angu-
2335 lus tamen medii celi prerogatiuam merito habet propter eius
influentiam propinquiorem | et manifestiorem in producendo   V132v
res ad notitiam hominum et ad famositatem. Quoniam igitur
duo superiores infra terminos coniunctionis sunt circa hunc
angulum una cum stella fixa supra nominata secundum dispo-
2340 sitionem, inquam, superius expositam, nec potest aliquis aspectus frustrare coniunctionem nec est aspectus Solis ad ipsos omnino contrarius propter latitudinem Iouis et Saturni supra Solem eleuati, et habet se Saturnus in hoc aspectu et Sol, quemadmodum et domus ipsorum, quibus de causis contrarietates
2345 aspectuum minorantur iuxta sapientes. Vnde **Hispalensis** : *etsi*

2323 primi] primum *P* | si] *om. P* | latitudinem] -nis *P* | a cinctura] a centura *V*
ac cineturam *P* acactura ? *S*   2324 uel] ut *P* | in²] *om. PV*   2325 pertinget] -git *S*
2327 fortunati] infortunati *V*   2329 angulo medii] medio *PV* | Angulus...celi]
om. S   2333 dixit] dicit *P*   2335 propter] papa *sic V*   2336 propinquiorem] in
producendo res ad notitiam propinquiorem *add. V (cf. mg. P)* | et
manifestiorem] *om. P* et manifestiorem in producendo res ad notitiam
propinquiorem et manifestiorem *mg. add. P²* | producendo] per- *PV*
2338 infra] inter *V*   2339 una] *om. PV* | nominata] nomina *V*   2340 nec
potest] ut possit *S* | aspectus] ascendens *P*   2341 frustrare] frustra *V* | nec]
neque *P* uidelicet *V*   2342 contrarius] *om. PV*   2343 habet] habebit *PV*
2344 contrarietates] -tas *V*   2345 minorantur] -atur *PV*

2327 Albumasar...2328 ascendente] Sadan, *Excerpta* 3, p. 300 | 2329
Angulus...2333 oppositum] Ibn Ezra, *Te'amim I*, §3.5:6-7, pp. 64-65, quod Bate
sic interpretatus est: "conueniens igitur est ut sit fortitudo maxima angulo qui in
linea medii celi est et angulo primo qui est gradus ascendentis. Dicit enim
Messehallah quod hic fortior est eo qui in linea est medii celi. Ptolomeus vero
dicit contrarium et ipse quidem ius habet et verum dicit" (MS Leipzig 1466, fol.
66rb:23-30) | 2345 etsi...2347 suos] Iohannes Hispalensis, *Epitome*, sig. M2r:3-
5

ascenderit *Aries, et Sol* ibi fuerit *Saturno coniunctus uel contrarius uel*
quartus, *honorabitur super omnes parentes suos*. Merito uidetur hoc
aliquod singulare et magnum significari, licet retrogradatio
difficultates adducat, inuolutiones, iacturas et desperationem
non in rebus anime, sed in hiis que corpori atribuuntur, de   2350
quibus in hiis que de prima domo habitus est sermo magis
diffusus. Sed hoc a mente non labatur quod retrogradatio
superiorum non est perfecta debilitas, secundum quod supra
tactum est. Notandum quoque est quod Iupiter et Saturnus in
eodem gradu coniunctionis sunt secundum medios motus   2355
ipsorum, ratione cuius uirtus configurationis eorum maior esse
debet, prout testatur Hispanus **Abraham** cognomine **Princeps**
in suo tractatu CONIUNCTIONUM. Scriptum quidem enim est in
libro 9 IUDICUM quod *Saturnus in decimo* constitutus *grauem*
apportat angustiam, otio quidem et difficultati implicat et a rege   2360
detrimentum inducit - longos enim minatur carceres -, sed *Venus* loci
domina *non mortem, sed subitum incutiet malum*. Item **Iulius** : *si per*
noctem in medio celi fuerit Saturnus, *infelicitates decernit*. Et iterum
Auenezre : Saturno in medio celi existente per noctem
S20r   significatur natus | passurus semper timorem et iacturam ex   2365
parte regum ac consimilium ; at infortunia Saturni per bonitates
loci et Iouis refrenata in melius reformantur, ut dictum est
supra. Et hoc innuit **Iulius** in eadem parte qua loquitur de
infelicitate Saturnina. In libro quoque 9 IUDICUM consimiliter
habetur quod *Iupiter in decimo laudis et profectus operum et facultatis*   2370
facit, iudicium de omnibus quoque *uenerandum efficit*. Item alibi :

2346 ascenderit Aries] *inu. S* | ibi] *om. S* | fuerit] sit erit *V*   2347 hoc] quod *P*
2348 significari] *om. V*   2350 atribuuntur] asscribuntur *V*   2352 hoc] hec *SV*
om. P | labatur] labitur *S*   2354 est²] *om. P*   2355 coniunctionis] *om. S*
2358 enim] *mg. S* autem *PV*   2359 libro] *om. S* | quod Saturnus] *om. S*
grauem] *om. P*   2361 inducit] indicat *S* | enim] *om. PV* | Venus *scr. cum Libro 9*
iudicum] Venere *PSV*   2363 noctem] mortem *PV*   2365 passurus] passiuus *PV*
iacturam] iacta *P*   2366 ac] et *S* | at *scr.*] aut *PSV* | infortunia] -na *V*   2367 et]
cum *P*   2370 et¹] *om. S* | facultatis] -tes *S*

2357 Hispanus…2358 Coniunctionum] Abraham Bar Ḥiyya ha-naśi, *Megillat ha-*
Megalle, p. 117:16-19 | 2359 Saturnus…2360 angustiam] *Liber novem iudicum*,
A.116 (MS Vat. lat. 6766, fol. 9vb) | Saturnus…2362 malum] *Liber novem*
iudicum, A.116 (MS Vat. lat. 6766, fol. 9vb-10ra) | 2362 Iulius…2363 decernit]
Firmicus Maternus, *Math.* III 2, 21, p. 102:30-31 | 2364 Saturno…2366
consimilium] Ibn Ezra, *Moladot*, III x 2, 5, pp. 174-175 | 2368 Iulius…2369
Saturnina] Firmicus Maternus, *Math.* III 2, 21, p. 103:3-6 | 2370 Iupiter…2371
efficit] *Liber novem iudicum*, A.117 (MS Vat. lat. 6766, fol. 10ra)

Iupiter in decimo ditationem et collationem substantiarum significat et laudis honestatem, subtilitatem quoque ac honorem in omnibus. Hoc ergo modo infelicitas Saturnina refrenatur. In hoc enim omnes
2375 conuenerunt astrologi quod bonitas Iouiana remedium constat infortuniis Saturninis ; alioquin ipsorum coniunctio summam boni non portenderet sublimitatem, quod tamen omnes astrologi confitentur. Ex coniunctione enim Iouis cum Saturno capiunt originem populi, regna, leges et prophetie. Preterea
2380 quia **Iulius** et **Auenezre** et **ceteri** dicunt Saturnum magis infortunatum de nocte quam de die, in hoc proposito causa est defectus a suo haym | siue a sua similitudine seu conditione,   V133r pro tanto quod ipse est planeta diurnus ; sed hec causa insufficiens esse uidetur, ubi deterioribus corrumpatur
2385 impedimentis. Nam semper uidetur stella habere maiorem uirtutem *supra terram* existens quam subtus siue *de nocte* siue *de die*, quod et fatetur **Auenezre** in LIBRO RATIONUM. Vnde **Auicenna** : *natus* quidem *erit odibilis et mali animi,* cum in natiuitatibus nocturnis fuerit Saturnus *in ascendente uel in angulo*
2390 *terre,* quod de angulis supra terram non dicit. Adhuc dicit idem quod exaltatio et regnum et ualitudo considerari debet in natiuitatibus diurnis a Sole et in noctibus a Saturno, quod quidem inconuenienter dixisset si nocturnitas uirtutem sue ualentie et exaltationis sibi prorsus adimere posset. At uero, ut
2395 | ad omne dicatur, totum impedimentum huius partis ex   P41r

---

2373 laudis honestatem] *inv. S* | subtilitatem] *om. S* et *praem. P*   2374 modo] *om. V*   2375 constat] s't in *P*   2376 ipsorum coniunctio] *om. PV* | summam] summa *PV*   2377 non] nature *P* | tamen] cum *P*   2378 coniunctione] -nibus *PV*   2379 populi] *om. PV* | leges] reges *S*   2380 quia *scr.*] quod *PSV del. Par.* et[1]] *om. S*   2382 sua similitudine] *inv. S*   2384 ubi] suis *S*   2385 impedimentis] elementis *praem. S* | habere maiorem] *inv. S*   2387 et] *om. P* | Vnde] cum *add. V*   2389 natiuitatibus] -ate *P*   2390 terram] *om. P* | idem] *om. PV*   2392 noctibus] nocte *PV*   2393 quidem] si *add. P* | nocturnitas] nocturnus *V* | sue] *om. P*   2394 prorsus] *om. S* | uero] non *V* | ut] *om. S*

2372 Iupiter...2373 omnibus] *Liber novem iudicum,* A.117 (alia translatio incognita) | 2380 Iulius...2381 die] Firmicus Maternus, *Math.* III 2, 21, p. 103:7, et III, 2, 26, p. 104:29 | Auenezre] Ibn Ezra, *Teʿamim II,* §7.2:10, pp. 246-247 | 2385 semper...2387 die] Ibn Ezra, *Teʿamim I,* §2.7:2, pp. 46-47, quod Bate sic interpretatus est: "Dederunt autem fortitudine soli quia de die apparet de die eius virtus et posuerunt Iouem de nocte quia de nocte supra terram esse potest" (MS Leipzig 1466, fol. 63vb:10-13) | 2388 natus...animi] Albohali, *De nativitatibus,* c. 29, sig. l2v:10-11 | 2390 Adhuc...2392 Saturno] cf. Albohali, *De nativitatibus,* c.30, l3v:6-9

retrogradatione Iouis et Saturni causatur, de qua satis dictum
est superius. Hiis igitur ita se habentibus dicamus quod, cum
dominus ascendentis fuerit in medio celi, significat hoc natum commixtum fore *regibus*, ut dicit **Auicenna**. Item cum *dominus
ascendentis* sit de superioribus et sit in medio celi *dominus eius*   2400
applicatus, domino quidem exaltationis, dicit idem hoc *significare*
natum esse *commixtum tam nobilibus quam regibus* aut circa dignitatem eum consistere. Asserit enim idem dominum exaltationis
in hoc negotio prerogatiuam habere et magis ualere quam
dominum domus, quod et confirmat **Iulius**. Dicit igitur **Aui-**   2405
cenna quod talis applicatio significat proficuum adipisci ex
regibus per inquisitionem nati. Amplius Iupiter et Saturnus coniuncti in domo decima significant magnam sapientiam siue *magnum*
sapientem, ut habetur in LIBRO RATIONUM, et quod natus *hono-*
rem habebit propter leges, iudicia et fidem iuxta testimonium   2410
Auenezre in LIBRO NATIVITATUM. Et ut ad unum dicatur,
secundum significationem Iouis et Saturni honorificabitur
natus quantum ex hac parte, sed propter retrogradationem
occurrent difficultates laboriose ita ut uix ad exaltationes
perueniatur nisi post desperationem et retardationem. Nam   2415
retrogradatio contra significat siue contraria, ut dicit **Alkindus**, et
est minarum contradictionis et corruptionis, ut dictum est
supra. Quapropter significatum est natum sibi timere in suis
exaltationibus. Preterea cum Saturnus in exaltatione sua existens sit dominus secunde domus et habeat partem in prima,   2420

2396   causatur] cautus *V* | dictum…superius] superius est dictum *S*
2400 dominus] domino *PV* 2405 et] *om. P* 2408 siue] *om. PV* 2409 honorem
habebit] *inv. P* 2410 leges] et *add. S* | iuxta] legem *add. P* 2411 unum] omne *S*
2413 natus] *om. P*   2414 ut] quod *S*   2417 minarum] *lectio suspecta, an* minax
scrib.? 2418 significatum] signatum *V*

2397 cum…2399 Auicenna] Albohali, *De nativitatibus*, c.10, sig. f1v:25-26 |
2399 Item…2402 regibus] Albohali, *De nativitatibus*, c.32, sig. m1r:5-7 | 2403
dominum…2405 Iulius] Firmicus Maternus, *Math.* II 3, 4, p. 44:3-6. | 2406
talis…2407 nati] Albohali, *De nativitatibus*, c.31, sig. l4r:4-7 | 2407
Iupiter…2409 sapientem] Ibn Ezra, *Te'amim II*, §5.4:10, pp. 228-229, quod Bate
sic interpretatus est: "Cum Saturno autem super magnum sapientem significant
eo quod ambo superni sunt" (MS Leipzig 1466, fol. 56va:36-38) | 2409
natus…2410 fidem] Ibn Ezra, *Moladot*, III x 2, 7, pp. 174-175 | 2416
retrogradatio…Alkindus] *Liber novem iudicum*, II.3, p. 422a: "gressus directus
equalitatem retrogradatio contra significant" | 2417 ut…2418 supra] vide ll.
32-36

significat hoc secundum **Auenezre** natum *exaltari* inter *creaturas* propter personam suam et quod *acquiret substantiam per reges* seu principes, sed non erit hoc sine contradictione et difficultate propter retrogradationem. Item quoniam Saturnus partem

2425 habet in domo tertia secundum gradus equales, significatur etiam aliquod *honorificum sibi euenire occasione fratris* aut uiarum propinquarum seu eorum que sunt domus tertie. **Alkindus** tamen uult | quod ratione domini prime domus significatur   S20v dignitas *acquiri proprio labore*, ratione uero domini secunde

2430 domus *per ministros et per propriam pecuniam*, sed ratione *tertii a fratribus et multimodo discursu*. Insuper Sol in exaltatione sua | V133v existens dominusque triplicitatis ascendentis partem habet in domo octaua et nona. Mercurius quoque maior none dominus uim suam Soli commisit. Quamobrem significatur iuxta

2435 eundem **Auenezre** natum *honorem* consequi ex eis que a *mortuis* proueniunt, per *scientias* quoque et per ea que de *fide*. Sed quia natiuitas nocturna est, minuetur aliquantulum hec uirtus Solis in exaltando natum, secundum quod dicit **Auicenna**. Rursum dicit **Abraham Compilator** : *si in natiuitate aliquem planetam in*

2440 *domo sui honoris inueneris, uide naturam illius planete et in quota domo sit ab Oriente, per hoc sciturus quibus ex rebus honor ille continget.* Sol autem reges significat et magnates, Saturnus uero seniores et summates. Amplius dicit **Aomar** quod *omnis stella in propria domo aut regno inuenta regiam* aut excellentem *significat dignitatem*. In

2445 proposito autem Venus in propria domo est domina existens decime domus, ratione cuius iuxta **Alkindum** significatur acquiri dignitas per *mulieres uel mulierum beneficia* necnon per amicitias. Vult quoque **Aristoteles** in 9 IUDICUM quod cum

---

2422 substantiam] -tias *P* -tia *V*   2423 hoc] *om. S*   2425 significatur] signatur *V*   2430 sed] *om. S*   2431 multimodo] multitudo *V*   2432 triplicitatis] triplicitas *P* triplicantis *V*   2433 nona] contra *V*   2435 eundem] *om. S*   2436 quoque] quorum *P*   2441 Oriente] Ariete *S*   2442 et summates] mammates *S* 2444 regno] regna *V* | regiam] regum *PV*   2446 decime] id *V*

2421 Auenezre…2423 principes] Ibn Ezra, *Moladot*, III X 2, 9, pp. 174-175 | 2424 quoniam…2426 fratris] Ibn Ezra, *Moladot*, III X 2, 9, pp. 174-175 | 2428 ratione…2431 discursu] *Liber novem iudicum* X.6, p. 554a | 2435 natum…2436 fide] Ibn Ezra, *Moladot*, III X 2, 9, pp. 174-175 | 2436 Sed…2438 natum] Albohali, *De nativitatibus*, c.42, sig. o2v:17-20 | 2439 si…2441 continget] Ibn Ezra, *De nativitatibus*, c.5, sig. c3r:6-8 | 2443 omnis…2444 dignitatem] *Liber novem iudicum* X.4, p. 552a | 2447 acquiri…2448 amicitias] *Liber novem iudicum* X.6, p. 553b | 2448 cum…2451 dignitatem] *Liber novem iudicum* X.10, p. 555a

Iupiter ascendentis dominus *none dominum respiciat* sitque noni
dominus in cardine repertus, significatur natus infra natiuam   2450
regionem *prouehi ad ecclesiasticam dignitatem*. *Iupiter* enim, ut uult
Ptolomeus, dignitates adducit *per fidem et per prefecturas et per
sacerdotalia*. Ad hoc etiam cooperari uidetur pars subite exaltationis, secundum **Albumasar** in ascendente, 20° uidelicet gradu
Sagittarii, locata, in termino quidem Mercurii, domini none   2455
domus et domini uigoris habetque Mercurius partem in natura
stelle fixe, de qua supra tactum est, cum hoc quod Venus habet
in ea partem, ut dicunt **Auenezre** et **Ptolomeus** et reliqui.
Venus igitur secundum hec et alia nato prosperitatem confert
in Venerianis, Mercurius uero in Mercurialibus, licet cum   2460
occultatione. Ceterorum quoque, Saturni scilicet, Iouis, Solis et
Lune, uirtutes et influentie secundum dispositiones preostensas
non sunt in proposito minus efficaces, solus autem Mars
propter inconnexionem eius cum ascendente et debilitatem
eius suas affectiones et accidentia nato non infundit. Denique   2465
rememorandum est signanter quod gradus coniunctionis
magne, que fuit in Libra, ut predictum est, prope angulum
consistit medii celi. Adhuc idem est hic ascendens cum ceteris
domibus quod fuit in oppositione Solis et Lune immediate
precedente coniunctionem que incepit in Aquario per mutatio-   2470
nem triplicitatis super longitudinem Machlinie et latitudinem
eius anno Domini 1225. Gradus autem coniunctionis illius fuit
hic in domo secunda, cuius *mysteria* multa sunt, quemadmodum
dicit **Albumasar** in SADAN de natiuitate prophete accidisse.
Adhuc et signum profectionis ab hoc loco coniunctionis perue-   2475

2449 none] noni *S* | sitque] sit *S*   2452 per²] *om. PV* | per³] *om. P*   2453 Ad
hoc] *post corr. S*   2454 ascendente] ab'nte *V in add. P* est *add. S*   2456 domini
scr.] domino *PSV*   2457 tactum] dictum *S*   2458 partem] parte *PV* | et¹] *om. S*
2459   nato] *om. V*   2461   quoque] que *S* | Saturni scilicet] *inv. S*
2466 rememorandum] -ando *V* | est signanter] *om. PV*   2467 predictum] supra
dictum *P* | prope] proprie *P*   2468 Adhuc] ad hoc *V* | ascendens] ascendentis
V | cum] *om. PV*   2470 incepit] incipit *PS*   2471 Machlinie] Mahilinie *V*
Magh'lie *S*   2474 dicit] *om. S*   2475 profectionis] perfectionis *P* | loco] *om. V*

2451 Iupiter...2453 sacerdotalia] Ptol., *Quad.* IV.2, trans. Guilelmi, p. 278:34-35
| 2453 pars...2455 locata] Albumasar, *Introductorium maius*, VIII.4 (vol. 8, p.
163:528-530) | 2458 Auenezre...reliqui] Bate referre videtur ad Ibn Ezra,
Reshit Ḥokhmah, §2.14:8, pp. 134-135; Ptol., *Quad.* I.9, p. 175:438-442 | 2473
in...2474 Sadan] Sadan, *Excerpta* 21, p. 315

nit in anno natiuitatis ad Libram, ratione quorum omnium significata est quedam altitudo | gradus siue status nati respectu conditionis parentum eius, secundum quod testantur sapientes, nisi quantum nocturnitas Solis et Saturni

2480 exaltationem huius offuscant. Retrogradationes quoque Saturni et Iouis tribulationibus et contradictionibus et desperationibus etiam propter Solis aspectum rem inuoluunt. Dicitur enim in 9 IUDICUM quod *omnium retrogradatio ducum, cum eorum significatio spem acquirendi iam incitet, pericula et impedimenta anteponit.* | Et

2485 iterum **Hermannus** in LIBRO RERUM ABSCONDITARUM *retrogradus* rem *inuoluit.* Ad hunc ergo modum erit exaltatio nati. Quando autem et qualiter hoc fiet cum precisione declarabunt annorum reuolutiones. |

    Opus uero nati professio et magisterium preter id quod ex

2490 domo decima de significatione trahunt et a Marte et Venere et Mercurio gubernantur. Mars autem in proposito parum potest, ut patet ex predictis, propter quod *tolerantia laboris* et *agilitas* seu festinatio et huiusmodi per Martem significata, ut dicunt **Auenezre** et **Compilator** et ceteri, huic nato est ablata. Venus

2495 autem domina domus decime propter laudabilem eius dispositionem, quantum in se est, opus nati gratiosum reddit et placidum, ut uolunt philosophi, precipue autem in *canendo* et *saltando* et *iocando* iuxta **Hispalensem**. Nam hec ars eius est et opus, deliciis scilicet indulgere et amori et ceteris Venerianis. Sed ut

2500 ad unguem sit dicere, Mercurio plurimum huius negotii incumbit, cum sit de prepotentibus in figura, opus autem et professio

V134r

P41v

S21r

2476 omnium] omnia *S*   2477 quedam] quidem *S*   2478 secundum] *om. P*
2480 huius] eius *S* | Retrogradationes] retrogradatio *P* retrograda *V* | quoque]
tamquam *V om. S* 2481 contradictionibus] conditionibus *P* 2482 Dicitur] dicit
V | in…Iudicum] *om. S* 2486 rem] *om. S* 2490 et[2]] *om. S* 2492 tolerantia]
tolleratur *S* 2493 et] in *S* 2494 ceteri] cetera *S* 2496 est] *post* quantum *S* cum
V | placidum] placide *V* 2497 autem] *om. PV* | et saltando] *mg.* P[2] *om. V* et
psaltando *S* | et…iocando] *om. P add a. m. mg.* 2499 et[1]] *om. S* | et[2]] ac *S*
2500 Mercurio] mentio *V* 2501 sit] *om. P* | prepotentibus] -tioribus *S* | autem]
scilicet *P*

2483 omnium…2484 anteponit] *Liber novem iudicum*, II.3, p. 422a | 2486
retrogradus…inuoluit] Hermannus, *De occultis*, p. 274:2 | 2492
tolerantia…2493 significata] Ibn Ezra, *Moladot*, III x 3, 4, pp. 176-177 | 2494
Compilator] Ibn Ezra, *De nativitatibus*, sig. c3r:10 | 2497 in…2498 iocando]
Iohannes Hispalensis, *Epitome*, sig. M3v:5 | 2501 opus…2502 est] Ibn Ezra,
Moladot, III x, 3, 6, pp. 176-177

Mercurii seu magisterium, ut dicit **Auenezre**, *sapientia* est, que
consimiliter ab existentibus in medio celi consignificatur propter ipsorum dispositionem supra dictam, quod etiam per hoc
confirmatur quod Saturnus est dominus *partis fortune* in hoc   2505
negotio magnam uim habens in *natiuitatibus nocturnis*, ut dicit
Auicenna. Erit ergo natus secundum hoc philosophie professor et eorum operi et magisterio [se] immiscens que ad ipsam
consequuntur. Item confirmatur hoc idem per hoc quod dicit
Auicenna de applicatione Lune ad Mercurium in natiuitatibus   2510
nocturnis et iterum per hoc quod dicit **Hispalensis** et **Benneka Indus** de applicatione Lune cum Mercurio corporaliter in
coniunctione luminarium natiuitatem precedente, cum scilicet a
Sole Luna separetur. Sed cum *Mercurius* sit *sub* luce *Solis*, significat hoc iuxta **Hispalensem** quod natus *sciet plus quam facere*   2515
posset, presertim cum Mercurius tantam uirtutem et talem
habeat in figura quanta et qualis est supra declarata. Aspectus
uero Martis ad Mercurium supra expositus significat natum
physicum, diuinuum, ingeniosum et calidum, ut uult **Auicenna**,
innuens consimiliter quod cum Mercurius Soli coniunctus sit   2520
nec impeditus a combustione, *significat natum esse alti magisterii*

2502 est] *om. P*   2503 consignificatur] configuratur *S* consignator *V*   2504 per]
propter *S*   2505 quod] quia *P*   2506 habens] habentis *PV*   2507 hoc] hec *S*
2508 se] *delevi*   2509 confirmatur] -mant *PV*   2511 Benneka Indus] Alkindus
Par Auicenna *p. corr. L*   2513 natiuitatem] -te *V*   2514 separetur] -atur *V*
2516 posset] possit *P*   2519 ut...Auicenna] *om. V*   2521 magisterii] ingenii *PV*

2505 Saturnus...2506 nocturnis] Albohali, *De nativitatibus*, c.33, sig. m1v:25-28
| partis...2507 Auicenna] Cf. Albohali, *De nativitatibus*, c.29, sig. l2v:11-12 "pars
fortune in natiuitatibus diurnis et nocturnis", et vide supra 2388-2390 | 2509
hoc²...2511 nocturnis] cf. Albohali, *De nativitatibus*, c.29, sig. l2v:5-7: "si Luna
fuerit in natiuitatibus nocturnis, significat quod natus erit astronomus, peritus
diuinationum ac futurorum annunciator." | 2511 Hispalensis...2514
separetur] Cf. Iohannes Hispalensis, *Epitome*, sig. I2v:14-19 | Benneka...2512
Indus] Cf. Ibn Ezra, *Liber nativitatum*, fol. 67r30-v3 : " Dicit Bonneca Alhendi:
respice semper ad loca Lune in puncto coniunctionis aut opposicionis Solis, que
scilicet eorum est ante nativitatem nati, et cui stelle dabit fortitudinem, et
naturam stelle recipientis fortitudinem dabis nato." Bonneca Alhendi, idest
forsan Kanakah al-Hindi, qui ut "Benneka Indus" citatur in tractatu
pseudo-Alkindi ab Henrico translato: vide MS Pal. lat. 1407, f. 59v15 et 61r22.
| 2514 Sed...2516 posset] Iohannes Hispalensis, *Epitome* (MS Erfurt, Ampl.
O.84), fol. 19r:5-6 | 2517 Aspectus...2519 Auicenna] Albohali, *De
nativitatibus*, c.33 sig. m2r:10-12: "erit physicus uel uates uel nigromanticus,
astutus et prouidus in suis operibus" | 2519 Auicenna...2522 eos] Albohali,
De nativitatibus, c.33 sig. m2r:12-16

maximeque subtilitatis ac scriptorem regum plurisque pretii apud eos.
Idem quoque uult **Auenezre** cum hoc quod aspectus Iouis et
Saturni super Solem et Mercurium professionem nati afficiant
2525 secundum dispositiones suas. Item pars operis in 15° gradu
locata Leonis, quamuis secundum domorum equationes in
domo cadat octaua, secundum tamen gradus equales incidit
none sub aspectu trino secundum gradus equales tantum sui
Solis. Sed quia Sol de se *propter | sue nature altitudinem non est*   V134v
2530 *operum significator*, ut dicit **Auenezre**, quia tamen Mercurium
recipit, opera et magisteria Mercurialia nobilitat et exaltat. Huic
etiam cooperantur domini triplicitatis huius domus, qui idem
sunt cum dominis triplicitatis luminaris, cuius est auctoritas, de
quibus satis est dictum supra. Preterea scriptum est in CAPITU-
2535 LIS ALMANSORIS quod *perfectus medicus erit cui Mars et Venus*
fuerint in 6°, secundum quod Mars hic se habet, Venus etiam in
sexta domo cadit per gradus equales. Verum Martis infortunium in hoc loco impedimentum adducit. Insuper dicit **Aui-**
cenna : *scito quod in anno quo ascendens radicis peruenerit ad signum*
2540 *medii celi, si fuerit in eo aliquis ex planetis magisterium significantibus,*
renouabit natus magisterium suum secundum naturam substantie planete
qui ibi fuerit. Hic autem 35° anno a radice peruenit profectio ad
Libram. Et similiter perueniet ad Libram anno 47° a natiuitate
necnon et 69° Et hec de decima domo dicta sufficiant.

4.12. <Domus undecima>

2522 subtilitatis] sublimitatis *ed.* | plurisque] plurimique *ed.*   2524 super] supra
PV   2527 cadat] -dit *P* | tamen gradus] *inv. post corr. S*   2528 tantum] t'm *P*
d'm *S* dictum *V*   2529 Sed] et *V*   2530 tamen] cum *P*   2531 recipit] recepit *S*
exaltat] exultat *P*   2532   etiam] enim *S* | cooperantur] quo operantur *V*
triplicitatis] -tum *S* | qui idem] quidem *PV*   2533 auctoritas] -ris *S*   2534 satis
est] *inv. P*   2536 6°] sexta *ed.* | quod] *om. P*   2537 cadit] -dat *S* | Verum] uero *P*
2539 scito] *om. S*   2540 aliquis] aliqua *P*   2541 planete] per *praem. V*   2542 a
radice] *om. S* | profectio] perfectio *S*   2543   Et similiter] consimiliter *P*
Et…69°] *om. S* | 47°] 74° *V*   2544 decima] 10. *s. l. P* | sufficiant] sunt *PV*

2523 aspectus…2525 suas] Ibn Ezra, *Moladot*, III x, 3, 7, et III x, 3, 10, pp. 174-
177 | 2529 Sol…2530 significator] Ibn Ezra, *Moladot*, III x, 3, 11, pp. 176-177
| 2535 perfectus…2536 6°] *Capitula Almansoris*, c. 28, sig. 120vb | 2539
scito…2542 fuerit] Albohali, *De nativitatibus*, c.33, sig. m2r:25-m2v:1

Vndecima uero domus nominata est a **Iulio** *agathos demon* 2545
siue *bonus demon* eo quod super bonam fortunam significat et
super amicos ; in qua quidem | secundum gradus equales
accepta coincidunt Saturnus et Iupiter in coniunctione continentes inter se partem amicorum, ratione cuius amicitiam
habebit natus et bonam fortunam cum senioribus et iudicibus 2550
et consimilibus de significatione Saturni et Iouis, non tamen
sine tribulationibus propter retrogradationem. Vnde **Auicenna**
hoc confirmat, cum partem habeant in ascendente existentes in
undecima, dicens Saturnum significare amicitiam cum senioribus, seruis et ancillis, Iouem uero cum nobilibus, diuitibus et 2555
principibus. **Auenezre** ucro dicit *Saturnum* significare *seruos et*
huiusmodi *homines despectos nisi fuerit in exaltatione sua.* Nam, cum
ex hoc eius conditio nobilitetur, ascendet eius significatio ad
magnos sapientes, ut prius dictum est. Item in LIBRO PAR-
TIUM : *pars amicorum* in medio celi *amicos parat nominatissimos* et 2560
regios. Insuper dicit **Hispalensis** *quod si una de domibus Iouis as-*
cenderit et Iupiter consideret ascendens quocumque aspectu, puer fit semper
fortunatus. Sed ut ad omne dicatur, *illa que fortunium significant,*
prout habetur in CAPITULIS ALMANSORIS, *sunt Iupiter, pars fortu-*
ne et pars diuinationis, idest pars futurorum, *domus quoque secunda et* 2565
qui in ea fuerit eiusque dominus, dominus etiam triplicitatis, cuius fuerit
auctoritas, necnon dominus domus decime et qui in ea fuerit, de quorum
omnium dispositione dictum est sufficienter. Preterea hec

2547 secundum] et super *S*   2548 coincidunt] quo incidit *PV*   2551 significa-
tione] signo uero *V*   2552 propter retrogradationem] in -tione *S*   2553 hoc]
hec *V* | existentes] existens *P*   2555 uero] non *V om. SP* | nobilibus] -lioribus
S et *add. P*   2556 uero] *om. P*   2557 homines despectos] *inv. a. corr. S* | despec-
tos] dispositiones *V* | nisi] non *S*   2558 ascendet] -it *S* | eius²] *om. P*   2559 dic-
tum est] *trsp. V*   2561 Iouis] *om. S*   2562 consideret] -rat *S* | aspectu] -tum *V*
puer] peruerso *S* | semper] super *P*   2563   fortunatus] formosus *ed.*
significant] -cat *P*   2565   diuinationis] donationis *ed.* | idest] et *V*
2566 dominus² *scr. cum ed.*] domini *PV* dominii *S* | etiam] et *SV* | triplicitatis]
luminaris *add. ed.*   2568 sufficienter] supra *PV*

2545 Vndecima...2546 demon] Firmicus Maternus, *Math.* II 16, 2, pp. 59:27-
60:2 | 2552 Vnde...2556 principibus] Albohali, *De nativitatibus,* c.35, sig.
m3v:16-20: "Si...Saturnus, significat quod plures amicorum eius erunt senes,
serui et captiui; sed si Iupiter fierit, erunt plurimi eorum nobiles ac principes
hominesque bellicosi" | 2556 Saturnum...2557 sua] Ibn Ezra, *Moladot,* III XII
1, 5, pp. 179-180 | 2560 pars...2561 regios] Ps.-Ptol., *De iudiciis partium,* fol.
46va | 2561 Hispalensis...2563 fortunatus] Iohannes Hispalensis, *Epitome:,* sig.
M4r:15-16 | 2564 Capitulis...2567 fuerit] *Capitula Almansoris,* c. 40, sig. 120vb

domus equata initium sumit a 4° gradu Scorpionis, cuius | $_{P42r}$
2570 dominus Mars ipsam non aspicit nec aliquis planetarum preter
Venerem. Cum igitur signa naturam habeant suorum dominorum, ut dicunt astrologi, uisum est natum amicos habere Martiales, cum Mars sit dominus Scorpionis, sed propter debilitatem Martis non aspicientis hanc domum, quamquam sit in
2575 gaudio suo, euanescet hec amicitia et fortuna. Verum quia
Venus hanc domum ex oppositione aspicit illustrando partem
Veneream in 13° gradu Scorpionis contentam, domine quidem
triplicitatis eius, ex hoc delectabilior fit huius domus conditio | $_{V135r}$
iuxta proprietatem Veneream, sed quoniam hec domus est
2580 locus meroris Veneris signumque casus eius, ob hoc *extrem*a
huius amicitie *luctum* concludunt et merorem, secundum quod
innuunt sapientes. Dominus uero triplicitatis huius domus
primus, Mars uidelicet, secundum dispositionem eius amicos
Martiales reddit ineptos, secundus autem et tertius, Venus
2585 scilicet et Luna, secundum esse suum meliora portendunt. Hec
sunt igitur significationes domus undecime.

4.13. <Domus duodecima>

Locus autem *cacodemonis* siue *mali demonis* secundum **Iulium** domus est duodecima, que merito sic uocatur, nam ex
hac domo inimicorum significatio trahitur. Cacodemones
2590 autem humane nature inimici sunt, quorum filii seu consan-
guinei conuenienter dici possunt qui hostilitates et inimicitias
captant cum pacificis exercere. Huius autem diabolici loci
dominus infortunatus Mars in casu suo existens et cadens ab
angulo suam domum contrario aspicit aspectu in hac proposita

2569 initium] *om. S* 2570 Mars] est *praem. S* 2575 euanescet] -cit *S* | quia]
quod *V* 2577 13°] 3° *P* | contentam] contentum *V* contemptum *P* | domine
scr.] domino *PV* domina *S* 2578 triplicitatis] -tati *P* | delectabilior] delectatior *S*
declarabilior *V* | huius] *om. P* 2579 Veneream] Venerianam *S* | quoniam]
quando *V* 2580 signumque…eius] casus eius signumque casus *V* | hoc] hec
V | extrema] extranea *V* 2581 luctum] uictum *P* iunctum *V* 2583 Mars] *om.*
P 2585 scilicet] uidelicet *S* | portendunt] pro- *S* 2586 domus undecime] *inu. S*
2587 cacodemonis] caca- *S* | siue…demonis] *om. S* 2588 que] quod *V* | sic
uocatur] sit uocatus *V* 2589 Cacodemones] caca- *S* 2591 dici possunt]
decipiunt *S* | et] *om. S* 2592 autem] *om. PV* 2593 ab] in *S*

2580 extrema…2582 sapientes] *Prov.* 14,13 | 2587 Locus…2588 duodecima]
Firmicus Maternus, *Math.* II 17, 1, p. 60:13-16

natiuitate nec impedit ascendens aut dominium eius, quare   2595
significat debilitatem inimicorum et impotentiam respectu
conditionum nati. **Auicenna** dicit hoc significare *aduersitatem
inimicorum* et infortunium *et malum* esse ; et quia Mars significator ipsorum est, erunt tales inimici qui pacem habebunt odio et
bella diligent et rixas iuxta Martialem naturam. Item dicit   2600
Auenezre quod *cum ascendens fuerit Sagittarius, plures contentionum
nati erunt cum bellicosis,* et hoc propter Scorpionem. Amplius cum
prima pars Sagittarii signi ascendentis cadat in hac domo,
significat hoc contrarietatem habere natum in se ipso propter
S22r   dominium | eiusdem planete super hec loca, ut testantur sa-   2605
pientes. Et quoniam Iupiter habens partem in fine huius domus ipsam amico aspectu aspicit secundum gradus equales
dominus existens ascendentis et committens uim suam Saturno, consimiliter ascendentis dominus arbitrandus est bonitatem Iouis hostilem inimicitie naturam et rancoris mitigare,   2610
quatenus conuenienter dicere possit natus : *cum hiis qui oderunt
pacem eram pacificus* etc. Ad idem etiam cooperatur aspectus
Iouis trinus secundum gradus equales ad partem inimicorum
casum minantem a domo septima, cum omnino non ceciderit
et dominus eius Mercurius sit in dispositione alia quam in   2615
domo septima, ut supra tetigimus. Sane non multum ualere
poterit Mercurius ratione partis, cum ipsam non aspiciat, et
iterum pars inimicorum alio modo accepta, secundum quod
cadit in fine Arietis, similiter parum ualet ad propositum cum
in illius sit aspectu. Quapropter de significatione huiusmodi   2620
partium non est multum curandum in hac parte nisi quantum

2597 conditionum] -nis *S* | Auicenna dicit] dicit enim Auicena *S* | aduersita-
tem] diuersitatem *P* 2598 inimicorum] *om. PV* 2599 qui] quia *S* 2600 Martia-
lem] naturalem *P*   2601   fuerit] fuit *V* | Sagittarius] Saturnus *PV*
contentionum *scr.*] contemptionum *S* cond'onum *P* concessionum *V*
2603 Sagittarii] *om. PV* 2604 hoc] hic *S* 2605 sapientes] et super hec loca *add.*
S 2606 habens] habet *V* 2608 existens] *om. S* 2609 dominus] domino *PV*
arbitrandus] arbitrand' *P* arbitrandum *SV*   2610   naturam] *post* rancoris *S*
2611 quatenus] et *praem. V* | dicere] dicit *S* 2612 etiam] et *PV* | cooperatur] -
etur *S* 2613 trinus] 3us *S* | partem] partes *V* casus *praem. S* 2614 omnino non]
inv. S 2615 sit] *om. V* | alia] *om. PV* | quam…septima] *om. S* 2616 ut] iam
PV | ualere poterit] *inv. P* 2620 in illius] nullius *V* | huiusmodi partium] eius
PV

2597 Auicenna…2598 esse] Albohali, *De nativitatibus*, c.36, sig. m4v:25-n1r:7 |
2601 cum…2602 Scorpionem] Ibn Ezra, *Moladot*, III XII 3, 2, pp. 180-181 |
2611 cum…2612 etc] *Ps.* 119,7

prediximus. De equitaturis uero sibi timeat natus propter dispositionem Martis infortunatam. Bonitas tamen Iouis pro secunda parte rem emendat, insuper *pars auctoritatis et magni*
2625 *nominis* iuxta **Albumasar** cadit in fine huius domus. Et licet hec pars ratione domus | ob inimicitias deturpetur, aspectus tamen   V135v Iouis ipsam saluat cum receptione. Et hec de duodecima domo sufficiant.

4.14. <Mors nati>

Vltimo quidem igitur huic principali proposito finem
2630 concludentes de fine nati et termino uite eius conclusiuo secundum presuppositam celestium harmoniam auctorum sentencias subiungamus. Quoniam igitur hec natiuitas post coniunctionem luminarium euenit, erit mors nati post opposi-tionem secundum dicta Persarum, et quia ascendens mundum
2635 est ab aspectu malorum et octaua similiter necnon et Luna, significat hoc, ut uult **Abraham Princeps**, mortem domesti-cam. Dicit tamen idem **Abraham** quod, cum dominus octaue domus dederit uim suam domino domus none, significat hoc natum moriturum extra natale solium. Luna autem in propo-
2640 sito domina domus octaue pro prima parte a Mercurioque recepta maiorem partem habente in domo nona dispositionem suam pulsat eidem. Item dicit **Hispalensis** quod, cum *dominus octaue domus* eandem non aspexerit secundum quod Luna se habet in proposito, *morietur* natus *extra* locum natiuitatis, quod
2645 etiam affirmat **Auenezre** et **Abraham Compilator**. Sol tamen

---

2622   prediximus] diximus *PV* | uero] *om. S* | timeat] caueat *P* retineat *S* 2626 ob inimicitias] ab inimicis *PV*   2627 receptione] acceptione *P*   2628 suffi-ciant] *om. S*   2629 quidem] quid *V*   2630 concludentes] -dens *P* | nati] *om. PV* 2631   presuppositam] propositam *PV*   2632   sentencias] -tiis *S* sermonis *V* igitur] ergo *PV*   2634 mundum] mondi *P*   2635 octaua] octauum *S* | et²] *om. P* 2637   tamen] *om. P*   2638   dederit] *post* suam *S*   2639   solium] solum *PV* 2640   domina domus] *inv. P*   2641   nona] contra *V*   2642   eidem] eodem *S* 2643 domus] dominus *S*   2645 affirmat] confirmat *S*

2624 pars...2625 Albumasar] Cf. Albumasar, *Introductorium maius*, VIII.4 (vol. 8, p. 163:530-533) | 2636 significat...domesticam] Ibn Ezra, *Liber nativitatum*, fol. 65v:13-17 | 2637 cum...2639 solium] Ibn Ezra, *Liber nativitatum*, fol. 65v:17-18 | 2642 Hispalensis...2644 natiuitatis] Iohannes Hispalensis, *Epitome*, sig. N1v:24-26 | cum...2644 natiuitatis] Ibn Ezra, *Moladot*, III VIII 3, 4, pp. 166-167 | 2645 Abraham Compilator] Ibn Ezra, *De nativitatibus*, sig. b8v:18-19

partem habens in octaua ipsam aspicit saltem per gradus equales, sed, quia consimiliter partem habet in nona, uidetur trahi
significatio mortis secundum hoc ad exitum a prima secundum
testimonium **Abrahe Principis**. Item dicit idem **Princeps**
quod, cum dominus octaue domus fuerit in opposito ascen-   2650
dentis aut domini eius, secundum quod hic se habent Luna et
Sol, significat hoc quod natus cadet ab alto et morietur. **Auenezre** quoque ait : *cum prepotentia super loca mortis fuerit in Geminis
cum Mercurio, significat hoc natum casurum ab alto et sic moriturum*. In
proposito autem Luna non est corporaliter coniuncta Mercu-   2655
rio, sed per aspectum. Item dicit idem quod testimonia Lune
per se recipienda non sunt *quousque perquisita fuerint testimonia
domini domus septime* et loci in quo est Luna, ut etiam dicit idem.

P42v   Mercurius autem dominus domus septime, in qua est Luna, |
nondumque egressus terminos combustionis receptus est a   2660
Sole, ut dictum est supra, quod quidem, ut dicit **Princeps
Abraham**, natum occulte moriturum significat ita quod exitus
eius dubius erit et ignotus secundum dispositionem Mercurii
occultati. Sed ut certitudo huius iudicii euidentiorem habeat de-
clarationem, consideremus ad reliqua mortis testimonia a iam   2665
dictis discrepantia quatenus partem possumus eligere saniorem
et certioribus fultam testimoniis. Dicit igitur **Auenezre** quod
*loca mortis sunt hec: domus octaua et locus domini eius et pars mortis et
locus Lune* necnon et domini horum. Ex hiis enim scitur species

S22v   mortis. | Et hoc idem affirmat per **Alkindum. Auicenna** uero   2670

2646   in octaua] 8. domo *P* | saltem] tamen *P*   2648   significatio] sermo *S*
secundum[1]] in *S* | a prima] apr'ia PV apetru' *S* | secundum[2]] iuxta *S*
2650   domus] alias sexte domus *add. S*   2651   aut] in opposito *add. S*
2652   significat] -cant *P* | hoc] hec *V*   2653   prepotentia] prepotencior *V*
potencior *P*   2655   non est] *post* coniuncta *post corr. S*   2658   domini] *om. S*
etiam dicit] *inv. S*   2660   nondumque] nondum *S*   2663   dubius] indubius *S* | et]
om. S   2665   mortis...possumus] *om. S*   2667   fultam] fulcitam *PV*   2669   Lune]
om. P | Ex] et *S*   2670   mortis] *om. V* | idem] *om. P* | affirmat] confirmat *S*
per Alkindum] Akind' *P*

2649 Princeps...2652 morietur] Ibn Ezra, *Liber nativitatum*, fol. 66r:21-23: "Et si
fuerit dominus octave in opposito domus prime aut in opposito grado domini
ascendente aut in opposito loci potentis, cadet natus ex loco alto et morietur" |
2653 cum...2654 moriturum] Ibn Ezra, *Moladot*, III VIII 1, 7, pp. 164-165 |
2656 Item...2658 Luna] Ibn Ezra, *Moladot*, III VIII 1, 5, pp. 164-165 | 2662
natum...2664 occultati] Ibn Ezra, *Liber nativitatum*, fol. 66r:11-16 | 2668
loca...2669 horum] Ibn Ezra, *Moladot*, III VIII 2, 2, pp. 164-165 | 2670
Auicenna...2671 eius] Albohali, *De nativitatibus*, c.37, sig. n1r:18-19

superaddit hiis *ascendens et dominum eius*, secundum quod facit **Princeps**, insuper et aspicientes dominum domus mortis. Item addit dominum *triplicitatis anguli terre* primum et dominum *septime domus* et *octauum signum* a loco Lune ; cum fuerit nati-
2675 uitas nocturna, addit et dominum huius signi, | hoc affirmans quod si *plures eorum qui habuerunt dignitatem in* hiis *predictis locis salui fuerint, significat* non *extraneam mortem* nati, si e contrario, mala morte uitam suam finiet natus. Dicit igitur **Auenezre** quod *si dominus octaue domus in bono loco fuerit nec aspexerit ipsum*
2680 *maleficus, morietur natus in lecto suo ex egritudine sibi superueniente secundum partitionem significatorum qua Aries caput significat,* Taurus collum et Gemini humeros et brachia. In proposito autem Luna bene se habet in omnibus, nisi quod opponitur ascen-denti, et, quamuis ascendenti opponatur, dominus tamen
2685 ascendentis non contrariatur, secundum quod Sol ascendenti, licet dominus eius contrarietur. Propter quod temperandum est illud dictum superius de Luna in domo septima iuxta dictum **Abrahe Compilatoris** sic dicentis: *si dominus octaue orientem uel dominum eius male respexerit,* puta aspectu contrario, *timore et an-*
2690 *gustia natum significat affligendum et, si quidem bene aspexerit, timore solo sine angustia affligetur natus.* Non poterit igitur secundum hoc remanere quin natus hic timorem mortis ex casu aut timorem huius cum angustia patiatur, presertim cum dominus partis mortis cadat ab angulo, nec aspiciat ipsam Venus, cum ipsam
2695 aspiciens, licet ex opposito, significationem tamen eius in melius commutat. Item octaui signi a Luna dominus Saturnus magis est saluus quam impeditus, ut prehabitum est, quemad-

V136r

2672 insuper…aspicientes] *om. P* | mortis] *om. S* | Item] et *add. V* 2675 addit] ad h'c *PV* | signi] *om. S* | hoc] hic *S* 2676 eorum] illorum *PV* | habuerunt] -int *S* hominum *V* | predictis] pro dictis *P* dictis *S* 2677 significat] *om. P* 2678 natus] *om. S* 2680 superueniente] proueniente *P* 2681 significatorum] signorum *V* 2682 et Gemini] geminis *S* 2683 opponitur] --nit V*om. S* 2684 et] *om. S* | ascendenti] -tis *P* | dominus] terminus *S* 2687 dictum²] illud *praem. S* 2689 dominum eius] dominus orientis *S* 2690 affligendum] *om. S* | si quidem] sicos de *S* 2691 solo sine] suo siue *S* 2692 hic] *om. PV* | aut] *post* mortis *P* 2693 patiatur] -etur *PV* 2694 nec] non *S* | cum] tamen *V* 2695 licet] sed *P* | tamen] *om. PV*

2671 secundum…2672 Princeps] vide supra ad l. 2649-2650 | 2672 Item…2674 Lune] Albohali, *De nativitatibus,* c.37, sig. n1r:22-24 | 2674 cum…2678 natus] Albohali, *De nativitatibus,* c.37, sig. n1r:25-nv1.:8 et n2v:20-21 | 2679 si…2682 brachia] Ibn Ezra, *Moladot,* III VIII 3, 2, pp. 166-167 | 2688 si…2691 natus] Ibn Ezra, *De nativitatibus,* sig. b8v:14-17

modum et Iupiter dominus triplicitatis anguli terre primus, cum
sit natiuitas nocturna. Amplius, ut dicit **Auicenna** : *si fuerit ali-*
qua fortuna cum domino domus septime *in angulo terre significat* 2700
mortem suauitatis ; Sol autem in exaltatione sua existens taliter
se habet, ratione cuius, ut uult **Auicenna**, erit mors nati inter
parentes et proximos. Hiis igitur significationibus in se consi-
deratis et in comparatione mutua ad inuicem libratis, quamquam plures eorum salui et magis fortunati quam infortunati 2705
mortem significent non extraneam, uehementia tamen significationis et fortitudo illorum qui mortem innuunt extra locum
natiuitatis ex precipitatione seu casu timenda est et quantum
possibile est precauenda. Nam ut dicit **Ptolomeus** in CENTI-
LOQUIO : *anima sapiens cooperatur celesti effectui, sicut optimus agricola* 2710
cooperatur nature per arationem et purgationem. Et hoc est quod dicit
Ptolomeus in QUADRIPARTITO capitulo tertio primi inquirens
quod *huius artis maximas uires Egyptii monstrauerunt, quoniam in*
omnibus libris medendi scientiam stellarum pronosticationi coniunxerunt.
Propterea quod hec huiusmodi cognouerunt nec in eadem hora illa in simul 2715
coniungerunt ut incantationes et medicinas facerent ad delendum impedi-
menta presentia seu futura generalia seu particularia per corpus circum-
dans accidentia, nisi quoniam opinati sunt quod inde prouenta nec muten-
tur nec conuertantur. Alia uero translatio que de greco melius
habet hoc modo : *Egyptii qui maxime talem artis uirtutem produ-* 2720
xerunt, coniunxerunt ubique medicinalem cum pronosticatione per astro-
nomiam. Non enim umquam utique institutissent in contrarium regimina
aliqua et preseruatoria contra dispositiones continentis superuenientes aut

---

2698 et] *om. P* 2701 mortem suauitatis] bonitatem mortis *ed.* 2702 Auicenna]
om. P 2703 et] *om. S* | igitur] *om. P* | in se] inter *S* 2704 in] *om. S* | mutua] *post*
inuicem *S* 2706 uehementia] -tiam *PV* | tamen] cum *P* | significationis] signis
P 2708 precipitatione] precipitio (-ne *s.u. P*) etiam *PV* | quantum] quam *S*
2709 Nam] *om. S* | Centiloquio] -gio *P* 2710 cooperatur] cooperabitur *V*
2713 artis] operis *ed.* | monstrauerunt] -uerat *S* 2714 pronosticationi] pre- *S* -
nibus *ed.* 2715 Propterea...cognouerunt] *om. S* | in¹] *om. S* 2716 coniunge-
runt] -ret *S* -rent *V ed.* 2718 prouenta] per- *S* prouentura *ed.* 2720 qui] quidem
praem. S | maxime] *om. V* 2722 umquam] numquam *V* | institutissent] consti-
S 2723 continentis] -tes *S* | superuenientes] super eminentes *P*

2699 Amplius...2701 suauitatis] Albohali, *De nativitatibus,* c..37, sig. n3r:4-8 |
2701 Sol...2703 proximos] Albohali, *De nativitatibus,* c.37, sig. n1v:25-28 |
2709 Ptolomeus...2711 purgationem] Ps.-Ptol., *Cent.,* trans. graeco-latina, v. 8
| 2712 Ptolomeus...2719 conuertantur] Ptol., *Quad.* I.3, trans. Platonis
Tiburtini, sig. a4v:37-r:5 | 2720 Egyptii...2725 opinio] Ptol.., *Quad.* I.3, trans.
Guilelmi, p. 169:279-284

presentes uniuersales et particulares si qua ipsis immutabilitatis et ineuita-
2725 *bilitatis euentorum inesset opinio.*

Sed reuertamur ad intentum principale et compleamus sermonem conclusiuum. Dicamus igitur quod cum timendum sit nato de casu seu precipitio et hoc extra locum natiuitatis, ut pretactum est, et Mars dominus domus duodecime, domus
2730 inquam equitaturarum, in detrimento suo sit cadens ab angulo, ut predictum est, item cum Sagittarius ad hoc cooperetur, ut dicunt philosophi, tanto magis | sibi caueat natus in equitando, precipue cum Mars sit dominus partis mortis. Nam, ut ait **Auicenna**, significator huius propositi cadens ab angulo mor-
2735 tem minatur per casum ab altiori loco. Iupiter tamen partem | habens in domo equitaturarum rem emendat, ut predictum est. Sed bonitas eius non tantum ualet contra impedimentum Martis quantum Veneris. Venus autem partem mortis aspicit, ut predictum est, et in hoc est consolatio. Preterea dicit **Hispa-**
2740 **lensis** quod *Indi considerant dominum hore* torte *in qua* fuit natiui-tas ad sciendum *totam naturam* eius, quemadmodum *alii domini astronomie considerant idem ab ascendente et domino* suo *in illa hora ; et quia dominus | prime hore et octaue idem est,* iudicant per primam sicut per octauam locum. In proposito autem *dominus* hore
2745 *Iupiter* est significans iuxta dispositionem suam supra expositam *bene mori* secundum **Hispalensem**. Postremo uero omnium non debet nos latere illud dictum **Hispalensis** quod scilicet **Ptolomeus** rectius omnibus dicit: qui considerat loca concisi-onis super alhyleg, a quo uitam sumpsimus, et considerat natu-
2750 ram planete uel stelle abscidentis et naturam signi et qualiter se

S23r

V136v

P43r

2724 et¹] aut *P* | immutabilitatis] -bilibus *S* mutabilitatis *PV* 2725 inesset] non esset *P* inesse *S* 2727 conclusiuum] conclusionum *P* 2729 domus²] *om. P* 2731 predictum] supra dictum *P* 2732 in] *om. P* 2736 predictum] supra dictum *P* 2737 eius] *om. P* 2738 quantum] *om. P* 2739 predictum est] supra dictum est *P* dictum est supra *S* | et...hoc] in hoc quidem *S* 2740 torte] certe *P* 2741 eius] *om. P* 2743 prime] primus *P* | iudicant] iudicatum *S* 2745 suam] *om. PV* 2749 super] supra *V* | naturam...et] *om., sed mg. rest. P* 2750 uel] seu *V* | abscidentis] -ndentis *PV*

2733 Nam...2735 loco] Albohali, *De natiuitatibus*, c.37, sig. n2r:24-25 | 2740 Indi...2744 locum] Iohannes Hispalensis, *Epitome*, sig. N2v:4-8 | 2745 significans...2746 Hispalensem] Iohannes Hispalensis, *Epitome*, sig. N2r:17-19 | 2748 qui...2751 postponit] Iohannes Hispalensis, *Epitome*, sig. N1r:26-27: "Ptolemaeus dicit, quod est considerandus locus sectionis vitae, et in quo fit signo, et cuius naturae signum sit, et quis planeta locum sectionis aspiciat"

habeant, hiis dispositionem quoque Lune non postponit. Igitur
faciendo commixtionem significatorum qualitatis mortis iam
exquisitorum secundum naturam prepotentium super loca
mortis et secundum naturam stelle abscidentis, iuxta quod
Ptolomeus innuit, necessarium est uti directionibus a locis uite   2755
sue hyleg secundum doctrinam sapientum respectu habito ad
annorum numerum ab alkocoden collatorum non omissis
tamen annorum reuolutionibus huic annexis negotio quatenus
de qualitate mortis et termino cum omni precisione iudicium
integraliter compleatur. Sed hoc quidem conuenientius suis   2760
incidet locis ; quapropter ad suum tempus differatur. Rationabilius enim est secundum ordinem naturalem annos reuoluere
quam saltus faciendo et interruptiones tempus et ordinem
preposterare. Antequam tamen ulterius in speciali procedamus,
uideamus id quod dicit **Abraham** una cum **Hispalensi** et   2765
ceteris sapientibus, scilicet quod post mortem corpus sine
sepultura eius a quarta domo, anima uero a decima diiudicatur,
hoc quidem sic intelligendo uidelicet qualiter post mortem sit
corpori quantum scilicet honoris uel uituperii sibi fieri debeat,
consimiliter quoque de anima qualis quidem ipsius memoria   2770
seu fama reuerentie aut confusionis hominum celebretur in
ore. Dictum est autem supra de dispositione domus decime ac
domine eius, scilicet Veneris, et quoniam retrogradatio fauora-
bilis est anime, ut preostensum est, tanto magis conditio domus decime pro hac parte laudabilior fit. Item dispositio   2775
domus quarte laudabilis est consimiliter, ut predictum est.

2751   hiis] hii *S* | dispositionem] -oni *V* | postponit] -positam *S*
2752 significatorum] signatorum *S*   2753 super] supra *V*   2754 secundum]
supra *V* | abscidentis] -ndentis *PV*   2757 ab] *om. S*   2758 tamen] cum *P*
2759 iudicium] iudicum *S*   2760 hoc] hic *S* | conuenientius] conueniens *S*
2761 incidet] -dit *S*   2763 faciendo] et *add. PV* | et[1]] *om. S* | et[2]] *om. S*
2764 Antequam] ante *S* | tamen] cum *P* enim *V* | procedamus] et *add. S*
2765 id] illud *P*   2767 quarta] decima *S* | decima] -mo *S*   2768 quidem sic]
idem sit *P*   2770 memoria] -rie *V*   2772 ac] *om. S*

2753 secundum…2755 innuit] Cf. Ptol., *Quad.* IV.9, 1, pp. 334-335 | 2765
Abraham…2767 diiudicatur] Cf. Ibn Ezra, *Liber nativitatum*, fol. 67v:21-24:
"Dixerunt sapientes legis quod prepositus super locum principii domus decime,
qui aspiciet eum, erit super animam illius per mortem, quemadmodum erit
prepositus super principium quarte domus qui respicit eum super corpus suum
et illud quod accidit ei in fovea sua" | una…Hispalensi] Bate referre videtur ad
Iohannem Hispalensem, *Epitome*, sig. N1v:29-30

Quapropter quoddam singulare significatum est huic nato post
mortem, in anima scilicet et corpore, secundum dicta astrologorum. Hec sunt igitur iudicia philosophorum ad inuicem
2780 concordata super iudicio preposite natiuitatis serui Dei gloriosi
et sublimis.

5. <Reuolutiones natiuitatis annorum 35 et 36

Nunc autem tempus est ut ad annorum reuolutiones
perueniamus natiuitatis date. Nam ut dicit **Albumasar** in
LIBRO REVOLUTIONUM ANNORUM NATIVITATUM : *si sciuerimus*
2785 *dispositiones figurarum que sunt in natiuitatis principio et nesciuerimus*
eas que sunt in reuolutione non poterimus diligenter aut distincte *diffi-*
nire significationes earum. Et quoniam de reuolutionibus annorum
preteritorum satis est dictum supra, quantum necesse erat
propter concordantiam iudiciorum cum rebus sensatis, super-
2790 est opportunum reuoluere annum presentem et conuenienter
alios futuros. | Reuolutionis autem anni presentis qui est   S23v
trigesimus quintus a natiuitate hec est figura que sequitur:

2777   quoddam] quidem *P* quidam *V*   2780   concordata] -dantia *S*
2781   sublimis] Explicit natiuitas. Incipiunt reuolutiones annorum presentis
natiuitatis *add. S*   2782 autem] *om. V*   2789 concordantiam] concordiam *P*
discordantiam *S* | superest] super *PV*   2792 est] *om. P* | que sequitur] *om. PV*
sequitur] *sequens figura deest in V, vice cuius Par usus sum*

2783 Albumasar…2787 earum] Albumasar, *De revol.*, p. 212b:34-38

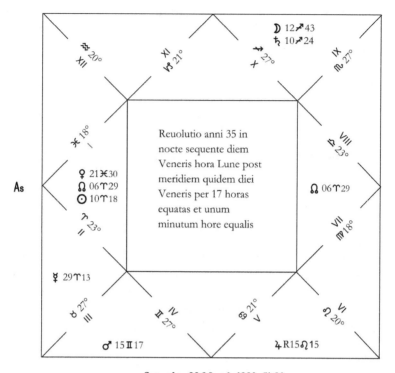

Saturday 23 March 1280, 5h01

5.1. <Revolutio anni 35ⁱ>

Reuolutio anni 35ⁱ in nocte sequente diem Veneris hora Lune post meridiem quidem diei Veneris per 17 horas equales et unum minutum hore equalis.

2795

I. Piscium 18 ; Venus 21.30 ; Sol 10.18 ; Caput (Draconis) 6.29.

II. Arietis 23 ; Mercurius 29.13

III. Tauri 27 ; Mars 15.17

2793 anni 35i] annorum 35 *S* | in...Lune] *om. M* | hora...Veneris] *om. S sed mg. add.* post meridiem quidem diei   2794 quidem] *om. M* | Veneris] *om. M* | 17] 27 *S* | equales] equales equatas *PParS*   2795 unum] septimum *S* numerum *Par* equalis] equales *Par*   2796 21.30] 12.30 in Ariete *L* | Sol 10.18 | Sol...6.29 *in domu I posui cum S: cet. codd. in domu II posuerunt, sed del. L et mg.* Sol in Ariete 10.18 *ad domum I refert L* | 10.18] 19.18 *S*   2797 6.29] 39 *S*   2798 29.13] 20.13 *LP* 2799 27] 20 *L* | Mars 15.17] Geminorum (-ni) *add. LMParS*

2800   **IV.** Geminorum 27

           V. Cancri 21 ; Iupiter 15.15 retrogradus

           VI. Leonis 20

           VII. Virginis 18 ; signum profectionis Cauda (Draconis)
           6.29

2805   **VIII.** Libre 23

           IX. Scorpionis 27 ; Luna 12.43 meridionalis ; Saturnus
           10.24 septentrionalis

           X. Sagittarii 27

           XI. Capricorni 21

2810   **XII.** Aquarii 20

           Latitudo Saturni septentrionalis 2 gr. 11 minutorum

           Latitudo Iouis meridionalis 1.11

           Latitudo Martis meridonalis 0. gr. 56 min

           Latitudo Lune meridionalis 4 graduum

2815 | Cum igitur in reuolutionibus annorum natiuitatum   V137r
           multa requirantur consideranda, ut patet per **Albumasar** et per
           Hispanum Abraham et **Auenezre** et **Hispalensem** de hiis
           tractantes, ponamus quidem ad presens illa cum precisione ut
           pro radice sint annis sequentibus. Primum quidem horum est
2820   annorum directio multiplex secundum locorum multiplicitatem
           a quibus dirigere conuenit. Facta igitur directione a gradu
           ascendente natiuitatis peruenit directio hoc anno 35° incipiente
           ad 13^m gradum Capricorni, uersus finem scilicet eius, ad 6
           minuta uel circiter, in termino quidem Iouis. Item dirigendo a
2825   gradu hyleg, a gradu scilicet Lune latitudinem habentis
           septentrionalem fere 4 graduum, ratione cuius dirigendum erat
           a gradu cum quo celum mediabat Luna secundum doctrinam

---

2801   Iupiter…retrogradus] *perperam in domu VI pos. omnes codd., huc transposuimus*
15.15] 15 *M*   2803   VII…18] *domus vacua in M* | signum…6.29] *in domu VIII*
posuit L (qui 6.29 legit), deest in MPPar 6.39 *S*   2806   IX Scorpionis] *om. S*
meridionalis] *om. LMPPar*   2807   10.24] 10.14 *S* | septentrionalis] retrogradus
LPPar om. M   2815 Cum] utrum *S*   2816 per^2…et^2] *om. S*   2817 Hispalensem]
ypsalensis *P* yspal' *V* | hiis *scr. cum Par*] huius(modi) *PSV*   2819 quidem] autem
S   2820 annorum] *om. S*   2822 ascendente] asc' *V*   2824 Item] iterum *S*

2826   ratione…2828 Albategni] Albategni, *Canones tabularum* (ed. 1537), cap.
LIV, sig. 82r-83v

Albategni, Auenezre et reliquorum, peruenit directio hoc
anno ad principium 20^i gradus Cancri, | et hoc quidem in ante
dirigendo. Verum quia non solum hoc requiritur in proposito,
sed ut directio fiat consimiliter retro, ut dicitur supra, dirigendo
retrorsum peruenitur hoc anno ad 21 gradum Tauri, utrobique
quidem ad terminos Iouis. Item dirigendo a parte fortune
peruenitur hoc anno ad 15 gradum Arietis, terminum scilicet
Mercurii. Adhuc dirigendo a gradu medii celi peruentum est
hoc anno ad 18 gradum Scorpionis, consimiliter terminum
Mercurii. | Preterea si Solem ponamus alkocoden siue datorem
annorum, gubernabit adhuc Mercurius primam uite tertiam ex
parte dominorum triplicitatis Lune cuius est auctoritas ; si uero
Mercurius sit annorum dator, erit Saturnus huius secunde tertie
dominus. Eodem quoque modo se habet de domino nouene
secundum Indos uitam in nouem partes diuidentes. Secundum
enim quod Sol est alkocoden, est adhuc natus in nouena tertia
cuius domina Venus, alio uero modo est in nouena quarta
cuius dominus est Iupiter. Item secundum annos **Ptolomei**
gubernat Sol natum, unde Sol dominus est periodi secundum
dicta **Albumasar**. Rursum hic annus in firdaria Martis est cum
participatione Veneris. Item profectio ab hyleg peruenit ad
Arietem et profectio a domino hore natiuitatis peruenit ad
Saturnum ; profectio quoque a domino ascendentis natiuitatis
ad eundem peruenit Saturnum. Item profectio a sorte fortune
peruenit ad 19 gradum Sagittarii, ubi partem subite exaltationis
reperit. Amplius signum profectionis ab ascendente natiuitatis
est hoc anno Libra, 13us scilicet gradus eius, ubi erit stella fixa
de qua dictum est supra. Vnde **Albumasar** : *cum fuerit tempore*
reuolutionis aliqua stella fixa de hiis que prosperitatem significant in
gradu signi, ad quod annus applicuerit, significat prosperitatem in illo
anno secundum complexionem scilicet illius stelle. *Venus* autem

Margin: P43v, S24r

Line numbers: 2830, 2835, 2840, 2845, 2850, 2855

2829   principium] *om. S* | quidem] quidam *V*   2831   fiat] *om. S*
consimiliter…dirigendo] *om. PV*   2832 peruenitur] -nit P   2834 peruenitur] -nit
PV   2835 Adhuc] ad hoc *V*   2840 secunde] *om. S*   2842 Indos] numeros inno
(?) *S*   2845 est] *om. S*   2850 profectio…Saturnum] *om. PV*   2852 gradum] *om. S*
2853 Amplius] item *praem. V* | natiuitatis] *om. S*   2854 scilicet] *om. P* | erit] est
P et *V*   2855   est] *om., sed rest. s.u. ante* dictum *P* | supra] *om. S* | tempore]
tempus *P*   2856 que] ad *add. S*   2858 scilicet] suam *praem. sed exp. S*

2828 Auenezre] cf. Ibn Ezra, *Moladot*, III I 11, 1-4, pp. 114-115 | 2841
domino…2842 diuidentes] cf. Albumasar, De revol., p. 261b:14-16 et cf. infra
3154-3156 | 2855 Albumasar…2858 anno] Albumasar, *De revol.*, p. 258b:11-17

partem habens in complexione huius stelle *domina anni* est, que
2860   quoniam in natiuitate fortis et laudabilis dispositionis fuit, ut | v137v
supra patuit, et nunc in exaltatione sua et gradu lucido consi-
stens in ascendente significat iuxta **Albumasar** quod *ille cuius est*
reuolutio erit in iocunditate et ludis uel tripudiis et cantilenis et quod
habebit familiaritatem cum amicis et alios acquiret amicos et ducet
2865   *uxorem,* supple : si in natiuitate hoc significatum fuisset. Qualitercumque autem hoc se habeat, iudicium proportionandum
est secundum exigentiam materie. Non enim huiusmodi significatio frustrari potest ex toto. Item significatum est quod *habebit*
gratiam ab habentibus potestatem atque principibus et augmentabitur
2870   *gloria eius et diuitie et in hostiis regum perseuerabit et gaudebit in mulieri-*
bus et obtinebit desideria sua et augebitur eius immobilis substantia, sed
quia *retrograda est* hic *Venus, significat* hoc iuxta eundem quod
natus quidem *obtinebit predicta ex modis uerumtamen inhonestis.* Item
quoniam *a Marte* aliqualiter *impedita* est per aspectum quartum
2875   secundum gradus equales, significat hoc, ut uult idem et
Auenezre cum ipso, quod natus *tristabitur gratia mulierum* et
quidam obloquentur de eo et contentiones habebit cum quibusdam et
tristitias et anxietates de uita et corpore, secundum quod ascendens significare habet secundum etiam impedimenta nature
2880   Martialis. Necessarium est enim quod Mars soluat promissum,
de quo supra dictum est in domo sexta. Adhuc cum idem Mars
secundum gradus equales angulum terre possideat, significat
hoc timorem de morte mulieris, ut dicit **Albumasar** et *rixas*
cum feminis et accusationem de fornicatione, sed quoniam iuxta
2885   domorum equationem Mars est cadens ab angulo, maior erit
timoris immissio quam impedimenti lesio. Mars enim impediens cum fuerit cadens ab angulo, parum impedit, ut dicunt

---

2860 dispositionis fuit] *inv. S*   2861 et²…lucido] *om. S*   2863 reuolutio] *om. PV*
et¹] *om. S* | ludis] laudis *PS*   2864 ducet] -cit *S*   2866 iudicium] *om. S*
2871 sua] *om. PV* | immobilis] in mobil' *V*   2872 quia] *om. V s.v. P* | hic] *om.*
PV   2875 et] *om. S*   2876 ipso] hoc *S*   2877 contentiones] contemptiones *S*
2881 Adhuc] ad hoc *V*   2885 maior…2887 angulo] *om. S*   2886 impediens…-
fuerit] *om. P*

2862 Albumasar…2865 uxorem] Albumasar, *De revol.,* pp. 237b:49-238a:3 |
2868 habebit…2873 inhonestis] Albumasar, *De revol.,* p. 239b:9-19 | 2873
Item…2876 mulierum] Albumasar, *De revol.,* p. 239b:25-26 | 2876
Auenezre…2878 corpore] Ibn Ezra, *Moladot,* III III 1, 4, pp. 130-131 et
Albumasar, *De revol.,* p. 239b:22-24 | 2883 ut…2884 fornicatione] Albumasar,
De revol., p. 257b:17-18

astrologi, sed timorem immittit et anxietatem. Vnde **Auenezre**: *malus aspectus Martis ad Venerem uituperium significat et angustiam magnam pro mulieribus in tempore quo Mars* in sua firdaria *Venerem sibi assumperit conparticipantem*, maxime si in natiuitate Venus consimiliter disposita fuerit. Sed quia non sic est in proposito, propter hoc huiusmodi impedimentum Veneris tolerabile est, secundum quod uolunt sapientes, quemadmodum infamia et suspicio praua non habens aliud in effectu. Adhuc receptio Veneris a Marte, cum sit in termino triplicitatis et facie Martis, amplius et in eius duodena particula, item et presentia Martis in termino Veneris et in eius nouenaria nocumenta Martis reddunt multo minora. Preterea presentia Veneris in gradu sui sextilis aspectus equati in radice natiuitatis *mouere* debet *significationem* ipsius *secundum propriam naturam* ex natiuitate insinuatam, ut dicit **Albumasar**, et per hoc quidem fortificabitur significatio Veneris supra dicta. Amplius, cum Iupiter sit dispositor siue diuisor, ut preostensum | est ex directionibus a gradu hyleg ante et retro et ab ascendente, similiter significat hoc, ut uult **Albumasar**, eum de quo est sermo *coniungi optime uxori in tempore* huius *diuisionis et loqui cum principibus et dignitatem* acquirere et *diuitias*, nisi quod debilis est in reuolutione et cadens ab angulo, per que uirtus eius diminuitur. Sed quoniam secundum gradus equales Ioui participat Saturnus, significat hoc impedimenta circa *diuitias* et alia et *contristari* in *egrotari* et *conualescere*. Sane *participatio Solis* duplex *significat ipsum dominari in aliqua dignitate uel opere et* | *augmentari diuitias suas et prosperitatem et gloriam et loqui cum principibus*. Item *participatio Veneris* in hoc loco potentioris pluribus de causis *significat ipsum coniungi uxori probe consanguinee uel nobili*, ut dicit **Albumasar**, *et habebit filium bonum*

Margin line references: 2890, 2895, 2900, 2905, 2910, 2915. Margin labels: S24v, P44r

---

2889 aspectus] *om. P*   2890 in tempore] *inv. S*   2891 conparticipantem] *om. S* in] *om. S*   2892 consimiliter] sic *S* | fuerit] fuit *S* | non sic] *inv. V* | proposito] opposito *P*   2893 hoc] *om. S*   2894 sapientes] *om. S*   2895 Adhuc] ad hoc *V* 2896   termino triplicitatis] triplicitate *S*   2897   duodena] duodenaria *S* 2899   minora] maiora *S*   2903 Iupiter] *om. PV* | dispositor siue] *mg. P* 2906 eum] cum *S*   2908 acquirere] acquiret *P*   2909 eius] *mg. P*   2910 Ioui] Iouis P rem *S*   2911 et²] *om. V*   2912 duplex] habet *V*   2915 ipsum] om. *V*

2889 malus…2891 conparticipantem] Ibn Ezra, *Moladot*, IV 12, 5, pp. 192-193 | 2900 mouere…2901 naturam] Albumasar, *De revol.*, p. 277b:30-32 | 2906 Albumasar…2908 diuitias] Albumasar, *De revol.*, p. 254a:29-38 | 2911 circa…2914 principibus] Albumasar, *De revol.*, p. 254b:1-11 | 2914 Item…2918 prosperitates] Albumasar, *De revol.*, p. 254b:18-24

et gratulabitur in mulieribus et habebit utilitatem per eas et perseuerabit
in cantilenis et ludis et delectationibus et obtinebit prosperitates. Rursum
directione facta a parte fortune | necnon a gradu medii celi   V138r
2920   diuisor est Mercurius cum participatione Saturni, Iouis, Martis,
Solis et Lune. Vnde **Albumasar**: ratione *participationis Saturni*
erit languidus corpore et egrotabit egritudine pessima et operationes eius
impedientur, erit etiam piger et difficile mobilis et diuersa pericula ac
contentiones incurret, sed propter Iouem hec mala mitigantur. Item
2925   ratione *participationis Martis significatur languor et calumnie et fatigatio*
ingenii super lesione quorundam et uituperari a pluribus et morbum
euenire in capite. Sed quia secundum natiuitatem non configuratur Mars hiis terminis ex contrario, idcirco minuitur eius
significatio in predictis. Item *participatio Solis significat obtentum*
2930   *dignitatis et augmentum glorie et augebuntur eius diuitie et quod erit*
industrius et reuelabuntur ei secreta scientie. Participatio Lune significat
quod augmentabitur eius scientia et doctrina et cogitabit de rebus diuinis et
celestibus et prophetica scientia et astronomia et prosperabilis erit atque
tractabilis in omnibus que incepit, habebit utilitatem ex eis et aug-
2935   *mentabuntur diuitie sue et thesauri.* Preterea disponit Mars hunc
annum ratione sue firdarie una cum Venere, de quo **Albu-**
masar : *et in huiusmodi* quidem *dispositione perseuerabit in melodiis et*
iocunditatitibus et habibitabit cum mulieribus et rixabitur cum eis *et*
habebit familiaritatem cum latronibus et utilitatem ab eis. **Hispalensis**
2940   dicit huiusmodi firdariam significare laborem causa mortis
mulieris. Sed quoniam in reuolutione proposita omnes dis-
positores preter Solem et Mercurium aliquo saltem impedimento sunt impediti, idcirco significationes dicte debiliores
effecte sunt iuxta impedimentorum conditiones. Vnde **Albu-**

2918 delectationibus] dilectionibus *V* | prosperitates] -tem *S*   2919 a²] et *V*
2920   Iouis Martis] *inv. PV*   2921   Solis] *om. PV*   2922   erit] est *S*
2924   contentiones] contemptiones *S* intentiones *V*   2925   calumnie] -nia *S*
2926 quorundam] *om. PV*   2928 idcirco] *et add. V*   2931 Participatio] autem
add. PV   2934 incepit] incipit *S* | et] *om. S*   2938 mulieribus] meretricibus *ed.*
eis] uxore sua *ed.*   2939 latronibus] mulieri *praem. V*   2941 quoniam] quia *S*

2921 ratione…2924 incurret] Albumasar, *De revol.*, p. 256b:29-34 | 2925
participationis…2927 capite] Albumasar, *De revol.*, pp. 256b:48-257a:4 | 2929
Item…2935 thesauri] Albumasar, *De revol.*, p. 257a:14-37 | 2936
Albumasar…2939 eis] Albumasar, *De revol.*, p. 271b:22-27 | 2940
huiusmodi…2941 mulieris] Iohannes Hispalensis, *Epitome,* sig. Ov:18:
""Septima fridaria est Martis (...). In communi Veneris, dolet propter obitum
mulieris" | 2944 Albumasar…2951 damnum] Albumasar, *De revol.*, p. 259b:12-
20

masar : *cum fuerit dominus anni ac diuisor beniuoli tempore uero reuolu-* 2945
tionis anni in malo loco locati aut retrogradi fueritque in reuolutione
aliquis de duobus planetis in ascendente, secundum quod in proposito se habet, Venus quidem retrograda in ascendente Iupiterque
retrogradus et cadens ab angulo, *significat malitiam anni et diffi-*
cultatem et inimicorum uictoriam et uulnus a ferro uel precipitium ab alto 2950
loco ac damnum. Porro non uidetur hoc dictum rationabile; nam
si aliud non esset in causa significandi dicta infortunia quam
retrogradatio aut casus beniuolorum supra dictum dominium
obtinentium, nequaquam maliuoli consimilem habentes dispositionem magis aut tantundem possent impedire secundum 2955
quod apparere potest intuenti dicta sapientum Quapropter
opinandum est illum sermonem **Albumasar** corruptum esse
aut truncatum, ut sit talis littera: *cum fuerit dominus anni* et infra
fueritque in reuolutione aliquis de duobus planetis malis in ascendente uel
in medio celi etc. Hoc enim modo recipit illud dictum uerifica- 2960
tionem conuenientem, uidelicet ut inimicorum uictoria et
uulnus a ferro Marti, precipitium uero ab alto et damnum
Saturno attribuatur. Huic enim dicto subest ratio et consensus
philosophorum. In proposito quidem nullus malorum est in
angulo, Iupiter tamen impeditus est et Saturnus cum Luna. Vn- 2965
S25r de bonitas significationis Iouis et Lune minorata est | hoc anno
et defalcanda in parte propter retrogradationem et casum Iouis
ab angulo et propter dispositionem Lune infortunatam per
luminis diminutionem et numeri ac per latitudinem meridianam. Item et per coniunctionem Saturni in gradu ascendente 2970
radicis una cum dispositione Martis a loco in quo fuit Luna
hyleg in natiuitate. Vnde **Albumasar** : *oportet autem aspicere et*
signum in quo est Luna tempore reuolutionis. Habet enim equalem
potentiam horoscopo anni et cum *fuerit in domo Iouis mali esse*
existentis, ut est hic, *indicat merores diuersos et accusabitur ab ali-* 2975

2945   ac…anni] *om. PV*   2951   non] omnino *S* | rationabile] rationale *S*
2952 aliud] illud *S*   2956 quod] *om. PV, s.u. add. P* | sapientum] *om. S*   2960 etc
scr.] et cum *PV* responsio *(in abr.) S*   2961   ut] non *S* | uictoria] -am *S*
2962 Marti] Marte *S* | precipitium] precipimur *S*   2964 quidem] autem *add. S*
2968   Lune…diminutionem] *om. P*   2970   ascendente] ascendentis *S*
2971 dispositione] appositione *S*   2972 in natiuitate] *om. S* | oportet autem]
oportunum autem est *S* | et] *om. S*   2973 equalem] -liter *P*   2974 potentiam]
planetam *ed.* | esse] *om. P*   2975 merores] mores *V* | et] quod *add. PV*

2972 Vnde…2976 anno] Albumasar, *De revol.*, p. 242a:37-b:4

quibus, nec erit bonum in illo anno. Dicit enim **Ptolomeus** quod *singulariter impedit Lunam* Saturni coniunctio et Martis diametrizatio, cui consonat **Auenezre** in LIBRO LUMINARIUM, ubi quidem innuere uidetur quod fortunatarum aspectus in

2980 huiusmodi fortunio parum aut nihil | ualeant nisi Sol Lune ~V138v~ succurrat per aspectum. Quamquam igitur Luna taliter disposita et infortunata *egritudines significet et tristitias et angustias,* ut uult **Albumasar,** et contentiones *occasione mulierum* et tribulationes et cum hoc cogitationes eleuet propter ingressum eius in

2985 ascendens radicis, amplius et ratione oppositi aspectus Martis et Saturni *casum in manus inimicorum et egritudinem de qua medici* | ~P44v~ *dubitabunt et habebit natus caput intemperatum ac corpus* precipue propter contrarietatem Lune et ascendentis. Quia tamen Saturnus nunc ingressus est radium Iouis in radice, Iupiter quoque

2990 Lunam aspiciens et Saturnum cum receptione *soluit* hec *mala,* ut dicit **Albumasar,** aut saltem diminuit, nisi quia retrogradus est et cadens ab angulo in hac reuolutione, in natiuitate quoque non erat multum fortis. Nam consimiliter retrogradus fuerat, ut prehabitum est. Licet autem nunc sit debilis et impeditus satis,

2995 tamen uidetur fortis esse ut impedimentis Lune posset succurrere, cum malefactores eius consimiliter sint cadentes. Quapropter non habent magnam *potentiam ad nocendum,* ut dicit **Albumasar,** sed timorem immittunt maiorem quam lesionem, ut predictum est, cum etiam quod Mars est occidentalis. Item

3000 quia in natiuitate cadens erat et impotens ad nocendum, nunc autem ingressus septimum natiuitatis impediensque locum aduersariorum et mulierum, eapropter casus nati in manus

---

2978 diametrizatio] diametratio *S*   2979 fortunatarum] for^arum^ *P* fortunarum *SV* 2980 fortunio] infortunio *P*   2983 contentiones] contemptiones *S*   2985 oppositi] et *add. P*   2986 manus] manibus *V*   2987 dubitabunt] dubitant *S* | et] quod *add. PV*   2988 tamen] cum *V* | Saturnus] *om. S*   2989 nunc] tunc *P* | radium] radius *S* | quoque] -que *S*   2991 est] *om. S*   2993 fuerat] est *S*   2994 Licet] hec *P*   2995 posset] possit *P*   2996 consimiliter] similiter *PV post* cadentes *P* 2997 potentiam] potestatem *P*   2999 cum] licet *add. s.v. P*

2976 Ptolomeus...2978 diametrizatio] Ptol.., *Quad.* III.11, trans. Guilelmi, p. 247:397-399 | 2978 Auenezre...2981 aspectum] Ibn Ezra, *Me'orot,* §32:1, pp. 478-479 | 2982 egritudines...2983 Albumasar] Albumasar, *De revol.,* p. 277b:8-9 | 2983 contentiones...mulierum] Albumasar, *De revol.,* p. 234a:2 | 2986 casum...2987 corpus] Albumasar, *De revol.,* p. 257a:9-13 | 2990 soluit...mala] Albumasar, *De revol.,* p. 257a:13-14 | 2997 potentiam...nocendum] Albumasar, *De revol.,* p. 225a:27-28

inimicorum non est multum formidandus. Nam ut dicit **Albumasar**, *si reuolutio sola aliqua signauerit aliquid cum debilitate, erit
modicus et debilis eius euentus aut erit motus solummodo imperfectus.* 3005
Mulieres tamen propter Martis dispositionem infamabuntur.
Item cum sit Mars in termino Veneris tendatque ad eius aspectum, ut prediximus, mitigatur ex hoc eius impietas. Ingressus quoque eius in locum Lune et ex hoc *egrotationem* significans
et *contristationem* occasione mulierum et impedimenta ab 3010
hominibus prouenientia propter Geminos et Sagittarium, ut
uolunt philosophi, contemperatur per Venerem et Iouem et
maxime per Solem qui potens est Lune succurrere ab utrisque
infortuniis impedite, secundum quod supra dictum est, presertim cum sit in ascendente dominus existens periodi. Item Luna 3015
in diuersa existens latitudine cum Saturno et separata iam ab
ipso non effectum realem, sed cogitationes et uerba euenire
significat iuxta **Hispalensem**. Vnde **Hermannus**: *si infortuna
secundo iam gradu precesserit, nil esse* significat preter *metum*. Adhuc
et magnitudo latitudinis diuerse testimonium Lune causat, ita 3020
quod in eo non est confidendum, prout testatur **Auenezre** in
LIBRO LUMINARIUM. Mars quoque meridianus a loco Lune in
natiuitate septentrionalis existentis, que nunc meridiana existens a Marte perfecta oppositione non aspicitur, ad impedimentorum alleuiationem cooperatur, quatenus huiusmodi no- 3025
cumenta in cogitationes mutentur et in uerba, secundum quod
innuunt sapientes. Amplius figura natiuitatis huiusmodi malis
non concordat neque directio similiter. Euadet igitur diuina

3004   si reuolutio] siuolutio *S* | sola] *om. PV*   3005   eius euentus] *inv. P*
3007   Item] iterum *PV*   3009   locum] loco *P*   3010   ab hominibus] *om. P*
3011 prouenientia] uenientia *S* | Sagittarium] Saturnum *PV*   3012 contempera-
tur] -antur *P* | per] propter *S*   3014 impedite] impedire *V*   3015 ascendente]
ascendens *S* | existens] *om., sed mg. rest. P* | Luna] *om. P*   3017 cogitationes…-
uerba] *inv. P*   3018   si infortuna] in fortuna *S*   3019   Adhuc] ad hoc *V*
3020 diuerse testimonium] *om. P* | causat *scr.*] cassat *PV* cessat *S*   3021 in eo]
om. P   3022 meridianus] mundianus *V*   3023 existentis] existens *S* | que] qui
V | meridiana] mundiana *V*   3024 impedimentorum] -tum *S*   3027 Amplius]
om. S   3028 neque] nec *S* | similiter] *om. S*

3003 Albumasar…3005 imperfectus] Albumasar, *De revol.* 225b:17-20 | 3009
egrotationem…3010 mulierum] Albumasar, *De revol.*, p. 275a:39-40 | 3015
Item…3018 Hispalensem]   vide supra 1826-1827 | 3018 si…3019 metum]
Hermannus, *De occultis*, pp. 316:25-317:1. | 3019 Adhuc…3022 luminarium]
Ibn Ezra, *Me'orot*, §20:3, pp. 466-467 | 3025 huiusmodi…3027 sapientes] vide
supra 1826-1827

fauente | gratia hic seruus Dei mala huiusmodi, bona uero per
3030 Iouem significata moderata debent ad presens esse dictas ob
causas. Insuper impedimenta Martis super Lunam per ingressum eius ad locum Lune significata per 40 dies durare debent
iuxta doctrinam **Albumasar** et quia Mars Lunam aspicit, significat hoc durationem duplicari per alios 40 dies secundum
3035 orbes ipsorum mediocres.

Vt autem ad omne dicatur, secundum mentem **Albumasar** de quinque significatoribus corporis quatuor boni sunt,
Luna uero sola infortunata, de 8 quidem significatoribus anime
tantum duo aut tres bene sunt dispositi. Quare necessarium est
3040 hunc seruum | Dei in anima conturbari magis quam in cor-
pore. *Quinque* autem *significatores corporis* sunt hii: *signum profectionis, terminus directionis ab horoscopo, terminus directionis ab hyleg,
Luna* et *horoscopus reuolutionis. Octo uero* significatores *anime* hii
sunt: *dominus* scilicet *anni, dominus termini directionis ab ascendente,*
3045 *dominus termini directionis ab hyleg, comparticipans eis per corpus aut per
aspectum, dominus firdarie, dominus periodi, planeta recipiens coniunctionem Lune uel coniunctionem domini domus sue* et *dominus horoscopi reuolutionis anni.* Iupiter igitur *dominus horoscopi reuolutionis* et
dispositor siue diuisor biformis aut triformis iuxta dis-
3050 positionem eius supra expositam parum ualere potest hoc anno
de se nisi quod aliqua mitigat impedimenta, ut prehabitum est.
Et quoniam horoscopus reuolutionis anni regiratus est ex
domo tertia radicis natiuitatis, item ascendens natiuitatis subin-
gressum est nonam reuolutionis domum, rationabiliter hoc
3055 uisum est itinera portendere in quibus utique timendum est
propter Gradiuum Martem in tertia et Saturnum in nona simul
cum Luna infortunata in domo lamentationis sue. Sed Iupiter

3029 fauente gratia] *inv. P* | Dei] de *S* 3031 super] supra *S* 3032 ad locum] a
loco *S* 3036 ad] *om. PV* 3037 boni] bona S 3038 infortunata] infortuna *PV*
3039 aut] uel S 3040 conturbari] contristari S 3041 corporis] corporum *S*
profectionis] perfectionis *S* 3042 directionis[1] *scr. cum ed.*] diuisionis *PSV* | ho-
roscopo] hyleg *PV* | directionis[2] *scr. cum ed.*] diuisionis | hyleg] horoscopo *PV*
3043 hii sunt] *inv. S* 3044 directionis *scr. cum ed.*] diuisionis *PSV* | ascen-
dente…ab] *om. S* 3045 directionis *scr. cum ed.*] diuisionis *PV* 3047 Lune…con-
iunctionem] *om. PV* 3049 aut] et *S* 3051 de se] *om. P* | quod] *om. S* | aliqua
mitigat] *inv. P* 3052 Et] *om. S* | regiratus] retrogradus *S* 3053 item…natiui-
tatis] *om. PV* 3054 hoc] *trsp. post* est *S* 3055 portendere] protendere *S*

3031 Insuper…3033 Albumasar] Albumasar, *De revol.*, p. 272b:46-50 | 3041
Quinque…3048 anni] Albumasar, *De revol.*, II.2, p. 219a:4-22

et Venus periculum uidentur releuare, ut pretactum est, una
cum Solis adiutorio, qui, cum sit *dominus periodi* significans
exaltationem et sit in ascendente, fortior omnibus aliis,
peregrinationem significat bonam, ut dicit **Albumasar**, *cum sit in
Ariete boni esse* propter angularitatem *habeatque dignitatem in anno*,
cum sit *dominus periodi* et *comparticipans* seu communicans diuiso-
ribus et receptor ipsorum, precipue Iouis, *domini horoscopi reuolutionis.* Amplius secundum directionem factam a parte fortune et
a gradu medii celi in ante, ut predictum est, dispositor siue
diuisor Mercurius est existens in succedenti angulum, in domo
scilicet secunda, iam ingrediens Taurum, cum sit in 30 gradu
Arietis, in gradu scilicet lucido, et Iouis duodenario, ubi partem
itinerum inuenit peruenitque diuisio a parte fortune prope
partem substantie in radice, cui etiam Mercurius corporaliter
iunctus fuerat. Nunc autem stat diuisio consimiliter in duodenario Mercurii, ratione quorum, cum in radice fuerit
dominus uigoris, ut prehabitum est, proficuum innuere uidetur
in substantia. Superfluum autem et inutile mihi uisum est directionem retrorsum facere a parte fortune, secundum quod
aliqua translatio | CENTILOQUII sonare uidetur ac secundum
quod **Ptolomeo** imponitur a pluribus. Correcta namque littera
que de translatione Greca non sic habet, neque in QUADRI-
PARTITO consimiliter hoc reperitur usquam, nisi quando gradus
hyleg in quarta occidentali fuerit, ut pretactum est, et occasione
huius forsan sumpsit exordium error ille, qui ex prauis transla-
tionibus que de Arabico processit. Cum igitur Mercurius et
Venus prosperitatem stelle fixe continentes et naturam de qua

3060

3065

3070

3075

3080

P45r

3058 releuare] reuelare *V*   3062 boni esse] bonum est *S* | anno] alio *S*
3063 diuisoribus] derisoribus *S*   3069 duodenario] -ria *S*   3072 consimiliter]
similiter P | duodenario] -ria *S*   3073 cum] *om. S*   3074 innuere uidetur] *inv. P*
3075 directionem] directio non *S*   3077 Centiloquii] -gii *PS* | sonare uidetur]
inv. S   3078 pluribus] plurisque *S*   3079 neque] nec *S*   3082 huius forsan] *inv. P*
3083 de] *om. PV* | igitur] *om. P*

3061 peregrinationem…3062 anno] Albumasar, *De revol.*, p. 275b:34-36 | 3077
aliqua…3078 pluribus] cf. Ps.-Ptol.., *Cent.*, v. 25: "Diriges significatores cum
fuerint in medio celi cuiuslibet civitatis per ascensiones circuli directi, et cum
fuerint in gradu ascendentis per gradum ascensionum eiusdem civitatis. In eis
que sunt inter illa, fac in ascensionibus graduum secundum quantitatem casus
eorum, et duo loca eis opposita, secundum quantitatem illius. Partes vero
diriges *retrorsum*, et quanto magis crescunt, tanto motus principiorum
retardantur." Nota quod ultima pars ubi de directione retrorsum loquitur, deest
in versione Graeca.

3085 mentio facta est supra, sint in quarta, que est ab angulo terre
usque ad ascendens, Venusque domina anni sit in angulo ascendentis una cum Sole honorem insinuante, dicit **Albumasar**
huiusmodi bonum euenire uersus finem anni.

Adhuc cum perueniat annus ad angulum decime domus
3090 initii natiuitatis, ubi duo superiores infra terminos coniunctionis fuerant simul cum stella fixa et cum parte amicorum in
domo quidem Veneris, que nunc domina est anni et particeps
diuisionis, cum in radice natiuitatis tante fuerit dignitatis, ut
supra declaratum est, uidetur huiusmodi proficuum siue honor
3095 ex hiis significatoribus insinuatus secundum concordiam philosophorum procedere a mulieribus personis alti gradus seu
regalibus, et hoc uersus finem anni. Huiusmodi impedimenta
uero et infortunia per Lunam et Saturnum significata secunde
quarte anni ascribuntur propter ipsorum presentiam inter
3100 angulum medii celi et occidens et ad instar huius manifestabitur
uirtus Iouis in tertia quarta anni. Impedimentum quoque Martis
quantum in se est afficiet seruum Dei uersus ultime quarte
principium. Circa illud itaque tempus caueat sibi propter
coniunctionem Martis cum Saturno prope gradum ascendentis
3105 radicis et propter oppositionem amborum ad locum hyleg et
propter aspectum eorum ad ascendens reuolutionis. Dicit
tamen **Albumasar** | quod propter contrarietatem ipsorum   V139v
conuentus fit fortunatus et disputat contra dicentes oppositum.
Auenezre autem partim huic consentiens in INITIO SAPIENTIE
3110 negat eufortunium ex ipsorum conuentu generari, sed affirmat

---

3086 domina] dominus *V*   3089 Adhuc] ad hoc *V abhinc usque ad figuram anni*
36⁵ textus multo diversus invenitur in S: vide appendicem I. In hac parte notatur L quando
confirmat P 3096 mulieribus] muliebribus *P*   3105 et[1]...hyleg] *om., sed mg. rest. P*
3108 disputat] disputatus *LP*

3087 dicit...3088 anni] Bate referre videtur ad Albumasar, *De revol.*, p. 260b:21-
25 | 3106 Dicit...3108 oppositum] Albumasar, *Introductorium maius*, VII.5 (vol.
8, pp. 134:287-135:311) | 3110 negat...3111 impediri] Ibn Ezra, *Reshit*
Hokhmah, §7.4:3, pp. 198-199. Ibn Ezra, *Commencement*, p. 101: "quant il se
conjoignent, les anciens ont dit qu'il enseignent sur bien. Et le voir est que
chascun destourbe l'oevre de son compaignon, et par ce sera garanti li nés de
domage. Et donques n'ensegnent il mie sur bien fors que bien qu'il ne
domachent mie", quod Bate sic interpretatus est: "quando coniunguntur
dixerunt antiqui quod significant bonum. Veritas autem est quod eorum
utrorumque opus destruit alterius et per hoc salvatur natus a nocumento,
quapropter non significant bonum nisi quod non nocent" (MS Leipzig 1466,
sig. 17ra:26-30)

propter contrarietatem mutuam infortunia illorum impediri.
Vnde in LIBRO NATIVITATUM dicit quod gradus in quem
coincidunt radii ambarum infortunarum *non abscidit uitam, sed
facit egritudinem generari secundum naturam alterius.* Et quia Saturni
coniunctio magis potest quam aspectus Martis in reuolutione,   3115
cum hoc quod Saturnus supra Martem eleuatus est et in reuolutione et in coniunctione ipsorum, idcirco caueat homo Dei
ab egritudine Saturnina, puta quartana aut tertiana, propter
caliditatem Sagittarii et Martis. Cauendum est etiam a constipa-
tione uentris propter presentiam Saturni circa augem excentrici   3120
sui iuxta testimonium **Auenezre** et aliorum, aut oculorum
nocumento propter impedimentum Lune a Saturno in loco
sagitte in Sagittario, que oculorum significant impedimenta,
adhuc et totius capitis, ut supra tactum est, propter ascendens
radicis infortunatum, nisi quia directiones et ea que prius dicta   3125
sunt hiis non concordant. Quapropter periculi grauitas remitti-
tur et magnitudo, non oberit tamen, si precaueatur secundum
Hermetis consilium in FLORIBUS suis sic dicentis: *esto sollicitus
atque suspiciosus quando beniuolus fuerit cum maliuolo neque ualde
confidas quod mali malum penitus auertatur.* Dicit quidem enim   3130
Auenezre in LIBRO LUMINARIUM quod coniunctio Lune cum
Saturno et Marte ualet minus medietate significationis male.
Nam alter alterius significationem corrumpit. Erit autem circa
Natale Domini in hoc anno Luna coniuncta ambobus. Verum
quia Mercurius eisdem infortuniis consimiliter associabitur ad   3135
idem tempus, tanto magis est timendum, cum dicat idem in
eodem quod Mercurius infortunatus a Saturno et Marte peior
est aliis et maioris periculi significatiuuus, nisi fortassis ita sit
iudicandum de Mercurio cum ambobus infortuniis quemadmodum de Luna. Item timendum est ad idem tempus propter   3140
combustionem Veneris et propter priuationem aspectuum ad
dictam coniunctionem. Verumtamen Mercurius a Saturno et

3113   coincidunt] concidunt *P*   3118   puta quartana] *om., sed mg. rest. P*
3123   significant] -at *V*   3124   adhuc *scr.*] ad hoc *LPV*   3130   enim] *om. LP*
3131 Lune] *om. V*   3140 propter] *om. P*

3112 gradus...3114 alterius] Ibn Ezra, *Moladot*, III I 12, 5, pp. 116-117 | 3119
constipatione...3121 Auenezre] Ibn Ezra, *Me'orot*, §24:8, pp. 470-471 | 3128
esto...3130 auertatur] Hermes, *Cent.*, c. 78, sig. 117vb:55-57 | 3131
Auenezre...3132 male] Ibn Ezra, *Me'orot*, §32:1, pp. 478-479 | 3137
Mercurius...3140 Luna] Ibn Ezra, *Me'orot*, §8:1-2, pp. 460-461

Marte defluens Ioui applicabit cum mutua receptione, ratione cuius consolandum est de periculi parte maiori. Preterea
3145 sperandum est de meliori uersus finem anni, ut dictum est, et eo fortius propter restitutionem Veneris in locum, in quo erat in reuolutione, necnon et in gradu exaltationis suae cum aspectu Iouis et propter Solis ingressum ad partem fortune et postea ad ascendens reuolutionis anni. Hec est enim doctrina
3150 **Albumasar**. Vnde motus significationis huius esse debet ex causa precedenti propter esse Veneris in radice prosperitatem promittentis. Item Solis propinquitas cum Capite Draconis in loco in quo est suum exauget promissum. Postremo autem directione facta per nouenas particulas secundum doctrinam
3155 Indorum, quam pro secreto habebant Indi, ut refert **Albumasar**, peruenit hoc anno post 150 dies et duas horas ab hora reuolutionis ad nouenarium Veneris stabitque dispositio in diuisione huius nouenarii per 3 annos, 24 dies et 8 horas, cuius pars tertia unum annum continet, 8 dies, 2 horas, 40 minuta
3160 hore. Disponet igitur Venus principaliter primam tertiam huius diuisionis et hoc iuxta dispositionem eius in duobus temporibus, radicis uidelicet et reuolutionis, ut prehabitum est, conparticipantibus sibi Mercurio et Saturno cum suis dispositionibus supra dictis. Rursum cognitio domini anni | ex
3165 nouenariis secundum opinionem Indorum hoc anno nos perducit ad Venerem. Nam ipsa domina primi nouenarii signi Libre ad quod annus applicuit. Vt igitur ad unum sit dicere, summa prosperitatis huius Veneri incumbit cum qua hunc annum sigillauimus.

P45v

5.2. \<Revolutio anni 36^i\>

3170 Figura reuolutionis 36^i anni que die Solis ante meridiem per unam horam equalem et 11 minuta hore et 30 secunda. dominus hore Iupiter

---

3153 in quo] *om. V* 3158 annos] et *add. P* 3159 unum] *om. V* | 2] et *V* 3163 conparticipantibus] cum participantibus *V* | sibi] *om. V* 3165 Indorum] iudeorum *P* 3168 prosperitatis] prosperitas *P* | huius] *om. V* 3170 Figura] *sequens figura non inuenitur in M et V, ante figuram* Latitudo Lune septentrionalis .3. gr. 34 min. Latitudo Veneris meridionalis .0. gr. 36 min. *inseruit S* 3171 secunda…Iupiter] *om. Par* 3172 dominus] quasi *praem. S*

3154 secundum…3156 Albumasar] Albumasar, *De revol.*, p. 261b:14-16

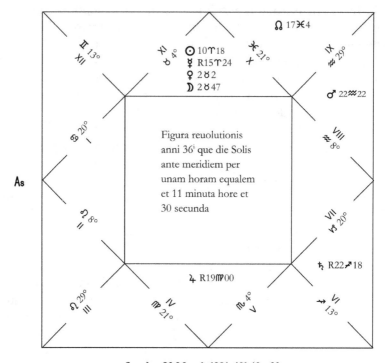

Sunday 23 March 1281, 10h48m30s

I. 20 Cancri

II. 8 Leonis

III. 29 Leonis   3175

IV. 21 Virginis ; Iupiter 19 retrogradus

V. 4 Scorpionis

VI. 13 Sagittarii ; Saturnus retrogradus 22.18

VII. 20 Capricorni

VIII. 8 Aquarii ; Mars 22.22   3180

IX. 29 Aquarii ; Caput 17.4. Piscium

X. 21 Piscium ; Sol 10.18 Arietis ; Venus 2.2 ; Luna 2.47 ;
Mercurius 15.24 retrogradus

3175   Leonis] cauda 17.4 uirginis *add. L*   3176   19] 10 *LP* 19.0 *Par* 18 *S*
3178   22.18] 18.22 *L* 22.28 *Par*   3181   Caput...Piscium] caput 17 *P*
3182   Venus...247] *huc transposuimus, in domu XI posuerunt LPParS (forsan propter exiguitatem loci domus X)*   3183 15.24 *scr.*] 25.24 *LPParS*

XI. 4 Tauri

3185 **XII.** 13 Geminorum

| Hec quidem reuolutionis figura 36^i anni prosperitatem $_{V140r}$ significare uidetur et alacritatem, secundum quod testantur sapientes. Vnde bonum in fine precedentis anni insinuatum consummationem recipiet testante **Albumasar** in prima quarta

3190 huius anni propter presentiam significatorum inter ascendens et angulum medii | celi. Promissa namque prosperitas in radice $_{S27r}$ secundum dispositiones Solis et Lune ac Veneris in hoc tempore uidetur ostendenda iuxta philosophorum assertiones. Etenim Luna hyleg natiuitatis nunc uero ascendentis domina in

3195 loco bone fortune et amicorum locata in gradu quidem exaltationis sue aucta lumine et numero in coniunctione cum Venere simul cum mutua receptione ambarum in domo ac exaltatione ac duodenario Veneris atque cum bona dispositione utriusque in ambobus temporibus bona significat et gloriam, ut dicit

3200 **Albumasar**, maxime quidem a mulieribus personis. Nam *Venus locum* natiuitatis ingrediens *renouat ea que significat in receptione et augebitur thesaurus eius*, ut dicit **Albumasar**. Luna quoque signum ingressa Veneris *significat esse in requie et delectatione et immobilem adipisci substantiam*, precipue propter coniunctionem

3205 Lune cum Venere in reuolutione et propter ambarum esse promittens felicitatem in initio et propter septentrionalem eleuationem Lune supra Venerem, quod quidem bona exaugebit. Vnde **Albumasar** : si tempore reuolutionis *Luna fuerit in proprio signo boni esse, omnia quecumque inceperit* is cuius est reuolu-

3210 tio *euenient sibi prospera*. Item aspectus Veneris et Lune ad ascendens una cum aspectu Iouis ad signum uidelicet exaltationis sue conditiones anni condecorabit, presertim cum Iupiter sit diuisor, ut habitum est, in reuolutione anni precedentis et erit in angulo secundum domorum equationes, quamquam eius

3215 retrogradatio aliquam importet contradictionem. Item terminus

---

3186 Hec] Deinde *V* de *P* | 36i] 6^i *V*   3189 testante] teste *S*   3190 inter ascendens] ascendentis *P*   3192 dispositiones] promissiones *PV*   3194 uero] non *P*   3195 exaltationis] locationis *V*   3197 ambarum] -borum *S* | ac] et *S* 3201 receptione] conceptione *S*   3203 signum ingressa] *inv. P*   3206 promittens felicitatem] *inv. S*   3210 euenient] eueniens *S*   3212 condecorabit] eum decorabit *P* concordabit *V*

3200 Nam…3202 Albumasar] Albumasar, *De revol.*, p. 276a:38-41 | 3208 Albumasar…3210 prospera] Albumasar, *De revol.*, p. 242a:40-42

diuisionis in ante a gradu hyleg in ascendente cadet sub dictis
aspectibus stabuntque diuisiones ab hyleg in ante et retrorsum
in eisdem terminis, in quibus in reuolutione precedente, sed
erunt participantes fortiores et melioris dispositionis quam in
reuolutione precedente preter Mercurium, qui erit retrogradus.   3220
Circa principium retrogradationis erit tamen in angulo medii
celi, qui licet non | multum proderit, impedire tamen poterit,
cum sit receptus in angulo honoris et non combustus. Immo
secundum dispositionem eius forsan significabit aliquod
bonum Mercuriale, ex modo tamen inhonesto aut cum infama-   3225
tione, secundum quod dicit **Albumasar** de retrogradatione
Veneris. Et quoniam tunc associabitur parti scientiarum, ex
hoc eius significatio maior erit precipue in hiis que ad scientias
pertinent. Preterea Iupiter dispositor | ratione diuisionis ab
hyleg angularis existens in proprio termino et gradu lucido   3230
dominus erit exaltationis ascendentis ubi cadit diuisionis terminus circa gradum ascendentem, ratione cuius Iouis significatio tanto magis uigorabitur, nisi quantum diminuitur ratione
detrimenti sui in quo erit. Amplius Sol dominus periodi cum sit
in angulo medii celi in exaltatione sua et conditione cum sit   3235
reuolutio diurna nec impedietur ab aliquo, sicuti nec Venus
neque Luna, iuxta quod in radice spoponderat, honorem augmentabit. Etenim cum fortis in natiuitate fuerit in illa reuolutione, adhuc fortior erit et cum hoc partem habebit in ascendente ac maiorem in secunda, ratione cuius substantiam   3240
augmentabit. Sed quia secundum gradus equales cadit in nona
cum sit eius gaudium, parum obesse poterit aut nihil, presertim
cum secundum hanc uiam Venus cum Luna sit in domo
decima. Porro secundum directionem factam ab ascendente
intrabit hoc anno diuisio terminum Veneris, 15. uidelicet gradu 3245
Capricorni, exeundo uidelicet terminum Iouis, de quo **Albu-**

V140v

P46r

3216 a¹] *om. P*   3219 participantes] -tis *P*   3221 Circa...retrogradationis] *om. S*
3225   aut...infamatione] *om., sed mg. rest. P*   3230   proprio termino] *inv. V*
3231 ubi] cum *S* | cadit] cadet *S*   3234 detrimenti] doctrine menti *P*   3235 sit]
om. P   3236 nec¹] necque *S* | impedietur] -ditus *P*   3237 neque] nec *P* et *S*
3239   hoc] *om. S*   3240   ac] et *P*   3241   augmentabit] ampliabit *S*
3242 presertim] *om. PV*   3245 terminum] *om., sed mg. rest. P* | uidelicet] scilicet *S*

3223 Immo...3227 Veneris] Albumasar, *De revol.*, p. 239b:17-19 : "obtinebit
quidem predicta, ex modis uerumtamen inhonestibus"

masar: hoc enim *durabilem* felicitatem significat et a felicitate in felicitatem *mutationem*. Vnde Venus disponet annum illum et septem alios sequentes una cum participatione Saturni, Iouis,

3250 Solis et Mercurii secundum aspectus graduum eqalium in radice. Et quoniam in natiuitate Venus fortis fuerat et expedita, ut prehabitum est, et in hoc anno reuolutionis erit consimiliter, idcirco dignitas eius et uirtus manifestanda est illis diebus, secundum quod testantur astrologi. *Tunc enim quilibet planetarum,*

3255 ut ait **Albumasar**, *operationes suas quas secundum natiuitatem significabat, manifeste ostendit quando manifestat ipsas diuisio. Et si planeta ipse fuerit in natiuitate in signo firmo,* secundum quod se | habet in   S27v proposito, *erunt* eius significata *tempore diuisionis immutabilia.* Igitur dispositio Veneris secundum utraque tempora, ut

3260 testatur **Albumasar**, significat *perseuerare in melodiis et cantibus et tripudiis et alacritatibus et coniungi mulieribus et obtinere multa bona a uiris effeminatis et mulieribus et loqui cum preexistentibus uiris et loqui etiam coram eis in conuentibus doctrine. Participatio* autem *Saturni* cum *Venere,* licet *contentiones et discordias* in rebus muliebribus ac

3265 tristitias significet, quantum in se est, bonitas tamen Iouis, qui tempore natiuitatis Saturnum mitigabat, in reuolutione quoque illa potentior existens Saturno eius mala soluet. *Participatio* uero *Solis* maxime propter dispositiones eius in utrisque temporibus *significat gloriam et meritum a regibus et principibus et utilitatem ab eis et*

3270 *a parentibus.* Ratione autem *participationis Mercurii* significabitur *iuuamentum occasione discipline et occultorum documentorum et obtinere utilitatem pro mulieribus et delectari in eis ; tamen cum eis patietur conuitia occasione meretricum,* dicit **Albumasar.** Sed quia huiusmodi participationes sunt tantum propter aspectus graduum

3275 equalium et non secundum equationes, idcirco uirtus earum minoratur nisi quantum dispositiones planetarum in reuolutionibus uigorantur. Et hinc est quod Luna Veneris induens

---

3248 illum] *om. S*   3251 Et...expedita] *om., sed mg. rest. P* | quoniam] quando *S* et] *om. S*   3254 testantur] attestantur *V*   3255 operationes] oppositiones *S* suas] *om. PV*   3260 testatur] attestatur *V*   3261 mulieribus] cum *praem. S* et³...mulieribus] *om. S*   3264 contentiones] contemptiones *S* | muliebribus] muli'bus *S*   3266 mitigabat] -bit *P*   3273 quia huiusmodi] huius quia *P* huius quia huius *V*   3276 reuolutionibus] -nes *S*

3247 hoc...3248 mutationem] Albumasar, *De revol.*, p. 257b:18-22 | 3254 Tunc...3258 immutabilia] Albumasar, *De revol.*, p. 257b:23-29 | 3260 Albumasar...3264 discordias] Albumasar, *De revol.*, p. 256a:7-20 | 3267 Participatio...-3273 Albumasar] Albumasar, *De revol.*, p. 256a:50-b:11

esse mulieres anteponit et *iuuamentum occasione mulierum et per-*
uenire ad dignitates et diuitias. Facta autem directione a gradu
medii celi deuenietur hoc anno ad 19um Scorpionis gradum   3280
cuius duodenam particulam Venus in radice possidebit, ratione
V141r | cuius testimonia honoris recipiunt incrementum iuxta doctri-
nam **Albumasar**. Rursum Venus erit domina nouenarii, ut
prius <dictum est,> disponetque annum conparticipantibus
sibi Mercurio et Saturno usque ad 158 dies, 4 horas et 40 minu-   3285
ta hore. Abhinc uero incipiet disponere Mercurius cum Saturno
et Venere. Item erit et Luna anni domina secundum opinionem
Indorum ex nouenariis ratione quorum ambe, Venus scilicet et
Luna, maius consequentur dominium in illa reuolutione. Sane
Mars dominus fidarie in hoc anno habebit Mercurium condis-   3290
positorem, ratione cuius, ut dicit **Albumasar**, significabitur
habere nocumenta et peregrinare et contristari propter furtum uel damnum
uel *amicis suis inimicari et forte perire ab aliquo infortunio.* Sed quia
significatores contrarie partis fortiores sunt et plurium testimoniorum in bonitate, idcirco certior et maior erit promotionis   3295
bonitas quam infortuniorum impedimenta, precipue cum in
radice Mars fuerit impotens nec in reuolutione in loco erit a
quo ualeat multum impedire. Aliquam tamen operationem,
licet debilem, ostendet Mars hoc anno propter dominium anni.
Itaque dicit **Albumasar** : *si fuerit aliquis de maliuolis in quadratis*   3300
ascendentis anni, ipse uero dominus ascendentis in bono loco configuratus
cum beniuolis et aspexerit ascendens, plures de aduersitatibus aufert que
significauit maliuolus. Preterea profectione facta ab hyleg per-

---

3278 mulieres] -ris *V* | anteponit] -net *S*   3279 directione] directe *S*   3280 celi]
om. S | deuenietur] perueniatur *S*   3281   duodenam] duodenariam *S*
possidebit] -bat *S*   3283 erit] erat *S*   3284 dictum est] *addidi (vide l. 1667-1668)*
conparticipantibus] cum participantibus *V*   3285   et^1] *om. V*
3289 consequentur] -quantur *S*   3292 contristari] tristari *S*   3298 ualeat
multum] *inu. S*   3299   ostendet] -dit *PV*   3300   Itaque...anni] *om. S*
3301 configuratus] figuratus *P*   3303 significauit maliuolus] significat beniuolus
S | profectione] perfectione *S*

3278 iuuamentum...3279 diuitias] Albumasar, *De revol.*, p. 256b14-16 | 3281
ratione...3283 Albumasar] Bate referre videtur ad Albumasar, *De revol.*, p.
238a:7-13: "Considerandum est et radiationes et partes et duodenas particulas
quibus coniungitur Venus uel configuratur in duobus temporibus, quod si fuerit
conuenienti figura, indicat sospitatem et prosperitatem secundum
significationem ipsorum" | 3291 Albumasar...3293 infortunio] Albumasar, *De*
revol., p. 271b:30-34 | 3300 Albumasar...3303 maliuolus] Albumasar, *De revol.*,
p. 243a:34-40

ueniet annus ad Taurum cuius domine, Veneris scilicet, dis-
3305   positio iam sepius est dicta. Item secundum profectiones a
domino hore natiuitatis et a domino ascendentis eiusdem
perueniet annus ad Iouem cuius dispositio similiter est predicta. Amplius secundum directionem ab ascendente perueniet
annus ad Scorpionem, dominum scilicet amicorum in | radice   P46v
3310   ad gradum scilicet partis amoris. Propter quod Mars dominus
erit anni, qui, quoniam impeditus erat et debilis in radice nec
aspexerit ascendens aut eius dominum, parum ualere poterit
eius dispositio et dominium in reuolutione, maxime cum non
aspiciat etiam ascendens reuolutionis nec Venerem aut Lunam
3315   impediat neque Iouem. Verum quia receptus est et orientalis in
proprio termino, magis uidetur proficere quam nocere in illo
anno secundum doctrinam sapientum. Vnde utilitas a mortuis
et hereditatibus significata per Martem in octaua domo reuolutionis modica erit quantum ex hac parte propter locum Martis
3320   debilem et propter ultimam partem signi profectionis que cadet
in 12^a radicis. In reuolutione uero cadet in quinto totum
signum profectionis. Fortificabitur tamen huiusmodi significationis testimonium per partem fortune cadentem in octauo sub
lumine Martis, | item et per retrogradationem octaue domus   S28r
3325   radicis in ascendens reuolutionis cum aspectibus et testimoniis
supra dictis. Quamquam autem Saturnus propter retrogradationem impeditus supra Martem eleuetur, cuius latitudo
meridiana erit, Saturni uero septentrionalis, non tamen uidetur
Mars multum impediri ab ipso propter receptionem et as-
3330   pectum sextilem, presertim cum Saturnus cadat ab angulo,
timorem potius minatur quam lesionem. Significat autem
huiusmodi configuratio Saturni cum Marte *desidiam et periculum
in fratribus*, ut uult **Albumasar**. Saturnus igitur ascendens radicis ingressus sextam reuolutionis domum occupabit, domum

---

3304 scilicet] est *S*   3305 iam…est] sepius iam *S* | profectiones] perfectiones *S*
3307 Iouem…3309 ad] *om. PV*   3315 impediat] impedita *P* | neque] nec *S* | et]
om. P   3317 Vnde] *om. P* | utilitas] fit *add. S*   3320 ultimam] lunam *S*
profectionis] perfectionis *S*   3321 cadet] -dit *S*   3322 profectionis] perfectionis
S | tamen] cum *V*   3324 item] iterum *PV* | et] *om. PV* | retrogradationem]
regirationem *PV* aliter reuersionem *mg. P^x* | domus] *om. V*   3326 propter] per *S*
3327 eleuetur] eleuatus *P* | cuius] in *praem. V*   3329 aspectum sextilem]
aspectus sestilitatem *S*   3331 minatur] inmaturus *S*   3332 configuratio] -tu *S*
3333 in] *om. S*   3334 occupabit domum] *om. PS (sic)*

3331 Significat…3333 Albumasar] Albumasar, *De revol.*, p. 223a:14-16

scilicet infirmitatum, sua dispositione morbos significante   3335
afficiens locum uite. Quare uidetur hoc, quantum in se est,
morbum significare Saturninum, precipue propter quartum
aspectum Saturni, secundum gradus equales in radice ad
gradum diuisionis illum disponentem annum. Quia tamen dicit
Compilator Abraham: cum fuerint ductus siue directiones per   3340
ascensiones, debent etiam aspectus accipi secundum domorum
partitiones, et cum fuerint directiones siue ductus per gradus
equales, aspectus consimiliter accipiendi sunt secundum gradus
equales, ut singula singulis correspondeant. Si hoc sit uerum,
tunc nihil est ad propositum de quarto aspectu Saturni super   3345
gradum diuisionis anni illius. Adhuc in radice Iupiter infra
terminos coniunctionis erat cum Saturno proiciens consimiliter
V141v   suos radios uersus locum aspectus Saturni. | Item Venus
domina termini in initio suum terminum amicabiliter illustrabat
aspectu trino. Amplius in reuolutione aspiciet Iupiter eundem   3350
terminum et cum hoc erit Saturnus ab ipso receptus et Mars a
Saturno et Mercurius a Marte, ita quod omnes impeditores
recepti erunt et sub aspectibus amicitie, ratione cuius ipsorum
impedimenta relaxantur secundum testimonia philosophorum.
Propter quod impedimenta Saturni et Martis non oportet   3355
multum formidare, quinimmo Mars ipse, ut dictum est, magis
uidetur non obesse. Vnde **Albumasar**: *si fuerit dominus anni in*
duobus temporibus impeditus in *locis ascendens non aspicientibus,* ut est
sextus et octauus, *erit malum clandestinum occultum et incognitum*
uniuersis. Verum quia aspicitur a Mercurio ex domo decima,   3360
uidetur quod debeat apparere post occultationem, ut asserit
idem, nisi quod ille Mercurius, qui occultatiuus in radice, tunc
iterum incipiet radios Solis subintrare, per quod ocultatio

3335 infirmitatum] -tem *S* | morbos] domos *S*   3336 hoc] *om. S* | in] de *S*
3337 Saturninum] Saturnum *S*   3339 tamen] cum *P*   3340 fuerint] fuerit *PV*
siue] *om. S*   3342 fuerint] fiunt *PV*   3343 consimiliter] similiter *PV*   3345 est]
om. S   3346 Adhuc] ad hoc *V*   3347 terminos] *om. V*   3349 terminum] *om. S*
amicabiliter] -bilem *S*   3353   cuius] domus *S*   3355   et Martis] *om. P*
3356   quinimmo] qui in initio *P*   3357   uidetur] u'r *S* uidebitur *PV*
3362 nisi…ille] *om. PV* | ille] est *add. S*

3340 Compilator…3342 partitiones] Ibn Ezra, *De nativitatibus,* sig. a8r:22-24:
"quod si feceris ductus cum gradibus equalibus, fac quoque respectus cum
gradibus equalibus" | 3357 Albumasar…3359 incognitum] Albumasar, *De*
revol., p. 220a:50-b:7 | 3360 quia…3361 occultationem] Albumasar, *De revol.,* p.
220b:8-11

consimiliter insinuatur. Martis quidem igitur dispositio secunde
3365   quarte deputatur, Saturni autem tertie et consimili ratione in
ultima quarta manifestabitur uirtus Iouis. Ingressus quoque
Iouis in *locum proprium* necnon et ad partem futurorum ubi
fuerat in radice, *renouabit prosperitates que per natiuitatis initium
iudicabuntur*, ut dicit **Albumasar**, *necnon prebebit diuitias ab in-*
3370   *sperato emolimento*. Hic autem ingressus eueniet uersus finem
Septembris illius anni. Item Veneris operatio post principium
Aprilis manifestabitur, si Deus uoluerit. Tunc enim restituetur
in proprium gradum natiuitatis. Item et uersus finem Maii
operabitur aliquid. Nam tunc ingredietur ascendens reuolu-
3375   tionis presertim post principium Iunii, cum erit in primo duodenario. Amplius sperandum est semper de bono in tota reuolutione illa quotiescumque Luna perueniet ad Cancrum et
consimiliter ad Taurum. Item sperandum est a medio Iulii
usque ad medium Augusti propter ingressum Solis in Leonem,
3380   in quo partem operis inueniet. Specialiter autem sperandum est
ex ingressu Solis in primam duodenam Leonis. Nam in radice
Sol duodenam propriam que Leoni competit possidebat, cuius
uirtutem tunc ostendet. Consimiliter quoque per totum Au-
gustum erit Venus in Libra in qua loca Iouis et Saturni et
3385   partem futurorum et inimicorum peruagabit aspicietque dominum anni et signum eius in reuolutione necnon et ascendens
radicis. Diuersis tamen diebus fient hec, ratione quorum in
bonis erit hic cuius est reuolutio, si Deus uoluerit. | E   S28v
conuerso autem timendum est et cauendum aliqualiter uersus
3390   principium Iulii propter retrogradationem Saturni ad gradum
oppositum gradui hyleg, sed magis uidetur cauendum esse circa
principium Septembris. Tunc enim cum hoc quod Saturnus
directus existens repetet dictum gradum, erit et Mars in opposito ledens ipsum hyleg gradum et non aspiciet tunc Iupiter
3395   aut Venus aliquem illorum. | Insuper cauendum est in Decem-   P47r

---

3364 igitur] *om. S*   3368 renouabit] remouebit *S*   3370 ingressus] egressus *P*
3371 operatio] oppositio *S*   3373 et] *om. P*   3374 operabitur aliquid] compara-
bitur idem *S* | ingredietur] egredietur *P*   3376 est] *om. S*   3377 illa] *om. S*
3381 ex] in *S* | duodenam] duodenariam *S* | Leonis...propriam] *om. S*
3382 Leoni] locum *S*   3385 inimicorum] amicorum *S*   3389 conuerso] diuerso
S   3391 gradui] gradum *P*   3393 et] *om. P*   3394 aspiciet] -ent *S*
3395 Decembre] -bri *PV*

3367 locum...3370 emolimento] Albumasar, *De revol.*, p. 274b:4-7

bre propter reditum Martis per retrogradationem ad gradum hyleg.

Hec sunt igitur significationes reuolutionis 36^i anni et que tunc euenient, si Deus uoluerit, secundum quod ex dictis astrologorum perpendere possumus ad presens.

3400

3396 per] propter *S*   3398 sunt] *om. P* | que] *om. S*   3399 euenient] -et *S* 3400   presens] Explicit deo gratias; Laus tibi Christe quoniam liber explicit iste *add. S* Explicit natiuitas magistri Henrici Machliniensis cum quibusdam reuolutionibus *post aliam nativitatem que sequitur add. LP*

Appendix I. Versio altera in codice Segoviensi, bib. cath. 84

Preconsideratis hiis et anteuisis nunc euentus anni huius notabiliores per ordinem subiungamus; in cuius quidem principio post dies tres aut circiter perrexit hic cuius est reuolutio una cum domino terre sue ad quoddam monasterium sancti-
5 monialium in Brabantia, ubi illam familiarem consiliariam regine Francie inueniens dominus exortatus est ipsam tamquam debentem exorans | ut de promotione huius serui Dei promissum non frustraret, quod etiam ipsa constanter annuebat. Sed ut breuius transeamus, tota prima anni quarta deliciis
10 indulgens et gaudio uitam duxit amenam hic aliquis secundum concupiscentias quidem corporis multiformes, nisi quod circa Pascha Domini passus est in faucibus apostema. Postmodum uero inualescebat fama et diuulgatum est apud notos et ignotos quod hic, cuius erat reuolutio, satur alme philosophie,
15 repudiata dignitate celi bellans Iouis fetum, honestam Paladem, sub Plutonis machinaretur pedibus conculcari adnatam philosophie predignitatem in libertatem coniugalem, immo uerius in subconiugalem captiuitando seruitutem; in quandam dementiam prolapsus esse dicebatur, ut non solum dignas Mercurii et
20 Philosophie nuptias, de quibus tam digne quam reuerenter anominatus **Capella Martianus** cecinit, detestaretur, uerum sanctificati legalisque coniugii turpe diuortium machinando ipsum quidem Mercurium cum infernali, quod absit, adulterantem Proserpina simul apud inferos demergi procuraret.
25 Circa principium autem secunde quarte anni exorta est accusatio et infamia super quam credi posset cum obligationibus innumerabilibus occasione mulieris ita quod aliqui coram regina Anglie et suis familiaribus conati fuerunt eius infamiam magis ac magis deturpare. Amplius et creuit

S26r

App1,1 Preconsideratis] *haec versio invenitur* post "versus finem anni" *usque ad figuram anni 36ⁱ in cod. Segovensi, f. 25v-26v. Vide introductionem,* 1.1.2   5 Brabantia *scr.*] Brabantiam *S*   6 ipsam] dominus *add. S*   9 prima *scr.*] primi *S*   13 diuulgatum] nota que de illo dicebantur *mg. S*   14   alme philosophie] *scr.*] alme'phoe *S* 15 bellans *scr.* bellare *S*   19 esse *scr.* est *S*   22 sanctificati *coni. Guldentops*] fastigati *S*   24 Proserpina *scr.*] proserina *S*

---

19 non…21 cecinit] Martianus Capella, *De nuptiis Philologiae et Mercurii* II 160

ranchor et inuidia in maliuolis plurimorum, et amicorum   30
auctoritate supersederunt inimicantes et literati et mercatores.
Vnde contra huiusmodi cautum et munitum oportebat esse
seruum dei. Durauit autem feruor huius infortunii quasi per
tres menses. Vnde hoc tempore edidit illud rhitmicum in
uulgari super infortuniorum nimietate multiplici inopinabilium,   35
in uestibulo quidem cordis dicens deo: *domine quam multiplicati
sunt qui tribulant me; multi insurgunt aduersum me* etcetera. Item
passus est hiis diebus soda siue dolorem capitis inordinatum et
frequenter totius corporis discrasiam, de qua medici dubitant
ob ignorantiam cause, et maxime circa tertie [et] quarte   40
principium. Tunc enim passus est hic aliquis inflationem circa
oculum sinistrum et quasi per totam maxillam ex apostemate in
sinistra parte nasi. In hac uero quarta anni tertia, cum
peruenisset Venus ad signum profectionis, arripuit iter uersus
Parisius, exiens in illa in qua natus fuit hora, qua signum   45
profectionis septimam domum subintrabat Cancro Lunam
continentem in angulo terre. Antequam autem Parisius
perueniret, incommoda quam plurima substinuit et tedia,
quamquam precautus fuerit quam ualeret. Post recessum uero
a terra sua per 3 dies, tempore uidelicet quo Venus coniuncta   50
est Marti in Scorpione, noua consurrexit infamia occasione
infortunii honeste quondam mulieris arte fraudulenta
circumuente et decepte, sed propter euidentissimam infamie
falsitatem confestim ignoscentia emicuit accusati. Preterea
Saturno gradum ascendentis tenente radicis passus est hic   55
aliquis constipationem inconsuetam in uentre, amplius et
capitis debilitatem cum tinitu continuo et aurium sibilo necnon
et   quadam   conturbatione   uertiginali.   Item   tempore
coniunctionis Mercurii cum Marte et Saturno passus est
difficultatem loquendi propter impedimentum lingue et ali-   60
qualem eius dolorem in sinistra parte et hoc precipue cum
Luna ipsis coniuncta fuit quasi per triduum ante Natale Domi-

---

30 maliuolis] *scr.*] maliuolentiis *S* | et² *scr.*] n'c *S* | amicorum auctoritate *scr.*] ani-
marum austeritate *S*   31 supersederunt *corr. Guldentops*] supercederunt *S* | litera-
ti *scr.*] lrati *S*   32 munitum *scr.*] inimicum *S*   39 discrasiam *scr.*] distrasiam *S*
40 et² *delevi*   44 profectionis *scr.*] perfectionis *S*   46 profectionis *scr.*] perfectionis *S*   50 terra *scr.*] tertia *S*   53 circumuente *scr.* circumuemente *S*

---

36 domine…37 etcetera] *Ps.* 3,2

ni. Adhuc passus est hoc tempore relaxationem uuule et ante
hoc tempus parum fuit inchoata passio oculorum, sed obui-
65 atum est sibi per regimen et dieta. Vt autem ad omne' dicatur,
detrimentum principii est passus, capitis Arietis quippe, cum de
hiis que magis repugnant capiti sit constipatio uentris incon-
sueta. Demum uero apud ultime anni quarte principium non
affuit egritudo febrilis aut grauior, propter quod experimento
70 inuestigari potest quod annorum reuolutiones | natalium non
magnam superaddunt radici fortitudinem nisi per directionum
et consimilium consonantiam specialiter fuerint roborate. Item
Saturni et Martis impedimenta inuicem dexid (?) satis propor-
tionabiliter suam hoc tempore significationem impleuerunt.
75 Nam bis in hac anni quarta euenit in nare sinistra passio
apostema, leuis tamen, et sibilus quidem aurium et capitis
discrasia usque ad annum sequentem est continuata. Maxime
autem passa est auris dextra propter Saturnum et naris sinistra
propter Martem, quibus quidem conueniunt dicta sapientum ;
80 oculi autem hoc tempore non sunt infirmati. Materia namque
huius debens fore causa ad aures et nares satis detinebatur.
Saturno etiam ad stationem appropinquante incepit uentris
constipatio cessare. Sane expertum est sufficienter ex euentibus
tam propositis quam aliis quod uerum dicit **Auenezre** et reliqui
85 in hoc quod significatorum latitudo coniunctorum magnam
partem fortitudinis subtrahit testimoniorum. Sed compleamus
annum. Circa medium quidem Februarii est quidam Hoiensis
cum magna instantia ex parte nepotis cuiusdam regis propter
sibi faciendam societatem et, licet ante, circa festum scilicet
90 Sancti Nicholai, habitus fuerit sermo super eadam materia, non
reputatum fuit euenire, cum tamen, ut postea compertum est,
ille nobilis firmum habuisset propositum ex intima amicitie
beniuolentia a longo tempore preconceptum. Responsum
autem ultimo facere ardenti petitioni conueniens protelando
95 amicis imponebatur. Insuper secundo die Martis, dominica
uidelicet ad brandones, hora diei quasi 12ª, habitus est sermo

S26v

---

63 uuule *scr.*] ubule *S*   66 passus *scr.*] passa *S* | Arietis *scr.*] ariud' *vel* arind' *S*
73 dexid] dexidera (?) *sed* -ra *del. S an* relaxantia *scrib. ?*   77 discrasia *scr.*]dist'sia *S*
81   detinebatur *scr.*] detinebat *S*   85   in hoc] *lectio incerta in S* ml' *(*magistri *?)*
87 Hoiensis *scr.*] hoie'm *S*   93 preconceptum *scr.*] preconcepta *S*   96 brandones
scr.] brabandones *a. corr. S*

---

85 significatorum…86 testimoniorum] Ibn Ezra, *Teʿamim I*, §7.1:6-8, pp. 88-89.

ab homine cum regine consiliaria, secundum quod in anni
principio, et iterum in die Iouis sequente hora quasi 3ª uel 4ª
repetitum et idem promotionis colloquium. Ipsa autem primo
in aliquibus deuians tandem quidem apponendo concilium   100
promisso fidelius intendere repromisit, et tunc infra triduum
terminatus est annus 35ᵘˢ.

In quadam margine libelli a quo translata fuit ista natiuitas
fere uersus finem libri erat scriptum hoc: "postquam Saturnus   105
gradus ascendentis radicis ingressus fuit quousque Sagittarium
egressus, est passus in brachiis lesionem in motu et quandam
impotentiam cum quodam dolore per uices redeunte". Vide
ubi debeat intrare quod non erat signatum.

Appendix II: Digressio in Libro Rationum Auenezre
ab Henrico Bate translato

Textus Auenezre [ed. Sela §6.2:5-8]. **Nam c**um planeta
remotus est a terra, tunc recipit fortitudinem magnam a superioribus stellis. Vnde si prefuerit stella seu planeta super res anime, que subilis est res, tunc multa erit nato scientia in omnibus
manieribus; si autem presul fuerit aut almutas super res corpo-   5
ris, tunc erit statura parua et breuis et non erit ei robur et fortitudo conueniens. Quod si fuerit planeta in loco depressionis
sue seu in opposito augis et sic presul super animam, tunc significat quod natus erit fatuus et ignorans. Si uero presul fuerit
super corpus, tunc significat quod erit ei corpus magnum et ro-   10
bustum. Et huius quidem sermonis ueritatem expertus sum
multis uicibus. Causa enim quare est planete fortitudo in sta-
tione sua secunda est quia a loco illo incipit esse directa in suo
cursu.

Inquit translator. Ecce quomodo planeta circa augem   15
existens fortitudinem significat circa res anime, in opposito

---

App2,5 aut] seu *Lm* | almutas] almubtam *Lp* almustam *Lm*   6 statura] statu *Lm*
et³] seu *Lm*   7 Quod] *om. Lm*   12 planete fortitudo] *digressio Henrici inuenitur in
cod. Lips. 1466, fol. 69va:6-70rb:4; in cod. Lemov. 9, fol. 37v in fine-39r:19; sed verba
"inquit translator" erronee inserta sunt in medio digressionis post verba "philosophie
adaptamus"* (l. 67)

uero augis, et hoc est cum motus eius uelocior est contra motum generalem quantum ad deferentem eius, fortitudinem et
bonum esse corporis significat. Et hoc dicit ipse expertum esse.
20 Et hoc autem aduerti potest quod simili modo debet esse ratione illius motus quem uocant astrologi motum in epiciclo,
scilicet directionem et retrogradationem, ut quidem directio
super bonam dispositionem et esse corporis significet, retrogradatio uero super esse anime, cum motus generalis, scilicet
25 hic qui est ab oriente in occidens super esse et conseruationem
entium uirtutem habeat et causalitatem, ut uult **Philosophus**,
motus uero in obliquo circulo, qui contrarius est primo, scilicet
secundum successionem signorum, generationis est causa et
corruptionis. Et quia generatio et corruptio proprie passiones
30 sunt corporis, igitur huiusmodi causa fortis, motus scilicet
directionis secundum astrologos, qui secundum **Alpetragium**
et secundum ueritatem potius deberet appellari retrogradatio,
cum sit contra intentionem generalem, conuenienter debet
fortitudinem causare corporis, propinqui inquam generationis
35 et corruptionis subiecti ex contrarietatibus elementorum
constituti. Motus uero ille qui ab astrologis retrogradatio uocatur secundum hanc uiam corporis debilitatem et impedimenta
significabit. Vnde quemadmodum *fortes* corpore *ineptos mente*
uidemus, sic iuxta **Philosophum** *molles carne* et passibiles *aptos*
40 mente frequentius experimur ; propter quod dogna **Platonis** et
uniuersaliter omnium philosophantium tenet hoc quod ad operationes intellectus libere extendas : necessarium est corporales
uires subigi et tamquam infortunatas in se seruiliter captiuari.
Vnde et **Philosophus** in octauo POLITICORUM : *labor quidem*
45 *corporis impediens est intellectum, qui autem huius corpus.* Hoc idem
quoque tamquam nature legem existimans tanto euenientem in
maiori parte dixit ingenio pollet cui uim natura negauit. Hac
uero de causa conuenientius est magis quod res diuinior, motus
scilicet ille qui primo similior est, uirtutem habeat super illam
50 partem hominis, per quam ad operationes diuinas, que sunt ratione uti et intellectu, aptius disponatur. Rationis enim per-

21 quem] *scr.* quam *LmLp* 44 octauo] -ua *Lp* 51 intellectu] -tus *LmLp*

38 fortes...40 experimur] Arist., *De an.* II 9, 421a25-26 | 44 labor...45
corpus] Arist., *Polit.* VIII 4, 1339a9-11

fectio, ut dicit **Plato**, et *intellectus* est *Dei propria et paucorum admodum* animalium, uerbi gratia, *hominum*. Vnde **Philosophus** in decimo ETHICORUM : *Vita* autem que *secundum intellectum* est *melior uita quam <secundum> hominem. Non* enim *secundum quod* 55 *homo est, sic uiuit, sed secundum quod diuinum aliquod in ipso existit.* Consonum est ergo rationi quod planeta directus fortitudinem corporis et anime detrimentum significet, e contrario retrogradus utendo nominibus ab astrologo usitatis, sicut satis apparere potest intuenti. Sciendum autem est quod in proposito 60 sustentatus sum super principia philosophie Aristotelis non ponendo ecentricos et epiciclos, ut dicatur planeta aliquando propinquior terre, aliquando remotior, sed modum motus planetarum considerantes solum quantum ad conuenientiam eius cum motu primo et differentiam uelocitatis quoque eius secun- 65 dum hoc et tarditatem principiis philosophie adaptamus. Bone quidem fortune ab astrologis uocate sunt prosperitates in bonis exterioribus secundum quandam excellentiam, prout etiam apud uulgares consuete sunt reputari. Quamquam igitur opus sit aliquali prosperitate exteriori homini enti, nihilominus 70 tamen communiter uocate prosperitates, secundum quod etiam ab astrologis appellantur, impedimenta sunt ad speculationem, ut testatur **Philosophus** et rei ueritas, et in hoc etiam sensu omnes philosophi conuenerunt. Vnde sexto ETHICORUM: *Anaxagoram* inquit et consimiles *sapientes quidem, non prudentes* 75 *autem aiunt esse, cum ignorantes uideantur conferentia sibi ipsis, et superflua quidem et admirabilia et difficilia et diuina scire ipsos aiunt; inutilia autem quoniam non humana bona querunt.* Item in quarto: *et accusant,* inquit, *fortunam quoniam maxime digni existentes nequaquam ditantur.* Vnde et fortune ymago ceca depingitur. *Contingit autem* 80 *non irrationabiliter hoc,* ut ait **Philosophus.** *Non enim possibile pecunias habere non curantem ut habeat quemadmodum neque in aliis.* Non solum autem hoc ita se habet in felicitate speculatiua, sed

---

56 existit] *mg. Lp* 67 uocate] -ta *Lp* 73 sensu] sensui *Lp* 77 scire ipsos] *inu. Lm* 78 Item] et *add. Lm* 80 depingitur] pingitur *Lm* 81 irrationabiliter] n. rationabiliter *Lp* 82 curantem] *ex* curantur *corr. Lp* | habeat] hebeat *Lp*

---

52 ut...53 hominum] Plato, *Timaeus* 51E (translatio Calcidii, p. 50,9-10). Cf. Bate, *Speculum divinorum*, XVI, c. 6, 118-121 | 54 Vita...56 ipso] Arist., *Eth. Nic.* X 7, 1177b26-28 et 1178a6-7 | 75 Anaxagoram...78 querunt] Arist., *Eth. Nic.* VI 7, 1141b4-8 | 78 et...82 aliis] Arist., *Eth. Nic.* IV 1, 1120b17-20

etiam in actiua. *Existimandum* namque *non est multis et magnis*
85 *indigere felicem futurum. Non enim in superabundantiis per se sufficiens*
neque iudicium neque actio. Possible autem et non principes terre et maris
bona agere. Ydiote enim, ait **Philosophus**, *potentibus non minus stu-*
diosa uidentur agere, sed et magis. Idem quoque patet quarto POLI-
TICORUM. Quemadmodum igitur bona fortuna appetitui sen-
90 suali attributa planetarum directioni proportionatur secundum
astrologos, secundum quod et inferior spera contra superiorem
mouendo aliquando uincit, ut innuit Philosophus tertio DE ANIMA,
sic et bona fortuna beatitudinis, que in appetitu consistit intel-
lectuali, planetarum retrogradationi proportionanda relinquitur,
95 secundum quod inferior spera superiorem pro posse suo
consequitur in motu. *Natura autem que sursum semper principalior*,
ut ibidem ait **Philosophus**. Et hoc quidem sensui consenta-
neum est, rationi etiam secundum mentem astrologorum,
prout hic apparet in textu. Cum enim secundum principia phi-
100 losophie impossibile sit ecentricos esse stellarum circulos, in
quibus mouentur, quid aliud esse potest locus augis et eius
oppositum nisi loca in quibus contra motum supremum uelo-
cius aut tardius mouetur stella. Quanto autem mouetur tardius,
tanto supreme spere similius, et tunc, ut ait **Actor**, anime signi-
105 ficat perfectionem. Cum itaque per retrogradationem planeta
motum spere superioris perfectius consequatur ac eidem magis
assimiletur et melius quam per motum alium, relinquitur illam
in rebus anime sublimitatem importare non obstantibus tamen
impedimentis que in rebus corporis adducit. Vnde quomodo
110 tristitias et contradictiones et cetera impedimenta corporalia
causat retrogradatio, sic et accidentia tribulant et conturbant
beatum. Tristitias enim inferunt et impediunt multis operatio-
nibus in quibus oportet esse uirum *tamquam tetragonum sine uitu-*
perio. Et hinc alibi scriptum est *uerti me ad aliud uidique sub Sole*
115 *nec sapientum panem nec doctorum diuitias nec artificum gratiam* et
cetera. Sed reuertatur ad textum.

---

84 in] *om. Lm* 85 superabundantiis] -tia *Lm* -tiam *Lp* 93 consistit intellectuali]
inv. Lm 108 importare] imponere *Lm* 112 beatum] *post* tribulant *trsp. Lm*
116 Sed…textum] *om. Lm*

---

84 Existimandum…88 magis] Arist., *Eth. Nic.* X 9, 1179a1-8 | 91
secundum…97 Philosophus] Cf. Arist., *De an.* III 11, 434a12-13 | 113
tamquam…uituperio] Arist., *Eth. Nic.* I 10, 1100b21-22 | 114 uerti…116
cetera] *Eccl.* IX,11

Index fontium ab editoribus allegatorum

III IV, 5, 3, pp. 142143	1642-1648
III V 7, 2, pp. 148-149	1663-1666
III VI 10, 2, pp. 154-155	1716-1718
III VI 10, 3, pp. 154-155	328-331
III VI 11, 3, pp. 154-155	1719-1720
III VI 11, 4, pp. 154-155	564-567
III VII 1, 13, pp. 158-159	1766- 1768
III VII 3, 3, pp. 160-161	1899-1902
III VIII 1, 5, pp. 164-165	2656-2658
III VIII 1, 7, pp. 164-165	2653-2654
III VIII 2, 2, pp. 164-165	2668-2669
III VIII 3, 2, pp. 166-167	2679-2682
III VIII 3, 4, pp. 166-167	2644-2645
III IX 2, 2, pp. 170-171	2242-2244
III X 2, 4, pp. 172-173	602-603
III X 2, 5, pp. 174-175	2364-2366
III X 2, 7, pp. 174-175	2409-2410
III X 2, 9, pp. 174-175	2421-2423
III X 2, 9, pp. 174-175	2424-2426
III X 2, 9, pp. 174-175	2435-2436
III X 3, 4, pp. 176-177	2492-2493
III X, 3, 11, pp. 176-177	2529-2530
III X, 3, 6, pp. 176-177	2492-2493
III X, 3, 7, et III X, 3, 10, pp. 174-177	2523-2525
III XII 1, 5, pp. 179-180	2556-2557
III XII 3, 2, pp. 180-181	2601-2602
IV 12, 17, pp. 192-193	1032-1034
IV 12, 5, pp. 192-193	2889-2891
IV 29, 2, pp. 202-203	741-745

ʿOlam I [*Liber revolutionum annorum mundi* aut *Liber coniunctionum*] (ed. Sela)

§ 22:1, pp. 66-67	2049-2051
§ 23:1, pp. 66-67	380-382
§ 38:1-24, pp. 76-79	233-235

Reshit Ḥokhma [*Liber initii sapientiae*] (ed. Sela)

§ 2.3:23, pp. 74-75	249-250
§ 2.7:33, pp. 100-101	984-987
§ 2.7:33, pp. 100-101	1349-1351
§ 2.9:26, pp. 112-113	821-825
§ 2.9:28, pp. 112-113	825-827
§ 2.9:30, pp. 112-113	827-829
§ 2.9:33, pp. 112-113	829-831

Iudicium nativitatis cuiusdam (MS Leipzig 1466)
    fol. 60va:18-22   707-710

ABRAHAM COMPILATOR / ABRAHAM IUDAEUS [re vera ipse Ibn Ezra]
   Liber de nativitatibus (ed. 1485)

sig. a2v: 21-25	179-203
sig. a3r:1821	1270-1273
sig. a6r:8-11	1146-1148
sig. a7v:2527	673
sig. a8r:12-14	713-715
sig. a8r:2224	3344-3342
sig. a8r:2628	659
sig. b2v:1314	1682-1683
sig. b4r:17-20	1543-1545
sig. b6a:8-9	332-333
sig. b6v:3335	1538-1540
sig. b8v:1417	2688-2691
sig. b8v:1819	2644-2645
sig. c1r:1013	2287
sig. c1v:22	2175-2176
sig. c3r:10	2494
sig. c3r:68	2439-2441

ABRAHAM PRINCEPS [re vera ipse Ibn Ezra]
   Mishpetei haMazzalot (ed. Sela)

§ 29:1, pp. 512-513	694-697

   Mivḥarim III [*Liber electionum*] (MS Erfurt, Ampl. O.89)

fol. 41v:17-42r:4	86-87
fol. 42r:6-14	106-117
fol. 44b:31-45a:1 1	1919-1920
fol. 45r:9-13	603-604

   Moladot II [*Liber nativitatum*] (MS Erfurt, Ampl. O.89)

fol. 55r:21	681-68
fol. 57r:230	735-736
fol. 57r:3-6	602
fol. 57v:12	735-736
fol. 58r:1922	673
fol. 58v:28-29	578-580
fol. 59r:21-24	658-659
fol. 59v:2528	812-814
fol. 60a:2830	1196-1200

fol. 60b:2-3	1054-1057
fol. 61v:9-11	1584-1586
fol. 63a:19	1595-1596
fol. 64v:1718	1454-1455, 1787-178
fol. 64v:1922	1774-1776
fol. 64v:2527	1684
fol. 64v:25-27	1759-1760
fol. 65r:2-3	1802-1804
fol. 65v:1318 (Benneka Indus)	2639
fol. 66r:1116	2662-2664
fol. 66r:21-23	2649-2652, 2672
fol. 66v:4	2250-2252
fol. 67r:30-v3	2511-2512
fol. 67v:21-24	2765-2767
fol. 68r3-4	1739-1740

ALBATEGNI [al-Battānī]
    Canones tabularum (ed. 1537), c. LIV   2826-2828

ALBENAIACH
    Vide *Librum novem iudicum*

ALBOHALI [Abū ʿAlī al-Khayyāṭ] qui dicitur Avicenna
    De nativitatibus (ed. 1546)

c.2, sig. b4v:24-27	669-672
c.5, sig. c2r:21-24	1130-1134
c.5, sig. c3r:4-11	1035-1040
c.5, sig. c3v: 20-21	1128-1130
c.7, sig. d1v:21-25	1442-1446
c.7, sig. e2v:13-23	1425-1428
c.9, sig. e4r:15-17	1474-1475
c.9, sig. e4v:2-3	1469-1471
c.9, sig. e4v:23-27	1498-1500
c.9, sig. f1r:7-9	1500-1501
c.10, sig. f1v:25-26	2397-2399
c.10, sig. f1v:25-28	1462-1466
c.11, sig. f2v:8-10 et f4r:4	1415-1417
c.11, sig. f4r:5-7	1419-1421
c.15, sig. g3r:15-18 et 20-21	1512-1514
c.21, sig. i1r:16-18	1662-1663
c.24, sig. i4r:12-18	1711-1716

c.25, sig. i4v-k1v	1810-1814
c.25, sig. k1r:1-5	1755-1757
c.25, sig. k1v:8-10 et c.26, k3r:7-9	1804-1807
c.26, sig. k2r:3-8	1784-1787
c.26, sig. k2v:7-9	1776-1778
c.26, sig. k2v:11-12	1761-1762
c.26, sig. k2v:22-23	1762-1764
c.29, sig. l1r:20-22	2210-2211
c.29, sig. l1r:24-l1v:4	2213-2219
c.29, sig. l1v:13-15	2219-2223
c.29, sig. l2r:5-7	2211-2213
c.29, sig. l2v:5-7	2507-2511
c.29, sig. l2v:10-11	2388-2390, 2505-2506
c.29, sig. l2v:15-25	2235-2242
c.30, sig. l3v:6-9	2390-2392
c.31, sig. l4r:4-7	2406-2407
c.32, sig. m1r:5-7	2399-2402
c.33, sig. m2r:10-16	2517-2522
c.33, sig. m2r:25-m2v:1	2539-2542
c.35, sig. m3v:16-20	2552-2556
c.36, sig. m4v:25-nr:7	2597-2598
c.37	2127
c.37, sig. n1r:18-19	2670-2671
c.37, sig. n1r:22-24	2672-2674
c.37, sig. n1r:25-n1v:8 et n2v:20-21	2674-2678
c.37, sig. n1v:25-28	2701-2703
c.37, sig. n2r:24-25	2733
c.37, sig. n3r:6-8	2699-2701
c.42, sig. o2v:17-20	1602-1603, 2436-2438
c.43, sig. o3r:15	2179-2180
c.43, sig. o3v:12-14	1776-1778
c.43, sig. o3v:21-25	1687-1689
c.45, sig. p1r:4-6	1790-1792
(locus non inventus)	176

ALBUMASAR [Abū Ma'shar]
De magnis coniunctionibus (ed. Burnett/Yamamoto)

I.1 (vol. 2, p. 9:106-107)	209-211
I.4.7 (vol. 2, p. 131)	971-981
II.4 (vol. 2, pp. 45-46)	2305-2306
III.4 (vol. 2, p. 114)	1057-1060

Metaphysica
    XII 8, 1073b1 sqq   360-362
    XII 8, 1073b32 sqq.   717
Politica
    III 9, 1280a15-16   5-6
    III 15, 1286a15 et 17-18   21-23
    III 16, 1287a41-b3   15-17
    VIII 3, 1338a1-3   1331-1332
    VIII 3, 1338a9-11   1332-1334
    VIII 4, 1339a9-11   *App. II*, 44-45
    VIII 5, 1339a21-26   1322-1326
    VIII 5, 1339b21-25   1328- 1331
    VIII 5, 1340a3-5   1334-1336
    VIII 6, 1340b22-25   1336-13
    VIII 6, 1340b35-39   1339-1343
    VIII 6, 1341b3-4 et 6-8   1295-1298
Rhetorica
    I 2, 1358a9-10   1386-1387
    II 1, 1377b31-1378a3   9-14
    II 1, 1378a20-21   14-15
    II 10, 1387b23-24   2084-2085

ARISTOTELES (pseudo-)
Secretum secretorum (ed. Steele)
    pars I, c. 4, p. 41:17-19   1202-1305

ARISTOTELES ASTROLOGUS
    Vide *Librum novem iudicum*

AVERROES [ibn Rusd]
    In De Caelo II, c. 68, 144G-H   1000-1002
    In Metaphysicam XII, c. 45, 329H-M 355-356

BENNEKA INDUS [Kanakah al-Hindi]
    Vide Abraham Principem, *Liber nativitatum*

BIBLIA SACRA
    Ecclesiastes 9,11   *App. II*, 114-116
    Malachias 4,2   2164
    Proverbia 10,14   1867
          14,13   1686, 1687, 2580-2582

Psalmi 3,2	*App. I,* 36-37
18,5	2164-2165
119,2	1937-1938
119,7	2611-2612

CAPITULA ALMANSORIS (ed. 1493)

c. 10	581-582
c. 11	1078-1080
c. 16	1173-1175
c. 20	1541-1542
c. 27	2309-2311
c. 28	2535-2536
c. 33	1697
c. [35bis]	2201
c. 40	2564-2567
c. 56	1080-1082
c. 64	292-294
c. 95	1527-1528
c. 103	1398-1400
c. 113	1044-1046
c. 128	851-852

DOROTHEUS [Doritheus qui et Doronius]
  Vide *Librum novem iudicum*

FIRMICUS MATERNUS
  Matheseos (ed. Kroll/ Skutsch)

I 6, 2, p. 18:10-24	1885-1895
II 3, 4, p. 44:3-6	1597-1599, 2403-2405
II 13, 6, pp. 56:30-57:1	855-857
II 14, 3, pp. 57:31-58:2	1391-1392
II 16, 2, p. 59:22-25	2128-2129
II 16, 2, pp. 59:27-60:2	2545-2546
II 17, 1, p. 60:13-16	2587-2588
II 19, 2, p. 61:12-13	840-841
II 19, 11, p. 64:10-12	994-995
III 1, 18, p. 96:25-26	996
III 2, 19, p. 102:10-11	898-899
III 2, 21, p. 102:30-31	2362-2363
III 2, 21, p. 103:3-6	2368-2369
III 2, 21, p. 103:7	2380-2381

III 2, 26, p. 104:29	2380-2381
III 5, 17, pp. 132:27-133:7	1615-1616
III 6, 10, pp. 145:20-146:3	1691-1694
IV 1, 1, p. 197:4-9	805-810
IV 9, 8, p. 211:1-8	790-795
IV 19, 24, p. 251:27-29	1193-1195
IV 19, 32-33, pp. 254:16-255:3	1118-1128

G<small>ERGIS</small>
De significatione septem planetarum in domibus (ed. 1564)
    sig. F1v   1613-1615

G<small>UILLELMUS</small> A<small>NGLICUS</small>
De urina non visa (ed. Moulinier-Brogi)
    c.1, p. 137-140   1217
    c.4, p. 148   333-334

H<small>ALY</small> (et Abuiafar Hamet)
expositor *Centiloquii*
    v. 71, v. 78, v. 83   811, 1029, 1077

H<small>ALY</small> E<small>MBRANI</small> ['Alī b. Aḥmad al-'Imrānī]
De electionibus horarum (ed. Millás Vallicrosa)
    p. 329   231-233
    p. 333   2102-2104
    p. 335   887-888
    MS BnF lat. 16204, 532a-b 1856-1857

H<small>ERMANNUS</small>
De occultis, (ed. Low-Beer)
    p. 274:2   2485-2486
    pp. 316:25-317:1   2063-2065, 3018-3019
    (locus non inventus)   211-215

H<small>ERMES</small>
Centiloquium (ed. 1493)
    c. 1   542
    c. 20   1526-1527
    c. 27   848-849
    c. 59   1406-1408, 1671-1672

c. 86	1406-1408
c. 78	3128-3130
c. 99	1414-1415

IERGIS
Vide *Librum novem iudicum*

IOHANNES HISPALENSIS
Epitome totius astrologiae (ed. 1548)

Ysagoge, c. 7, sig. B4r:30-31	963-965
Ysagoge, c. 9, sig. C1r:14-15	831-832
Ysagoge, c. 11, sig. C1v:31-C2r:1	1185-1187
Ysagoge, c. 24, sig. E1r:2122	740-741, 1826-1827, 2064-2065, 3015, 3025-3027
Ysagoge, c. 26, sig. E2v	660-666
Quad., c. II.2, sig. H4v:16-21	577-580
Quad., c. II.4, sig. I2r:23-24	1232-1233
Quad., c. II.4, sig. I2r:26-27	833-834
Quad., c. II.4, sig. I2v:11-13	1349-1351
Quad., c. II.4, sig. I2v:14-19	2511-2516
Quad., c. II.4, sig. I2v:17-18	1200-1202
Quad., c. II.4, sig. I2v:23-24	1179-1180
Quad., c. II.6, sig. I4r:12 et passim	672-673
Quad., c. II.6, sig. I4v:8-12	719-723, 730
Quad., c. II.6 (alia versio)	732-734
Quad., c. II.9, sig. K1v:30	1196-1200
Quad., c. II.11, sig. K4r:24-27	1536-1537
Quad., c. II.11, sig. K4v:15-16	1593
Quad., c. II.14, sig. L3r:23-25	1770-1771
Quad., c. II.14, sig. L3v:5-7	1772-1774
Quad., c. II.15, sig. L4v:28	2177
Quad., c. II.15, sig. M1r:8	2160
Quad., c. II.16 (in MS Erfurt, Ampl. O.84)	2514-2516
Quad., c. II.16, sig. M2r:3-5	2345-2347
Quad., c. II.16, sig. M2r:11-15	2313-2316
Quad., c. II.16, sig. M3r:3-12	2321-2327
Quad., c. II.16, sig. M3v:5	2497-2498
Quad., c. II.17, sig. M4r:15-16	2561-2563
Quad., c. II.18, sig. M4v:13-14	1198-1200
Quad., c. II.19, sig. N1r:26-27	2748-2751
Quad., c. II.19, sig. N1v:24-26	2642-2644

Quad., c. II.19, sig. N1v:29-30	2765
Quad., c. II.19, sig. N2r:17-19	2745-2746
Quad., c. II.19, sig. N2v:4-8	2740-2744
Quad., c. II.21, sig. N4v:17-19	1740-1741
Quad., c. II.21, sig. Ov:18	2940-2941
Quad., c. III.12, sig. Q2r:33-Q2v:2	1638-1639
(alia versio Vat. Reg. lat. 1452, fol. 66 ra)	914-916

LIBER ALDARAIA SIVE SOYGA (ed. Kupin)

16, p. 172	1189-1192
22, p. 251	1187-1188

LIBER DE VITA ET GENERE ARISTOTELIS

§ 43	2074-2076

LIBER NOVEM IUDICUM (ed. 1571 et MS Vat. lat. 6766)

A.75, fol. 4vb:26-27 (Aristoteles)	1356-1357
A.98, fol. 6ra:34-35	567-569
A.99-100, fol. 6rb (Alkindus)	1822-1825
A.99, fol.7va:15-16	1577-1578
A.112, fol. 9ra:5-7	607-609
A.116, fol. 9vb	2359-2362
A.117, fol. 10ra	2370-2373
A.118, fol. 10rb (Iergis)	1729-1731
A.119, fol. 10rb (Iergis)	1610-1612
A.120, fol 10va	1695-1696
A.122, fol. 10va-vb	1788-1790
A.125, fol.11vb:13-14 (Alkindus)	1578, 1825-1826
I.1, p. 418	771-773
II.3, p. 422a	1460-1461, 2416, 2483-2484
VI.9, p. 454b	1725-1728
VII.1, p. 467b	1800
VII.37, p. 475b (Zael)	1986-1988
VII.38, p. 475b (Aomar)	1985-1986
VII.39, p. 476a (Alkindus)	1970
VII.40, p. 476a (Albenaiach)	1970
VII.41, p. 476b (Dorotheus)	1969
VII.42, p. 477b	1957- 1958
VII.45, p. 478a (Albenaiach)	1996-1998
VII.46, p. 478b (Dorotheus)	2026-2027, 2037-2038
VII.47, p. 479a (Aristoteles)	2023-2024

VII.49, p. 480a (Aomar)	1958-1959, 1964-1969, 2109-2111
VII.148, p. 514a	1982-1986
VII.149, p. 514b (Albenaiach)	2118-2122
VII.153, p. 515a (Aomar)	2122
VII.153, p. 515a (Zael)	2121
VII.160, p. 516b (Zael)	1061-1063
VII.160, p. 516b (Albenaiach)	1988-1990
VII.160, p. 516b	2002-2005
VII.171, p. 522b (Alkindus)	2024-2025, 2040-2041
VII.178, p. 583b (Alkindus)	2021-2022
VII.203, p. 530b (Aomar)	1633-1636
IX.36, p. 547b (Aomar)	2265-2270
IX.36, p. 548a (Aomar)	2173-2175
X.4, p. 552a (Aomar)	2443-2444
X.6, p. 553b (Alkindus)	2447-2448
X.6, p. 554a (Alkindus)	2428-2431
X.10, p. 555a (Aristoteles)	2448-2451
XII.4b, p. 575a	1550-1552
(locus non inventus)	910-912

Martianus Capella
De nuptiis Philologiae et Mercurii

II, 160	*App. I*:16-24
II, 214	1361-1364

Messahallah [Māshā'allāh] (ed. 1549)
De revolutionibus annorum mundi

c. 20, sig. C4r:15-17	907-910

Epistola de rebus eclipsium

c. 9, sig. G2r:25-30	955-960

Liber receptionis

c.1, sig. M1r:31-M1v:1	1555-1557
c.2, sig. N1v:6-8	609-610
c.5, sig. O1r:3-5	1574-1576

Plato
Timaeus 38 D1-2   717

51 E5-6 (translatio Calcidii)	*App. II*, 52-53

Proverbia *sententiaeque Latinitatis* (ed. Walther)

14513	1949-1950

| 16974 | 2015-2016 |
| 29931 | 2089 |

PTOLEMAEUS
    Almagesti (ed. 1515)

sig. 1r:38	1929-1930

    Quadripartitum (translatio Guillelmi, ed. Vuillemin-Diem/Steel)

I.3, p. 18:314-316	1872-1873
I.3, p. 169:279-284	2720-2725
I.9, p. 175:438-442	2458
I.24, p. 196	962-964, 991-994
II.8, p. 217:498-499	965-967
II.9, pp. 217:520-218	523 553-557
III.10, 4, p. 205:575-577	651-654
III.10, 9, p. 209:623-625	658
III.11, p. 247:397-399	2976-2978
III.12, p. 248:448-450	1450
III.13, p. 258:701-703	779-782
III.14, p. 262:816817	250-252
III.15, p. 264:873-876	1134-1139
IV.2, p. 278:25-26	388
IV.2, p. 278:34-35	2451-2453
IV.5, p. 283:177-179	1752-1754, 1835
IV.5, p. 283:182	1801-1802
IV.5, p. 284:192	1793-1794
IV.9, pp. 334-335	2748-2751
(trans. Platonis ed. 1484)	
I.3, sig. a4v:37-r:5	2712-2719
III.2, sig. c8vb-d1ra	83-84, 153-157
IV.8	2127

PTOLEMAEUS (pseudo-)
    Centiloquium (ed. Boer)
        trans. graeco-latina

v. 5	1871-1872
v. 8	2709-2711
v. 12	7-9, 1283-1284
v. 27	1698-1700
v. 29	2311-2313
v. 38	1074-1078
v. 51	87

Editiones et manuscripta fontium
ab editoribus allegata

Abraham Bar Ḥiyya, *Sefer: Megillat ha-Megalle*, eds. Adolf Poznanski and Julius Guttmann (Berlin: Verein Mekize Nirdamim, 1924).

Albategnius, *De scientia stellarum* [trans. Plato Tiburtinus] in: *Rudimenta astronomica Alfragani (...) Albategnius (...) de motu stellarum (...)* (Nürnberg: Johannes Petreius, 1537), sigs. ar-y6r.

Albohali, *De nativitatibus* [trans. Johannes Toletanus] (Nürnberg: Johannes Montanus & Ulricus Neuber, 1546); MS Oxford, BL, Digby 51, s. XII, fols. 114vb-130rb [trans. Plato Tiburtinus].

Albumasar in Sadan: Gabriella Vescovini, "La versio Latina degli Excerpta de Secretis Albumasar di Sadan" in: *Archives d'Histoire Doctrinale et Littéraire du Moyen Age*, vol. 65(1998), pp. 273-330.

Albumasar, *De magnis coniunctionibus*: Keiji Yamamoto and Charles Burnett 2000. *Abū Maʿsar on Historical Astrology: The Book of Religions and Dynasties (On the Great Conjunctions)* [*De magnis coniunctionibus*], 2 vols. (Boston/Leiden: Brill).

Albumasar, *De revolutionibus nativitatum* in: ΕΙΣ ΤΗΝ ΤΕΤΡΑΒΙΒΛΟΝ ΤΟΥ ΠΤΟΛΕΜΑΙΟΥ ΕΧΗΓΗΤΗΣ ΑΝΩΝΥΜΟΣ *(...) praeterea Hermetis Philosophi De Revolutionibus Nativitatum (...)* (Basel: Henricus Petreius, 1559), pp. 211-279.

Albumasar, *Introductorium maius*: Albumasar, *Liber introductorii maioris ad scientiam judiciorum astrorum*, ed. Richard Lemay, 9 vols. (Naples: Istituto universitario orientale, 1995-1997).

Albumasar, *Ysagoga minor*: Charles Burnett, Keiji Yamamoto and Michio Yano 1994. *Abū Maʿshar: The Abbreviation of the Introduction to Astrology, together with the Medieval Latin Translation of compleAdelard of Bath* [*Ysagoga minor*] (Leiden/New York: Brill).

Alcabitius, *Introductorius*: Charles Burnett, Keiji Yamamoto and Michio Yano 2004. *Al-Qabīṣī (Alcabitius), The Introduction to Astrology* (London: Warburg Institute).

Alpetragius [al-Biṭrūjī], *De motibus celorum. Critical edition of the Latin translation of Michael Scot*, ed. Francis J. Carmody (Berkeley/Los Angeles: University of California Press, 1952).

Aomar, *De nativitatibus* in: Firmicus Maternus, *Astronomicωn libri VIII* [*Mathesis*] (Basel: Joannes Hervagius, 1533), pp. 118-141.

Averroes, *In Metaphysicam* in: *Aristotelis Opera cum Averrois Commentariis* (Venetiis: apud Junctas, 1562), vol. 8, fols. 1r-340r.

Averroes, *In De Caelo* in: *Averrois Cordubensis commentum magnum super libro De celo et mundo Aristotelis*, eds. Francis J. Carmody, Rüdiger Arnzen and Gerhard Endress, 2 vols. (Leuven: Peeters, 2003).

Capitula Almansoris [trans. Plato Tiburtinus] in: Ptolemy, *Quadripartitum* [1493], sig. 120v-122r.

Conradus de Mure, *Fabularius*, ed. Tom van de Loo (Turnhout: Brepols, 2006).

Abraham Ibn Ezra, *Commencement*: Raphael Levy and Francisco Cantera 1939. *Le Commencement de Sapience* [*Reshit Hokhmah*] in: *The Beginning of Wisdom. An Astrological Treatise by Abraham ibn Ezra (1148)*, (Baltimore: Johns Hopkins Press), pp. 31-125.

Abraham Ibn Ezra, *Liber de nativitatibus* (Venice: Erhard Ratdolt, 1485).

Abraham Ibn Ezra, *Liber electionum*: Ms. Erfurt, Amplon. O.89, fols. 39v-46v.

Abraham Ibn Ezra, *Liber nativitatum*: Ms. Erfurt, Amplon. O.89, fols. 53r-68v.

Abraham Ibn Ezra, *Me'orot*: Shlomo Sela 2011. *Abraham Ibn Ezra on Elections, Interrogations, and Medical Astrology. A Parallel Hebrew-English Critical Edition of the Book of Elections (3 Versions), the Book of Interrogations (3 Versions), and the Book of the Luminaries* [*Sefer ha-She'elot I*], [*Sefer ha-She'elot II*], [*Sefer ha-She'elot III*], [*Sefer ha-Mivharim I*], [*Sefer ha-Mivharim II*], [*Sefer ha-Mivharim III*], [*Sefer ha-Me'orot*] (Leiden: Brill).

Abraham Ibn Ezra, *Mishpetei ha-Mazzalot*: Shlomo Sela 2017. *Abraham Ibn Ezra's Introductions to Astrology. A Parallel Hebrew-English Critical Edition of the Book of the Beginning of Wisdom and the Book of the Judgments of the Zodiacal Signs* [*Reshit Ḥokhmah*], [*Mishpeṭei ha-Mazzalot*] (Leiden: Brill).

Abraham Ibn Ezra, *Mivharim*: Shlomo Sela 2011. *Abraham Ibn Ezra on Elections, Interrogations, and Medical Astrology. A Parallel Hebrew-English Critical Edition of the Book of Elections (3 Versions), the Book of Interrogations (3 Versions), and the Book of the Luminaries* [*Sefer ha-She'elot I*], [*Sefer ha-She'elot II*], [*Sefer ha-She'elot III*], [*Sefer ha-Mivharim I*], [*Sefer ha-Mivharim II*], [*Sefer ha-Mivharim III*], [*Sefer ha-Me'orot*] (Leiden: Brill).

Abraham Ibn Ezra, *Moladot*: Shlomo Sela 2014. *Abraham Ibn Ezra on nativities and continuous horoscopy: a parallel Hebrew-English critical edition of the Book of nativities and the Book of revolution* [*Sefer ha-Moladot*], [*Sefer ha-Tequfah*] (Leiden: Brill).

Abraham Ibn Ezra, *'Olam*: Shlomo Sela 2010. *Abraham Ibn Ezra. The Book of the World. A Parallel Hebrew-English Critical Edition of the Two Versions of the Text* [*'Olam I*], [*'Olam II*] (Leiden: Brill); Ms. Leipzig, UB, 1466, fols. 25r-30v.

Abraham Ibn Ezra, *Reshit Hokhmah*: Shlomo Sela 2017. *Abraham Ibn Ezra's Introductions to Astrology. A Parallel Hebrew-English Critical Edition of the Book of the Beginning of Wisdom and the Book of the Judgments of the Zodiacal Signs* [*Reshit Ḥokhmah*], [*Mishpeṭei ha-Mazzalot*] (Leiden: Brill); Ms. Leipzig, UB, 1466, fols. 2r-23v.

Abraham Ibn Ezra, *She'elot*: Shlomo Sela 2011. *Abraham Ibn Ezra on Elections, Interrogations, and Medical Astrology. A Parallel Hebrew-English Critical Edition of the Book of Elections (3 Versions), the Book of Interrogations (3 Versions), and the Book of the Luminaries* [*Sefer ha-She'elot I*], [*Sefer ha-She'elot II*], [*Sefer ha-She'elot III*], [*Sefer ha-Mivharim I*], [*Sefer ha-Mivharim II*], [*Sefer ha-Mivharim III*], [*Sefer ha-Me'orot*] (Leiden: Brill).

Abraham Ibn Ezra, *Te'amim*: Shlomo Sela 2007. *Abraham Ibn Ezra. The Book of Reasons. A Parallel Hebrew-English Critical Edition of the Two Versions of the Text* [*Te'amim I*], [*Te'amim II*] (Leiden: Brill); Ms. Leipzig, UB, 1466, fols. 49v-73v.

Firmicus Maternus, *Mathesis* in: *Matheseos libri VIII*, eds. Wilhelm Kroll and Franz Skutsch, 2 vols. (Stuttgart: B.G. Teubner, 1968).

Gergis, *De significatione septem planetarum in domibus* in: *Astrologica opuscula antiqua* (Prague: Georgius Melantrichus, 1564), sig. F1v-G2r.

Guilielmus Anglicus, *De urina non visa*: Laurence Moulinier-Brogi 2011. *Guillaume l'Anglais le frondeur de l'uroscopie médiévale (XIIIe s.)* [*De urina non visa*] (Genève: Droz).

Guilelmus Peraldus, *De eruditione principum*, in: Thomas Aquinas, *Opera omnia*, 25 vols. (Parma: Pietro Fiaccadori, 1852-1873), vol. 16, pp. 390-476.

Haly Embrani, *De electionibus horarum*: Millás Vallicrosa 1942. *Las traducciones orientales en los manuscritos de la Biblioteca Catedral de Toledo* (Madrid: Instituto Arias Montano), pp. 328-339;   Ms. Paris, BnF, lat. 16204, pp. 507a-534b.

Hermann of Carinthia, *De occultis*: Hermann of Carinthia 1979. *Hermann of Carinthia: The Liber Imbrium, the Fatidica, and the De Indagatione Cordis*, ed. Sheila Low-Beer (PhD dissertation: City University of New York), pp. 260-344.

Hermes, *Centiloquium* in: Ptolemy, *Quadripartitum* [1493], sig. 117r-118r.

Hyginus, *Fabulae*, ed. Peter Marshall (Stuttgart: Teubner, 1993).

Ioannes Hispalensis, *Epitome totius astrologiae* (Nürnberg: Johannes Montanus and Ulricus Neuber, 1548).

Liber de Vita et Genere Aristotelis in: Ingemar Düring, *Aristotle in the Ancient Biographical Tradition* (Göteborg: Elanders Boktryckeri Aktiebolag, 1957), pp. 151-158.

Liber novem iudicum in: Haly Abenragel, *De iudiciis* (Basel: Henricus Petreius, 1571), pp. 411-586 [lacks the first 126 chapters]; Ms. Vatican, BAV, Vat. lat. 6766, s. XIV, fols. 1ra-48ra [fols. 1ra-12rb for the first 126 chapters].

Liber Soyga, ed. Jane Kupin in: "Aldaraia sive Soyga vocor", *Esoteric Archives*, retrieved 12 July 2017: http://www.esotericarchives.com/soyga/Book_of_Soyga_8x10.pdf.

Messahallah, *De receptione* in: Messahallah, *Libri tres* (Nürnberg: Johannes Montanus and Ulricus Neuber, 1549), sig. Liiijr-Riijv.

Messahallah, *De revolutione annorum mundi* in: Messahallah, *Libri tres* (Nürnberg: Johannes Montanus and Ulricus Neuber, 1549), sig. Br-Fijv.

Messahallah, *Epistola*: in: Messahallah, *Libri tres* (Nürnberg: Johannes Montanus and Ulricus Neuber, 1549), sig. Fiijr-Liijv.

Proverbia sententiaeque Latinitatis Medii Aevi, ed. Hans Walther, 6 vol. (Tübingen: Vandenhoeck&Ruprecht 1963-1969)

Ps.-Aristotle, *Secretum secretorum cum glossis et notulis; tractatus brevis et utilis ad declarandum quedam obscure dicta Fratris Rogeri*, ed. Robert Steele (Oxford: Clarendon, 1920).

Ps.-Ptolemy, *Centiloquium* in: Ptolemy, *Quadripartitum* [1493], sig. 107r-116v [trans. Plato Tiburtinus]; ed. Aemilia Boer in: *Claudii Ptolemaei Opera Quae Exstant Omnia*, vol. III.2 (Leipzig: B.G. Teubner), pp. 37-69.

Ps.-Ptolemy, *De iudiciis partium* in: Ms. Munich, BSB, Clm 3857, fols. 43vb-46vb.

Ptolemy, *Almagestum* [trans. Gerardus Cremonensis] (Venezia: Petrus Liechtenstein, 1515).

Ptolemy, *Quadripartitum* (Venezia: E. Ratdolt, 1484); (Venezia: Bonetus Locatellus, 1493); ed. Wolfgang Hübner (Stuttgart/Leipzig: B.G. Teubner, 1998); Gudrun Vuillemin-Diem and Carlos Steel, *Ptolemy's Tetrabiblos in the Translation of William of Moerbeke: Claudii Ptolemaei Liber Iudicialium* (Leuven: Leuven University Press, 2005).

Publilius Syrus, *Sententiae*, ed. Eduard Woelfflin (Leipzig: B.G. Teubner, 1869).

Sela, Shlomo (forthcoming b). "Calculating Birth: Abraham Ibn Ezra's Role in the Creation and Diffusion of the *Trutina Hermetis*" in: *Pregnancy and Childbirth from Late Antiquity to the Renaissance*, eds. Costanza G. Dopfel and A. Focati (Turnhout: Brepols).

Tunnicius Antonius., *Die älteste niederdeutsche Sprichwörtersammlung*, hrsg. von Hoffmann von Fallersleben (Oppenheim: Berlin 1870).

Zael, *De interrogationibus* in: Ptolemy, *Quadripartitum* [1493], sig. 127r-138r.

Zael, *Fatidica* in: *Hermann of Carinthia, The Liber Imbrium, the Fatidica, and the De Indagatione Cordis*, ed. Sheila Low-Beer (PhD dissertation: City University of New York, 1979), pp. 138-253.

Zael, *Introductorium* in: Ptolemy, *Quadripartitum* [1493], sig. 122v-126r.

Zael, *Quinquagenta praecepta* in: Ptolemy, *Quadripartitum* [1493], sig. 126r-127r.

CPSIA information can be obtained
at www.ICGtesting.com
Printed in the USA
LVHW081805010319
609209LV00012B/338/P